THE WORLD ENCYCLOPEDIA OF
ARMOURED
FIGHTING VEHICLES

THE WORLD ENCYCLOPEDIA OF
ARMOURED
FIGHTING VEHICLES

An illustrated guide to armoured cars, self-propelled artillery, armoured personnel carriers and other AFVs from World War I to the present day - Jack Livesey

JACK LIVESEY

LORENZ BOOKS

Contents

Introduction

Armoured Fighting Vehicles (AFVs) form one of the most complex groups of machines to be found on a modern battlefield. Excluding the tank, the AFV manifests itself in a wide and diverse variety of machines that are multi-tasking and multi-functional. They form the core of the armoured division and can be found in greater numbers around the world than the tank, even replacing the tank in some armies.

Before the invention of the internal combustion engine, man had tried to devise various ways of using wagons as crude mobile fighting platforms. Some of these performed quite well but most were ill-conceived. After 1900, AFV use and development started to move quickly, and developed into three main types. The armoured car was the first of the AFVs to be deployed by the armed forces with the Self-Propelled Gun (SPG) and the Armoured Personnel Carrier (APC) following on more slowly.

The biggest debate that surrounds the AFV is the choice of wheels or tracks as a form of mobility. At first wheeled vehicles had very poor cross-country ability when compared with that of the tank. However, today the wheeled vehicle has very good cross-country ability, is air-portable, and can be used in an urban area far more easily than the tank and with greater flexibility. The armoured car has always used wheels but from time to time light tanks have been developed to be used in the same primary reconnaissance role. The SPG is usually mounted on tracks but wheeled SPGs have also been developed on occasion, especially by the Russians. The APC

TOP: **The Marksman SPAAG (Self-Propelled Anti-Aircraft Gun) was developed by BAe Systems for the British Army but it was not taken into service. As yet it has only been sold to Finland.** ABOVE: **Saloon car converted by the British Home Guard into an AFV by fitting armour to the windows and radiator.**

started life as a battlefield taxi for the infantry, initially with a mix of wheels and tracks, and was known as the half-track. Being such a useful and versatile vehicle, it was very quickly adapted into other roles such as command, armoured ambulance, and supply vehicle.

The armoured car has taken over from the cavalry as one of the main Armoured Reconnaissance Vehicles (ARVs) on the battlefield. The ARV has to be well armed and armoured, and be capable of travelling at relatively high speed. The main work of this vehicle is to serve as the eyes of the army well in advance of its own frontline. It has to rely on speed and agility to get out of trouble if observed by the opposing forces. As the destructive power of anti-tank guns has increased, armoured cars have become much larger, surrendering speed for increased crew protection.

The APC has undergone a metamorphosis and emerged as the Infantry Fighting Vehicle (IFV). Starting life as an open-topped box for transporting infantry to the edge of the fighting, the infantry then had to leave the vehicle and attack the enemy position on foot with support from the vehicle. With the modern IFV, the infantry can attack from the safety of a vehicle that can fight its own way into the enemy position and then disgorge the troops.

SPGs are frequently confused with tanks by the general public. Their role is to support tank attacks with high-explosive rounds. The early tanks did not have an adequate long-range gun which could fire a high-explosive round making the SPG essential. In early SPGs, the gun was mounted in an open box on the top of a tracked vehicle, leaving the gun crew very exposed. Since then the gun calibre has grown in size and the range of the gun has increased, becoming very sophisticated and accurate, with missiles beginning to replace the gun on the battlefield in some cases. Crews are now much better protected from both the weather and enemy action.

This book contains a wide selection of armoured fighting vehicles from around the world dating from the early 20th century to the present day. The selection of machines is confined to those that are of interest and importance and which particularly demonstrate the diversification of the AFV. This is not a definitive book but will give the reader a good insight into why the AFV plays such a crucial role in military forces around the world today.

ABOVE LEFT: **The Gepard Flakpanzer 1 emerged in the late 1960s as an indigenous SPAAG for the West German Army. The Contraves turret mounts twin 35mm/1.38in Oerlikon KDA cannon. The Gepard chassis is based on the Leopard 1 MBT.** TOP: **The Fox FV 721 armoured car entered service with the British Army in 1973 as a replacement for the Ferret armoured car. It is armed with a 30mm/1.18in RARDEN cannon which can destroy light armoured vehicles at 1,000m/3,281ft.** ABOVE: **The Commando M706 armoured car was built by Cadillac Gage for the US Army. Originally intended as an export vehicle for police forces around the world, it saw extensive service during the Vietnam War with both the South Vietnamese and US armies as a convoy escort vehicle.** BELOW: **The LAV-25 8x8 APC is a copy of the Swiss MOWAG Piranha, one of the world's most successful armoured personnel carriers. The LAV-25 is built by General Motors of Canada and has been sold to many countries around the world, including the USA.**

The History of Armoured Fighting Vehicles

In just over 100 years, the armoured fighting vehicle has undergone many transformations. The first vehicles were created by designers who were unsure of what it was that the army required, or indeed how to produce a machine that would usefully replace the horse. Once armies had acquired useful vehicles, they then spent the next 30 years learning how to use these new weapon systems. Men such as Sir Basil Henry Liddell Hart and Heinz Guderian would be fundamental in devising and developing the theory of mechanized warfare.

In 1914, armoured vehicles were improvised using boiler plate and this was quickly improved upon by the introduction of armour plate. The modern vehicle is constructed from composite materials, making it very light and fast yet giving the crew adequate protection.

After 1945, the Cold War arms race started and new weapons, nuclear and chemical, made their debut on the modern battlefield. Armoured fighting vehicles would not only deliver these but would also have to protect their crews and infantry from these unseen threats. This is vital because, as the saying goes, it takes 20 days to produce a vehicle but 20 years to grow a soldier. The priority is clear.

LEFT: **The American DUKW served in many different theatres in World War II. Here "Pistol Packen Mama" takes US troops over the Rhine in 1945.**

LEFT: **In 1902, F. R. Simms designed and built a "war car" which had a crew of five. One man drove the vehicle while two operated the Maxim 1pdr "pom-pom" gun in the rear and two men operated the two forward machine-guns.** BELOW: **One of the early development vehicles designed to act as an infantry fighting vehicle. Made from an old steam boiler, the cab and engine were also covered in boiler plate. The engine was not powerful enough to handle the weight of all this armour.**

Evolution

Probably the earliest significant use of the AFV was in 1125 when the army of the Sung dynasty halted the advance of the invading Tartar forces in Northern China using iron-plated armoured "cars" to break up the Tartar cavalry. The next time that AFVs make an appearance on the battlefield is between 1420 and 1431 during the peasant rebellion in Bohemia (the modern Czech Republic). Jan Zizka led a peasant army of 25,000 against the might of the 200,000-strong Imperial German army. Zizka came up with the idea of putting sheets of iron on some of his wagons. Inside were men armed with handguns, crossbows and large axes and could fire from the wagons through slits in the iron plates.

The AFV did not come into its own until the 20th century, with each type developing separately. First was the armoured car, followed by the Self-Propelled Gun (SPG) and finally the infantry carrier. Mr F. R. Simms, a British motoring enthusiast, came up with the idea of mounting a machine-gun on the front of a quadricycle and installing a small petrol engine at the rear. The Simms machine was widely publicized and spurred others on to design "war cars" of one sort or another, and even Henry Ford got in on the act and mounted a machine-gun on the front of a Model T. France produced a Charron armoured car in 1906 and a Hotchkiss car in 1909. These were basic touring cars with a sheet of armour bent around the tonneau. These early machines represent the first attempts to bring a new measure of speed and mobility to the battlefield.

SPGs made slow progress. The first ones to be developed were mobile anti-balloon guns such as the German Rheinmetall of 1909. The idea of these vehicles was to provide a highly mobile defensive force, capable of rapid deployment against a very mobile enemy. By December 1914, trenches ran from the Swiss border to the North Sea and siege warfare had started. In Britain there were no mobile Anti-Aircraft (AA) guns at the start of World War I, so a crash programme was put in place. The 5.9kg/13lb gun, weighing 457kg/9cwt was placed on Thornycroft and Peerless trucks as a makeshift response, but once established it built up a sound reputation. When the rains came to the Flanders area and the earth turned into a sea of mud, horse-drawn transport with its narrow steel-rimmed wheels ground to a halt. In particular, the movement of guns was almost impossible. After a successful attack, the infantry would be without close artillery support, as horse-drawn artillery could not cross the mud of No Man's Land. They needed this support to keep the momentum of the attack going. As a result, Gun Carrier Tanks were developed and an order for 48 units was placed. They arrived in France in 1917 but were only deployed a few times before being relegated to the supply role. The main problem was that these new vehicles did not fit the established way of handling guns in the British Army, namely, with horse teams.

For centuries, the infantry have had to march to the battlefield and then go into battle on foot. Railways were to change the face of warfare in Europe, by enabling armies to move over large distances very quickly and to arrive on the battlefield in good order. The Franco-Prussian War of 1870–71 was the first example of transportation by rail. In 1914, the French garrison of Paris was loaded into taxis and moved to the front to help stop the German advance. The British Army came up with the idea of moving troops to the front line by putting them into imported London buses, the sides of which were covered in heavy timber to give the troops some protection from shell splinters. In 1917, the British Army asked for a supply tank that could carry 10.16 tonnes/10 tons of supplies or 30 armed men. Being a converted tank, it could keep up with a tank assault and deliver the infantry into the German lines. The first of these machines did not arrive in France until October 1918, in readiness for the attacks planned for 1919, which were to prove to be unnecessary.

TOP: **F. R. Simms demonstrates his Quadricycle Maxim Gun Carrier at Roehampton in 1898. The ammunition was carried in a tray under the gun. The manoeuvrability of the machine left a lot to be desired.** ABOVE: **A British idea for a "war car" designed in 1855. Called the Cowen Battle-Car, it had several retractable scythes fitted to the sides of the vehicle.** BELOW: **The armoured traction engine of Fowler's Armoured Road Train. This was sent to South Africa in 1902 during the Boer War to pull armoured wagons full of British troops. The idea did not work as well as expected.**

ABOVE: **The Holzschuher car of 1558 was conceived as a mobile "war car" that would be pulled into position by a team of horses, unhitched and left to pour fire into the flanks of an enemy.**

> "Operations of war require 1,000 fast chariots, 1,000 four-horse wagons covered in leather and 100,000 mailed troops. Now when an army marches abroad the treasury will be empty at home."
> Sun Tzu, c.500–320 BC

Components of an Armoured Division

The basic components of an armoured division have not changed a great deal since 1934. These are armoured reconnaissance, tanks, motorized infantry, self-propelled artillery, engineer and signal units.

During World War I, there was no formal tank formation – a set number of tanks would be assigned to a particular attack. The infantry and the supporting artillery assigned to the attack might never have worked with tanks before. As a result of the lack of training with this new weapon there were large numbers of unnecessary infantry casualties that could have been avoided. Aerial photographs provided forward reconnaissance, as armoured cars could not breach the German trenches.

During World War I and until the formation of the integrated armoured force, the tank was felt to be purely an infantry support vehicle, with the French continuing to believe this until World War II. In 1926, the British government decided to establish an experimental armoured force consisting of an armoured reconnaissance battalion, made up of one company of light tanks and two companies of armoured cars, a medium tank battalion and an infantry battalion. Other supporting units were a towed motorized artillery detachment, a battery of SPGs, a machine-gun company, an engineering company and a signals company. This unit was the first complete armoured formation in the world and would be widely copied. Wound up in late 1928 having been led in a restricted and conventional way, the unit allowed the army to learn some very useful lessons in the detailed handling of armour and mechanized infantry. In 1931, the British had another go at an armoured formation by creating the 1st Armoured Brigade which remained in service and was sent to France with the British Expeditionary Force in 1939.

The theory had been developed in Britain by military theoreticians such as J. F. C. Fuller and Sir Basil Henry Liddell Hart, but the real father of the armoured division was Heinz Guderian. He had learnt the theory from the British and had built up practical experience at the German training school in Russia. A German armoured brigade was formed under his command in 1934, and one year later Germany would have three full armoured divisions.

The strength of a standard British armoured division in 1944 was 15,464 men and 3,464 vehicles, made up of 343 tanks, 261 tracked carriers, 100 armoured cars and 2,710 other vehicles. The large number of AFVs is significant; the roles they play were and are vital within the division's makeup.

> "Designed to convey, under the most trying conditions imaginable, accurate and balanced information to the general's battle map."
> Sir Arthur Bryant (on the armoured car), 1950

ABOVE: **In the foreground is an FV 432 armed with a single 7.62mm/0.3in machine-gun turret. Behind is a line-up of ten different types of the basic FV 432 vehicle, all of which were built by GKN Sankey.** LEFT: **Part of the 7th Armoured Division before the start of the 1991 Gulf War. In the front is a CVR(T) while behind it are two Centurion AVRE tanks armed with the 165mm/6.5in demolition charge projector. On the left is an FV 434 engineer's vehicle.**

LEFT: **Part of a Soviet battle group. In the foreground are six ACRV M1974/1, in the middle are T-72 MBTs, while in the rear are a mixture of Zil and Ural trucks.**

ABOVE RIGHT: **A Black Hawk helicopter picking up a British Light 105mm/4.13in field gun during a combined exercise. Behind it is a Land Rover.** LEFT: **Two Willys Jeeps lead a Sexton SPG past a stationary convoy of British carriers, during the fighting in Normandy in June 1944. The leading Jeep has additional fuel in jerry-cans fixed on the bonnet.** BELOW: **A British Chieftain MBT passing an FV 432 APC during an exercise on Salisbury Plain. The Chieftain is fitted with Still Brew armour while the FV 432 has a 7.62mm/0.3in gun turret fitted to it.**

Tanks are the main offensive unit of the division and supply the armoured punch to smash through an enemy's defence. However, some tanks were converted into anti-aircraft vehicles (to give the division some protection from the air) and command vehicles.

The purpose of reconnaissance is to provide the commander with an accurate assessment of what the enemy is doing, its strength and position. Reconnaissance takes the form of aerial, ground and signals information and this intelligence helps the commander make tactical decisions. The armoured car performed the ground reconnaissance role for many years within the British Army until replaced by the light tank.

Motorized infantry specifically trained in the art of armoured warfare co-operate in action with the tanks. The job of the infantry is to attack enemy anti-tank guns and to clear infantry defensive positions that would normally stop the armour.

The SPGs give covering fire to the initial assault of the division. The bombardment must be short and not churn up the ground. Artillery can also give covering fire to engineers or infantry as they move forward. SPGs are essential as getting towed artillery into position is slow and very time consuming and they can easily become bogged down when off-road on difficult ground.

The engineers supply the bridging equipment, mine-field clearing and many other specific roles that now can be carried out from specialized AFVs. The British Army leads the world in this type of vehicle development.

Without signals or radio communications, the division could wander aimlessly over the battlefield as was the case in World War I. Now a divisional commander can keep control of 3,500 vehicles spread over many miles of the battlefield.

World War I

The story of the AFV in World War I is the story of the armoured car, and in particular its use by the British Royal Naval Air Service (RNAS). When the Germans overran Belgium in 1914, they came up against a few improvised armoured cars being used by the Belgian Army. These vehicles, the first AFVs to see action, were basic touring cars with boiler plate fitted to them and armed with one or two machine-guns. They did excellent work in slowing the German advance. The RNAS based at Dunkirk had 18 cars for aircraft support and downed-pilot rescue, and, on hearing about the Belgian success with armouring touring cars, armed two of their own and used them effectively against German cavalry.

The RNAS continued producing these home-made armoured cars and the Royal Naval Armoured Car Division (RNACD) was officially formed in October 1914, taking part in the land battles in Flanders over the next year. The Division would eventually consist of 15 armoured car squadrons and a Divisional HQ. Each armoured car squadron consisted of three sections, each with four cars. The Navy pushed on converting more and more vehicles including several trucks, but this led to problems with maintenance and spare parts. A basic armoured body with full body and overhead protection and mounting a turret with 360-degree traverse was developed so that it could be fitted to several makes of car. The two main chassis used were the Rolls-Royce and the Lanchester. The first of these new designs started arriving in France by Christmas 1914.

> "'The Chase' was the unit's especial type of war, and went into it with all the dash and efficiency that its long training had produced."
> RNAS Armoured Car Section Commander, 1915

TOP: **One of the British Gun Carriers developed to move heavy guns forward after a successful attack in World War I. The two-wheel trailer at the rear of the vehicle was to aid steering, but this idea was quickly dropped. The doors in the rear of the vehicle are the main entrance and exit for the gun crew.**
ABOVE: **A British RNAS Seabrook armoured car of 1915. This 10,160kg/10-ton vehicle had a crew of six and was armed with a 3pdr gun and a Vickers machine-gun. All these early RNAS vehicles were built as "one-offs". Most were later handed over to the British Army.**

Once the Western Front had settled into stagnant trench warfare, there was very little for the RNACD to do and in October 1915 the last section returned to Britain for re-assignment. RNACD squadrons Nos.3 and 4 were first redeployed to Gallipoli, where they did nothing, and then to Egypt, where the British Army reluctantly took charge of them and used them for patrolling the Suez Canal and in western desert operations. The army broke up the naval units and formed the Light Armoured Motor (LAM) Batteries of the Motor Machine Gun Corps, standardizing on the Rolls-Royce armoured car as it was very reliable. The British Army in

FAR LEFT: **London buses shipped over to France were used to move British troops up to the front line. At first they carried their London bus livery, but this was quickly removed along with all the window glass.**
ABOVE: **The front view of the British Gun Carrier. The driver's station is on the left and the vehicle commander's on the right, with the field gun in the middle, mounted on its carriage from which the wheels have been removed.**
BELOW: **Senior British officers inspecting a line-up of Royal Naval mobile anti-aircraft guns. The guns mounted on these vehicles are French 75mm/2.95in AA guns.** BOTTOM: **British officers inspecting a Thornycroft mobile anti-aircraft gun. These vehicles were formed into mobile brigades and were moved around the battlefield to cover any major attack.**

general was not sure how to deploy the armoured car but individual officers discovered their worth and used them with imagination and panache. The desert proved to be an excellent operational area for the armoured car, but it also had significant success against German forces in German South West Africa and British East Africa. No.1 squadron RNACD, which was sent to Russia in June 1916 to help fight the Germans in that country, had covered 85,295km/53,000 miles from the White Sea to the Crimea in their operations by the time of their return to Britain after the Russian surrender in late 1917.

The armoured car also showed its value in India, particularly on the Northern Frontier, where demand for troops in other theatres had weakened the forces used for peacekeeping. Armoured vehicles of all types were found to be a very satisfactory substitute for both infantry and cavalry against marauding tribesmen. Armoured cars had speed and endurance, and could be adapted to suit local conditions. One was even fitted with a ten-barrelled Gatling gun, while others had pom-pom guns fitted. Some trucks were converted to the SPG role having 76mm/2.99in guns fitted to them.

Other AFV developments of World War I were comparatively minor. They included early SPGs – guns mounted on trucks for mobile Anti-Aircraft (AA) defence, such as the Thornycroft, or in the support role for armoured car operations. One tracked SPG was developed by the British but only used a few times, as it did not conform to standard army procedure. Infantry carriers were under development and if the war had gone on into 1919 would have been deployed in action against the Germans. All of these were minor developments compared to the armoured car, and it was undoubtedly due to the ingenuity of the RNAS that the armoured car played such an important role in World War I.

Between the wars

After the developments in armoured vehicles by France and Britain during World War I, many military men felt that the days of the horse were numbered, and between 1920 and 1939 there was a general move towards the mechanization of armed forces. Britain continued to build and experiment with more tanks, armoured cars and carriers than any other nation and would lead the world for many years in this development. French and British light tanks and armoured cars would be sold to many countries, becoming the nucleus of many virgin armoured units. In 1929 Britain made two significant developments in the use of the AFV: the fitting of short-range two-way radios to all AFVs, and the development and use of the smoke mortar, both of which would become standard equipment in practically all armies.

Under the Treaty of Versailles that ended World War I, Germany was not allowed to build any AFVs. They were allowed unarmed armoured cars for policing duties, and some of these were borrowed by the army for exercises. Nevertheless, some tanks and armoured cars were built secretly both in Germany and in a German-controlled factory in Sweden, and a German-Soviet pact enabled the Germans to open a testing establishment in Kazan in 1926. Heinz Guderian made the most of this test area and companies like Daimler-Benz, Rheinmetall and Bussing sent armoured cars and other AFVs for testing. By 1927–28 the Germans had developed a number of very good half-track vehicles for towing artillery. Although Guderian had most of the components of an armoured division either in place or under development by 1936, it would not be until the spring of 1939 that the armoured half-track Sd Kfz 251 infantry carrier would start to come into service.

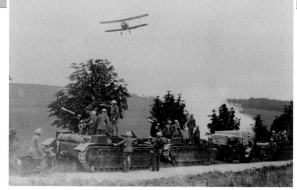

TOP: **In 1928, Vickers Armstrong were experimenting with the idea of the wheel-cum-tracked vehicle. The vehicle in the picture has the tracks deployed and is armed with a single Vickers machine-gun. Only two machines were built.** ABOVE: **Two Birch Gun SPAAGs of 20 Battery deployed on the roadside during an exercise on Salisbury Plain. These vehicles were not very reliable and were quickly dropped by the British Army.**

Russia had bought a large number of British armoured cars during World War I and more were sent to aid the White Russians, but these early cars had great problems with the rough Russian roads and were badly maintained by the Russian peasants who used them. The Soviet Union developed several very good armoured cars and other AFVs in this period, but not armoured infantry carriers and SPGs. The Soviets felt that the infantry could travel on the outside of the tanks, as with almost unlimited manpower life was cheap – Mother Russia was all.

The Americans sat back and did practically no AFV development between 1919 and 1930. There was great debate between the cavalry and the infantry over what they wanted and how it was going to be used. However, between 1930 and 1939, development went into overdrive and 48 projects were on

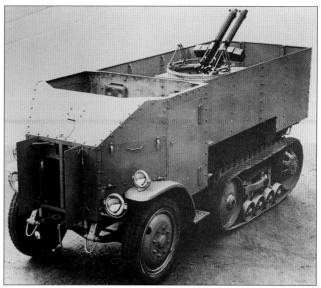

ABOVE: **A Light Tank Mk II fitted with collapsible pontoons. The exhaust pipe on the left has been raised and the driver's visor has been smeared with sealant. The man on the rear of the vehicle is operating the outboard motor, which was attached to the rear of the tank.**

trials with the army, but only six would eventually see service. With the start of World War II, the Americans very quickly discovered that they had been left far behind by developments in Britain and Germany and so they swiftly set about improving the standard of the AFVs in service with the US Army.

Italy had undertaken some armoured car development during World War I, but this was now considerably increased by the Fiat Company. In addition, the Italians had bought several of the new Carden-Loyd small fast tanks from Britain.

By the end of World War I it was considered very desirable to have SPGs and they were under development in many countries but few would see service, like the Birch guns in the British Army. It would not be until 1940 that the first real SPG would appear. In the meantime the Portee was developed. This was a basic truck that the small field gun or anti-tank gun would be winched up on to. There was room for the gun crew on the vehicle, which would be driven to where the gun was required. The gun and crew would then leave the vehicle that would move off to a place of safety.

Many traditionally inclined army officers and men around the world had been greatly opposed to the introduction of mechanization and the loss of the horse, but nothing could withstand the power of the armoured formation which Guderian and his Panzer Divisions would demonstrate to the world with the invasion of Poland in 1939.

TOP: **An armoured Burford-Kegresse machine-gun carrier B11E5. It was based on the company's 1,524kg/30cwt half-track chassis. The gun-mounting could be removed and the vehicle turned into a personnel carrier.** ABOVE: **The Burford-Kegresse Half-track Portee vehicles of the 9th Light Battery. The 94mm/3.7in howitzers are carried complete on the rear of the vehicle. The loading ramps can also be seen on the rear deck.** BELOW: **An Indian Pattern armoured car and a Crossley Mk 1 on display at the Bovington Tank Museum. These large armoured cars were developed to help police the Empire, especially in areas such as the North West Frontier in India.**

> "The German system consists essentially of making a breach in the front with armour and aircraft, then to throw mechanized and motorized columns into the breach."
> General A. Armengaud (analysis of the Blitzkrieg on Poland), 1939

Dad's Army

After the withdrawal of British and French forces from Dunkirk in June 1940, there was a real threat that the Germans would invade Britain once France had been defeated. There was a great shortage of AFVs in Britain as the British Expeditionary Force (BEF) had left all its heavy equipment behind so an urgent programme of rearmament was started. In the meantime, a number of makeshift designs were used, based on standard civilian saloon cars and trucks.

Many Home Guard units produced their own armoured cars. Some were very good and would have performed well against the enemy, but most were death traps to their users and would have been all too easily brushed aside by the Germans. One unit based at Chiswick in London converted several buses, by removing the bus bodywork and replacing it with a steel shell that had several firing slits in it. These unorthodox armoured cars and trucks were officially discouraged by the high command as they did not fit into the designated role of the Home Guard and the use of these unsupported AFVs would have been a disaster. Two of the better armoured cars were the Beaverette and the Humberette, based on the standard Humber Super Snipe chassis, built at the insistence of Lord Beaverbrook (the Beaverette was named after him). Sir Malcolm Campbell, the land and water world speed record holder, was the provost company commander of the 56th London Division, Home Defence Force, and he designed and then built the prototype of the Dodge armoured car which was

unofficially known as the "Malcolm Campbell" car. Seventy of these were built by Briggs Motor Bodies of Dagenham and were ready by the end of August 1940. To increase the fire-power of these cars and trucks, the Home Guard would often fit captured German machine-guns from crashed bombers to their vehicles, the only problem being fresh supplies of ammunition! Some units managed to get hold of a few World War I 6pdr tank guns and fitted them to the Malcolm Campbell cars.

ABOVE: **Two 762kg/15cwt civilian vehicles converted for the use of the Home Defence Force in 1940. Each vehicle has a crew of three, one driver and two for the single machine-gun mounted in the open-topped rear.**
BELOW: **A Humber saloon car converted for the Home Guard. Six men could be carried in the vehicle. The windows have been removed and replaced with metal plates with a firing slit cut in them.**

"Armadillos" were a large group of AFVs designed and built by the London Midland and Scottish Railway (LMS) workshop at Wolverton. Several prototypes were developed using different types of boiler plate as armour, but these were rejected in favour of a wooden box structure. The wooden box armour was made up as a sandwich with 76mm/3in wooden planks front and back, with a 152mm/6in thick filling of gravel between the planks. The box had an open top with an AA machine-gun mount and all-round armoured firing slits in the sides, and was bolted to the flat bed of many different types of truck. It was proof against small arms fire but nothing else. The cab had the glass removed and mild steel plate inserted which gave the driver some protection but was not bullet-proof. Some 700 Armadillos of three different marks were built. Concrete was also used as armour on several types of truck, known as "Bison". These were bullet-proof and proof against small anti-tank rounds and were basically concrete pillboxes mounted on truck flat beds. The Beaver Eel, known to the RAF as "Tender, Armoured, Leyland Type C", was built by Leyland for the protection of aircraft factories and airfields. These vehicles were based on the Leyland Retriever 3-ton truck and by the end of September 1940, Leyland had produced 250 and LMS 86 of this type. The last major conversion type was the Bedford type OXA which was officially the "Lorry, 30cwt, Armoured Anti-Tank,

ABOVE LEFT: **A heavy truck chassis has been used for this large armoured infantry carrier. This conversion has been carried out by the LMS workshops. It carried a crew of two plus an infantry section of ten men.** ABOVE: **A civilian 1,524kg/30cwt truck converted into an armoured car in 1940. It has been named "Flossie" by the crew. The vehicle had a crew of eight and was armed with a single light machine-gun and small arms. Only the driver's position was equipped with a visor.**

Bedford". These had a custom-made armoured cab and body for the truck and were fitted with the Boys anti-tank rifle and several machine-guns. All these truck conversions could take up to five men in the fighting compartment and some of the larger conversions could take a full section of ten men.

By the summer of 1942 as the threat of invasion diminished and more conventional vehicles were available, all the truck conversions had reverted back to their normal role, and the light armoured cars were by now relegated to airfield defence, some even being passed over to the American 8th Air Force.

ABOVE: **A Humber Saloon car being used by the British Home Guard in 1940. This car has had a hatch cut in the roof above the passenger's seat and a larger removable hatch over the rear section so the men in the back could stand up and fire from the car.** RIGHT: **A Bedford 1,524kg/30cwt truck converted and issued to the British Army in 1940. This vehicle was called a Lorry Armoured Anti-Tank as the vehicle carried a Boys anti-tank rifle and light machine-guns.**

The coming of age of the Self-Propelled Gun

The SPG is a motorized or tracked artillery piece which unlike the tank does not have to be in visual range of its target. A number of countries had tried SPGs before World War II but nothing had come of it, either because they were not reliable or because they did not conform to basic army modes of operation. The rise of the SPG can be attributed to the impact of the tank on the battlefield, as demonstrated by Guderian's new formation that swarmed all over Poland, France, and later the Soviet Union. Supporting forces now had to move at the same speed as the tank and go where the tank went. Two distinct ideologies of how the SPG should be used in action came to the fore during World War II. One regarded the SPG as an extension of basic artillery doctrines, developing and using these guns as platforms to deliver indirect supporting fire in the usual way. The other school believed that the SPG should be used as a mobile gun to deliver close support to armour, and this theory, favoured by the Germans, led to the development of the Assault Gun.

Guderian knew he needed an SPG to support his tanks and infantry. The Germans started development in 1938 of the 15cm/5.91in sIG on a Panzer I chassis. This was an infantry

ABOVE: **A Churchill Mk 1 SPG armed with a 76.2mm/3in anti-aircraft gun. Originally 100 of these vehicles were ordered, but this was reduced to 50 with deliveries starting in July 1942. The vehicle had a crew of four and none of them saw active service. Later in the war some were converted into experimental Snake Demolition Carriers.**

gun mounted on top of the tank chassis with very basic protection and first saw action during the invasion of France in 1940. The Germans would go on to produce some very good SPG mounts and some extraordinary mounts that were just plain crazy. The largest production run was for the Sturmgeschutz III, often mistaken for a tank, as it very often had to fill the role of the tank. As the war turned against Germany there was a mad scramble to get more and more guns on self-propelled mounts.

By 1941 there was an urgent need for SPGs for the British forces, both for the Home Defence Forces and for the 8th Army in the deserts of North Africa. For the Home Forces, the Churchill 76.2mm/3in Gun Mk 1 was developed. An order for 100 vehicles was placed but only 24 were produced before the order was cancelled. They were very quickly transferred to the training role and did not see action. The Bishop was developed for the British 8th Army, with which it would see extensive service in North Africa and later in Sicily. These guns were very quickly phased out of service by the American M7, which in turn was replaced by the Sexton.

> **"Unleash the God of War!"**
> Marshal Zhukov's order to the Soviet artillery in front of Berlin, 1945

Like the Germans, the Italians very quickly took to the idea of the SPG and put it into production and service with the Italian Army. The majority of the Italian SPGs were known as Semovente. These were very good vehicles and were also used in large numbers by the Germans. They were used to equip several reformed Italian units after World War II.

The Japanese were well behind in the development of armour compared to the other combatants of World War II and even further behind in the development of the SPG. They did come up with a few designs but these were never produced in any large numbers. The most numerous type was the Type 4 HO-RO 150mm/5.91in SPG. These vehicles were hand-built and no production facility was ever set up. Very few records survive about these vehicles in action and deployment.

After the destruction of the Soviet armoured forces during the German invasion of the Soviet Union in June 1941 (Operation "Barbarossa"), the Russians had to start rebuilding their armoured formations almost from scratch. They took the idea of the SPG to heart and produced it in great numbers, concentrating on the assault gun types as these fitted into Soviet armed forces doctrine better than the indirect artillery support of Western design.

World War II would see the meteoric rise of the SPG both as an important weapon system in its own right and as part of the armoured formation, and would go on to replace the towed gun in many armed forces around the world.

TOP LEFT: **A British prototype SPG developed during World War II that never went into production. The chassis was from a Crusader tank and the gun was a 140mm/5.51in medium gun.** TOP RIGHT: **An Italian mobile anti-aircraft vehicle developed in 1915. A Lancia I Z lorry chassis was used with a 75/30 gun mounted on the rear. There was only room for the driver and gun commander on the vehicle, the rest of the crew travelling in a separate one.** ABOVE LEFT: **A Carden-Loyd Mk VI carrier armed with a 47mm/1.85in gun. Development started in 1927. However, the British Army preferred the machine-gun armed carrier, so the 47mm/1.85in version was only sold abroad.** ABOVE RIGHT: **An American prototype SPAAG vehicle. The T53E1 used the Sherman tank chassis and mounted a 90mm/3.54in anti-aircraft gun. The top of the turret was open to allow for maximum elevation of the gun and the vehicle had four stabilizers fitted to the running gear.** BELOW: **The rear of the AMX GCT 155mm/6.1in SPG. The chassis of this vehicle is the AMX-30 MBT. The rear ammunition bins hold 42 mixed rounds, which can be reloaded in about 30 minutes. It has a crew of four.**

LEFT: **A DUKW, usually pronounced "Duck", emerging from the water on to an Italian beach. It has its trim vane raised on the front of the vehicle. Derived from the GMC 6x6 2,540kg/2.5-ton truck, but fitted with a boat-shaped hull, a total of 21,000 of these vehicles were built.**
BELOW: **A DUKW on shore in hostile territory. This vehicle has been fitted with a machine-gun mount above the co-driver's position. Operating the machine-gun was very dangerous as there was no protection for the gunner.**

Amphibious Infantry Assault Vehicles

There are several ways for a vehicle to cross a water obstacle such as a river; it can go over a bridge, be ferried across by boat, swim across under its own power or drive across the river bed fully submerged and out the other side. For amphibious landings on an enemy coastline, vehicles have to swim ashore under their own power or be landed by special landing craft.

Amphibious vehicles did not make an appearance until World War II, but since then great strides have taken place in many armoured forces around the world. During World War II there were many variations on a theme, some vehicles being designed to carry loads from ship to shore while others were designed to take a section of 35 men and put them on a beach. A British idea for producing an amphibious tank involved using a flotation screen, which was also used on several post war vehicles. At first the DD (Duplex Drive) Sherman tank (as these first models were known) were not liked by the Navy and it took the intervention of General Eisenhower himself to get the project moving. Eventually, some 300 of these tanks were built to take part in the D-Day invasion.

The Americans were to produce two of the best and most numerous amphibious vehicles of the war, both of which would soldier on for many years after it finished. The first was the DUKW amphibious truck based on the GMC 6x6 2,540kg/ 2.5-ton truck – one of the most important weapons of World War II as far as General (later President) Eisenhower was

concerned. The letters DUKW (pronounced "Duck") explain the vehicle's specification. D stands for a 1942 vehicle, U is for amphibious, K indicates that it is all-wheel drive and W denotes that it has twin rear axles. Most of these vehicles were not armoured, but some were converted into special support vehicles, like the rocket-firing version known as the Scorpion, while others had field guns firing from the cargo area. The second vehicle was the Landing Vehicle Tracked (LVT) which was to play a very important role in the island-hopping campaign in the Pacific and in the crossing of the last great water barrier in Europe: "The Rhine Crossing". The LVT was to be found in many different variations from the basic troop transport and cargo carrier to vehicles fitted with tank turrets

LEFT: **A DUKW entering the Rhine and about to take American troops over into Germany. The DUKW had a central tyre inflation system so the driver could raise or lower tyre pressures from the driving position.** ABOVE: **An LVT (A) 1 demonstrating its full firepower during a night exercise. The vehicle had a crew of six and was armed with one 37mm/1.46in gun, one 12.7mm/50cal machine-gun in a turret and two 7.62mm/30cal machine-guns in pits behind the turret.**

giving close support to the invading forces. These vehicles would remain in service with armed forces around the world until the 1970s.

The Germans and the Japanese both dabbled in developing amphibious vehicles, the Germans with greater success. They produced a very effective amphibious version of the Kubelwagen called the *Schwimwagen* which proved to be a very useful vehicle. They also tried to give tanks like the Panzer III *Tauchpanzer* a snorkel device and converted some 168 vehicles, which were used once in 1941 at the crossing of the river Bug in Soviet Russia. The Japanese went for amphibious tanks such as the Type 2 Ka-Mi light tank developed by the Japanese Navy. Used several times very successfully, the big problem, as with all Japanese armour, was the lack of numbers, and so these were used in penny packets. Most ended their life as dug-in pillboxes on various Pacific islands.

During the "Cold War", NATO forces went for specialized armoured vehicles to bridge water obstacles, while the Soviet forces concentrated on amphibious vehicles. The Soviets designed and produced vehicles such as the BMP-1, BTR-60, 2S1 and the SA8 – a whole family of amphibious vehicles that used a water jet propulsion system when in the water. The main battle tanks use the snorkel system and take a large amount of time to ready for the water crossing, but once ready are driven into the river and the crew and engine draw air into the vehicle down the snorkel tube. The largest amphibious force in the world is the US Marine Corps, the branch of the United States Armed Forces responsible for conducting expeditionary and amphibious operations.

ABOVE: **The LVT was also used by the British Army where it was known as the Buffalo. These two Buffalos are being loaded with Universal Carriers.**
BELOW: **Seven British LVT Buffalos are being readied for an operation to cross the Rhine. These vehicles are armed with three machine-guns and a single 20mm/0.79in cannon, and had a crew of four.**

Wartime developments

Great strides in AFV design and development were taken during World War II. The SPG went from a makeshift development into a sophisticated weapon system in the Allied armies, while the Axis forces scrambled to place as many guns as possible on to tracked or wheeled chassis. The British Army ended World War II with the medium 25pdr Sexton and the M40 155mm/6.1in heavy gun as the main SPGs and these would remain in service until the early 1960s. The Americans had several new designs in development at the end of the war that came into service during the 1950s.

The infantry carrier started as a lightly armed and armoured vehicle and was only capable of taking troops to the edge of the fighting. The British and Canadians came up with the idea of using the redundant SPG Priest vehicles in this role – by removing the gun and plating over the opening 12 men could be carried in safety. These were known as "unfrocked Priests" and were first used by the Canadians during their attack on Caen in 1944. The British also used a redundant tank chassis as an armoured infantry carrier. The Kangaroo, as it was called,

TOP: **A Morris Commercial C9/B portee armed with a 40mm/1.58in Bofors AA gun. The seats and windscreen could be folded forward to give the gun a full 360-degree traverse. It had a crew of four.**
ABOVE: **A 6pdr (57mm) anti-tank gun portee. This vehicle was a conversion of a Bedford truck. It is passing a burnt-out Panzer IV in North Africa during a British advance in 1942.**

was a conversion of the Canadian Ram tank; by removing the turret and the internal fittings there was room for ten men. Two regiments were kitted out with this vehicle and some 300 of these were used in north-west Europe by the Allies. In Italy, the Allies converted a further 177 vehicles. The one big disadvantage was that the infantry had to disembark over the top of the vehicle leaving them very exposed to enemy fire; this and other faults would be rectified in post-war development. The Russians did not develop any form of Armoured Personnel Carrier (APC) during World War II, feeling that the infantry could ride on the outside of the tank, and it would not be until the 1950s that they would start to develop APCs. The Americans looked at the Kangaroo and could see its shortcomings so stayed with the half-track infantry carrier until the mid-1950s.

> "Behind this armoured and mechanized onslaught came
> a number of German divisions in lorries."
> Winston Churchill (description of Blitzkrieg in France),
> June 1940

The armoured car had started World War II for the Allies as a small vehicle that was fast but poorly armed and armoured. They learnt quickly, and bigger and better cars did come into service by the war's end. In Britain they came up with the idea of making a wheeled version of the Sherman tank called the Boarhound. This was an eight-wheeled monster, 6.1m/20ft long and weighing 26,416kg/26 tons, which never went into service. The Germans went down the road of developing their eight-wheeled armoured car even further and putting larger and larger guns on the same chassis. In America the M6 and M8 armoured cars had been developed and saw extensive service during the war and further development post-war until replaced by modern armoured cars in the 1960s.

The rocket was beginning to make a name on the battlefield with many armies during World War II, and a number of special vehicles were developed to carry this new weapon. The main players in the rocket weapon system were the Germans, Russians and the Americans. The Germans put several different types of rockets on various half-tracks, but the biggest was the Sturmmörser. The Russians developed the Katyusha rocket system and would go on to develop several other systems post-war. The Americans also developed several systems, one being the T34 Calliope mounted on the Sherman tank. They also developed the artillery rocket further and designed several new vehicles post-war.

One of the most important vehicles to be developed was the armoured command truck or tank. These were often only lightly armed with just machine-guns, but would carry several extra radio sets so that commanders could keep in touch with their fighting units in the front line. These vehicles were developed further post-war and now are even more important on the battlefield. The story of the AFV in World War II clearly demonstrates the principle that the pace of development of new weapons and vehicles is very fast during a time of war while in times of peace it is long and slow.

ABOVE: **A German Sd Kfz 263 heavy armoured radio car. Above it is the large frame aerial that on later vehicles was replaced by a rod aerial. It carried a long-range radio transmitter and receiver and had a crew of five. The turret was fixed and had a machine-gun fitted in the front.**

ABOVE MIDDLE: **Two British LVT Buffalos entering the Rhine. These vehicles were operated by the 79th Armoured Division. The rear machine-gun positions have gun shields to protect the gunners from enemy fire.** ABOVE: **Two DD (Duplex Drive) tanks being readied to take to the water as part of a training exercise. One of the flotation screens has been fully inflated while the other is about half-raised.** LEFT: **A German RSO fitted with a PaK40 75mm/2.95in anti-tank gun. Designed and built by Steyr, the gun was directly mounted without its wheels and trails on to the wooden body at the rear of the vehicle.**

"Divisional reconnaissance units should be armoured and preferably contain 2-pounder guns."
General Bartholomew, July 1940

The adaptation of soft-skin vehicles

The average soldier around the world is very good at adapting to local terrain and conditions, and at adapting his vehicles to do the same. This has gone on since motorized vehicles first appeared on the battlefield. The RNAS armoured car section was one of the first units to do this and were very good at this type of conversion. They did a number of local conversions of cars and trucks, and would scrounge, beg or borrow weapons which they would fit to whatever vehicle was suitable, for example, 6-pound naval guns fitted to Peerless trucks to give the armoured cars better support.

During World War II, there was wholesale conversion of vehicles, which started with the British forces after the withdrawal from France in 1940. The shortage of vehicles made the troops very ingenious at adapting what they could, and turning them into some form of AFV. The Home Defence forces and the Home Guard made many local conversions of vehicles, which were frowned upon and openly discouraged by high command but not stopped. The British 8th Army in North Africa became real experts in the local adaptation of soft-skin vehicles into AFVs. With the constant advance and retreat by opposing forces, large numbers of enemy vehicles fell into each other's hands. One unit in particular would make its name from its vehicle conversions: the Long Range Desert Group (LRDG). This group took vehicles such as the Chevrolet truck and the Jeep and fitted them with a large number of cannon and machine-guns. The Jeeps carried up to five heavy machine-

> "Very largely the story of mechanization is the story of adaptation of commercial motoring to military purposes."
> Professor A. W. Low (in Modern Armaments), 1939

guns, while the trucks had the heavier weapons such as 20mm/0.79in cannon and several heavy machine-guns fitted. They then took these vehicles far behind the German lines and created havoc in the German supply routes. The LRDG worked very closely with another new unit called the Special Air Service (SAS), who would take their converted Jeeps into Sicily, Italy and finally into north-west Europe where they continued to work deep behind the German front line.

The Germans were better known for their conversion of captured enemy armour, but they did do a number of conversions to their half-tracks and other soft-skin vehicles, mounting various different types of captured field guns on them. A large number of these vehicles were used by the German *Afrika Korps* in the fast flowing mobile warfare conducted in the deserts of North Africa.

The Americans were and still are great innovators and converters of soft-skin vehicles. During World War II, they converted the Jeep from a light utility vehicle into a heavily armed AFV by fitting armour plate and numerous heavy machine-guns to the vehicle. Some were fitted with rocket launchers. During the Battle of the Bulge, the American paratroopers surrounded at Bastogne turned a number of Jeeps into armoured cars and used them as a mobile fire-fighting unit rushed to any position under great pressure from

ABOVE: **A British AEC 10,160kg/ 10-ton truck that has been converted into an SPG in 1940. A number of these vehicles were built to help bolster the coastal defences of Britain. They were armed with a range of obsolete naval guns.**
RIGHT: **An American pick-up truck has been converted into an AFV by fitting a single Lewis gun in the rear cargo area. The standard road wheels have been replaced with railway wheels so the vehicle can be used to patrol the railway.**

RIGHT: **HMS Aniche is a Talbot armoured car. This is a modified version of the first Admiralty Pattern vehicle that was built for the RNAS in 1914–15. There are two spare tyres on the rear of the vehicle.**
BELOW: **This bulldozer has been converted into an armoured vehicle by being covered with steel plate and having two machine-guns fitted to the front of the vehicle.**

a German attack. To put more rocket batteries into action the Americans mounted launch tubes on the back of "deuce and half" (GMC 2,540kg/2.5-ton) trucks. These trucks were also fitted with the M45 quad 12.7mm/50-caliber mounts to give supply convoys some protection from both air or ground attacks. In the island-hopping campaign of the Pacific war, the Jeep proved to be an excellent support AFV. Fitted with heavy machine-guns and rockets, it could go where other vehicles could not. During the Vietnam War, the Americans had a real shortage of armoured cars and other escort vehicles for their supply convoys which were constantly attacked. The men of the transport battalions started putting armour plate on some of their trucks, the favourite being the 5,080kg/5-ton M54A2. They then fitted them with a wide variety of weapons such as the M45 quad mount, mini guns. In a few cases, the complete hull of M113 APCs minus the tracks and running gear were placed on the back of the truck.

No matter where they are, troops will continue to adapt and convert their vehicles officially or unofficially to meet local circumstances, often with remarkable success.

ABOVE: **A line-up of three Austin vehicles. Two have been converted into AFVs by attaching steel plate around them. Each armoured car has an open roof so that a light machine-gun can be fitted on a pedestal mount. The middle vehicle is an ambulance.** BELOW: **An armoured 3,048kg/3-ton truck that has been converted into an APC using steel plate. The side-skirts covering the wheels are hinged to allow access to the tyres and fuel tank.**

The Cold War

World War II finished in 1945. The Cold War, which started in 1946 between the NATO countries (USA and most of Western Europe) and those of the Soviet-led Warsaw Pact, would last for some 45 years. The two sides never actually came to blows, each no doubt deterred by the military might of their opponents. The Cold War would see the greatest arms race in Man's history; it would cover land, sea, air and space. Money for research and development into better weapon systems was freely available at first, but with crippling debts from World War II, most countries had to drop out of the race leaving the Americans and the Soviet Union as the front runners.

The Soviets placed large numbers of men in highly mechanized units and machines along the border with Western Europe – the infamous "Iron Curtain". The idea was that the Soviets would launch an NBC (nuclear, biological or chemical) attack first, then the mechanized forces would flood through in a Blitzkrieg-style attack on the NATO forces.

The members of NATO decided to try for standardization throughout their armed forces. A large number of members could not afford to develop new weapons and so looked to

TOP: **An American cruise missile TEL system on exercise in Britain. The vehicle had a MAN Cat I AI 8x8 tractor unit and a separate trailer which carried four Tomahawk missiles. It had a crew of four.** ABOVE: **A Soviet Scud B missile system being driven to a site. The launch vehicle was known as the 9P117 and the MAZ-7310 LTM. It has a crew of four and can only carry one missile at a time.**

America to act as the main weapon supplier. Ammunition was standardized, and the same thing was done to vehicle types. The idea was that you developed one engine and chassis and then this basic vehicle filled many roles. In Britain, the 432 chassis was produced as a basic APC with 12 different models and an SPG. The Land Rover became a multipurpose vehicle, being produced in reconnaissance, anti-tank, signals and ambulance roles. In America, the M113 was produced and sold to over 40 different countries (not all members of NATO), with some 40 different types being created due to local modifications. Some models of both the 432 and the M113 were turned into anti-tank weapons. In the late 1950s and early 60s the guided missile started to make an appearance on the battlefield. At the time this new lightweight weapon was

> "An iron curtain has descended across the Continent."
> Sir Winston Churchill, March 5, 1946

ABOVE LEFT: **A German Leopard passing an M113 APC. The troops are riding on the outside of the vehicle, which is a very common practice of infantry using this type of carrier.** ABOVE RIGHT: **A Lance missile is about to be launched from an M752 TEL. This vehicle uses many of the parts of the M113 APC. It has a crew of four and is still in service with many countries.** LEFT: **A column of Soviet BMP-1 IFVs crossing a river, demonstrating that it is fully amphibious. When this vehicle first entered service it gave NATO a real fright. It has a crew of three and carries an infantry section of eight men in the rear of the vehicle.** BELOW: **A Berlin Brigade British FV 432 APC. On the top of the vehicle is a wire basket for additional storage. To the rear of the basket is a yellow flashing light which is carried on military tracked vehicles when travelling on public roads. British troops are no longer based in Berlin.**

supposed to sound the death knell of the Main Battle Tank (MBT). It could be mounted on just about any type of AFV and turn that vehicle into a tank killer. In the same way, the contemporary guided missile was expected to end the threat of fighter aircraft.

Vehicles and weapons were becoming very sophisticated and so required a higher degree of training for the troops who were to use the system in battle. In the West this weighted the balance in favour of professional volunteer armies. After World War II, America stopped conscription only to reintroduce it during the Vietnam War. Britain ceased conscription in 1962 and concentrated on developing a small but very professional army. This army would develop a very good reputation around the world and in 1982 would fight a war in the Falkland Islands that most of the world felt they could not win. Again during the Gulf War, Britain would demonstrate how professional and highly trained its armed forces were. The Soviet Union for the most part stayed with a conscripted army, as it decided to

make its weapons more basic and simpler to use. Consequently they were able to sell their weapons far and wide outside the Soviet Union and some of these have continued to be used long after becoming obsolete in the Cold War scenario.

Another major change in tactics and basic army doctrine was the introduction of the helicopter into service and its effect on military operations. The helicopter has changed the speed at which troops can be moved from one part of the battlefield to another. During the Vietnam War, the Americans fitted their transport helicopters with machine-guns and rockets, and this has now been taken one stage further with the development of the helicopter gunship. Heavy lift helicopters are also capable of moving artillery and light AFVs around the battlefield and newer vehicles are being developed to make the most of this capability.

With the collapse of the Soviet Union and the end of the Cold War in the early 1990s, a number of former Warsaw Pact countries have joined NATO, and now former enemies work and train together.

LEFT: **British Saracen 6x6 APC. This is a tropical version of the Saracen with raised engine intakes on the engine housing. The turret has been fitted with an additional four smoke dischargers.**
BELOW: **Rhodesian mine-protected vehicle called the Leopard. This is built using a Volkswagen beetle chassis. It has no fixed armament and relies on the small arms of the men inside the vehicle.**

The battlefield taxi with NBC and mine protection

Nuclear, Biological and Chemical (NBC) warfare is a new and terrifying type of war that has come to Man with the onset of the Cold War. Open-topped vehicles offered little protection for the crew from this new type of warfare. At the same time a lot of time and money was being spent on training these men because armies after World War II were becoming smaller and more professional. Here was a great incentive to develop protection for vehicle crews and infantry as quickly as possible.

The first modern APCs in the Soviet armed forces were open-topped such as the BTR-152. They gave the crew very little protection from incoming fire or the weather and were not very different from what the Allied forces had used during World War II. By the early 1960s this mistake had been rectified by the Soviet designers and new vehicles such as the BTR-

60 and the BMP-1 came on to the scene. The BTR-60 was no danger to the NATO forces, but the BMP-1 was a very different matter and frightened the life out of NATO commanders. The BTR-60 and the BMP-1 are both fully amphibious and have a full NBC system fitted to protect the crew of the vehicle and the infantry section being carried. The Soviet NBC system first draws the outside air into a multi-filter that removes all the dangerous agents, then passes it through a heater if necessary and then into the crew compartment. The air pressure in the vehicle is also kept several atmospheres higher than the outside pressure, which ensures no chemicals or other agents can leak into the vehicle through the side gun-ports.

The first British APCs, such as the Humber "Pig" and the Saracen, did not have any form of NBC protection for the crew or the infantry section. This fault was put right when the 432 came into service. The vehicle was fully NBC protected just as other more modern vehicles have continued to be to this day. The Americans took a very different approach with the M113 and only protected the vehicle crew of the driver and commander and two others. The other nine men in the vehicle have to use their own respirators. Even in a more modern vehicle like the Bradley there is no protection for the infantry in the back of the vehicle. Crews for the open SPGs like the M110 had no NBC protection at all except for their own personnel NBC clothing.

LEFT: **Soviet BMP-1 MICV. This shows the back of the vehicle with the bulged rear doors, which is one of the major weaknesses of the vehicle as they contain fuel tanks. The low profile of the turret can be clearly seen and the very narrow tracks which give the vehicle a high ground pressure.**

LEFT: **Two American M113 APCs. The driver's hatch is in the open position, with the vehicle's 12.7mm/50cal machine-gun beside it. The commander's position is to the rear of the machine-gun. The M113 has been sold to over 60 countries around the world and has already racked up more than 60 years' service.**

BELOW: **An American M2 Bradley halted and debussing its infantry section. The great height of the vehicle shows up clearly here and is a major weakness of the design. The M2 has had several upgrades to help improve its performance and armoured protection.**

The anti-tank mine has always been a problem for wheeled and tracked vehicles. Designers have tried to give wheeled vehicles some form of survivability by making these vehicles bigger with six or eight wheels so if one is destroyed the vehicle can still get the crew to a place of safety. In Zimbabwe and South Africa between 1972 and 1980 there was a proliferation of armoured vehicles designed to protect the occupants from mines. The main body was shaped to direct the blast from the mine down and away from the vehicle, as with the 5-ton Crocodile which could carry up to 18 men in the troop compartment. Vehicles such as the Hippo were designed with the main body of the vehicle raised up off the chassis and again shaped to direct the blast away from it. A Land Rover-based product Ojay was produced for the domestic market. In Russia the BTR-80 and 90 have been designed to operate with several wheels damaged or blown off. The Germans have also developed this system for their heavy wheeled vehicles like the Luchs and the Fuchs. The American M113 has a very weak floor. During the Vietnam War, a large number of men were injured riding in the vehicle, so the floor was covered with sandbags and the men remained on top until fired upon. The Russians had the same problem in Afghanistan with the BMP-1 and 2, and their crews also rode on top until attacked.

ABOVE: **Soviet troops climbing into the rear of a BMP-1. The eight-man infantry section sit back-to-back with the main fuel tank between them, and the rear doors also act as fuel tanks. As can be seen, Soviet mechanized infantry had very basic webbing and personal equipment.**

> "The bullets entered our half-tracks and rattled around a little killing all inside."
> General Omar Bradley to General George Patton (Kasserine Pass), 1942

LEFT: **British FV 432 APC** travelling in convoy and at speed through a forest. The vehicle commander is standing up in his position giving instructions to the driver, who has his seat in the fully raised position. The hatches above the mortar are also in the open position.

BELOW: **French AMX VCI** armed with a 20mm/0.79in cannon and coaxial 7.62mm/0.3in machine-gun. This was an optional extra that could be fitted to the vehicle. An infantry section of ten men is carried in the rear of the vehicle, each man having his own firing port.

The birth of the Infantry Fighting Vehicle

Mechanized infantry tactics up till the late 1950s used the APC as a battlefield taxi, taking the infantry to the edge of the fighting. The infantry would then debus and go into action on foot. Both the British and the Americans were developing replacements for their ageing APCs, which resulted in 1960 with the Americans putting the M113 into production, followed in 1962 by the British with the 432, but these new vehicles would not herald any great change in tactics. The Soviets were also working on a new vehicle which would change infantry tactics for ever and which caused NATO grave concern.

This new vehicle was the BMP-1 Infantry Fighting Vehicle (IFV). It was the first Soviet vehicle to be designed with the nuclear battlefield in mind from the start. The BMP-1 was one of the most significant innovations in AFV design in the latter half of the 20th century. Development started in the early 1960s, with trials commencing in 1964. In 1966, as the vehicle was about to be placed into production, the Soviet leader Nikita Khrushchev felt the vehicle was too expensive and that troops could be taken into battle far cheaper by the basic truck. Khrushchev was replaced as leader in the same year by Leonid Brezhnev who now rescinded the cancellation and allowed the BMP-1 to go into production. The BMP-1 was the first vehicle

that could take troops right into the engagement zone. The men inside could fire their weapons from the safety of the vehicle at first, and then when in a suitable position, the troops would debus and fight on foot with close support supplied by the BMP-1's gun. In a major change in tactics, only 8 men could be carried in the rear of the vehicle. They sat in two rows of four facing outwards, each man having a firing port for his own personal weapon. This vehicle was first seen by the Western powers at the Moscow May Day Parade in 1967.

NATO had to find a way of combating this new threat. There was no way a new vehicle could be designed and developed from scratch, placed into production and then into service in the near future. The Germans were developing a multi-role chassis for a new family of vehicles including an IFV, the first prototypes of which were produced between 1961 and 1963. Eventually the vehicle went into production in 1970 and entered service with the German Army in 1971. Britain and America

> "The quickest and most effective way to exploit the success of the tank is by motorized infantry especially if the soldiers' vehicles are armoured and have complete cross country ability."
> General Heinz Guderian Achtung – Panzer!, 1937

were lagging far behind so they both went down the road of trying to turn the 432 and the M113 into IFVs from the APC. The Americans started development of the XM723 in 1972. In 1976, some changes were required to the basic vehicle out of which two vehicles would emerge: the XM2 IFV and the XM3 Cavalry Fighting Vehicle (CFV). The XM2 had a name change to the M2 Bradley and would enter service with the American Army in March 1983. In 1977, Britain started design and development of the MCV-80, which became the Warrior IFV, the idea being to replace most of the 3,000 432s in service with the Warrior. Orders were placed for 2,000 vehicles with the first entering service in 1987. As the Cold War ended, the order was cut back and the life span of the 432 was extended and variants remain in British Army service. In the US, the M2 Bradley and the M113 also serve on.

The BMP and the Bradley both have amphibious capability, but the British Warrior does not as it was felt it was not required. The real problem with these vehicles is that they are too heavy to be transported by air except in the largest transports. The Bradley and the Warrior both proved to be very reliable during the Gulf War and Operation "Iraqi Freedom", and have even taken on the role of light tank in some areas. Smaller, air-portable versions of the IVF have been considered for some time as part of the US Immediate Response Force.

ABOVE: **Soviet BTR-70 APC. This particular vehicle is not a standard infantry vehicle as it has several side hatches down the length of the vehicle. The trim vane can be seen in the stowed position under the nose of the vehicle.**

ABOVE: **This British Warrior is stopped and is covering the infantry section that has debussed from the vehicle during an exercise. Only half of the infantry section can be seen.** LEFT: **A West German Marder MICV. The vehicle commander and driver have their hatches open. The turret is fitted with six smoke dischargers. The box on the side of the turret is a laser sight.** BELOW: **A column of M2 Bradley MICVs passing over a temporary pontoon bridge during an exercise in Germany. The vehicle commander and gunner are almost out of the turret helping to give the driver information on the vehicle's position. Each pontoon has a single crewman looking after the pontoon's station-keeping.**

Playing catch-up

A rmies around the world have from time to time found themselves in the position of having to play catch-up against an enemy that out of the blue produces a new vehicle. There are two options open: either produce your own version of the new vehicle, or convert some of your existing stock into something similar to what the enemy has produced. The AFV seems to be capable of adjustments to meet almost any threat or need. These range from conversions done in the field to overcome a local problem, to production-line enhancements to fill the gap until more specialized vehicles become available. Its adaptability is truly amazing.

During World War II, the engineering officer of the German Panzerjager unit 653 converted a few of his unarmed Bergepanther recovery vehicles into armed vehicles by fixing Panzer IV turrets on them. The Germans took a number of old tank chassis like the Panzer II and placed the PaK40 anti-tank gun on some of these vehicles. They also did a large number of conversions on captured vehicles, turning them into mobile anti-tank guns or SPGs. The French Lorraine Schlepper chassis was used for two conversions, one to a 105mm/4.13in SPG and one armed with a PaK40 anti-tank gun.

The Israeli Defence Force have for many years been the masters of the vehicle conversion, turning old or captured vehicles into something new that they could use. The L33 SPG is a prime example of these conversions. They took the very old Sherman tank chassis and placed a 155mm/6.1in gun mounted in a very large box structure the size of a house on it. Another conversion was the Ambutank, also based on a

Sherman tank chassis but with the engine moved forward. It was developed so that the Israelis could evacuate their wounded while under fire – the rear area has been turned into an ambulance capable of taking stretcher cases.

A number of World War II vehicles were put into action during the 1992–95 conflict between Bosnian and Serbian forces in the former Yugoslavia. One of these was the M36 tank destroyer with "spaced armour". The M36 was never designed to withstand modern weapons like the RPG7 anti-tank rocket, so wooden batons were placed down the side of the vehicle and the space between them filled in with concrete. This

ABOVE: **British FV 432 APC armed with a 30mm/1.18in RARDEN cannon. Each mechanized British infantry battalion had 17 of these vehicles. This is the same two-man turret as that fitted to the Fox armoured car.** BELOW: **A 90mm/3.54in turret developed by Israel Defence Industries in 2004 to give the M113 a greater punch and extend its service life. This two-man turret has also been used to upgrade Chile's M24 Chaffee tanks.**

was then covered in heavy rubber sheeting that used to be conveyer belting in a factory. The other major change was in the engine. The old American engine was removed and with a little adaptation a Soviet T55 tank engine was dropped into the same space.

When the Soviets unveiled the BMP-1 at the May Day Parade in 1967, the British and Americans had only just brought the 432 and the M113 into service a few years previously and so had to make do with what they had until new vehicles like the IFV could be developed. The 432 and the M113 were the subject of a large number of conversions, both to improve the firepower of the basic vehicle and to give additional support to an infantry attack. Britain did a number of conversions to the 432 by putting RARDEN 30mm/1.18in gun turrets on the top of the vehicle, and some 432s were fitted with the Swingfire anti-tank missile to give the vehicle the ability to kill tanks. The Ferret armoured car was also fitted with two Swingfire missiles, one on each side of the

ABOVE LEFT: **British FV 432 APC fitted with a 120mm/4.72in Wombat Recoilless Rifle. The gun can be fired from the vehicle or dismounted, but the vehicle only carries 14 rounds of ammunition.** ABOVE: **American M113A2 Improved TOW Vehicle (ITV). This is a basic APC but fitted with the Raytheon TOW ATGW (Anti-Tank Guided Weapon). The vehicle carries ten missiles but no infantry.**

turret. Some 80,000 M113 vehicles have been produced since it went into production, a small number of which were converted on the production line, while others were converted by the different countries that bought them. The Australians at first placed old British Saladin armoured car turrets on some of their M113s and turned them into close-support vehicles. These were later upgraded with the British Scorpion 76mm/2.99in turret. The RARDEN 30mm/1.18in turret and the British Fox armoured car turret were also upgrade options. The Swiss fitted the 20mm/0.79in Hagglunds turret to some of their M113, and this conversion was also for sale to other M113 users.

LEFT: **A French AMX-30 chassis is used to mount the Euromissile Roland SAM system. The turret is in the raised position. The vehicle carries two missiles in the launcher and eight in the vehicle.** ABOVE: **American M163 Vulcan SPAAG. The vehicle has a crew of four but the turret is only a one-man operation. Developed by General Dynamics and entering service in 1965, the American Army had 671 of these vehicles in service by 1987.**

35

Peacekeeping around the world

Over the past half a century or so, armed forces around the world have found themselves undertaking the role of riot-control forces and internal security operations for which they were neither equipped nor trained. This has led to the development of many special vehicles that can protect the personnel using them whilst being, as much as can be possible, non-confrontational.

Full tracked vehicles such as the British 432, Warrior and Challenger tank are not suitable for this job, as they are very expensive to operate and maintain compared to a wheeled vehicle. Tracked vehicles like tanks and IFVs have very poor manoeuvrability in built-up areas, poor observation for the driver and commander, and can cause headlines in newspapers and on TV of "tanks on the streets". AFVs have proved their adaptability in these situations, with some conversions. The vision blocks of the vehicle have to be fitted with wipers and a cleaning fluid dispenser for a form of paint remover. Diesel is the preferred fuel for internal security vehicles as it does not burn as easily as petrol, and diesel engines have more economic fuel consumption.

When the "Troubles" started in Northern Ireland in 1969, the British Army had disposed of almost all its Humber 1-ton 4x4 wheeled APCs which were being sold off for scrap, to vehicle collectors or to the Belgian Army. These were all bought back at an increased cost and put back into service, and some of the 6x6

TOP: **British Warrior MICV armed with the 30mm/1.18in RARDEN cannon. All three of the crew can be seen. They have placed light blue UN covers over their helmets so they are easily visible and the vehicle has been painted white.**
ABOVE: **British Ferret Mk 2 in UN colours. The British Army has taken a full and active part in United Nations peacekeeping since World War II.**

Saracen APCs were also sent to Northern Ireland. The Humber 1-ton APC is better known as the "Pig" because it was a pig to drive. When in 1972 the IRA managed to acquire armour-piercing bullets, the Pig could not protect the troops from this new type of ammunition. All 500 Pigs were upgraded with better armour and armoured glass was put in the vision slits. Some Pigs were further converted with large gate-like structures covered in wire mesh that

RIGHT: The nickname for UN troops is the Blue
Helmets, and their vehicles are always painted
white so there can be no confusing the fact that
these men and women are on peacekeeping duties.
BELOW: British Saxon Patrol. This vehicle was
developed to replace ageing security vehicles such
as the Humber "Pig" in Northern Ireland. The Saxon
has been fitted with "wings" – riot-control screens
that can be deployed from side of the vehicle.

"Our country is going to be what our people have proclaimed
it must be – the Arsenal of Democracy."
Franklin D. Roosevelt, April 1916

ABOVE: Dutch Army AIFV in UN colours. The vehicle is an improved M113A1
and entered service in 1975 with the Dutch Army, who have bought 880.
The AIFV has a crew of three and can carry an infantry section of seven men.
BELOW: British Warrior on sentry duty at the city boundary of Sarajevo in Bosnia.
A large number of NATO forces were sent to the Balkans during the break-up
of Yugoslavia to act as peacekeepers.

were attached to the sides of the vehicle and then swung out to
give the troops protection from bottles, bricks and stones. This
winged appearance gave rise to the name "Flying Pig".

South Africa has developed a special internal security
vehicle in the Buffel. It has very high ground clearance, a
V-shaped body to deflect the explosive force from mines, and
a steel roof that can be folded down. The downside of this
vehicle is that it has a very high centre of gravity and so can
tip over when taking corners too fast or trying to cross rough
ground. In Britain, the Saxon has been developed to be used in
urban areas. Based on a Bedford truck chassis, the vehicle has
a good ground clearance and has been sold to several other
countries as an internal security vehicle.

The Shorts company of Northern Ireland built an internal
security vehicle called the Shorland for many years. It is based
on the Land Rover chassis and was sold to some 40 countries,
proving to be very cost effective and reliable. In America,
the Cadillac company produced the Commando III for use
with most police departments across the USA, as well as the
National Guard.

In the former USSR, no special internal security vehicles
were built. If there was a riot or demonstration then the police
would work alongside the army, and standard armoured
vehicles, including tanks, would be used against the unarmed
public, as happened in Hungary in 1956 and later in Poland.

The East Germans did produce an armoured water cannon
for the police and internal security forces. The vehicle was the
SK-2, based on the G5 6x6 heavy truck, which was used in
large numbers by the East German Army. The water cannon,
with a range of 70m/230ft, was mounted on the roof in a small
turret with a 360-degree traverse. It was reloaded by driving
the vehicle over a water main, opening a trapdoor in the floor,
and lowering a pipe to connect the vehicle to the water supply,
taking 10 minutes to refill the water tanks in the vehicle.

Air mobility

In 1930 the Soviets formed the world's first parachute force and commanders have tried ever since to give airborne troops an armoured capability. Trying to fit a tank into a transport aircraft has always been very difficult, due to the weight and size of the vehicle. During World War II, the Allies used Horsa and Hamilcar gliders to move heavy equipment to the landing zone of the parachute troops. These gliders could only carry small light vehicles such as the Jeep and the Universal Carrier (which was used to tow 6-pound anti-tank guns) until the British developed a small light tank. This was called the Tetrarch and was armed with a 2-pound gun and capable of being carried by the Hamilcar. The Germans meanwhile concentrated on powered flight and built the largest transport aircraft of the war that could carry 3-ton trucks and light tanks such as the Panzer II. After World War II, larger transport aircraft with large rear loading doors came into service with other armies, but as tanks have grown in size and weight they could still not be carried. In more recent times, the only aircraft capable of carrying a Main Battle Tank (MBT) were the USAF C5 Galaxy and the (former) Soviet AN 124 and even these aircraft, the biggest in the world, could only carry two MBTs. Since the Vietnam War, the heavy lift types of helicopter have changed the way troops, guns, vehicles and supplies move around the battlefield.

With the ending of the Cold War and the break up of the Soviet Union, the type of warfare that modern armies are training to fight has changed. Long gone are the massed ranks of Warsaw Pact tanks facing the NATO forces on the

TOP: **An American M551 Sheridan light tank being loaded on to a C-130 transport aircraft. This was designed to equip the American airborne divisions, but withdrawn from service after only five years due to its vulnerability.** ABOVE: **A Willys Jeep being unloaded from a British Horsa glider in front of General Montgomery. The bumpers have been cut down and all the tie-downs and handles have been removed.**

ground, and the battlefield of Western Europe has melted away to be replaced by the worldwide battlefield. Soldiers and their equipment have to be able to move very quickly and respond to a changing enemy with either low-technology weapons or good weapons but poorly trained operatives, or a mix of both. Troops used to be sent to the theatre of operations by aircraft with their heavy equipment following on in ships, but now soldiers and heavy equipment can be transported by air to theatre.

Vehicles like the British CVR(T) Scorpion can be airlifted to any part of the world and can then be slung under helicopters like the Chinook and delivered to the front line ready for battle. These fast light vehicles now carry a big punch and, being part of a fully integrated force, can respond to most situations that they come across. The sheer speed at which commanders can now get troops into a theatre does not give the enemy time to construct defences or build up ground forces and supplies. Also, as the response time is now hours and not days, the local defence forces stand a better chance of holding the attackers at bay until reinforcements and AFVs arrive.

AFVs can also be delivered direct to the battlefield by heavy-lift aircraft from which the vehicles can be delivered by parachute or Low Altitude Parachute Extraction System (LAPSE). This technique allows an aircraft such as the C-130 Hercules to come in very low and fast and deliver the tanks that are tied on to special air drop sledges. The Soviet Union had experimented with this system and others. One system they tried out was fitting an airborne AFV like the BMD to an air landing platform, with rockets fitted to the underneath and the crew inside the vehicle. The platform would be steadied on leaving the aircraft by a small chute, and a weighted rope would hang down from the platform. On striking the ground the rope would set off the retro rockets which would slow the descent of the platform and give the crew and the AFV a safe landing. Perhaps not surprisingly, the Soviets lost a number of men in these trials.

With more and more armies turning to rapid deployment forces, the heavy MBT is being cut back in numbers and replaced by lighter, faster and more agile light tanks or AFVs. Could this be the end of the MBT?

TOP: **Two M-1 Abrams MBTs loaded in the cargo area of a USAF C-5M Super Galaxy. The major problems with vehicles like this are the weight of the vehicle and the size of the transport aircraft required to move them by air.** ABOVE LEFT: **A Willys Jeep inside an American WACO glider. The front bumper has been shortened and only one headlight is fitted. The vehicle is shackled to the steel frame of the glider and only just fits inside.** ABOVE: **German Wiesel air-portable light tank inside a CH-53G heavy-lift helicopter. The crew of the vehicle varies between two and five, depending on its designated role. The German Army have some 400 of these vehicles in service.** LEFT: **Soviet BMD-1 airborne combat vehicle. The turret has been covered and the main parachute is fitted to the rear deck of the vehicle. Originally the crew were in the vehicle when it left the aircraft but they now drop separately.**

The multi-role family of vehicles

Long gone are the days of developing new vehicles from scratch, with new engines, chassis and weapons. These are very expensive, take a long time to come into service and require a lot of testing and training of new crews. World War II would see a new type of development where the vehicle "family" becomes more important. In Britain, the Churchill tank became the basic chassis for a number of new vehicles that would be known as the "Funnies". In the USA, several new vehicles such as the M10 and the M40, were based on the Sherman. The Germans turned the Panzer IV into a family of vehicles. Its well-tried and tested chassis gave rise to vehicles like the Hummel, Nashorn and Sturmgeschutz. The Soviets were a little behind on the idea of creating a basic chassis for several vehicles but the T-34 was used for several different vehicles including the SU100.

With the start of the Cold War and the birth of NATO with its ideas of standardization, the concept of a basic family of AFVs was born. In Britain the 432 was under development and would be produced in 19 variations, not including the SPG. In 1970

the CVR(T) Scorpion started its production run. This would lead to a new and revolutionary family of tracked vehicles that are capable of going were tanks cannot, and filling many of the MBT roles. Due to the very low ground pressure of the vehicle (less than an infantryman's foot in a size nine boot), this vehicle can even get to places on the battlefield where a soldier cannot. As a result, vehicles such as the Scorpion can traverse a peat bog with ease, and in safety. Alighting crews can however then be seen to sink up to their knees while the CVR(T) can sit on the top of the soft spongy ground! The CVR(T) was also the backbone of Britain's Rapid Deployment Force as two could fit into an RAF Hercules C-130 transport aircraft.

In the early 1960s, the Americans developed the M113 that would be produced in larger numbers than any other AFV since World War II with over 80,000 being built. It has been sold to 60 different countries around the world and there are 40 different variations on the basic vehicle chassis. These include bridge layers, flamethrowers, command, and anti-aircraft

> **"The full power of an army can be exerted only when all its parts act in close combination."**
> **British Field Service Regulations, Part 1, 1909**

ABOVE LEFT: **A line-up of British Spartan APCs. The cupola hatch opens to the rear and side and is the vehicle commander's position. The ambulance version of the Spartan family is called the Samaritan.** ABOVE: **British Spartan (FV 103) with Milan system on the rear of the vehicle. There are four of these vehicles per battalion. The vehicle has a narrow hull, blunt nose and a large sloping glacis plate. Two clusters of four smoke dischargers are mounted on the front.** LEFT: **Two British Spartan vehicles at speed in the desert during the Gulf War of 1991. All the personal kit of the crew and infantry in the vehicle has been stowed on the outside of the vehicle. Temporary storage boxes have also been fitted to the front of the vehicle.**

vehicles. The M113 has been in service for over 60 years and it is expected to remain in service for many more years with the US Army and many of its customers. For much of its existence, the US Marine Corps has had equipment older and inferior to that of the US Army. This changed when the Piranha Light Armoured Vehicle (LAV) entered USMC service in 1983, providing a vehicle as good as any in its class. The LAV has been developed into a family of vehicles that will remain in both US Army and Marine Corps service for some years to come.

The French have produced several very good families of vehicles such as the AMX VCI. This is based on the very successful AMX-13 light tank chassis and was in production from 1957. The early versions had an open machine-gun position on the top of the vehicle. By 1960, this had been replaced by a proper machine-gun turret and so could be regarded as the very first IFV. It was exported to 15 different countries and produced in 12 different variations of the basic vehicle. The AMX VCI was replaced in the French Army by the AMX-10P that has also been developed into numerous variations on the basic IFV.

The former Soviet Union produced several families of AFVs, which can still be found in service all over the world. These vehicles, such as the BRDM, have been in service since 1960 and because of their basic design and simplicity of maintenance were sold on to various developing countries, and many remain in service today.

The AFV family of vehicles has proved to be an excellent concept and has given military commanders more options and a flexibility in their tactical deployment of equipment and logistics on the battlefield.

TOP: **The Samaritan, like the other vehicles in the family, has no personal kit storage inside the vehicle, so in this case it is stored on the roof. The running gear can be clearly seen with the driving wheel at the front and the five large road wheels.**
ABOVE: **The British Striker SP ATGW (FV 102) launching a Swingfire missile. The rear launcher box is in the raised firing position, and holds five missiles. A further ten can be carried in the vehicle.**
LEFT: **The mother of the CVR(T) family is the Scorpion light tank. The three-man crew can be seen in their positions, with their personal kit stored on the outside of the vehicle. The turret is armed with a 76mm/2.99in main gun and coaxial 7.62mm/0.3in machine-gun.**

The future

It takes a very brave or very foolish person who will attempt to predict the future with confidence. Time and time again such predictions have been proved wrong and the history of the development of AFVs has plenty of examples of such mistakes.

During both World Wars, and the high-intensity conflicts that have since occurred worldwide, tanks and other armoured fighting vehicles proved themselves to be vital elements in fighting wars. In the 1950s the new guided anti-tank missile was going to make the battlefield a no-go area for the MBT yet the tank is still, at present, king of the battlefield in spite of this. AFVs continue to be as important as ever but things are definitely changing and all-new designs are gradually entering service, replacing vehicles developed during and for the Cold War that have in some cases (e.g. Snatch Land Rover, Warrior and FV430) been in service for a number of decades. These much-upgraded and modified vehicles have been adapted and up-armoured to fight counter-insurgency wars, not the predicted and practiced Third World War battles for which they were originally developed. Also, whereas the majority of AFVs in service around the world once predominantly originated in the Soviet Union, the US and Britain, there are now many more indigenous players in the field, producing vehicles designed

> "Infantry is the arm which in the end wins battles. To enable it to do so the cooperation of the other arms is essential."
> British Field Service Regulations, 1924

TOP: **American Multiple Launch Rocket System (MLRS) firing a salvo of missiles. This system was first tried in battle during the Gulf War of 1991. The large back blast from the missile can clearly be seen, but with a range of 30km/18.6 miles, it is not a problem.** ABOVE: **The MOWAG Piranha has become a very successful vehicle, being built in several countries around the world and in service with many others. It is expected to remain in service for some years to come.**

from the outset to meet the needs and challenges of battlefields in the 2020s and beyond.

In light of current and anticipated threats, the West has seen a declining market for Main Battle Tanks linked to favouring a more balanced force composition. While a heavy MBT, AFV and self-propelled gun (SPG) element still features prominently, there is an increasing requirement for a light element within a force that can be air-transportable in medium-range transport aircraft, such as the A400M Atlas, but that were also designed from the outset for urban warfare and counter-insurgency whilst having digital integration in terms of offensive and defensive

LEFT: In the early 2000s the Stormer SPAAM was developed with the Rapier missile system fitted to the rear of the vehicle – the version was not produced. The Stormer 30 was a development of the Stormer chassis as a tracked reconnaissance vehicle with a cannon-armed turret and TOW missile launchers. The version, yet to enter service, was fully air transportable in the C-130 and Sikorsky CH-53 helicopter. BELOW: Soviet BTR-80 BREM. This is the engineers' support vehicle and the turret has been fitted with a 3,048kg/3-ton "A"-frame. Behind the crane is storage for spare wheels and other heavy equipment. The BTR-80 is expected to remain in service for many years to come.

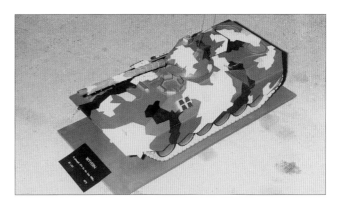

capability as well as communication. Non-conventional, lighter, composite armour has also been studied by numerous AFV manufacturers.

Armies around the world are undergoing major changes and restructuring at this time due to financial pressures and ever-changing technologies. There now seems to be no need for the old heavy tank formations that used to be lined up in Europe like great armoured juggernauts. In Britain, army units were amalgamated to form bigger and more flexible units. The heavy tank regiments armed with the Challenger MBT were cut back in numbers and re-equipped with the lighter CVR(T) type of vehicle. The British Army is one of the few in the world that has its light armoured fighting vehicles still mounted on full tracks, as most of the world's armies are going over to the cheaper all-wheeled vehicle.

In 1999, the US Army moved to reorganize into new types of units that could better deal with future deployments. The new units were to be called Objective Forces, equipped with new all-wheeled Future Combat Vehicles (FCV) able to fit into a Hercules C-130 transport aircraft and not weighing more than 20 tons. The US Army is now working on its Army 2030 strategy described as "a once-in-a-generation transformation", a comprehensive reorganisation and technical innovation based on lessons learned from fighting in Iraq and Afghanistan and in response to increasing threats from China and Russia. The transformation will include reorganisation of forces, the development of new equipment, and the adoption of new concepts on how to fight that allow the US Army to maintain superiority over any potential adversary and address the many current systems are enduring capabilities developed during the Cold War."

ABOVE MIDDLE: A development model of a Wyvern which was intended to be a principal AFV in the late 1990s. Although it failed to reach production, it does show the trend for smaller lighter vehicles that can be moved by air.
ABOVE: A possible development model for a future BMP-3 called Cossack. The body of the vehicle has cleaner lines for better performance in the water, but it still looks large and too heavy to be air-portable.

As part of this, faster, more-survivable fighting vehicles will replace older types. New equipment includes the Armored Multi-Purpose Vehicles (AMPV) – a US Army programme to replace the M113 armoured personnel carrier and family of vehicles. The first AMPV prototype was rolled out in December 2016 and at the time of writing, five variants of the AMPV are planned: M1283 General Purpose, M1284 Medical Evacuation Vehicle, M1285 Medical Treatment Vehicle, M1286 Mission Command, and M1287 Mortar Carrier Vehicle with an average cost of $3.7 million per vehicle.

Designers are looking at new propellants for munitions, as these at present take up a lot of space in the vehicle. If you can place more munitions in the vehicle then it can remain in action longer while logistical problems of re-arming a vehicle decrease.

ABOVE: **Soldiers from the US Army 9th US Cavalry Regiment complete field testing of the Armored Multi-Purpose Vehicle (AMPV) September 2018.**
BELOW LEFT: **Most AFVs have either petrol (gasoline) or diesel piston engines. Petrol is favoured less due to its flammability should the vehicle be hit. Gas turbines with their very high power-to-weight ratio offer poor fuel economy so have not been widely adopted. As a result, AFV engines have yet to see any major innovation beyond squeezing more power from fairly conventional engines. The Boxer's power pack consists of an MTU diesel coupled to an Allison transmission.**

One of the propellants under development is liquid explosive, which would be injected into the breech of a gun once the warhead had been loaded. This will increase the space available in the vehicle for more warheads and would make the use of automatic loaders a far better option. This will also either remove the need for a crew member or free them for other duties in the vehicle. This offers new design possibilities. New types of ammunition specifically designed for urban warfare environments have been developed, such as the American Multi-Purpose Anti-Tank round (MPAT). This will create breaches in buildings so assaulting troops can easily gain access.

Far more countries have developed their own wheeled AFVs, using basic truck chassis that can be bought "off the shelf" from many manufacturers. These might not have the sophistication of vehicles like the LAV III, but a high level of sophistication is not always required or desirable. Brazil used to be a major importer of AFVs but started to produce its own vehicles, such as the EE-11, while actively trying to sell them on the world market.

The tank remains the nominal king of the battlefield, but for how long? The vulnerability of MBTs was demonstrated during the 2022 Russian invasion of Ukraine when videos showed Russian tanks being destroyed by the defenders' APCs. The AFV can now pack the punch of the Abrams MBT, and has the ability to deliver a wide variety of munitions on target. 21st-century war demands increasing flexibility and agility that many new-generation AFVs can provide, in contrast to the MBT behemoths that cannot be flown where they may be most needed.

ABOVE: **The Ukrainian Varta Armoured Personnel Carrier (APC) has a main vehicle compartment made from specialized grade Swedish 560 steel which protects the crew from armour piercing incendiary ammunition of up to 7.62mm/0.3in calibre. The vehicle's windows provide crew and passengers with the same level of protection. While the v-shaped hull is a vehicle design approach that has been in use for some time in South Africa, the concept makes more and more sense as counter-insurgency actions and the threat of improvized explosive devices (IEDs) and rocket propelled grenades (RPGs) become more commonplace than tank battles.**

LEFT: **During 2021, Armored Multi-Purpose Vehicle prototypes underwent a high impact, multi-month evaluation at the US Army Cold Regions Test Center to test its cold weather capabilities. While the vehicle is a new design, it features the same powertrain and suspension system as the Bradley Fighting Vehicle and M109A7 self-propelled howitzer, which eases maintenance and logistics challenges for all three vehicles in the field.**

A–Z of World War Armoured Fighting Vehicles 1914–45

With the invention of the compression engine in 1892, military weapons developers around the world tried to fit it to various horseless carriages, resulting in some wonderful but impractical machines that were unusable on a battlefield.

The earliest practicable designs were produced in 1914 when the Belgian Army fitted machine-guns to touring cars which had been covered in boiler plate. These performed very well and were copied and developed further by the RNAS who used them aggressively in several different theatres. In World War II, the armoured car became the eyes of the armoured division.

There were a number of unsuccessful attempts to produce SPGs in World War I but it was not until World War II that this vehicle was really developed. Initially these were very crude conversions but by 1945, they had been developed into purpose-built, sophisticated weapons systems and had proved their worth on the battlefield.

The infantry carrier was developed in the 1930s from the early German half-track, which gave the infantry only basic protection, to the Kangaroo in the 1940s, which would give troops the protection of tank armour and allow them to fight alongside the tanks.

LEFT: **A column of British Bren gun carriers passing over a bridge.**

LEFT: **An LVT (A) 1 climbing out of the water. The rear machine-gun position can be seen manned behind the turret. This was a weakness as it let water into the vehicle.** ABOVE: **75mm LVT (A) 4 from above showing the position of the turret. The deck of the vehicle is fully covered, while the top of the turret is open to the elements. The ring mount for the 12.7mm/50cal machine-gun can be seen at the rear of the turret.**

75mm LVT (A) 4 Close Support Vehicle

The LVT (Landing VehicleTracked) was used for the first time in August 1942 during the amphibious operation to capture Guadalcanal. After this operation it was felt that some form of close support for the assault troops was required, and so in the Bougainville and Tarawa operations the LVTs were equipped with a number of machine-guns, typically three or four per vehicle. Following the Tarawa landings it was decided that a heavier support weapon was required and so the LVT Assault vehicle was developed and placed into production at the end of 1943. The LVT 2 chassis was used as the basis for a new vehicle called LVT (A) 1, which was completed by constructing the hull out of armour instead of mild steel, plating over the hull compartment and mounting

a 37mm/1.46in M3 light tank turret, with two machine-gun positions in the rear of the vehicle behind the turret.

The LVT (A) 1 first saw action during the ROI-Namur invasion in January 1943 when 75 of these vehicles were used. They proved to be very effective but an even heavier weapon was required to give the Marines better close support, so development started on the LVT (A) 4. Production commenced in March 1943 with its first combat mission being the invasion of Saipan in June 1944. The new vehicle had the complete turret from the M8 GMC; this was fitted with a 75mm/2.95in short-range howitzer and a single 12.7mm/50cal machine-gun. The LVT (A) 4 could carry 100 rounds of 75mm/2.95in ammunition and 400

rounds for the machine-gun. The Continental engine was mounted in the rear of the vehicle and used 4.55 litres/ 1 gallon of fuel per 1.6km/1 mile.

Total production for the LVT (A) 1 was 509 vehicles, and when production of the LVT (A) 4 ended in 1945, 1,890 of these vehicles had been built. A number of rocket launchers and flamethrowers were fitted to both the LVT (A) 1 and the LVT (A) 4. The LVT (A) 4 would take part in the Korean War and remained in service with the US Marine Corps until the late 1950s, when it was replaced by the LVTH-6 105mm Tracked Howitzer.

LEFT: **A 75mm/2.95in LVT (A) 4 on a beach with the crew on or beside the vehicle. The protruding track grousers can be clearly seen; these propel the vehicle through the water and help it to move across soft sand.**

LVT (A) 4 Close Support Vehicle	
Country: USA	
Entered service: 1943	
Crew: 6	
Weight: 18,140kg/17.9 tons	
Dimensions: Length – 7.95m/26ft 1in	
Height – 3.1m/10ft 2in	
Width – 3.25m/10ft 8in	
Armament: Main – 75mm/2.95in M2/M3 howitzer	
Secondary – 1 x 12.7mm/0.5in machine-gun	
and 1 x 7.62mm/0.3in machine-gun	
Armour: Maximum – 44mm/1.73in	
Powerplant: Continental W-670-9A 7-cylinder	
186kW/250hp air-cooled radial petrol engine	
Performance: Speed – Land 32kph/20mph;	
Sea 12kph/7mph	
Range – 240km/150 miles	

LEFT: **One of the first AEC Mk 2 cars in North Africa in 1941. The sheer bulk of the vehicle can be clearly seen, but the vehicle appears to have none of the extra crew-storage fitted in the field by combat crews.** ABOVE: **An AEC Mk 3 moving through shallow water during landing trials. The vehicle commander is standing in the turret giving directions to the driver, who has limited vision from his position.**

AEC Armoured Car

This was designed as a private venture by the Associated Equipment Company Ltd, which normally made London buses. Information sent back from North Africa indicated a need for a heavyweight armoured car. AEC were also producing the very successful Matador gun tractor and so from July 1941 they produced the AEC Mk 1 using many of the Matador chassis parts. The armoured hull was a simple design and had a 2pdr gun and coaxial Besa machine-gun in a turret, the same turret as that used for the Valentine tank. One hundred and twenty Mk 1s were produced before the improved Mk 2 came along. This had a 6pdr gun in the turret, a more powerful engine, and the crew was increased from three to four. This was a big improvement but the army still wanted a bigger punch and so the Mk 3 was developed.

The Mk 3 had an improved hull and the British copy of the American M3 tank gun fitted in a new turret that had improved ventilation. However, when the driver was hull-down his only view of the outside was through a periscope which gave him very poor visibility. The driver could select either two-wheel drive

RIGHT: **The improved frontal design to aid in obstacle clearing can be seen. The driver's hatch is large and opens towards the turret, so the gun barrel has to be offset to the left to allow him to enter or leave the vehicle. Mounted between the wheels are large storage panniers.**

to the front axial only, which was used for long road journeys to save fuel, or four-wheel drive for cross country or combat. In total, 629 of these heavy armoured cars were built.

Most of the Mk 1 and Mk 2 cars were sent to the 8th Army and saw action in North Africa, Sicily and Italy. The Mk 3 was at first issued to armoured car units that were destined to be used in north-west Europe as heavy support vehicles to the other armoured cars, as it had double the thickness in armour in comparison to these. A number of the Mk 3 armoured cars were used by the Belgian Army after the war and remained in service well into the 1950s.

AEC Mk 3 Armoured Car	

Country: UK
Entered service: 1942
Crew: 4
Weight: 12,903.2kg/12.7 tons
Dimensions: Length – 5.61m/18ft 5in
   Height – 2.69m/8ft 10in
   Width – 2.69m/8ft 10in
Armament: Main – M3 75mm/2.95in tank gun
   Secondary – Coaxial 7.7mm/0.303in Besa
   machine-gun
Armour: Maximum – 30mm/1.18in
Powerplant: AEC 6-cylinder diesel engine
   developing 116kW/155bhp
Performance: Speed – 66kph/41mph
   Range – 402km/250 miles

Archer 17pdr Self-Propelled Gun

In May 1942 the 17pdr anti-tank gun was approved for service. In June it was decided to mount this new gun on a self-propelled chassis to produce a tank destroyer. The first vehicle considered was the Bishop 25pdr SPG but this proved impracticable. The next was the Crusader tank but this was discarded due to reliability problems. Finally, it was decided to convert the Valentine chassis as used for the Bishop but with a different superstructure. However, there were a number of problems due to the length of the gun. This was mounted facing the rear and over the top of the engine deck of the vehicle in an open-topped fighting compartment, and had a limited traverse. A light steel roof was added to some vehicles at a later date, mainly post-war. Despite the length of the gun, a very compact vehicle with a low silhouette was produced. The fighting compartment was small for the four-man crew and 39 rounds of ammunition. The driver's position was left in the same place as it had been in the Valentine tank, but he could not remain in position when the gun was firing. The upper hull was of all-welded construction, with the lower hull, engine, transmission, and running gear being the same as on later Valentines. Secondary armament was the Bren gun, but no permanent mounting was provided on the vehicle. A popular crew conversion was to fit a 7.62mm/30cal Browning machine-gun to the front of the vehicle.

Firing trials were carried out in April 1943 and proved successful apart from a few minor changes. The vehicle was placed into priority production with an order for 800, but only 665 were produced, the first vehicle being completed in March 1944. It was issued at first to the anti-tank units of armoured divisions fighting in north-west Europe from October 1944. Later some were sent out to the 8th Army in Italy. While at first it was called the S-P 17pdr Valentine Mk 1, this was quickly dropped in favour of Archer.

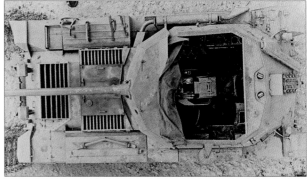

TOP: **An Archer fitted with deep-wading gear. The large ducting on the rear deck allows the vehicle to draw air into the engine from above the level of the water.**
ABOVE: **The front is to the right, the small fighting compartment is in the middle and the engine in the rear of the vehicle with the gun barrel passing over it.**

LEFT: **Some of the ammunition storage can be seen on the right beside the 17pdr gun breach inside the small and cramped fighting compartment. Between the front of the vehicle and the gun breach is the driver's position.**

Archer 17pdr SPG

Country: UK
Entered service: 1944
Crew: 4
Weight: 18,796kg/18.5 tons
Dimensions: Length – 6.68m/21ft 11in
    Height – 2.24m/7ft 4in
    Width – 2.64m/8ft 8in
Armament: Main – 17pdr OQF (ordnance quick-firing) (76.2mm/0.3in) gun
    Secondary – 7.7mm/0.303in Bren machine-gun
Armour: Maximum – 60mm/2.36in
Powerplant: GMC M10 diesel 123kW/165hp
Performance: Speed – 24kph/15mph
    Range – 145km/90 miles

LEFT: **A pair of Austin cars travelling at speed. The large bulk of these vehicles and the twin offset turrets can be clearly seen. The Russians have placed armour plate next to the guns to protect the barrels.**
ABOVE: **An Austin armoured car in Russian service. The turret gunners are taking the opportunity to get some air as it is very cramped and stuffy inside the car. The driver has also dropped his visor for better vision and ventilation.**

Austin Armoured Car

Before World War I, the Austin Motor Company Ltd was the largest supplier of cars and trucks to the Russian Imperial Army, and in 1913 won a contract to develop an armoured car for internal security duties in the large towns and cities. In 1914 an order was placed for 48 of these new armoured cars. The first armoured cars were built using the 22.4kW/30hp "Colonial" chassis, and had two machine-gun turrets mounted, one on each side of the rear of the vehicle. The wheels were all fitted with solid studded tyres. There were several problems with these early cars. Due to the height of the driver's cab, the machine-guns could not fire

to the front and were too close side by side for the gun crews to operate them efficiently. The Russians also wanted to increase the thickness of armour on the vehicle. Consequently, a number of improvements were put into place by the Russians and Austin. A 37.3kW/50hp engine was fitted to the vehicle to cope with the increased weight and the tyres were made pneumatic with the rear axle having dual wheels. The turrets were offset to improve the fighting efficiency and the driver's cab was lowered so the guns could fire to the front.

Austin also sent the Russians a large number of chassis which had their bodies fitted in the Putilov works in

Petrograd (now St Petersburg). About 200 of these new Putilov-Austin cars were built. One modification carried out by the Russians was the fitting of a rear driving position so that the car could be driven from the front or rear, and an auxiliary gear change was fitted.

Both the Austin and the Putilov-Austin were reliable cars, but like a number of early AFVs they suffered on the primitive Russian roads. In early 1917, all Austin production was switched to the Western Front and the 17th Battalion Tank Corps was equipped with these cars. The 17th Battalion with their Austins would lead the victorious British troops into Germany in November 1918.

LEFT: **In 1919, Britain urgently required armoured cars for duties in India and Ireland, so Austin-designed bodies were placed on other chassis. Peerless used their truck chassis to produce the Peerless 1919 Pattern armoured car.**

Austin/Putilov-Austin Armoured Car	

Country: UK
Entered service: 1914
Crew: 5
Weight: 5,384kg/5.3 tons
Dimensions: Length – 4.88m/16ft
    Height – 2.4m/7ft 10in
    Width – 1.95m/6ft 5in
Armament: Main – 2 x 7.7mm/0.303in machine-guns
    Secondary – None
Armour: Maximum – 8mm/0.315in
Powerplant: 37.3kW/50hp Austin petrol engine
Performance: Speed – 50kph/31mph
    Range – 200km/125 miles

LEFT: **The rear driver's position visor is in the open position. Next to this is the rear-facing machine-gun. The hatch in the rear of the turret lifts up.**
ABOVE: **The AB 41 was an all-riveted construction. This could become lethal for the crew inside when the car was hit, as the rivets would burst loose and fly around the interior, wounding them.**

Autoblinda AB 41 Armoured Car

In 1939, the Italian Colonial Police and the Italian cavalry had a requirement for a new armoured car, so both needs were combined and in 1940 production began with the Autoblinda 40. This had a four-man crew and was armed with twin machine-guns in a turret and one facing the rear of the vehicle. There was also a plan to build small numbers of a version armed with a 20mm/0.79in cannon as a support vehicle. It was quickly discovered that the cannon armament was far better in service than the machine-gun only armament, so production of the AB 40 was stopped and the AB 41 took over.

The AB 41 used a turret very similar to that of the L6/40 light tank, and had

a very advanced design for its time but suffered from one recurring problem with the four-wheel steering. The main armament was a Breda 20mm/0.79in modello anti-aircraft cannon with a coaxial machine-gun specially designed for use in AFVs. These vehicles could be fitted with a number of different wheels and tyres. One type was an extra wide sand tyre that was used when operating in areas such as North Africa. Another special feature was that the car could be fitted with wheels that would allow it to run on railway tracks. These were carried in the spare wheel area on the car and could be changed by the crew in less than 30 minutes. The vehicle had six forward and four reverse gears and

two driving positions, so two of the crew were designated drivers. The AB 41 was produced in larger numbers than any other Italian armoured car during World War II.

By the time of the Italian surrender to the Allies in September 1943, nearly 400 of these vehicles had been produced. When the Germans took over the campaign against the Allies in Italy, they captured 57 of these vehicles and also retained the car's production, managing to produce a further 120 AB 41 armoured cars for their own use.

RIGHT: **The side entrance door to the crew compartment can be seen clearly in the rear of the raised body of the car. The armoured headlight covers are in the raised position exposing the large lights. The driver's vision slot is in between the lights and has a very limited field of vision.**

Autoblinda AB 41 Armoured Car

Country: Italy
Entered service: 1940
Crew: 4
Weight: 7,518kg/7.4 tons
Dimensions: Length – 5.20m/17ft 2in
　　　Height – 2.48m/8ft
　　　Width – 1.92m/6ft 4in
Armament: Main – 20mm/0.79in Breda modello 35 cannon
　　　Secondary – Coaxial 8mm/0.315in and rear 8mm/0.315in modello 38 air-cooled machine-guns
Armour: Maximum – 17mm/0.67in
Powerplant: 60kW/80bhp SAP Abn 6-cylinder water-cooled petrol engine
Performance: Speed – 78kph/49mph
　　　Range – 400km/248 miles

Autoblindo Mitragliatrice Lancia Ansaldo IZ

The first Lancia Ansaldo IZ armoured car was not armed and was used as an artillery spotting vehicle but in 1915 the vehicle was dramatically redesigned and turned into an armoured car. The first version was armed with a single machine-gun mounted in a circular turret, but this was soon upgraded to a twin mounting for machine-guns. Another type of turret was tried on the vehicle and this had a second smaller turret mounted on top of the larger bottom turret and each had a single machine-gun mounted, each with a 360-degree traverse. Another unique feature of these cars was the twin steel rails that made up the wire cutter that extended from the top of the driver's cab forward and down and ended in front of the radiator. The wheels on later versions of the vehicle were protected by armoured shields. The rear wheels were dual and the tyres were all pneumatic. Armoured firing ports were placed around the top of the crew compartment to allow the extra men in the crew to fire small arms from the vehicle. There was also a mounting for a rear-firing machine-gun in the crew compartment. It had good ground clearance, and there was a rack for a bicycle on the rear of the vehicle.

For most of World War I, the Italian armoured car units played very little part in the fighting against the Austro-Hungarian forces in the mountains in northern Italy. However, a number of

these cars were used to help stop the Austro-Hungarian and German forces breaking through in that area in 1917. Those captured by the Germans were used to equip armoured car units of their own. This vehicle was also used for training and equipping American troops in Italy. A large number of these cars were sent to North Africa on policing duties. They proved to be very durable and were used by the Italian Army in the Spanish Civil War between 1936–39. Total production was only 120 vehicles.

TOP: **Lancia armoured car fitted with the single large turret armed with twin machine-guns. The wire-cutter frame can be clearly seen fitted to the front of the vehicle. This structure was far from robust and easily damaged.** ABOVE: **A Lancia car fitted with two turrets, each armed with a single machine-gun. Both turrets can be operated independently and both can traverse through 360 degrees.**

LEFT: **A Lancia car in North Africa armed with three machine-guns, two in the large turret and one in the top turret. A large single headlight is mounted forward in the front of the vehicle. A number of these cars were still in service at the start of World War II.**

Autoblindo Mitragliatrice Lancia Ansaldo IZ

Country: Italy
Entered service: 1915
Crew: 6
Weight: 3,860kg/3.8 tons
Dimensions: Length – 5.40m/17ft 9in
    Height – 2.40m/7ft 11in
    Width – 1.82m/6ft
Armament: Main – 3 x Fiat machine-guns
    Secondary – Small arms
Armour: Maximum – 9mm/0.354in
Powerplant: 26/30kW/35/40hp petrol engine
Performance: Speed – 60kph/37mph
    Range – 300km/186 miles

LEFT: **The gun crew are sitting on the top of the turret behind the forward opening hatch. The driver's side door is open allowing better ventilation. Spare wheels are carried on each side of the vehicle. The radiator shutters are in the open position.** ABOVE: **The BA-6 armoured car used the GAZ AAA truck chassis. The turret of this armoured car was very large and sat over the rear axles of the vehicle.**

BA-6 Armoured Car

The BA-6 replaced the BA-3 on the production line in 1935 after only 160 BA-3s had been built. The main differences between them were that the BA-6 was 1,000kg/2,205lb lighter and had a strengthened rear suspension and a modified transmission.

The BA-6 was a mixture of riveted and welded construction and was built on a shortened GAZ AAA chassis. The armour was increased in several places to 9mm/0.354in and the vehicle had fair cross-country ability. Tracks could be fitted over the double pairs of wheels on the rear of the vehicle and turn it into a form of half-track, which improved the off-road ability of the car. The turret was

the same as that fitted to the T-26 light tank except that the rear machine-gun port was covered over, and there was storage for 60 rounds of 45mm/ 1.77in ammunition in the vehicle. The combat debut of the BA-6 was during the Spanish Civil War where it made a very good impression, and in 1937 it would be used as a basis for the Spanish Autometralladoro Blindado Medio Chevrolet.

In 1936 an improved version of the basic BA-6 was introduced – the BA-6M. This had the new GAZ M1 engine. The weight was further reduced and an all-welded turret was fitted to the new vehicle. The ammunition storage was

reduced to 50 rounds and the 71-TK-1 radio was fitted as standard. There was also a railway version of the BA-6, but these were a lot heavier than the road car as there were hydraulic jacks mounted to the front and the rear of the vehicle so that flanged railway wheels could be fitted over the normal road tyres. However, the wheel change took only 30 minutes. In total 386 BA-20 and BA-20M were built, of which only 20 were the new BA-20M. These cars remained in production until 1939.

A large number of these vehicles were stationed on the Russian–Chinese border having been used against the Japanese, so missed the initial slaughter of the Soviet Army by the Germans in 1941, but by 1945 none was left in service.

LEFT: **A BA-6 in rare pre-World War II camouflage markings. The spare wheels also act as additional unditching wheels and stop the car getting stuck in soft ground. The front machine-gun is not fitted on this vehicle and the armoured shutters for the radiator are closed.**

BA-6 Armoured Car	

Country: USSR
Entered service: 1935
Crew: 4
Weight: 5,080kg/5 tons
Dimensions: Length – 4.9m/16ft 1in
    Height – 2.36m/7ft 9in
    Width – 2.07m/6ft 9in
Armament: Main – 1 x 45mm/1.77in M-1932 gun
    and 1 x coaxial 7.62mm/0.3in machine-gun
    Secondary – 7.62mm/0.3in DT machine-gun
Armour: Maximum – 9mm/0.354in
Powerplant: GAZ AA 4-cylinder 29kW/40hp
    petrol engine
Performance: Speed – 43kph/27mph
    Range – 200km/124 miles

BA-10 Armoured Car

By 1938, the Russians suspected that war with Germany was inevitable, despite political assurances to the contrary and the signing of the non-aggression pact between the Soviet Union and Germany. Consequently, a modernization of Soviet armoured vehicles was put in place. The BA-10 was already on the drawing board and would benefit from this acceleration in development. The vehicle used the GAZ AAA chassis, which was shortened and strengthened with the body being an all-welded construction. The main construction was done at the Izhorskiy plant where the body was built and then married to the GAZ chassis.

The BA-10 entered production in 1938 and would become the definitive as well as the most numerous form of the BA heavy armoured car. The layout was conventional with the engine at the front, driver and front gunner in the middle and a two-man turret at the rear. A modernized version of the BA-10 came into service in 1939, this improved design being called the BA-10M. The main improvements were an increase in armour for the vulnerable areas and a new 45mm/1.77in gun fitted in the turret – a simpler model with improved sights. The BA-10 and the BA-10M are often confused as there is very little difference between the two vehicles. The BA-10M has external fuel tanks mounted over the rear wheels and on both sides of the vehicle; these have often been mistaken for storage boxes. The BA-10 used the same turret as the BA-6 armoured car and was armed with the 45mm/1.77in M-1934 tank gun, together with a 7.62mm/0.3in DT machine-gun mounted

ABOVE: **Note the shelf on the rear of the BA-10 for the carriage of the "overall" tracks, which are used to improve its cross-country performance. The locking wires are still in place across the back of the vehicle.**

coaxially and another in the front of the car. The driver and front gunner sit side by side, with the vehicle commander and gunner in the two-man turret.

The BA-10/10M saw extensive service during the "Great Patriotic War" and large numbers of captured vehicles were put into service by the Finnish and German armies. Some 1,400 vehicles were produced of which 331 were the BA-10M version.

ABOVE: **A column of BA-10 cars. The crews are "buttoned up", but are not in a combat area as the radiator shutters are in the open position.**

ABOVE: **BA-10 cars in Poland in 1939, as Soviet crews show off their vehicles to German troops. Each car is carrying spare track-links on the side of the vehicle.**

BA-10 Armoured Car

Country: USSR
Entered service: 1938
Crew: 4
Weight: 5,080kg/5 tons
Dimensions: Length – 4.70m/15ft 5in
    Height – 2.42m/7ft 11in
    Width – 2.09m/6ft 7in
Armament: Main – 1 x 45mm/1.77in M-1934 tank gun and 1 x coaxial 7.62mm/0.3in DT machine-gun
    Secondary – 7.62mm/0.3in DT machine-gun
Armour: Maximum – 15mm/0.59in
Powerplant: GAZ M1 4-cylinder 38kW/52hp petrol engine
Performance: Speed – 55kph/34mph
    Range – 300km/186 miles

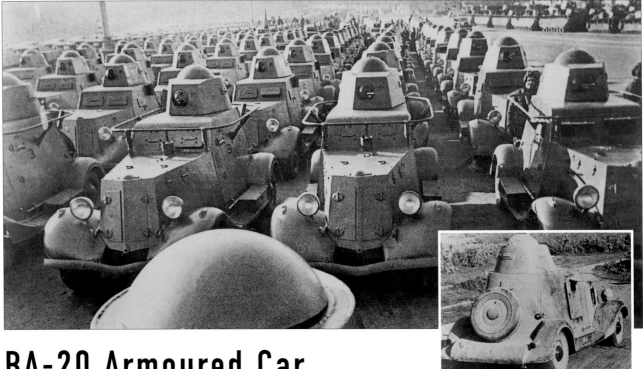

BA-20 Armoured Car

The BA-20 became the most numerous and popular armoured car in service with the Soviet Army in the late 1930s. Development for this car started at the GAZ factory in 1934 and under went trials in 1935. Once the vehicle had passed these trials it was accepted into service and placed into full production in late 1935.

The BA-20 used the GAZ M1 chassis which was built at the Novgorod factory, while the body was built at Vyksinskiy where the final assembly was also carried out. The original chassis had to be redesigned to accommodate the extra weight of the BA-20 body. The changes included a new differential and rear axle together with improvements to the suspension. The BA-20 normally carried

a crew of two but in the command version it had a crew of three. This was also the first Soviet armoured car to be fitted with an escape hatch in the floor of the vehicle. The BA-20 had an excellent cross-country performance and was especially good in soft going across marshy ground. The vehicle was also fitted with bullet-proof tyres and bullet-proof glass in the driver's vision block.

In 1938 the BA-20 was improved and became the BA-20M. It had a better turret and thicker armour and a three-man crew became standard. One interesting version of the BA-20 and the BA-20M was the ZhD. This car could change its road wheels for flanged steel railway wheels, which extended its range.

The BA-20 entered service in 1936 and remained in use until 1942, the BA-20M joining it from 1938 until 1942. The BA-20 first saw action in 1939 in the Battle of Khalkhin Gol against Japan, and later in the invasion of Poland and the Russo-Finnish war. The Finnish Army

TOP: BA-20M armoured cars lined up in Moscow for the November Parade in 1940. The front row of cars are the command version as they have the radio aerial around the body of the vehicle.
ABOVE: The rear of the vehicle showing the single spare-wheel storage. This position was also used to store the rail-wheels.

captured a number of these vehicles and put them back into service against the Russians. The Germans also captured a number of the BA-20M ZhD cars and used them for patrolling the rail network in an anti-partisan role. Both marks of the BA-20 proved to be very reliable and were well-liked by their crews.

LEFT: Captured BA-20 ZhD Drezine rail scout car. The Germans captured a number of these vehicles and used them to patrol the rear areas. A rail tow-link could be fitted to the spare wheel spigot to allow the car to be towed by a train.

BA-20 Armoured Car

Country: USSR
Entered service: 1936
Crew: 2 or 3
Weight: 2,341kg/2.3 tons
Dimensions: Length – 4.1m/13ft 5in
  Height – 2.3m/7ft 6in
  Width – 1.8m/5ft 9in
Armament: Main – 7.62mm/0.3in machine-gun
  Secondary – Small arms
Armour: Maximum – 6mm/0.24in
Powerplant: GAZ M1 4-cylinder 37kW/50hp petrol engine
Performance: Speed – 90kph/56mph
  Range – 350km/220 miles

BA-27 Armoured Car

Design work on the BA-27 started in 1924, with development models being produced in 1926. The first production model came out in 1927. The 1927 model was built on the 4x2 F-15 chassis and was very simple to maintain; it proved to be very reliable in service with the Soviet Army. There were several problems with the vehicle at first. When the armoured louvers were closed the engine would overheat very quickly, so a large fan was fitted behind the radiator that would draw air through slots cut in the armour and through the radiator to cool the engine. This helped but never really solved the cooling problems. The other big problem was the vehicle had large wheels with dual tyres on the rear axle, but the tyres were narrow and this caused the vehicle to bog down in any form of soft ground when the BA-27 went off-road.

Even when it went into production, the Russians did not stop development and in 1928 they produced the Model 1928 with the new Ford-AA chassis and a new engine, the GAZ four-cylinder 30kW/40hp. In the Model 1927 there was a crew of four but this had proved to be cumbersome in the very small fighting compartment, so in the Model 1928 the crew was cut back to three. This became the definitive production model of the BA-27. The turret came from the T-18 light tank and was fitted with a Hotchkiss 37mm/1.46in gun and a 7.62mm/0.3in machine-gun. While in the West the BA-27 would be classified as a light to medium armoured car, the Soviet designation was heavy, due to its armament.

The BA-27 is significant in that it was the first series of heavy armoured car to be produced in the Soviet Union since Putilov. It was in production from 1927 to 1931, by which time over 100 of these heavy armoured cars had been produced. It would see a lot of action against the Japanese along the Chinese border in the 1930s and 1940s. The main production plant was Izhorskiy near Leningrad (now St Petersburg).

ABOVE: **The BA-27M was based on the Ford Timken chassis and was built by Remontbaza No.2 (Repair base No.2). The cross-country ability of the BA-27 was supposed to be improved by adding an extra axle, but it did not work.**

ABOVE: **A BA-27M abandoned at a ferry crossing in 1941. The car is carrying a set of overall tracks on the rear of the car. One of the outer rear wheels is missing.** LEFT: **BA-27s on parade in Moscow in 1931 during the November Parade. The offset armament clearly shows up with the 37mm/1.46in gun. Under the front of the vehicle is an air scoop that forces air into the radiator.**

BA-27 Model 1927

Country: USSR
Entered service: 1927
Crew: 3
Weight: 4,400kg/4.33 tons
Dimensions: Length – 4.62m/15ft 2in
           Height – 2.52m/8ft 3in
           Width – 1.7m/5ft 7in
Armament: Main – 37mm/1.46in Hotchkiss gun
          Secondary – 7.62mm/0.3in DT machine-gun
Armour: Maximum – 8mm/0.315in
Powerplant: AMO F-15 4-cylinder 26.1kW/35hp petrol engine
Performance: Speed – 35kph/22mph
            Range – 270km/168 miles

LEFT: **The rear of a BA-64B. Above the spare wheel is the rear pistol port. The origins of the vehicle can be clearly seen, as the vehicle is an armoured Jeep. One defect of the BA-64B was a lack of adequate armament, so in 1943 the improved BA-64D was produced with the 12.7mm/0.5in heavy machine-gun.**

BA-64B Armoured Car

The first new Soviet armoured car design of World War II was the BA-64, designed and developed at the GAZ works. Production was started at the end of 1941 and went on until early 1942. This vehicle was based on the GAZ 64 Jeep. The vehicle had a coffin shape and an open pulpit-style machine-gun position, but production was slow due to the demands for the GAZ Jeep.

A troop carrier version was developed but never put into production as it was too small and could only carry six men.

In 1943 GAZ started to produce a new Jeep and the BA-64B armoured car was developed by using this new chassis. It was a better vehicle than its predecessor

as it was more reliable and had a wider chassis, giving it a better cross-country ability. It had an all-welded construction with steeply angled plates to give some form of deflection to incoming munitions. This design idea was copied from German vehicles such as the Sd Kfz 221 and Sd Kfz 222. The BA-64B also had a small one-man turret fitted to the top of the vehicle. These changes constituted a big improvement on the BA-64, but the greatest single improvement was four-wheel drive. Total production of both vehicles was 9,110 and while production would finish in 1945, it would remain in service with the Soviet Army until 1956 and later still with Soviet allies.

Various versions of the basic vehicle were built, one of these being a command car that was fitted with a radio and map boards fixed on special frames built on the top of the vehicle with the turret removed. This vehicle became very popular with all ranks of officer as a basic battlefield run-about and taxi. In another unusual version, the wheels were removed; the front wheels were replaced with two heavy-duty skis and the rear wheels were replaced by a Kegresse half-track. A large number of the basic armoured cars were upgunned in the field by their crews with the installation of the DShK 12.7mm/0.5in heavy machine-gun and captured German machine-guns and cannon. Its crews nicknamed the vehicle the "Bobik". Many of these cars saw action in the Korean War.

LEFT AND ABOVE: **Late production BA-64Bs: the vehicle above has all its pistol ports open, and the driver's periscope can be seen attached to the front hatch.**

BA-64B Armoured Car

Country: USSR
Entered service: 1943
Crew: 2
Weight: 2,359kg/2.3 tons
Dimensions: Length – 3.67m/12ft 4in
　　　　　　　Height – 1.88m/6ft 2in
　　　　　　　Width – 1.52m/4ft 10in
Armament: Main – 7.62mm/0.3in machine-gun
　　　　　　Secondary – Small arms
Armour: Maximum – 15mm/0.59in
Powerplant: GAZ MM 4-cylinder 40kW/54hp petrol engine
Performance: Speed – 80kph/50mph
　　　　　　　Range – 560km/350 miles

Beaverette Light Reconnaissance Car

After the withdrawal of the British Expeditionary Force from France in 1940, there was a proliferation of AFVs but only two were officially placed into production, one of these being the Beaverette. The vehicle was named after Lord Beaverbrook, Minister of Aircraft Production, on whose instance it was designed and placed into production within a few months.

The Beaverette was built by the Standard Motor Company Ltd of Coventry and used the chassis of the Standard 14 saloon car. The vehicle was covered in 11mm/0.43in mild steel, and was open topped, backed by 76.2mm/3in oak planks but with no rear protection for the crew. The driver had a small vision slot to the front and side, which was covered by sliding steel shutters and gave a very restricted field of vision. The Mk I had only just entered production when the improved Mk II was

introduced. As the restrictions on steel were being lifted extra armour could be fitted to the Beaverette giving the crew some rear protection, and the radiator grille changed from vertical, as in the Mk I, to horizontal.

In 1941, the Mk III came into service. This was a very different vehicle and gave the crew all-round protection. Armour plate was now being made available and although the thickness was reduced to 10mm/0.394in, the whole vehicle was now covered in it, which gave it a rear-end-down attitude while being driven. The only entrance to the vehicle was through the single large door at the rear. In front of the driver was a step in the armour which placed the driver a little further back in the vehicle than the turret. In the final version, the Mk IV, the step was done away with and the driver now sat in front of the turret so that the machine-gun crew had more room to operate. These cars remained in service for many years and some which had been used for airfield defence were handed over to the Americans in 1942.

LEFT: **The Beaverette Mk III with the single light machine-gun turret. This gave the gunner far better protection, but very poor vision. The large door in the rear of the Beaverette is the only entrance and exit from the vehicle.**

ABOVE LEFT: **A Beaverette Mk III armed with twin Vickers K machine-guns. The gunner is very exposed in this early turret. As well as the large opening in the front of the turret, the top is also open.**
ABOVE: **A column of Beaverette Mk I and II cars moving in convoy. The open-topped fighting compartment can be clearly seen. Because of this, the crew have to wear their steel helmets.**

Beaverette IV Light Reconnaissance Car

Country: UK
Entered service: 1940
Crew: 3
Weight: 2,540kg/2.5 tons
Dimensions: Length – 3.1m/10ft 2in
  Height – 2.03m/6ft 8in
  Width – 1.78m/5ft 10in
Armament: Main – 7.7mm/0.303in Bren light
  machine-gun
  Secondary – None
Armour: Maximum – 10mm/0.394in
Powerplant: Standard 14 4-cylinder 34kW/45bhp
  petrol engine
Performance: Speed – 65kph/40mph
  Range – Not known

Bedford Cockatrice

The Cockatrice was a mobile flame-thrower developed in 1940 by the Lagonda Company for airfield defence, using a Commer armoured truck as the prototype. The first production vehicles that came into service in early 1941 were built for the Royal Navy to act as airfield defence vehicles. Sixty of these vehicles were built using the Bedford QL 4x4 chassis. The armoured body was of a riveted construction, with the driver and engine at the front, the flame gun mounted in a small turret on the roof of the vehicle, and a machine-gun position at the rear with twin Vickers K guns. The flame projector used 36.4 litres/8 gallons of fuel per minute and had a range of 91.4m/300ft. The RAF were also looking at this type of vehicle but felt it was too small so asked for a vehicle to be developed based on the RAF's heavy fuel bowser which had an AEC 6x6 chassis. These were known as Heavy Cockatrice but only six of these vehicles were ever produced.

LEFT: **The Bedford Cockatrice has a very high ground clearance, with the flame gun mounted in the middle of the roof of the vehicle. The machine-gun position at the rear of the vehicle was open-topped.**

Bedford Cockatrice	
Country: UK	
Entered service: 1941	
Crew: 3	
Weight: N/A	
Dimensions: Length – 5.94m/19ft 6in	
Height – 2.59m/8ft 6in	
Width – 2.26m/7ft 5in	
Armament: Main – Flame Gun	
Secondary – 2 x Vickers K machine-guns	
Armour: Maximum – 11mm/0.43in	
Powerplant: Bedford 6-cylinder 53.7kW/72hp petrol engine	
Performance: Speed – 48kph/30mph	
Range – 370km/230 miles	

Bison Concrete Armoured Vehicle

Designed by Concrete Ltd which developed and built the vehicle, the Bison was a solution to the shortage of armoured vehicles in Britain in 1940. No two vehicles were the same, as any truck that could be scavenged was converted.

Leyland Lynx Bison	
Country: UK	
Entered service: 1940	
Crew: 5–10 men	
Weight: Variable	
Dimensions: Length – 6.1m/20ft	
Height – 2.74m/9ft	
Width – 2.28m/7ft 6in	
Armament: Main – Various small arms	
Secondary – None	
Armour: Maximum – 152mm/6in reinforced concrete, backed by 25mm/1in timber	
Powerplant: Leyland 6-cylinder 57kW/77hp petrol engine	
Performance: Speed – Variable	
Range – Variable	

The chassis were mainly pre-war civilian heavy trucks such as AEC, Dennis, Leyland, and Thornycroft. The vehicle was covered in wooden shuttering and fast-setting concrete was then poured over it to a depth of 152mm/6in, which made it bullet-proof and capable of withstanding hits from guns of up to 37mm/1.46in. There were two main variations. The first had a concrete-covered engine and cab with a separate pillbox mounted on the flatbed. The engine and cab were open-topped but protected by canvas covers as concrete tops would be too heavy. The second type had the whole flatbed and driver's cab covered in concrete, with no openings in the sides or top. Access was by a trapdoor under

ABOVE: **The Bison driver and vehicle commander have a very limited vision from the cab. The wheels and chassis were very exposed and there was no protection below the vehicle. As a result of this, these vehicles were mainly used as static armoured pillboxes.**

the vehicle. These vehicles carried a crew of between five and ten men and had a variety of armament, the heaviest being an LMG (light machine-gun).

LEFT: One of the final type of Birch Gun. Only two of these turreted vehicles were made. The turret has a high front and is really a barbette. This affected the elevation and maximum range of the gun.
BELOW: The four Mk II Birch Guns of 20 Battery Royal Artillery during an exercise on Salisbury plain. The Birch Gun was the first genuine self-propelled artillery. However, the gun shield on the vehicle gives the crew very little protection.

Birch Gun

The Birch Gun was named after the Master General of the Ordnance, General Sir Noel Birch. Officially known as the SP QF (quick-firing) 18pdr Mk I, this was the first self-propelled gun to go into production for the British Army. The vehicle used many of the parts from the Dragon Carrier and the Vickers Medium tank.

The first gun entered service in January 1925 and was attached to 28 Battery, 9th Field Brigade, but only one of this early type was built and it was used for trials. The vehicle was fitted with an Armstrong Siddeley air-cooled engine, which gave it a top speed of 24.1kph/15mph but when used cross-country the maximum speed of the vehicle fell to 16.1kph/10mph. The vehicle was open-topped and there was no protection for the crew from the

weather or from small arms fire. The gun was mounted on a pintle mount towards the front of the vehicle which gave it a 360-degree traverse and a maximum elevation of 90 degrees so it could be used in an anti-aircraft role. It had a very complex sighting system and the recuperator was fitted to the top of the barrel.

Late in 1925 an order was placed with Vickers for four more Birch Guns, but these had a number of improvements to both the gun and the sighting equipment. The recuperator was moved to underneath the gun barrel and a gun shield was mounted on the front of the gun to give the crew some protection. These vehicles were issued to the 20th

Battery of the 9th Field Brigade.

The third and final type of Birch Gun was ordered in December 1927 and was finished a year later but never issued. This model was equipped with a turret to give the gun crew some form of protection but this limited the maximum elevation and the range of the weapon.

The Birch Guns were used in the Experimental Mechanised Force manoeuvres of 1928, but by 1931 they had all been removed from service and the British Army would not get an SPG for another 11 years.

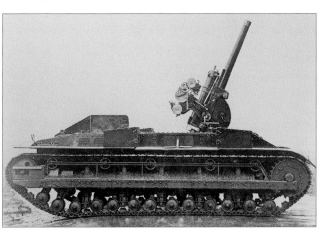

LEFT: The prototype Birch Gun showing the 18pdr at full elevation. The vehicle was given the designation of Mounting SP QF (quick-firing) 18pdr Mk I, but was better known as the Birch Gun.

Birch Gun	
Country: UK	
Entered service: 1925	
Crew: 6	
Weight: 12,192kg/12 tons	
Dimensions: Length – 5.8m/19ft	
Height – 2.3m/7ft 6in	
Width – 2.4m/7ft 9in	
Armament: Main – QF (quick-firing) 8.17kg/18pdr Mk I gun	
Secondary – Small arms	
Armour: None	
Powerplant: Armstrong Siddeley 8-cylinder 67kW/90hp petrol engine	
Performance: Speed – 45kph/28mph	
Range – 192km/119 miles	

Bishop 25pdr Self-Propelled Gun Mk 1

The successful use of self-propelled artillery by the German Army in the Western Desert led to urgent calls from the British 8th Army for something similar. It was suggested that the 25pdr gun could be mounted on a tank chassis and the best one for the job at this time was the Valentine. The Birmingham Carriage and Wagon Company were given the task of making this idea work in June 1941. A pilot model was ready for trials by August and an order for 100 vehicles was placed in November 1941.

The chassis was a basic Valentine Mk II tank with the standard turret replaced by a very large fixed box turret mounting a 25pdr gun. This gave the vehicle a very high silhouette, which was a great disadvantage in the desert. The gun could not be used to its maximum

elevation or range and so the vehicle was confined to the close-support role. Two large doors were mounted in the rear of the turret, which had to be open when firing the gun to give the crew extra room. The vehicle would often pull a 25pdr limber behind it for increased ammunition supply as it could only carry 32 rounds internally.

In early 1942, the British Tank Mission to America had seen a demonstration of the M7 and placed orders for it that March. However, production continued on the Bishop (the Royal Artillery gave its SPGs ecclesiastical names) and by July 1942, 80 of the first order had been built and a number had been shipped to the 8th Army in North Africa. As the last 20 were under construction, a further order for 50 was placed with the promise of

ABOVE LEFT: **The crew of a Bishop have come out of action. Before they can rest, they have to tend to the vehicle by refuelling, rearming, checking the engine and all the other parts that make up the Bishop.**
ABOVE: **A Bishop driving off a raised bank. These banks were dug to help increase the range of the gun, with the vehicle commander helping to direct the driver.**

an order for 200 to follow, but this was cancelled in favour of the M7.

By July 1942 the M7 was entering service with the British and would be used alongside the Bishop for another year. The 8th Army used the Bishop until the end of the campaign in Sicily when it was replaced with the M7 and relegated to the training role. Compared to the M7, the Bishop was crude and unsophisticated.

LEFT: **A group of British officers having an "O" (Orders) group, issuing orders for the next attack. The Bishop has been parked close to the trees to help camouflage it but the height of the fixed turret can be clearly seen. The vehicle is covered in personal kit.**

Bishop 25pdr SPG Mk 1	

Country: UK
Entered service: 1942
Crew: 4
Weight: 20,320kg/20 tons
Dimensions: Length – 5.62m/18ft 6in
   Height – 3.05m/10ft
   Width – 2.77m/9ft 1in
Armament: Main – 25pdr (87.6mm/3.45in)
   gun howitzer
   Secondary – Small arms
Armour: Maximum – 60mm/2.36in
Powerplant: AEC 6-cylinder 98kW/131hp
   diesel engine
Performance: Speed – 24kph/15mph
   Range – 177km/110 miles

LEFT: **The mantlet has been covered by a canvas cover to help keep dust out of the gun mechanism and the pistol port has been opened on the side of the fighting compartment. The side-skirts are still attached to this Brummbär.** ABOVE: **A knocked-out early Brummbär. The side skirt rails have been badly damaged. The vehicle is covered in *Zimmerit* paste to stop magnetic bombs being attached to the vehicle.**

Brummbär Sturmpanzer IV 15cm Self-Propelled Gun

As early as June 1941 a German Army paper suggested the idea of putting a 15cm/5.91in gun into an SP mount. In October 1942, Hitler was shown a plan drawn up by the firm Alkett for a close-support SPG using a 15cm short-barrelled gun mounted on the Panzer IV chassis. Hitler immediately insisted on the production of 40–60 of these vehicles, as he felt there would be a demand for them from the front-line troops, and on the development of a new high-explosive shell for the vehicle to use on buildings and other structures.

The first 60 vehicles were assembled by the Motor Vehicle Workshop in Vienna, the first 20 chassis being delivered in April 1943 with a further 32 in May. All were ready by June 1, 1943 and 50 were sent to Guderian on the Eastern Front, while 10 more were held back to be used at the Fuhrer's discretion. The Panzer IV Ausf F chassis required very little conversion: the turret was removed and a large box structure

was mounted on the top of the vehicle making it top-heavy. The frontal armour was increased to 100mm/3.94in and the driver's visor was at first the same as that in the Tiger 1, but later versions did away with this and replaced it with periscopes. At 28,651kg/28.2 tons, the vehicle was overloaded and the excessive weight caused suspension problems on the early vehicles, consequently the rubber-tyred wheels were replaced by steel-rimmed wheels on the first two bogie sets. Early service use showed that having no local defence machine-gun was a real handicap, so on later versions a machine-gun was mounted in the front of the hull above the driver. To increase the lower side protection for the vehicle, side plates called *Schürzen* (skirts) were hung from rails.

The Brummbär (Grizzly Bear) first saw action with *Sturmpanzerabteilung* 216 at Kursk, the largest tank battle of World War II, and later in Italy and in Normandy with units 217, 218 and 219.

ABOVE: **A late production Brummbär. The close-defence machine-gun port is mounted just above the driver's position on the front of the vehicle.**

Brummbär Sturmpanzer IV 15cm SPG

Country: Germany
Entered service: 1943
Crew: 5
Weight: 28,651kg/28.2 tons
Dimensions: Length – 5.93m/19ft 5in
Height – 2.52m/8ft 3in
Width – 2.88m/9ft 5in
Armament: Main – 1 x 15cm/5.91in StuH43 L/12
Secondary – 2 x 7.92mm/0.312in MG34 machine-gun
Armour: Maximum – 100mm/3.94in
Powerplant: Maybach HL 120 TRM 12-cylinder petrol engine 223.7kW/300hp
Performance: Speed – 40kph/24mph
Range – 210km/130 miles

Buffalo LVT Amphibious Assault Vehicle

When the US Marine Corps were looking for a vehicle capable of landing troops or supplies from the sea in 1940, they saw a vehicle designed and constructed by a Donald Roebling who wanted a vehicle to use in the Florida Everglades. He called it the "Alligator". They liked it, asked for a few changes, and then placed an order for 300.

The LVT 1 (Landing Vehicle Tracked) could carry 18 fully armed men ashore or 2,041kg/4,500lb of stores. The vehicle was propelled through the water by its tracks as these had special oblique shoes that also gave it good traction on land. The driver's position was in the front of the vehicle with the engines mounted in the side walls of the cargo compartment. A big drawback was that the men in the rear of the vehicle

had to climb up the side of the vehicle and then drop 2.1m/7ft over the side on to the ground with a full combat load on their backs. Development of the LVT 1 was frozen in 1941 but as the vehicle was needed urgently by the Marine Corps, 1,225 of these vehicles were built in 1942. They were first used in action in August 1942 during the invasion of Guadalcanal.

Early in 1943 production started on the LVT 2, an improved version of the LVT 1. The general hull of the vehicle was redesigned and given a better boat shape to improve its water handling. The engines were removed from the sides and placed in the rear of the vehicle. The tracks were fitted with new track grousers that were W-shaped which could be easily attached to the tracks of the vehicle. Troops still had to climb

ABOVE: **The rear ramp of this Buffalo LVT 4 is in the down position with a Weasel coming down the ramp. The grousers on the track, which move this very large vehicle through the water, can be clearly seen.**
LEFT: **A column of British Buffalos moving through the smokescreen to cross the Rhine in 1945. Some of the vehicles are still loading their infantry while the gunners of the leading Buffalo are getting their guns ready for action.**

the sides and drop down on to the beach, which was causing casualties among the Marines, so a better way of debussing had to be developed. Two thousand nine hundred and sixty three of these vehicles were built and their first operation was the invasion of Tarawa in November 1943.

Production of the LVT 4, basically an improved LVT 2, began in December 1943. The improvements were that the engine was moved from the rear to the front just behind the driver. A ramp was now fitted to the rear of the vehicle, a major change that would turn this vehicle into the most successful amphibious assault vehicle of the war with 8,348 being produced. The ramp was operated by hand-winch in normal conditions, but in combat the ramp would be released to fall under its own weight. The rear cargo area could now carry 35 fully armed men, an artillery gun or a Jeep. The driver's position was moved from the middle of the driver's compartment to the right-hand side and a bow machine-gun was fitted for the second crewman to use. The first American operation for this vehicle was the invasion of Saipan in June 1944.

The LVT 3 was due to go into production in early 1944 but due to a number of design faults this was delayed until late 1944. Like the LVT 4 it had a rear cargo ramp, and two engines were mounted in the vehicle, one in each side sponson. Apart from the twin engines the LVT 3's performance was the same as the LVT 4, but its water handling was better than the other marks of LVTs. The Americans named the vehicle the

"Bushmaster". Two thousand nine hundred and sixty three of these were produced and it was used by the Marine Corps and the US Army for many years, taking part in the Korean War and serving into the Vietnam War. The first combat operation for the LVT 3 was Okinawa in April 1945.

The Buffalo, as it was called in British service, was assigned to the 79th Armoured Division. Four hundred and twenty five vehicles from two marks, the LVT 2 and the LVT 4, were sent over from America and these would take part in several river crossings. The first British operation using it was the assault on the Breskens Pocket in October 1944, and it remained in service with the British Army until the late 1950s.

ABOVE: **British Buffalos landing on Walcheren island at the top of the Scheldt estuary in 1944. The Buffalo was one of the few vehicles that could cope with the sand and mud of the island.** LEFT: **An LVT 1 driving at speed over swampy ground. These vehicles were nicknamed the "Swamp Angel". The very large driver's window is in the raised position. It gave the driver excellent vision but in combat was a weakness.**

Buffalo Mk IV/LVT 4

Country: USA
Entered service: 1942
Crew: 2 plus 35 infantry
Weight: 12,428kg/12.2 tons
Dimensions: Length – 7.95m/26ft 1in
    Height – 2.46m/8ft 1in
    Width – 3.25m/10ft 8in
Armament: Main – 1 x 12.7mm/0.5in machine-
    gun
    Secondary – 3 x 7.62mm/0.3in machine-guns
Armour: Maximum – 13mm/0.51in
Powerplant: Continental W670-9A 7-cylinder
    air-cooled radial engine 186kW/250hp
Performance: Speed – Land 32kph/20mph;
    Water 12kph/7mph
    Range – 240km/150 miles

LEFT: **A column of Bren Gun Carriers, No.2, Mk 1, escorting soft-skin troop transports. The hood over the aperture for the Bren gun was to make room for the weapon's magazine. The driver has his seat in the raised position and is peering over the top to see where he is going.**

Carriers – Machine-gun

A great deal of development was carried out by Vickers Armstrong during the early part of the 1930s using the Carden-Loyd light tank as the base vehicle. A new suspension system was developed consisting of a two-wheel Horstmann type unit with a large coiled spring each side and a single wheel unit behind. The idler wheel was at the front with the drive sprocket at the rear. The first vehicle was a machine-gun carrier. This had the driver on the right and the gunner on the left. Behind them there was room for four infantrymen to be

carried, though with very little protection. The first trials vehicle was produced in 1935 and a number of changes were made before 13 more were manufactured in 1936. A further order was placed later in 1936 for an extra 41 carriers. It was decided that three more types of carrier would be developed during 1936.

A carrier was developed to transport the 7.7mm/0.303in Bren light machine-gun forward under fire, as the gun was just coming into service. When that point was reached, this weapon could be used either from the carrier or dismounted. A number of these Bren Gun Carriers were still in service during World War II and saw action in the desert with the British 8th Army.

The Carrier Cavalry Mk 1 and the Scout Mk 1 were developed for the new

role that the mechanized cavalry units would carry out. The Carrier Cavalry had a driver and gunner in the front with seats on the rear for six cavalrymen, three each side sitting back-to-back. The first contract for 50 vehicles was placed in 1937. A large number of these carriers went with the BEF to France in 1940 but their original role was soon abandoned as it was too dangerous for the troops on the rear of the vehicle.

The Carrier Scout, of which 667 were built, carried various weapons and a radio mounted in the rear of the vehicle. Often confused with the Universal Carrier, it would see action with the BEF in France and in the desert.

MIDDLE LEFT: **A pair of Carriers, Scout Mk 1. These vehicles had a crew of three and were armed with a Boys anti-tank rifle and a Bren gun.**

LEFT: **A group of four Bren Gun Carriers. The crew positions can be clearly seen, especially the third crew position behind the gunner. The suspension on each side has two road wheels in a Horstmann-type bogie which is sprung on coiled springs, a single wheel in a similar unit and the idler at the front.**

Bren Gun Carrier	

Country: UK
Entered service: 1937
Crew: 3
Weight: 4,064kg/4 tons
Dimensions: Length – 3.66m/12ft
  Height – 1.37m/4ft 6in
  Width – 2.11m/6ft 11in
Armament: Main – Bren 7.7mm/0.303in light machine-gun
  Secondary – Small arms
Armour: Maximum – 12mm/0.47in
Powerplant: Ford 48kW/65hp petrol engine
Performance: Speed – 48kph/30mph
  Range – 258km/160 miles

LEFT: **The heavy turret bolts stand out clearly on this Cromwell. The tank is covered in personal storage.**
ABOVE: **The crew of this vehicle have rigged up a rain shelter above their map boards. They are wearing the one-piece tank-suit, which was very warm.**

Cromwell Command/OP Tank

This was the simplest and yet one of the most important conversions of World War II. Due to the speed and danger of a modern mobile battlefield, forward commanders required an armoured vehicle that was capable of keeping up with the advance units, yet giving them some protection and the fullest possible access to communications relevant to their task. These vehicles were issued to formation commanders and forward observation officers of the Royal Artillery.

The Cromwell was chosen due to its good speed and reliability, although at first there were a number of problems with the engine. The speed and power was supplied by a Meteor V12 engine that was a development of the Rolls-Royce Merlin aircraft engine. The top

speed was initially 61kph/38mph but this was too much for the vehicle chassis to take, so the engine had a governor placed on it that reduced the speed to 52kph/32mph. From the outside, the vehicle would look very much like a conventional tank except for two map stands mounted on the top and towards the front of the turret. Inside the turret the whole main gun and its controls were removed, along with all the ammunition storage. The main gun barrel was replaced with either an aluminium or wooden copy to disguise the true purpose and configuration of this tank. This gave a lot of additional space for the extra radios that the vehicle carried. Three radios were placed in the turret area, two No.19 sets and one T43 Command radio set. In some vehicles,

the Command radios were replaced by a ground-to-air radio set. In addition, two-man portable sets were carried for use by the Observation officers when away from the vehicle. The radios would be operated and maintained by members of the Royal Corps of Signals.

Three marks of Cromwell were converted to Command and OP tanks, these being the Mk IV, VI and VIII. These vehicles were to see service mainly in north-west Europe, and would remain in British Army service for many years after World War II.

Cromwell Command Tank

Country: UK
Entered service: 1944
Crew: 4/5
Weight: 26,416kg/26 tons
Dimensions: Length – 6.35m/20ft 10in
　　Height – 2.5m/8ft 2in
　　Width – 2.92m/9ft 7in
Armament: Main – None
　　Secondary – 1 x Besa 7.92mm/0.312in
　　machine-gun, and 1 x Bren 7.7mm/0.303in
　　light machine-gun
Armour: Maximum – 76mm/2.99in
Powerplant: Rolls-Royce Meteor 12-cylinder
　　447kW/600hp petrol engine
Performance: Speed – 52kph/32mph
　　Range – 278km/173 miles

LEFT: **Two Cromwell Command tanks lead a column of Sherman tanks along a road. The map boards can be clearly seen on both Command tanks. The vehicles are clear of any personal clutter as they are on exercise in Britain.**

Crossley Armoured Car

In 1923, Crossley Motors of Manchester offered a new chassis that was very robust and cheaper than the Rolls-Royce, the main armoured car chassis used at this time. The Crossley six-wheeled chassis was used to produce a number of different armoured cars for the Royal Air Force (RAF) in the Middle East, the British Army in India, and a number of other governments in the 1930s.

The main contractor for building these vehicles was Vickers, which was able to build 100 six-wheeled armoured cars, most going to the British forces in India and Iraq. The first ones were based on the Crossley 30/70hp medium chassis and were over 6.1m/20ft long, so had a real problem with grounding in rough terrain. To overcome this problem Vickers mounted the spare wheels between the front and rear wheels so they hung below the chassis and could rotate freely, thus making it a four-axle vehicle which could withstand the rigours of less than perfect roads in the outlying

areas of India and Iraq. Another chassis was the 38/110hp Crossley IGA4 series with a six-cylinder engine. The body and turret were very similar to the Lanchester armoured car, but the turret was fitted with a single machine-gun. The Crossley 20/60hp light six-wheeled chassis was the basis for yet another armoured car. The first Crossleys were ordered from the Royal Ordnance Factory in 1928 and were armed with two machine-guns, one in a turret and one in the front hull. The turret was the same as a Vickers Mk 1 light tank.

Vickers produced a number of Crossley cars for export to several countries such as Argentina, Iraq and Japan. Most of these would see service for many years. The Iraqi cars were later commandeered by British forces and used by them in a training role until the

ABOVE LEFT: **Crossley armoured car on the 38/110hp chassis. This was known as the IGA4 series. The main customer for this car was the RAF.** ABOVE: **A Crossley 30/70hp chassis armoured car. The dome-shaped turret is very similar to the Indian Pattern armoured car and is armed with two Vickers guns.**

end of World War II. All Crossley cars in RAF service were equipped with ground-to-ground and ground-to-air radio sets. This proved very useful during combined operations in Iraq and India while trying to police the northern borders of these countries.

LEFT: **The pole frame above the vehicle carries the main aerial for the long-range radio, and for ground-to-air radio. The spare wheels were left free to rotate and so help the vehicle unditch itself.**

Crossley Mk 1 Armoured Car

Country: UK
Entered service: 1931
Crew: 4
Weight: 5,516.88kg/5.43 tons
Dimensions: Length – 4.65m/15ft 3in
　　Height – 2.64m/8ft 8in
　　Width – 1.88m/6ft 2in
Armament: Main – 2 x Vickers 7.7mm/0.303in
　　machine-guns
　　Secondary – None
Armour: Maximum – 10mm/0.394in
Powerplant: Crossley 52kW/70hp
Performance: Speed – 80kph/50mph
　　Range – 290km/180 miles

LEFT: **A Daimler armoured car opening fire in support of some infantry. This is not the normal role for this car as the main gun only fired solid shot.** BELOW: **The top hatch in the Daimler Mk 1 armoured car turret slides to the rear of the vehicle. A side hatch is situated between the wheels and storage boxes.**

Daimler Armoured Car

The Daimler Dingo was such a success that it was suggested that it could be scaled up into a wheeled tank. Development started in 1939 but due to a number of technical problems the armoured car did not enter service (as the Daimler Mk 1) until 1941.

The Daimler had many unusual and very advanced features for its time. There was no chassis to the vehicle and all the suspension components were attached directly to the armoured lower hull. Instead of a normal clutch, a fluid flywheel torque converter was used and also a pre-selector gearbox was fitted. The car had two driving positions, one in the front for the vehicle driver and one in the rear, which the vehicle commander could use to drive the vehicle away in reverse. The vehicle could use all five forward gears in reverse and was also

fitted with disc brakes some 20 years before any commercial vehicle. The turret mounted a 2pdr (40mm) gun. This was the first time that this gun was mounted in a British armoured car and was the same as that fitted to the Tetrarch light tank. The three-man crew meant that the vehicle commander had to act as loader for this weapon. Smoke dischargers were often fitted to the sides of the turret and some of the Mk 1 cars had a Littlejohn Adaptor fitted to their main armament. This was a squeeze bore muzzle adaptor that allowed the Daimler to achieve better armour penetration of enemy vehicles.

The Mk 2 came into service in 1943 with a number of improvements, including an improved gun mounting. The radiator was given better protection and improved to give better engine

cooling, and the driver was given an escape hatch. Apart from these modifications, the Mk 2 was the same as the Mk 1. Total production was 2,694 vehicles of all marks.

The Daimler soon developed a very good reputation for performance and reliability with the 8th Army in North Africa and it went on to serve with British forces in northern Europe. It remained in service until well after the end of World War II.

RIGHT: **A post-World War II Daimler Mk 1. A spare wheel has replaced the storage boxes on the side of the vehicle. This vehicle is shown in desert camouflage as used by the 7th Armoured Division in 1942.**

Daimler Mk 1 Armoured Car

Country: UK
Entered service: 1941
Crew: 3
Weight: 7,620kg/7.5 tons
Dimensions: Length – 3.96m/13ft
    Height – 2.24m/7ft 4in
    Width – 2.44m/8ft
Armament: Main – 2pdr (40mm) gun
    Secondary – Besa 7.92mm/0.312in machine-gun
Armour: Maximum – 16mm/0.63in
Powerplant: Daimler 6-cylinder petrol engine, 71kW/95hp
Performance: Speed – 80.5kph/50mph
    Range – 330km/205 miles

Daimler Dingo Scout Car

One of the requirements for the new armoured force that was being developed in the late 1930s was for a light 4x4 scout car for general duties and reconnaissance. The design was originally put forward by the BSA motorcycle company, but they were taken over by the Daimler car company. An order for 172 vehicles was placed with the new company in 1939.

The Mk 1 was a 4x4 open-top vehicle which only had armoured protection for the crew at the front of the vehicle and proved to be under-powered. The Mk 1A incorporated all-round armoured protection for the crew and a bigger and more powerful engine. It also had a folding metal roof. These Mk 1 vehicles had four-wheel

steering and this proved to be a liability in the hands of unskilled drivers.

The steering was changed to be front wheels only in the Mk 2, which made it considerably easier to handle. The basic layout would hardly change during the course of the vehicle's production. The two crew members sat side by side in an open-topped armoured box, while the crew compartment had only a folding metal roof for protection. The engine was at the rear.

The Mk 3 was the heaviest version of the scout car but was still well within the limits of the vehicle. The metal roof was done away with as it was hardly ever used operationally by the crews. The engine was also given a waterproof ignition system.

ABOVE LEFT: **This Dingo Mk 1 is in the "buttoned down" mode with all the hatches closed. The rear view mirror is mounted on the top of the front plate but was rarely fitted.** ABOVE: **The frame on the back of the Daimler is to support the crew compartment hatch. The front part of the hatch folds back, and then both parts slide back and on to the frame.**

The vehicle was armed with a Bren gun for all of its service history although there were a number of local crew modifications on the armament. The Daimler scout car proved to be a very reliable and rugged vehicle and has the distinction of being one of the few vehicles to be in service at the start of the World War II and to remain in service well after the war had finished, with 6,626 of all marks being produced. This car could be found in most British and Commonwealth units, even in units that were not supposed to have it on strength.

ABOVE: **A Dingo Mk 3 in the North African desert. The roof hatch has gone on this mark. The crew have increased the firepower of the car by adding a Vickers gun.**

Daimler Dingo Mk 3 Scout Car

Country: UK
Entered service: 1939
Crew: 2
Weight: 3,215.2kg/3.2 tons
Dimensions: Length – 3.23m/10ft 5in
　　Height – 1.5m/4ft 11in
　　Width – 1.72m/5ft 8in
Armament: Main – Bren 7.7mm/0.303in
　　light machine-gun
　　Secondary – None
Armour: Maximum – 30mm/1.18in
Powerplant: Daimler 6-cylinder petrol engine
　　41kW/55hp
Performance: Speed – 88.5kph/55mph
　　Range – 322km/200 miles

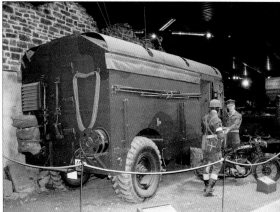

Dorchester Command Vehicle

The first command vehicle in British service was the Morris 762kg/ 15cwt. This came into service in 1937 but was far too small to be of any real use. The next vehicle was the 4x4 Guy Lizard which entered service in 1940 and most unusually had a Gardner diesel engine but again proved to be on the small side.

The Dorchester Command Vehicle was based on the AEC Matador chassis but with a few modifications. The fuel tank was moved and the winch was replaced with a generator for the radio sets that were carried in the vehicle. Two different marks of vehicle were produced, but there were no external differences between them – the changes were made to the internal fit

of the vehicle. The Mk 1 had a large single combined office and radio room, while in the Mk 2 there was a separate radio room. There were also two versions of each mark: the LP (Low Power) and HP (High Power) versions. The LP was fitted with No.19 radio LP and HP sets. The HP vehicle was fitted with an RCA (Radio Crystalline Amplifier) receiver and a No.19 set. The early versions of the vehicle were fitted with a canopy that, when unrolled, had side panels attached to form an extended working area. Later versions had a complete tent carried on the vehicle. There was normally a crew of seven with the vehicle, one driver, two radio operators and four officers.

Three Dorchesters were captured by the *Afrika Korps* in July 1941 and two

were given to Rommel to use as his own HQ vehicles. The official German designation for these vehicles was *Mammute* (Mammoths). The two vehicles used by Rommel were called "Max" and "Moritz" and were not recaptured by the British until the surrender of the German and Italian forces in Tunisia.

A new and larger vehicle did enter production towards the end of the war on the AEC 6x6 chassis. In all, 380 4x4 Dorchester command vehicles were produced from 1941–45. They would see service in North Africa, up through Italy and also in northern Europe.

Dorchester Armoured Command Vehicle

Country: UK
Entered service: 1941
Crew: 7
Weight: 10,500kg/10.33 tons
Dimensions: Length – 6.32m/20ft 9in
　　Height – 3.1m/10ft 2in
　　Width – 2.4m/7ft 10in
Armament: Main – Bren 7.7mm/0.303in light
　　machine-gun
　　Secondary – None
Armour: Maximum – 12mm/0.47in
Powerplant: AEC 6-cylinder 71kW/95hp
　　diesel engine
Performance: Speed – 58kph/36mph
　　Range – 579km/360 miles

LEFT: **The open side door of the vehicle has a blackout curtain on the inside, which was a standard fit. There is storage for several chairs on the back of the door. This door also gives access to the radio area and the driver's cab.**

LEFT: **Light Dragon Carrier Mk IIc. This was an improved vehicle having a new suspension system designed by Horstmann. The vehicle exhaust on the rear of the body has been fitted with a shield. The external shields for the return rollers can also be clearly seen as can the canvas roof for the vehicle which is in the raised position.**

Dragon Carrier Mk I

A number of experimental vehicles were designed at the Tank Design and Experimental Department commanded by Colonel P. H. Johnson. The origins of the Dragon lay in a number of experimental tropical tanks that were supply vehicles. The fourth vehicle of this series was sent to the 9th Field Brigade in 1922 for trials in gun-haulage. The army were not very impressed with these and so approached Vickers to produce three rival vehicles. One of these was built as a gun carrier for the 18pdr, the gun being carried on the top of the vehicle. It was hauled up ramps from the rear of the vehicle and positioned inside with the muzzle facing forward.

In 1922, the Royal Ordnance Factory at Woolwich produced two new vehicles called Artillery Transporters, which would be the prototypes for the Dragon Mk I. One was sent to India for trials and the other was sent to the 9th Field Brigade. An order was placed for 20 vehicles, 18 for the army and two for the RAF, and these entered service in 1923. The driver's compartment was down in the front of the vehicle next to the radiator. The vehicle commander sat next to the driver high up on the top of the vehicle and behind them was seating for a further 10 men who would man the gun. The crew compartment on the top of the vehicle was completely open to the elements, but a canvas tilt could be placed over the crew to protect them from rain. At the rear of the vehicle was storage for ammunition.

As soon as they were issued, the 9th Field Brigade began training with their new vehicles. In July 1923, they took part in a long-distance road march from Deepcut to Larkhill, a distance of 93km/58 miles. The march was completed in just 10 hours and all the crews arrived in good order. A horse-drawn battery would only have been able to cover 20 miles in the same time. However, the Dragon had a number of mechanical problems and was withdrawn from service in 1926.

ABOVE MIDDLE AND ABOVE: **A Dragon Carrier with the roof folded to the rear of the vehicle, but it could also be collapsed and stored on one side. The carrier is shown with an 18pdr gun and limber, its normal load. Note that the gun and limber are still fitted with wooden wheels.**

Dragon Carrier Mk I

Country: UK
Entered service: 1923
Crew: 2 plus 10 gun crew
Weight: 9,144kg/9 tons
Dimensions: Length – 5.03m/16ft 6in
Height – 2.13m/7ft – with tilt 3.05m/10ft
Width – 2.74m/9ft
Armament: Main – None
Secondary – Small arms
Armour: None
Powerplant: Leyland 6-cylinder 45kW/60hp petrol engine
Performance: Speed – 19kph/12mph
Range – 145km/90 miles

LEFT: **This is the armoured version of the Model T. The armoured body of the vehicle is very narrow at the front and just fits around the engine and the driver. The door for the cab is accessed from the rear of the vehicle.** BELOW: **A spare wheel is carried on the roof of the driver's cab. The machine-gun is mounted low in the rear of the vehicle, and had a very limited field of fire as it could not fire forwards due to the driver's cab.**

Ford Model T Scout Car

The Model T proved to be an outstanding scout and light armoured car, remaining in action long after other larger and more powerful armoured cars had broken down. There were two types of car built. The most numerous type used the basic Model T and was employed as a scout car. This was deployed mainly in the Middle East in countries such as Egypt and Palestine. The other type of car was a fully armoured version of the Model T and was used mostly in Russia and the Caucasus.

The scout car had a crew of two or three. In most of these, the machine-gun was mounted in the front of the car with the gunner sitting next to the driver. In some versions, a heavy machine-gun was mounted on the flatbed at the rear of the car. These vehicles had no armoured protection for the crew and no protection from the weather, while the machine-gun had very little traverse and none to the

rear. Nevertheless, due to its light weight and good reliability this vehicle proved to be well-liked by the men who used it. The American Army used several in Mexico and the Australians used them in Palestine and in Australia as they proved very good at covering large areas of dry, dusty ground.

The second car was developed by the British for the war in Russia, and designed by the Royal Navy, which had considerable experience with armoured cars. These vehicles were to replace a number of Lanchester armoured cars that had been damaged en route to Russia as they were all that was available at the time. Armour plate was placed around the engine and rear flatbed. The driver's cab was armoured except for the top which was canvas covered, and the Maxim machine-gun was mounted on a pintle mount on the rear flatbed with a 9mm/0.354in armoured shield fitted to

it. There was no forward field of fire for the machine-gun due to the driver's cab. These cars were ridiculed on arrival in Russia but soon proved far better than expected in service.

Ford Model T Scout Car	
Country: USA	
Entered service: 1914	
Crew: 2	
Weight: 508kg/10cwt	
Dimensions: Length – 3.42m/11ft 3in	
Height – 1.54m/5ft 1in	
Width – 1.28m/4ft 4in	
Armament: Main – 7.7mm/0.303in Vickers Maxim machine-gun	
Secondary – Small arms	
Armour: Maximum – 5mm/0.2in	
Powerplant: Ford 4-cylinder 16kW/22hp petrol engine	
Performance: Speed – 50kph/31mph	
Range – 241km/150 miles	

Grille 15cm Heavy Infantry Self-Propelled Gun Ausf M

LEFT: **The rear doors of the vehicle are in the open position; this was a common practice as the rear of the vehicle was used to store extra equipment. The crude armour around the crew compartment is very clearly shown in this picture. It gave the crew very little protection.** ABOVE: **An overhead view of the vehicle showing the very cramped fighting compartment. The driver's position is on the left below the gun-control wheels.**

By 1942 there was a growing demand for self-propelled artillery from the German Army so a number of chassis were considered for the task. The PzKpfw 38(t) was proving to be a very reliable and adaptable chassis and was used for a number of different gun platforms.

Development started in late 1942, and the prototype produced by Alkett using the 38(t) Ausf H chassis passed its acceptance trials. An order was placed for 200 units to be built on the Ausf K chassis, but this new chassis was not ready at that point, so construction started using the Ausf H. Production commenced in February 1943. After the initial production run was finished, it was agreed that all 38(t) chassis returned

for repair could also be converted into SPGs. Some of them were adapted to become the Grille, in which a 15cm/5.91in sIG 33 was mounted across the top of the body of the vehicle and bolted into place and an armoured superstructure was placed around the vehicle. This also covered the engine area to accommodate ammunition storage.

As soon as it became available, the Ausf M chassis was used for the bulk of the production of the Grille, which finished in September 1944. This new vehicle had a number of changes made to it. The rear engine in the H was moved forward to a mid position and the fighting compartment was moved to the rear of the vehicle. To protect the fighting

compartment, a large spring-loaded flap was used to cover the gun aperture when the gun was elevated.

Both versions of the Grille only carried 18 rounds of ammunition, so a further version was developed into an ammunition carrier using the Ausf M chassis. This was basically the same as the gun vehicle but without the gun, and consequently could be converted into the gun variant very quickly if needed. These vehicles were to see combat in Russia, Italy and northern Europe with many Panzer units of the German Army and the SS. In February 1945, there were still 173 Grille SPGs listed for combat.

Grille 15cm Heavy Infantry SPG Ausf M

Country: Germany
Entered service: 1943
Crew: 4
Weight: 12,192kg/12 tons
Dimensions: Length – 4.95m/16ft 3in
　　Height – 2.47m/8ft 1in
　　Width – 2.15m/7ft 1in
Armament: Main – 15cm/5.91in sIG 33/2
　　Secondary – 7.92mm/0.312in MG34
　　machine-gun
Armour: Maximum – 15mm/0.59in
Powerplant: Praga AC 6-cylinder 111kW/150hp
　　petrol engine
Performance: Speed – 42kph/26mph
　　Range – 190km/118 miles

LEFT: **A battery of Grille 15cm SPGs. The vehicle in the front of the picture is a late production variant, with the fighting compartment in the rear. The gun is at maximum elevation. When the weapon is in this position, a spring-loaded flap closes the gap in the gun shield.**

Guy Armoured Car Mk 1/1A

LEFT: **The driver's front hatch is in the open position, which improves the driver's vision. There are side hatches into the main fighting compartment just behind the front wheels on both sides. The very angular body and low ground clearance can be clearly seen.**

Following trials in 1938, the Guy Quad-Ant chassis was chosen to be the base for a "wheeled tank" as it was originally called. It was the first 4x4 vehicle to be specifically produced for the British Army. The engine was moved to the rear of the new vehicle, with a turret in the middle and the driver at the front. The other revolutionary thing about this vehicle is that it was of an all-welded construction for the hull and turret instead of riveted as specified for all other British AFVs at this time. An order was placed for 101 vehicles, one prototype and the remainder operational. The first 50 of these had one Vickers 12.7mm/0.5in and one 7.7mm/0.303in machine-gun. The next 50 vehicles had one Besa 15mm/0.59in gun and one 7.92mm/0.312in machine-gun. This configuration became the Mk 1A Guy Armoured Car. Only six of these went to France with the BEF and the rest remained in Britain with the Defence Force. All drawings were subsequently handed over to the Rootes Group.

Guy Armoured Car Mk 1/1A

Country: UK
Entered service: 1939
Crew: 3
Weight: 5,283kg/5.2 tons
Dimensions: Length – 4.12m/13ft 6in
Height – 2.29m/7ft 6in
Width – 2.06m/6ft 9in
Armament: Main – 12.7mm/0.5in Vickers machine-gun (Mk 1A 15mm/0.59in Besa machine-gun) Secondary – 7.7mm/0.303in Vickers machine-gun (Mk 1A 7.92mm/0.312in Besa machine-gun)
Armour: Maximum – 15mm/0.59in
Powerplant: Meadows 40kW/53hp petrol engine
Performance: Speed – 64kph/40mph
Range – 338km/210 miles

Guy Lizard Command Vehicle

Britain appears to be the only country to develop and use the armoured command vehicle during World War II. There was a clear requirement for a 4x4 command vehicle equipped with radio for use as a mobile headquarters. The development programme was awarded to Guy in 1939, as they had finished the development of a heavy armoured car for the War Office.

Guy used the new Lizard 3,048kg/3-ton 4x4 chassis that the company had just developed. It was powered by the Gardner diesel engine which was most unusual for military vehicles at this time. The prototype was basically an open box with the driver's position accessible from the command area at the rear. This would be modified in the AEC Dorchester command vehicles in which the driver's compartment was separated from the rest of the vehicle. The original contract was for 30 of these but only 21 appear to have been built.

The majority of these vehicles remained in Britain but some were sent to join the 8th Army and at least one was captured by the Italians.

RIGHT: **Very few pictures of these command vehicles exist due to their security classification. This vehicle has been pictured in a base workshop. The large number of roof hatches can be seen. The canvas roll on the side of the vehicle is a tent that can be used as an office.**

Guy Lizard Command Vehicle

Country: UK
Entered service: 1940
Crew: 6
Weight: 10,668kg/10.5 tons
Dimensions: Length – 6.48m/21ft 3in
Height – 2.67m/8ft 9in
Width – 2.44m/8ft
Armament: Main – Small arms
Secondary – None
Armour: Maximum – 12mm/0.47in
Powerplant: Gardner 6-cylinder 71kW/95hp diesel engine
Performance: Speed – 56kph/35mph
Range – 563km/350 miles

LEFT: **Humber Mk 4 armoured car armed with the American 37mm/1.46in gun. These vehicles belong to the 49th Division, the "Polar Bears", and are taking part in an exercise in Britain during 1944.**
ABOVE: **The angular design of the vehicle can be clearly seen along with its Guy heritage. The crew are leaving the vehicle by the turret hatches as these were easier to use than the hull doors.**

Humber Armoured Cars

The Humber was one of the most important British armoured cars of World War II, and the Rootes Group were to manufacture 5,400 of these, some 60 per cent of all British armoured cars used in that conflict. Rootes had taken over the design and development of the Guy Mk 1 and used the Karrier KT4 chassis, but Guy would continue to supply the turrets and hull as they had the special welding equipment. The new design was placed into production and renamed the Humber Mk 1, entering service with British forces in 1941.

The Humber had a short wheel base and even with this was not very manoeuvrable, which crews found frustrating at times. The Mk 1 was armed with one 15mm/0.59in and one 7.92mm/0.312in machine-gun and a total of 500

were built before it was replaced by the Mk 2. The improvements in the Mk 2 were confined to a better glacis plate at the front of the vehicle and improved radiator armour at the rear. The Mk 3 entered production in early 1942 and had a new type of turret that increased the crew to four men. A number of Mk 3 cars were converted into mobile artillery observation vehicles. The Mk 4 reverted to a crew of three and now mounted the American 37mm/1.46in gun in the turret as the main armament, becoming the first British armoured car to be fitted with this weapon. The driver was given a rear flap that he could open by a lever so that he could see when reversing or in an emergency.

The Canadians built 200 of these vehicles, calling them the Armoured Car

Mk 1 Fox 1, but the crews could not tell the difference except in armament. Another British version was the AA (anti-aircraft) Mk 1 armoured car, which came into service in 1943 but was decommissioned in 1944. The turret carried four 7.92mm/0.312in machine-guns.

The Humber began its service life in North Africa and then moved on up into Italy. The Mk 4 was to see extensive service in northern Europe. Some cars would remain in service with other countries until the early 1960s.

LEFT: **This Humber is leading a Dingo and a Jeep along a lane in northern France in 1944. The car is covered in additional personal storage and is armed with a 37mm/1.46in gun. The driver has fairly good forward vision when his front plate is raised.**

Humber Mk 2–4 Armoured Car		
Country: UK		
Entered service: 1941		
Crew: 3 (Mk 3 – Crew 4)		
Weight: 7,213kg/7.1 tons		
Dimensions: Length – 4.57m/15ft		
Height – 2.34m/7ft 10in		
Width – 2.18m/7ft 2in		
Armament: Main – 1 x Besa 15mm/0.59in, and 1 x coaxial Besa 7.92mm/0.312in machine-guns		
Secondary – Bren 7.7mm/0.303in light machine-gun		
Armour: Maximum – 15mm/0.59in		
Powerplant: Rootes 6-cylinder 67kW/95hp petrol engine		
Performance: Speed – 72kph/45mph		
Range – 402km/250 miles		

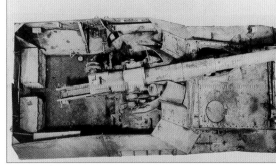

LEFT: **The eight wheels of the Panzer IV running gear can be clearly seen on this vehicle. It has the late production driver's position and radio operator's box structure, with improved forward vision.**

ABOVE: **The spacious fighting compartment can be seen here. The main gun is mounted on the top of the engine compartment. In action the crew have no protection from the weather.**

Hummel 15cm Heavy Self-Propelled Gun

Reports coming back from the Panzer Divisions showed a need for a heavy SPG on a fully tracked vehicle. It was originally intended to mount the 10.5cm/4.13in medium gun but experiments showed that the heavy sFH18 15cm/5.91in guns could be mounted on a tracked chassis. Development stated in July 1942 with Alkett doing the work, and by combining parts from the Panzer III and the Panzer IV a successful vehicle was developed. Nevertheless, as the Hummel had only limited traverse, this was an interim solution to the problem until an SPG with an all-round firing-arc such as the Waffenträger could be developed.

The prototype was shown to Hitler in October 1942 and was cleared for

production, with the first 100 being ready by May 1943 and 666 built by late 1944. The vehicle was given the name of Hummel (Bumble Bee) and would remain in production for the rest of the war. The gun barrel on the early vehicle was fitted with a muzzle brake at first but this was soon discarded as unnecessary. Another early feature was the long finger of the driver's position protruding forward. To ease production this was changed to an enclosed cab going from side to side of the vehicle. The engine was moved from the rear of the chassis to just behind the driver. The box-shaped armoured fighting compartment was roomy but gave very little protection to the gun crew, being only 10mm/0.394in thick with no protection from the weather, so

a number of crews fitted canvas covers to improve their conditions. As it could only carry 18 rounds of ammunition, 157 Hummel vehicles were converted into ammunition carriers. With their gun apertures plated over, they could carry 40 rounds. The vehicle was popular with both its crews and the unit commanders as it gave them a mobile heavy punch against enemy targets.

The Hummel was first issued to units on the Eastern Front in early 1943 for the big push at Kursk which resulted in the largest tank battle in history and from then on would see action on every German front until the end of World War II.

RIGHT: **Due to the size of the vehicle, crews tried to camouflage them with netting which was tied to the sides of the fighting compartment. The rear doors are covered in personal kit that has been moved from under the gun.**

Hummel 15cm Heavy SPG

Country: Germany
Entered service: 1943
Crew: 6
Weight: 24,384kg/24 tons
Dimensions: Length – 7.17m/23ft 6in
  Height – 2.81m/9ft 3in
  Width – 2.87m/9ft 5in
Armament: Main – 15cm/5.91in sFH18/1 L/30
  Secondary – 1 x 7.92mm/0.312in machine-gun
Armour: Maximum – 30mm/1.18in
Powerplant: Maybach V-12 198kW/265hp
  petrol engine
Performance: Speed – 42kph/26mph
  Range – 215km/134 miles

Indian Pattern Armoured Cars

Shortly after the outbreak of World War I, arrangements were made in India to form an armoured car unit for internal security duties and for work on the North West Frontier. A number of these cars were built on any available chassis at the East Indian Railway Workshops at Lillooah. More vehicles were required as the Indian armoured car units expanded and chassis used included Minerva, Quad and even Fiat trucks. These were very basic armoured cars, even by the standards of the early RNAS vehicles.

Improved vehicles were sought in the 1920s. The first chassis used were the Rolls-Royce Silver Ghost but these were very expensive and Vickers looked for a cheaper alternative after only 18 vehicles. Crossley Motors of Manchester were able to provide a good strong chassis at half the price of Rolls-Royce and production of a 4x2 armoured car, using a Crossley truck chassis, started in 1923. The armoured car had the engine located in the front and the fighting compartment in the middle of the vehicle, topped by a domed turret which had four machine-gun mountings but only carried two guns. On the top of the turret was a small observation dome, and on some vehicles a searchlight was fitted to the top of this. The inside of the vehicle was covered in a thick layer of asbestos which helped insulate the crew from the heat of India. The insulation also served to protect the crew from an electrical charge, as the crew could electrify the hull exterior when any enemy climbed on to the car. The footbrake acted directly on the propeller shaft of the vehicle and consequently made the car somewhat skittish on slippery roads. The vehicle was fitted with solid tyres and firm suspension, so the ride for the crew was very hard.

The chassis of these cars were worn out by 1939, but the bodies were still in good condition, so the Chevrolet truck chassis was used to refurbish the vehicle. These cars would remain in service until Indian independence in 1947. The new vehicle was also sent to Palestine and Syria in 1940.

TOP: **A pair of Vickers armoured cars built on the Crossley chassis outside the Erith plant in Kent. On the top of the turret is a fixed searchlight.**

ABOVE: **A group of three Crossley armoured cars, one of which has been unable to stop. These vehicles are fitted with solid tyres, so that they operate in the rough terrain of India.**

Indian Pattern Crossley Armoured Car

Country: India
Entered service: 1923
Crew: 4
Weight: 5,080kg/5 tons
Dimensions: Length – 5.03m/16ft 6in
　　　　　　　Height – 2.16m/7ft 1in
　　　　　　　Width – 1.83m/6ft
Armament: Main – 2 x 7.7mm/0.303in
　　　　　　machine-guns
　　　　　　Secondary – Small arms
Armour: Maximum – 8mm/0.315in
Powerplant: Crossley 6-cylinder 37kW/50hp petrol engine
Performance: Speed – 65kph/40mph
　　　　　　　Range – 200km/125 miles

ABOVE: **An Indian Pattern Crossley car in Africa crossing a river by pontoon ferry. This armoured car has been fitted with aerials for a command radio set.**

LEFT: **The IS II tank chassis can be clearly seen on this vehicle. The drums fitted to the rear are extended-range fuel tanks. The thickness of the gun mantlet is 160mm/ 6.3in. On the roof of the fighting compartment is the DShK 12.7mm/0.5in machine-gun mount. A number of these vehicles were captured and pressed into German service.**

ISU-152mm Heavy Assault Gun

The first chassis used for this vehicle was the KV-1S, at which point it was called the SU-152. It was developed and placed into production in just one month. The first vehicles were rushed to the Kursk salient as the Russians knew the Germans were going to attack at this point. The SU-152 used the 152mm/ 5.98in M-1937/43 howitzer mounted in a heavily armoured box on the front of the vehicle. At this stage of the war the Red Army made no difference between anti-tank and other SPGs, so the howitzer was used in the anti-tank role and relied on the weight of the shell to knock out the German tanks.

The new tank project called the IS (Josef Vissarionovich Stalin) was initiated and the gun tank developed from this was placed into production in December 1943,

followed very quickly by the ISU-152. The same chassis was also fitted with the 122mm/4.8in M-1931/44 gun and this became the ISU-122. No muzzle brake was fitted on the end of the barrel, which also had a screw breech. The vehicle could carry 30 rounds of main armament ammunition. A later model, the ISU-122A, was developed using the 122mm/4.8in 1943 model cannon (D-25-S) which was a tank destroyer of exceptional size and power. This had a large double-baffle muzzle brake and had a higher muzzle velocity than the 152mm/5.98in gun.

The ISU-152 had one weakness and this was that the vehicle could only carry 20 rounds of ammunition, but no armoured ammunition carrier was available. Extra ammunition was brought

up to the ISU-152 by basic open truck, but the risk involved in this was considered acceptable as the ISU was such an important vehicle to the Soviet infantry and armoured forces.

Each tank brigade would have 65 ISU-152s attached to it, which would take part in every major battle from Kursk to the fall of Berlin. These heavy assault guns would be in the vanguard of the Soviet Army entering Berlin in 1945 and would remain in service until early 1970 with the Soviet forces.

ISU-152mm Heavy Assault Gun

Country: USSR
Entered service: 1944
Crew: 5
Weight: 46,228kg/45.5 tons
Dimensions: Length – 9.05m/29ft 8in
Height – 2.48m/8ft 2in
Width – 3.07m/10ft 1in
Armament: Main – 152mm/5.98in M-1937/43 howitzer
Secondary – 12.7mm/0.5in DShK 1938/43 AA machine-gun
Armour: Maximum – 90mm/3.54in
Powerplant: 12-cylinder W-2-IS 388kW/520hp diesel engine
Performance: Speed – 37kph/23mph
Range – 180km/112 miles

LEFT: **This is one of the early SU-152 SPGs which has been knocked out by the Germans during the fighting at Kursk. The chassis is the KV heavy tank chassis.**

LEFT: **Developed in 1944 for operations behind the German lines in France by the Special Air Service (SAS), the driver and gunner have bullet-proof screens in front of them and extra large fuel tanks in the rear of the Jeep.** BELOW: **This is one of the last batch of Jeeps to be converted for the LRDG. It has been fitted with a twin and a single Vickers K guns plus a single 12.7mm/50cal heavy machine-gun. The vehicle is covered in extra fuel and water cans.**

Jeep Multi-Role Vehicle

The Jeep is the best known vehicle of World War II. Easily adapted into a light AFV, its reputation has gone from strength to strength and is as great today as it was in 1940. In the late 1930s, the US Army held a series of trials to find a new command and reconnaissance vehicle. The trials that were held in 1940 were won by the Bantam Car Company, their competitors being Willys Overland and the Ford Motor Company. All the companies were given small construction orders in 1940, but in July 1941 the contract for 16,000 vehicles was placed with Willys. It soon became very clear that Willys could not keep up with demand so the US Army insisted that they pass over the drawings and other details to Ford so they could also produce this vehicle. Between them, these two companies built 639,245 Jeeps between 1941 and 1945, but as the vehicle was developed in the post-World War II years, other companies would produce this remarkable little vehicle. By 1962, when American production finished, 800,000 of these ugly little vehicles had been built.

The Willys MB was the standard Jeep of World War II, and the first unit to turn the Jeep into an AFV was the British Long Range Desert Group (LRDG). These men began by liberating several Vickers K machine-guns from the RAF stores in Cairo and mounting them on their Jeeps and other vehicles. Most Jeeps were fitted with twin Vickers machine-guns in the front and twin Vickers machine-guns on a pedestal mount in the rear, while every third Jeep would have a 12.7mm/50cal heavy machine-gun fitted. The fuel tank was also doubled in size to 136 litres/30 gallons, and a condenser was fitted in the front of the radiator. The Jeep was often used by officers as a light reconnaissance vehicle in the desert campaign as it had a good turn of speed and was very small. The Jeep was still further modified by the men in the field and great assortments of weapons of various calibres were mounted on the vehicle during the war in the desert.

LEFT: **British paratroopers leaving the Horsa glider landing zone on D-Day, June 6, 1944. The Jeep is pulling a light trailer full of ammunition, and eight men have managed to get on the vehicle. The Jeep has no armament fitted to it.**

LEFT: **Lt Colonel David Stirling and some of the men from the LRDG. He found the Jeep ideal for long-range missions behind enemy lines. The vehicles are heavily overloaded with extra fuel, water and ammunition.** ABOVE: **This American Jeep is fitted with twelve 120mm/4.72in rockets. These vehicles had a crew of two. The man inside the vehicle is operating the elevation gear. The crew area has been protected by an armoured cover.**

Airborne forces were also looking at the Jeep as a light AFV that could be fitted into gliders and yet on landing could supply a fast moving, heavily armed vehicle to hit the enemy hard and to act as a reconnaissance unit, as the special Jeep squadrons did at Arnhem. The US 82nd Airborne trapped at Bastogne added armour plate to their Jeeps and mounted either one or two 12.7mm/50cal machine-guns on them. These vehicles had a crew of six men and acted as a mobile "fire brigade" that would move around the defensive perimeter from one hot spot to another. Other conversions produced in Europe were the mounting of twelve 114.3mm/4.5in rocket tubes on the back of the Jeep by the 7th US Army. The cab was covered with armour to protect the vehicle.

The US Marine Corps would also adapt the Jeep into a light AFV by placing 28 M8A2 rockets on the rear thus turning it into a rocket artillery support vehicle. However, the crew could not remain with the Jeep when firing as it was too dangerous. Others would have multiple machine-guns fitted as these

vehicles could get into the jungle better than heavier tanks and LVTs. In 1944 the Americans undertook a trial with the T19 105mm/4.13in recoilless rifle, turning the Jeep into an anti-tank weapons platform. This was a pointer to the future.

After World War II the Jeep was developed and became the Willys MC, and by 1950 the M38 was entering service and would be used alongside the Willys MB in Korea. In 1960 Ford started to produce the last version – the M151. This and the M38 would see extensive service in Vietnam and with the Israeli Defence Forces during the Arab-Israeli wars of the 1960s and 1970s. The M151, better known as the "Mutt", was withdrawn from service with the US forces due to its nasty habit of turning over. Now armed with TOW anti-tank guided missiles, the Jeep is very much a modern tank killer, but still carries a number of machine-guns for close support. The Jeep has proved over time to be a real multi-role vehicle but is now being replaced in service by the Humvee; however, it has attained cult status with private military vehicle collectors.

LEFT: **An American captain using the direct sighting device for the 120mm/4.72in rockets. This is the prototype vehicle and has only been fitted with six rockets. These vehicles carried no reload missiles, which were carried in a supply truck. These vehicles proved very popular as they could deliver a big punch close to the front line.**

Jeep MR LRDG Vehicle

Country: USA
Entered service: 1941
Crew: 3
Weight: 2,540kg/2.5 tons
Dimensions: Length – 3.33m/11ft
　Height – 1.14m/3ft 9in
　Width – 1.57m/5ft 2in
Armament: Main – 2 x twin Vickers K
　7.7mm/0.303in machine-guns
　Secondary – Bren 7.7mm/0.303in light
　machine-gun
Armour: None
Powerplant: Willys 441 or 442 Go Devil 4-cylinder
　45kW/60hp petrol engine
Performance: Speed – 104kph/65mph
　Range – 900km/559 miles

LEFT: **Side view of the Ram Kangaroo, clearly showing the forward storage boxes built into the hull of the vehicle. The running-gear on this vehicle is very similar to that on the Grant Mk 3 tank.**

ABOVE: **A Canadian Ram Kangaroo of the 79th Armoured Division. The driver's forward hatch is in the open position, and next to it is the close-defence machine-gun turret. There are storage boxes built into the front mudguards.**

Kangaroo Armoured Infantry Carrier

Just after D-Day, the Canadian II Corps deployed Priest SPGs with their guns removed as infantry carriers in Normandy. Each of these vehicles could carry 12 men, but there were problems with their height so the Canadians looked for a better alternative. They had been using the Ram tank as a training vehicle in Britain before being equipped with the Sherman, so some 500 tanks were sitting idle. The Canadians moved these to their base workshop in France, which was codenamed "Kangaroo", where they were converted into armoured infantry carriers. The turret, ammunition bins and any other unnecessary bits were removed and two bench seats fitted in the open turret space.

The Ram was built in Canada using many of the parts from the American M3 tank. The Ram Mk II versions had

an auxiliary machine-gun turret in the front of the vehicle that would be retained in the Kangaroo for close support and self-defence. Some later versions did not have this turret but a standard Sherman hull machine-gun. These vehicles were standard British right-hand drive with either the auxiliary turret or bow machine-gun on the left. Debussing was a problem because the troops were exposed as they jumped down from the top of the vehicle. However, the worst problem was getting the men into the vehicle, so very quickly climbing rungs were welded to the sides as a field modification. The infantry could not use their weapons from the vehicle and there was no overhead protection for the troops once inside. In addition to its infantry carrier role, the Kangaroo was also used for bringing forward

ammunition, fuel and other supplies to troops under fire.

The Ram Kangaroo entered service piecemeal with the Canadians in September 1944 but in December 1944, these minor units were combined to become the 1st Canadian Armoured Carrier Regiment, joining up with the British 49th Armoured Personnel Carrier Regiment, which came under the command of the 79th Armoured Division. The first operation for the Ram Kangaroo was the assault on Le Havre – the last one was taking the 7th Infantry Division into Hamburg on May 3, 1945.

Ram Kangaroo Armoured Personnel Carrier	

Country: Canada
Entered service: 1944
Crew: 2 plus 10 infantry
Weight: 25,400kg/25 tons
Dimensions: Length – 5.79m/19ft
    Height –1.91m/6ft 3in
    Width – 2.77m/9ft 1in
Armament: Main – None
    Secondary – 7.7mm/0.303in Browning machine-gun
Armour: Maximum – 60mm/2.36in
Powerplant: Continental R-975 298kW/400hp petrol engine
Performance: Speed – 40kph/25mph
    Range – 232km/144 miles

LEFT: **A Ram Kangaroo loaded with troops, moving through the Low Countries, 1944. The rear of the vehicle is covered with personal kit. The lack of any climbing ladders on the curved cast hull shows why the Kangaroo was difficult to climb into in full kit.**

LEFT: **A battery of Katyusha rocket vehicles being positioned for firing. The very simple M13 rockets were slid into position so that one rocket rides on the top of the rail while the other suspended on the same rail runs along the underneath.** ABOVE: **The 6x6 Studebaker chassis can clearly be seen along with the very basic rocket rail system. The armoured shield for the cab folds back on to the roof of the cab.**

Katyusha BM-13 132mm Rocket Launcher

The BM-13 rocket launcher was the first self-propelled artillery weapon produced in quantity by the Soviet Union. This system was given a number of cover names, one being Kostikov Guns, but was officially designated the Guards' Mortars. The popular nickname for the vehicle was "Katyusha", a diminutive form of Katerina, which was the title of a popular piece of music at the time.

Development started on the M-132 in 1938 and at first was not very successful, mainly because the rockets were fired over the side of the vehicle. The first chassis used was the ZiS-5 truck, and with the rocket rails now mounted longitudinally, it proved to be very successful and was placed on test in August 1939. Production started in 1940 with the Soviet Army designating the vehicle BM-13-16.

Several different truck chassis were used as rocket launchers for the Katyusha system, most of them lend-lease vehicles from Canada and the United States. The most common mount was the 2,540kg/2.5-ton 6x6 Studebaker truck of which over 100,000 had been sent to the Soviet Union. This vehicle was selected for its superior cross-country performance and reliability, with nearly 10,000 being converted into Katyusha. The Soviets used the chassis, engine and cab of the Studebaker, leaving the rear for the rocket rail system. The cab was covered in anti-blast armour that covered the windscreen to protect it from the rocket motor blast. The Studebaker and its Hercules JXD engine would be copied and built after World War II by the Soviet Union.

These vehicles were at first issued to special units under the control of the NKVD (Soviet Secret Police) with the first combat action taking place at Orsha in July 1941. It had a devastating effect on the average German soldier and was given the German nickname of "Stalin's Organ". The Soviets would mount several other types of rocket on the basic vehicle, the largest of these, the M-30 300mm/11.8in, entering service in 1944. The battle for Berlin in 1945 would see over 400 Katyusha batteries bombarding the Germans. This system finally left Soviet service in 1980.

Katyusha BM-13 132mm Rocket Launcher

Country: USSR
Entered service: 1941
Crew: 4
Weight: 6,096kg/6 tons
Dimensions: Length – 7.47m/24ft 6in
Height – 3.05m/10ft with rocket rails in the down position
Width – 2.21m/7ft 3in
Armament: Main – 16 x 132mm/5.2in rockets
Secondary – None
Armour: Maximum – 5mm/0.2in
Powerplant: Studebaker Hercules JXD 6-cylinder 65kW/87hp petrol engine
Performance: Speed – 72kph/45mph
Range – 370km/230 miles

LEFT: **The rear of the BM-13 showing the rear supporting jacks that were lowered when firing. The launching platform had very little traverse so the whole vehicle was aimed at the target.**

Kfz 13/14 Medium Armoured Car

This was a medium 4x2 car based on the chassis of the Adler Standard 6 passenger car. In 1932 the German Army issued a requirement for this kind of vehicle, and after extensive trials it was placed into production in late 1933, entering service in 1934. Being inexpensive and simple to produce, it very quickly appeared in relatively large numbers, being issued to cavalry units as a reconnaissance vehicle.

The engine was mounted in the front with a 4-speed gear box which drove a conventional rear axle. The hull was box-shaped with an open top and all-welded construction. The Kfz 13 had the driver in the front, with the vehicle gunner and commander sitting in the rear. The machine-gun was pedestal mounted and had a limited traverse with the main field of fire to the front. There was no radio set in the vehicle, and consequently all communication was done by means of flags. The Kfz 14 was an unarmed radio car with a crew of three, with a large frame aerial mounted above the crew compartment that when not in use could be folded down flush with the top of the crew compartment. These vehicles were known popularly by their crews as "*badewannen*" (bath-tubs). Being two-wheel drive the vehicle had a poor cross-country ability, which was not helped by also having a high centre of gravity. The 8mm/0.315in armour plate also gave very little protection to the crew.

These vehicles were built as training and reconnaissance cars for the new German Army. Normally a section of Kfz 13 reconnaissance cars would operate alongside one Kfz 14 radio car. Both vehicles were due to be replaced by the Sd Kfz 221 by 1939, but war came too soon and a large number of both the Kfz 13 and the Kfz 14 were still in front-line service. They would see action in Poland, the invasion of the Low Countries and France during 1939–40. Some were still acting as reconnaissance vehicles for non-motorized infantry units during the invasion of Russia in 1941.

TOP: **A mixed column of Kfz 13 and 14 armoured cars moving along a road. The very high radio aerial frame can be clearly seen on the second car.**

ABOVE: **The very clean and simple design of the car is apparent, but the wheels of this vehicle were very easily damaged.**

LEFT: **The driver of this vehicle has his seat in the raised position so that he has good all-round vision. The gunner is in his normal position which is a little exposed.**

Kfz 13/14 Medium Armoured Car

Country: Germany
Entered service: 1934
Crew: 2 (Kfz 13) and 3 (Kfz 14)
Weight: 2,235.2kg/2.2 tons
Dimensions: Length – 4.17m/13ft 8in
　　　　　　　Height – 1.45m/4ft 9in
　　　　　　　Width – 1.68m/5ft 6in
Armament: Main – 7.92mm/0.312in MG13 machine-gun (Kfz 13)
　　　　　　　Secondary – Small arms
Armour: Maximum – 8mm/0.315in
Powerplant: Adler 6-cylinder 45kW/60hp petrol engine
Performance: Speed – 70kph/44mph
　　　　　　　Range – 300km/186 miles

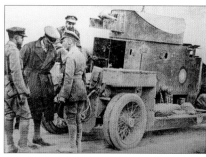

LEFT: **A Lanchester of the RNAS with all the hatches in the open position. Additional water storage for the radiator has been fitted to the side of the engine. The wire wheels were standard fit for this car.** ABOVE: **The rear of a Lanchester armoured car with the rear doors open; this was the main entrance and exit for all the crew. This vehicle is operating in Russia and has been fitted with additional armour to protect the gun barrel.**

Lanchester Armoured Car

After the Rolls-Royce, the Lanchester was the most numerous type of armoured car produced by the British in World War I. Designed by the Admiralty Air Department for the RNAS Armoured Car Section operating in France, the prototype was produced in December 1914, using the Lanchester Sporting Forty touring car chassis, with production following in early 1915.

A number of changes were made to the basic chassis, the main ones being that the suspension and chassis were strengthened to take the extra weight of the armour plate, and dual wheels were fitted to the rear axle to improve the vehicle handling. The Lanchester had sloping armour over the front and bonnet of the car and the engine was mounted beside the driver. While the engine was powerful and very reliable, and also used an advanced epicyclic gearbox, the Lanchester could never get over the problem of the weak chassis that would be its Achilles' heel.

In 1915 the RNAS armoured cars were handed over to the army, which looked at the great variety of cars it had acquired and decided to standardize on the Rolls-Royce. This standardization would make resupply of spare parts much easier. The Lanchesters were all sent back to Britain for overhaul before being despatched to Russia with No.1 Squadron RNAS Armoured Car Division. The squadron arrived in Russia in 1916 and would remain there for a year fighting in Persia, Romania and Galicia, and operating in climates ranging from desert to near-Arctic conditions. During their time in Russia these cars covered 85,295km/53,000 miles. The cars were deployed in a manner that would become the standard for AFV warfare in the 20th century. Acting as scouts and armed raiders, they operated well forward of the infantry following in their armoured trucks. When operating alongside the infantry, they would act as fire-support vehicles. Their final operation was as part of the unsuccessful Russian Brusilov Offensive of mid-1917. After this Russia descended into civil war and the RNAS Armoured Car Division was withdrawn back to Britain.

LEFT: **A Lanchester 6x6 Mk 1 armoured car. This was a vast improvement over the early 4x2 Lanchester. The new vehicle was armed with three machine-guns, two in the turret and one in the hull next to the driver.**

Lanchester Armoured Car	

Country: UK
Entered service: 1915
Crew: 4
Weight: 4,876.8kg/4.8 tons
Dimensions: Length – 4.88m/16ft
    Height – 2.29m/7ft 6in
    Width – 1.93m/6ft 4in
Armament: Main – Vickers 7.7mm/0.303in
    machine-gun
    Secondary – 7.7mm/0.303in Lewis gun,
    and small arms
Armour: Maximum – 8mm/0.315in
Powerplant: Lanchester 6-cylinder 45kW/60hp
    petrol engine
Performance: Speed – 80kph/50mph
    Range – 290km/180 miles

LEFT: **A Loyd Carrier towing a 6pdr AT gun and carrying the whole crew waits to pass a German Panther tank. The vehicle is overloaded with ammunition and personal equipment.** ABOVE: **The drive-shaft of the vehicle is in a very exposed frontal position, but this made it easy to maintain. The front of the carrier is very clean and well sloped. This vehicle has the canvas weather protecting roof in the raised position.**

Loyd Carrier

The Loyd Carrier was developed by Captain Vivian Loyd in 1939 as a simple cross-country tracked vehicle, using many existing components from various vehicle manufacturers. The basic vehicle was based on the 762kg/15cwt 4x2 Fordson truck, with tracks and suspension from Vickers light tanks.

The carrier used a basic Ford engine, radiator, gearbox and transmission, with the engine and radiator being mounted in the rear of the vehicle. The power from the engine was brought forward to the front sprockets, with brakes fitted to the front and rear sprockets. Steering was by means of steering levers that applied the front and rear brakes on one side of the vehicle or the other depending

on the direction of turn, but care had to be taken as a track could be easily broken or shed. The vehicle was a simple open box with access either side of the engine in the rear, or over the side to get into the driver's position. An order was placed with Captain Loyd's firm in late 1939 for 200 carriers.

Originally intended as an infantry carrier with a capacity of between eight and ten men, the Loyd was very quickly adapted into various specialist roles. This included mechanical cable laying for the Royal Signals units or as a starting vehicle for tank units, as the Loyd was fitted out as a battery slave unit that was capable of starting tanks or charging batteries. There were also several trials

using the carrier as an SPG mount for the 2pdr anti-tank gun and the 25pdr gun howitzer. However, the Loyd was mainly produced and used as a towing vehicle with infantry battalions for the 6pdr (57mm) anti-tank gun and the 107mm/ 4.2in mortar. These carriers were simple to maintain in the field and well-liked by their crews. They were built by the Vivian Loyd Company until 1941 but as demand increased during World War II, production was undertaken by five different companies in several different countries with Ford as the main manufacturer. Some 26,000 vehicles of this type were constructed during the war. A very adaptable vehicle, it was found in all British theatres of war.

RIGHT: **The rear of a Loyd Carrier. The engine can be clearly seen in the middle of the vehicle and takes up most of the space. The carrier has a 6pdr gun attached to the hitch. The lack of storage space can also be seen, as four men were carried in this area.**

Loyd Carrier

Country: UK
Entered service: 1940
Crew: Various
Weight: 4,064kg/4 tons
Dimensions: Length – 4.14m/13ft 7in
Height – 1.42m/4ft 8in
Width – 2.06m/6ft 9in
Armament: Main – None
Secondary – Small arms
Armour: None
Powerplant: Ford 8-cylinder 63kW/85hp
petrol engine
Performance: Speed – 48kph/30mph
Range – 193km/120 miles

Lorraine Schlepper 15cm Self-Propelled Gun

After the fall of France, the Germans captured a large number of AFVs from the French Army and at first placed them in storage. Among these were the Lorraine tractor units. The French had originally built 387 of these. The driver sat in the front, with the engine just behind and a large cargo area in the rear. Converting these vehicles into an SPG carriage was not difficult: the rear cargo area and suspension were strengthened to take the gun mount. The exact number of captured chassis is not known but over 300 were repaired and converted into self-propelled mounts as either an anti-tank weapon or gun howitzer.

In May 1942 the vehicle, armed with the 15cm/5.9in FH13, was demonstrated to Hitler who passed it for further conversion. Initially 60 chassis with 10.5cm/4.13in le FH18, 40 chassis with 15cm/5.9in FH13 and 60 armed with the PaK40 7.5cm/2.95in were converted. Each vehicle was fitted with an open-topped fighting compartment with the main weapon filling most of this area. Most crews fitted a canvas cover over the top that could be quickly removed when necessary. The superstructures were made by Alkett and shipped to Paris where they were fixed to the chassis and issued to German units in France. It was standard practice for captured vehicles to remain in German service in the country where they were captured. The

15cm/5.9in vehicle had a recoil spade fitted to the rear to help stabilize the vehicle during firing. The armour of the fighting area was very poor and was only just shell-splinter proof.

In July 1942, the first of these conversions arrived in North Africa. Ten were issued to the 21st Panzer Division and eleven to the 15th Panzer Division, and these would take part in the German attack on El Alamein. By November 1942, all the initial batch of vehicles had been destroyed or captured by the British. Large numbers of these vehicles were still available by D-Day, June 6, 1944, when 131 of the PaK40 conversion, 54 of the 15cm/5.9in FH13 and 37 of the FH18 with the 10.5cm/4.13in gun were serviceable.

TOP: A British Crusader tank towing a captured Lorraine Schlepper in the desert of North Africa. The small size of this SPG can be seen against the bulk of the tank. ABOVE: The rear of the Lorraine Schlepper showing the recoil spade in the raised position. When lowered into the ground, this helped to absorb some of the recoil from the gun.

LEFT: The diminutive size of the vehicle is clear in this picture. This allowed the vehicle to be easily hidden. The driver's position is below the gun barrel, with the engine immediately behind the driver.

Lorraine Schlepper 15cm FH13 SPG

Country: Germany
Entered service: 1942
Crew: 5
Weight: 8,636kg/8.5 tons
Dimensions: Length – 5.31m/17ft 5in
Height – 2.23m/7ft 4in
Width – 1.83m/6ft
Armament: Main – 15cm/5.91in sFH13/1
Secondary – 7.92mm/0.312in MG34 machine-gun
Armour: Maximum – 10mm/0.394in
Powerplant: Delahaye 6-cylinder 52kW/70hp petrol engine
Performance: Speed – 35kph/22mph
Range – 135km/84 miles

LEFT: **An M3 with the bad-weather roof-cover in place. This vehicle is fitted with a "pulpit" machine-gun mount over the vehicle commander's position. The armoured shutter for the windscreen is in the "up" position and has been used as a storage shelf for personal kit. The large whip aerial has been pulled over and attached to the front of the vehicle.**

M3 Half-Track Infantry Carrier

The Americans bought two French Citroen-Kegresse half-tracks during 1925 and purchased a further one in 1931. After a number of developments, they married the White Scout Car with the Kegresse suspension and came up with what would become the classic American half-track of World War II. The Car Half-Track M2 and the M3 Carrier Personnel Half-Track were two of the first half-track vehicles produced by the Americans in that conflict. The M2 was designed as a reconnaissance vehicle and as a prime mover for guns of up to 155mm/6.1in, while the M3 was designed as a personnel carrier for armoured divisions and motorized artillery. The distinction between the two vehicles very quickly disappeared once committed to action. These models were approved for production in October 1940 and entered service in 1941 with the American Army.

Under the competitive bidding system of the US Ordnance Department, the lowest bidder is awarded the construction contract. The Autocar company won the bid and secured the construction contract, but was very quickly joined by Diamond T and White. Total production would be 12,499 M3 vehicles of all marks, while 11,415 M2 carriers of all marks were built. It was agreed by the three manufacturers that as many parts as possible would be interchangeable between the M2 and M3.

The M3 could carry 13 men: the driver, commander and co-driver in the front with 10 infantry behind. The back of the vehicle had five seats on each side looking into the middle, with a large door in the rear. The armour on the rear crew compartment was only 7mm/0.28in thick, while that on the cab doors, windscreen shutter and radiator grill was 12.7mm/0.5in.

ABOVE: **The gunner's "pulpit" can be clearly seen on this vehicle, which is carrying four machine-guns. The vehicle exterior is covered with personal kit as there is no room inside to store the equipment of the ten-man crew.**

Armament was very varied and a lot depended on the crew of the vehicle. Officially there were to be two machine-guns, a 12.7mm/50cal in the front and a 7.62mm/30cal in the rear on a pintle mount. On the outside of the vehicle down each side of the rear compartment were two racks for carrying 24 anti-personnel mines.

In 1943 the M3A1 was developed and went into production in October of that year. The main improvement was to the armament of the vehicle. A M49 ring mount was fitted over the co-driver's position to take a single 12.7mm/50cal machine-gun. In the rear, three pintle sockets were installed each mounting a 7.62mm/30cal machine-gun. Diamond T was the main contractor and 2,862 of these vehicles were built before the contract was cancelled in January 1944. The last M2 was built in March 1944, and the last M3 was produced in February 1944 as sufficient of this type were stockpiled.

The M3A2 which was due to replace the M2, M2A1, M3, and M3A1 was going to be a universal carrier with movable storage lockers inside the vehicle. Depending on the role, it could be able to carry between 5 and 12 personnel with a great variety of weapons. The vehicle was passed by the Armoured Board in October 1943, but was never placed into serious production.

Production of brand new vehicles might have ceased in early 1944, but vehicle modification was still going strong with 2,270 M3 carriers upgraded to M3A1 standard. Personnel kit storage was very poor in the vehicle as it was never designed to act as a home-from-home for the section of men who lived and fought from their vehicle. The crews would personalize their vehicles by welding extra storage racks on the outside, in particular on either side of the door at the rear. The racks for mines on the side of the vehicle were converted to carry boxes of food and other important personal items.

One extremely important characteristic of these half-tracks was that the crew could fight from the inside of the vehicle in some safety. As more tracked gun tractors became available the half-track was passed over to the infantry. These vehicles could be found in every Allied army during World War II and on every front. In 1980 the M2/M3 could still be found in service with 22 different armed forces and some of these vehicles can still be found in service with the Israeli Defence Force reserve units.

TOP: The driver's cab in the M3 is relatively spacious and has a very simple layout. The driver and vehicle commander have very good vision from the cab of the vehicle, but it is roofless. ABOVE: Access to the engine of the M3 was very good and it was simple to work on or maintain. The armoured louvers of the radiator grill can be open or closed from the driver's position. LEFT AND BELOW LEFT: The front of these vehicles is fitted with a winch. The rack on the side of the crew compartment was originally intended for the storage of landmines. These vehicles are fitted with only a single machine-gun.

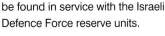

M3A1 Carrier Personnel Half-Track

Country: USA
Entered service: 1943
Crew: 3 plus 10 infantry
Weight: 10,160kg/10 tons
Dimensions: Length – 6.14m/20ft 3in
  Height – 2.69m/8ft 10in
  Width – 2.22m/7ft 3in
Armament: Main – 12.7mm/0.5in Browning machine-gun
  Secondary – 3 x 7.62mm/0.3in machine-guns
Armour: Maximum – 12.7mm/0.5in
Powerplant: White 160 AX 6-cylinder 95kW/128hp petrol engine
Performance: Speed – 64kph/45mph
  Range – 280km/200 miles

LEFT: **This vehicle is fitted with a roller on the front that helps the vehicle climb over obstructions. The crew of the M3A1 vehicle were very exposed in the rear of the car.**

M3A1 Scout Car

The forerunner of this car was designed in 1933 by White and was based on a 4x4 van chassis produced by their subsidiary Indiana. The prototype (T7) was an open-topped scout car, armed with two 12.7mm/50cal and two 7.62mm/30cal machine-guns, which carried a crew of four men. The vehicle was placed into production and was given the designation M1, with a total production of 76 cars.

The M2 followed in 1935. It was bigger and more powerful and could carry a crew of seven, but only 20 of these vehicles were produced. White went on to produce the M3 version of this scout car and had delivered 64 to the US Army by 1938. Marmon-Herrington also produced a number of these scout cars for Iran.

The M3A1 entered service in 1940 and would remain in production until 1944, by which time some 20,856 scout cars had been built. Fast and very reliable, it was well-liked by its crews, but its cross-country performance was poor and it was soon replaced by the half-track for many tasks. To help improve its off-road capability a roller was fitted to the front of the car. The open fighting compartment was a serious weakness – the men were very exposed and the rear was a grenade trap. However, it was fitted with the Tourelle skate rail that allowed the machine-guns to give all-round fire. General Patton used one as a command vehicle but had additional armour fitted and raised around the fighting compartment. The M3A1E1 was developed to increase the range and fuel economy of the vehicle. This model was fitted with the 58kW/78hp Buda-Lanova diesel engine and had a speed of

ABOVE: **This British M3A1 Scout car belongs to the 11th Armoured Division and was photographed in Normandy in 1944. The front of the vehicle has been fitted with a wire-cutter pole, and has had its roller removed.**

87kph/54mph. All of these vehicles, the total production of which was 3,340, were sent to Russia.

Most of the M3 scout cars in British service were used in a secondary role, being issued to units like the engineers, signals and medical corps. Some of these vehicles were to remain in service with a number of countries after World War II, particularly the French.

LEFT: **The driver's cab has a very simple layout. The dashboard has just two instrument dials and five switches, while the vehicle commander has a glove box. The wiper motors are mounted above the windscreen.**

M3A1 Scout Car

Country: USA
Entered service: 1940
Crew: 2 plus 6 infantry
Weight: 5,618kg/5.53 tons
Dimensions: Length – 5.62m/18ft 5in
Height – 2m/6ft 6in
Width – 2.03m/6ft 8in
Armament: Main – 12.7mm/0.5in Browning
machine-gun
Secondary – 2 x 7.62mm/0.3in Browning
machine-guns
Armour: Maximum – 12.7mm/0.5in
Powerplant: White Hercules JXD 6-cylinder
71kW/95hp petrol engine
Performance: Speed – 105kph/65mph
Range – 400km/250 miles

M3 75mm Gun Motor Carriage

The half-track served as the carrier for numerous self-propelled weapons, but relatively few of these would be standardized. The notable exception would be the anti-aircraft mounts that would remain in service for years after the end of World War II.

Development was started in June 1941 in response to a request from both the British and American armies for a mobile self-propelled anti-tank gun. The project was to mount the M1897 A4 75mm/2.95in gun in an M3 half-track. This gun was an American copy of the French 75mm/2.95in from World War I. The original gun mount was the M2A3, but there was a shortage of these and so the M2A2 was substituted on the M3A1 half-track conversion.

Autocar were given the first contract to convert these vehicles and built 86 in 1941. Fifty were sent to the Philippines to help bolster the forces there. Autocar produced a total of 2,202 of these conversions but due to a shortage of guns, 113 of these vehicles were converted back into personnel carriers.

A number of conversions were made to the basic carrier, these being the moving of the fuel tanks to the rear of

the fighting compartment and adding a new sub-floor to the rear of the fighting compartment, along with storage for 59 rounds of 75mm/2.95in ammunition. Initially the vehicle crew was four but this was quickly increased to five. The gun shield at first allowed the gun crew to stand full height behind the gun but this gave the vehicle a high silhouette so it was made smaller. First used in the defence of the Philippines against the Japanese, the vehicle proved to be a very good gun platform. The next major operation it was used in was "Torch", the invasion of North Africa by the Allies in 1943. In British service, these vehicles were known as "75mm SP Autocar" and were used by HQ troops of armoured car reconnaissance units. Even after being declared obsolete in September 1944, they would remain in service with many units until the end of the war.

ABOVE: **A US Marine Corps vehicle is landed on a beach from an LCT (Landing Craft Tank). The vehicle has been fitted with three extra machine-guns. The front of the half-track has also been fitted with a winch, which proved very useful in the jungle fighting.**

ABOVE: **A battery of American half-tracks armed with 75mm/2.95in guns belonging to Patton's forces in Sicily. Most of the personal kit has been placed at the rear of the vehicle and on the ground.**

LEFT: **A line-up of five gun half-tracks at their training ground in the USA in 1942. All the vehicles have been fitted with the unditching roller.**

M3 75mm Gun Motor Carriage

Country: USA
Entered service: 1941
Crew: 5
Weight: 10,160kg/10 tons
Dimensions: Length – 6.14m/20ft 3in
　　　　Height – 2.26m/7ft 5in
　　　　Width – 2.22m/7ft 3in
Armament: Main – 75mm/2.95in M1897 A4
　　　　Secondary – 7.62mm/0.3in machine-gun
Armour: Maximum – 12.7mm/0.5in
Powerplant: White 160 AX 6-cylinder
　　　　95kW/128hp petrol engine
Performance: Speed – 64kph/45mph
　　　　Range – 280km/200 miles

M5 Half-Track Personnel Carrier

Because demand was out-pacing production at the White Company factories building the M2 and M3, the M5 was built by the International Harvester Company (IHC). This new production facility started in April 1942 and produced 9,291 half-track carriers, most of them going to Lend-Lease. The M5 was similar in design to the M2 and M3 half-tracks, but their parts were not interchangeable as IHC used many of their own components in their vehicle. Obvious changes were the curved rear corners of the rear fighting compartment, the flat front mudguards and the use of homogeneous armour plate which increased the vehicle's weight.

The M5 entered service in December 1942 and remained in production until October 1943, when it was replaced by the M5A1. Like the M2A1 and the M3A1,

the improvement was in armament and the introduction of the M49 ring-mount. Between October and December 1943, 1,859 M5A1s were built, with a further extension to the contract of 1,100 vehicles with completion in March 1944. In April 1943 it was decided that IHC should produce a universal carrier to the same specification as the M2 and M3 carriers, but like these other universal carriers, the M5A2 was never put into production. The M5 itself would remain in production until June 1945.

The last version of this half-track was the M9A1 and this was the same as the M2A1. There was no basic version of the M9 as it was already fitted with the M49 ring-mount and the extra machine-gun mounts in the rear of the vehicle. Total production of the M9A1 was 3,433, with nearly all going into British service.

ABOVE LEFT AND ABOVE: **This M5 is covered in personal equipment, armed with three machine-guns and is fitted with a winch on the front of the vehicle. The shipping panel is still on this vehicle below the commander's door.**

Large numbers of M5 and M5A1 half-tracks were sent to the Soviet Union along with M17 anti-aircraft units. In British service, the M5 and the M9A1 were converted into several specialist roles such as radio and medical half-tracks. Other large users were the Royal Engineers (RE) and the Royal Electrical and Mechanical Engineers (REME). Large A-frames were fitted to the front so these vehicles could act as recovery vehicles in the field. They remained in British service until 1966.

LEFT: **Like the M3, the M5 was fitted with a storage rack for landmines but in combat it was never used for this purpose. The driver's side window is unglazed, having just a metal shutter with a very small vision slit cut in it.**

M5 Half-Track Personnel Carrier

Country: USA
Entered service: 1942
Crew: 3 plus 10 infantry
Weight: 10,668kg/10.5 tons
Dimensions: Length – 6.33m/20ft 9in
   Height – 2.31m/7ft 7in
   Width – 2.21m/7ft 3in
Armament: Main – 12.7mm/0.5in Browning
   machine-gun
   Secondary – 3 x 7.62mm/0.3in Browning
   machine-guns
Armour: Maximum – 10mm/0.394in
Powerplant: International Red 450B 6-cylinder
   107kW/143hp petrol engine
Performance: Speed – 61kph/38mph
   Range – 201km/125 miles

M8 Greyhound Light Armoured Car

Armoured cars have acted as the armed reconnaissance vehicle of the American Army for a long time. During 1940–41, the Americans were able to observe the war in Europe and study the new operational trends, and so develop a number of new vehicles. Four companies entered the competition for the new heavy armoured car, and in 1941 the Ford T22 was chosen for this role. It went into production in late 1942 with the first vehicles entering service in early 1943, but the 37mm/1.46in main gun was considered to be too small by 1942 for a "heavy" designation, so the new car was given the revised designation of Light Armoured Car. The M8 remained in production until 1945, by which time 8,523 vehicles had been built.

The M8 was a 6x6 lightweight vehicle of all-welded construction, with the driving compartment in the front, turret in the middle and engine at the rear. The turret had an open roof and was hand-operated by a crew of two, while the

other two crew members occupied the driver's position in the front of the vehicle. It had excellent cross-country ability, a low silhouette, and plenty of room for the crew. One weakness was its thin floor armour, so most crews covered the floor with sandbags to help protect themselves against the blast of a mine.

A variation on the M8 was the M20, which was basically the same vehicle except that the turret was removed. The fighting compartment was also cut away and fitted with a ring-mount for a 12.7mm/50cal machine-gun. The M20 was used as a reconnaissance and supply vehicle, and some 3,791 were built.

A few M8s were supplied to the British but it was not liked, as the armour was considered to be too thin. In 1973, the French demonstrated a new version of the M8 armed with the H90 90mm/3.54in turret. Some 22 countries still operated the M8 in 1976, and the Brazilian Army fitted their M8 cars with guided AT missiles.

ABOVE: **The clean lines of this vehicle are very apparent as is the two-man turret. It is one of the prototypes, and as such has no personal kit stored on the car.** LEFT: **The roof hatches above the driver's and co-driver's positions are open and folded to the side. The headlights have a protective frame over them and the turret has been fitted with a heavy machine-gun.**

M8 Greyhound Light Armoured Car

Country: USA
Entered service: 1943
Crew: 4
Weight: 8,128kg/8 tons
Dimensions: Length – 5m/16ft 5in
　　　　　　Height – 2.25m/7ft 5in
　　　　　　Width – 2.54m/8ft 4in
Armament: Main – 37mm/1.46in gun M6,
　　　　　and coaxial 7.62mm/0.3in machine-gun
　　　　　Secondary – 12.7mm/0.5in machine-gun
Armour: Maximum – 19mm/0.75in
Powerplant: Hercules JXD 6-cylinder 82kW/110hp petrol engine
Performance: Speed – 89kph/55mph
　　　　　　Range – 563km/350 miles

RIGHT: **The wheels and chassis of the M8 are well protected from damage by angled covers. The driver's and co-driver's hatches are fully closed and, as can be seen, the vision slits are small and making forward vision very limited. A tie-down rail is fitted around the middle of the turret.**

M8 75mm Howitzer Motor Carriage

The American Army made repeated requests for a close-support howitzer and these were met in early 1942 by the appearance of the T30 half-track howitzer. This was developed as an expedient project in 1941 and entered production very quickly, with some 500 contracted to be built. However, only 320 were actually produced. The vehicle used the M1A1 75mm/2.95in pack howitzer, mounting the weapon on a new tracked chassis that was just becoming available.

This new chassis was the M5 and the first test vehicle built was the T41 Howitzer Motor Carriage, in which the howitzer was mounted on the hull centreline.

The vehicle existed only as a mock-up and was abandoned in favour of a new design – the T47. This new vehicle, now named the M8, still used the M5 chassis, but this time the weapon, the M2 or M3 75mm/2.95in howitzer, was mounted in a rotating turret. The 75mm/2.95in turret was much larger than the M5 turret and so the hull had to be altered to fit it, with the driver's hatches moved forward on to the glacis plate. The M8 was fitted with two V8 Cadillac engines, and proved to be a reliable vehicle. A mock-up was produced in April 1942 and was approved, with production starting in September 1942. The total number of vehicles built was 1,778 with production finishing in January 1944.

As the M7, a 105mm/4.13in howitzer mounted on the Sherman chassis, began to appear in greater numbers, the M8 was replaced in armoured formations and passed to reconnaissance units to replace half-track mounted close-support weapons. The M8 was also passed on to the Free French forces and other Allied nations. In the Pacific, the M8 was used in the close-support role by the Marine Corps and was well-liked,

ABOVE LEFT: **The large glacis plate on this vehicle is very striking, and has the driver's and co-driver's hatches recessed into it. Above these hatches each man has his own periscope.** ABOVE: **Two M8 SPGs are leading two half-tracks and a 2,540kg/2.5-ton truck down a road in Britain. In combat these vehicles would be covered in personal kit and tow an ammunition trailer.**

as it could bring a large weapon close to enemy positions to help extract them from caves and other dug-in positions. The M8 was often fitted with an ammunition trailer in the European theatre of operations as it only carried 46 rounds in the vehicle itself.

LEFT: **An M8 caught up in a traffic jam with a column of Jeeps. The turret of this vehicle is fitted with a manual traverse only, as it is an artillery vehicle and not a tank.**

M8 75mm Howitzer Motor Carriage

Country: USA
Entered service: 1942
Crew: 4
Weight: 15,605kg/15.45 tons
Dimensions: Length – 4.41m/14ft 6in
  Height – 2.32m/7ft 7in
  Width – 2.24m/7ft 4in
Armament: Main – 75mm/2.95in M2 howitzer
  Secondary –12.7mm/0.5in Browning machine-gun
Armour: Maximum – 44mm/1.73in
Powerplant: 2 x Cadillac V8 series 42 82kW/110hp petrol engine
Performance: Speed – 56kph/35mph
  Range – 210km/130 miles

M12 155mm Gun Motor Carriage

The M12 was one of the earliest self-propelled mounts to be designed, but was one of the last weapons to enter active service in World War II. Development started in June 1941 with a test model being ready in February 1942. The vehicle was based on the M3 chassis and mounted a 155mm/6.1in gun, the M1918, an old French weapon used as a towed field gun by the Americans during World War I and then placed into storage as obsolete.

Originally this vehicle was rejected by the army as they could see no need for such a powerful weapon on a self-propelled mount. The army had plenty of towed guns which it felt would more than meet any future requirement. The Ordnance Department disagreed, feeling there was a specific need for this kind of piece, and ordered 50 vehicles in March 1942. This order was overruled by the

Supply Board until the vehicle had been fully tested by the Artillery Department. The Artillery Department reported back in agreement with the Ordnance Department that there was a need for the M12 and recommending that it should be placed into production. This started in late 1943, but for 100 vehicles only, and was completed in March 1944.

The vehicle had a two-man compartment at the front for the driver and the vehicle commander. The engine was in the middle of the vehicle just behind the driver's compartment with an open gun area at the rear. There was only room for 10 rounds of ammunition and so the rest of the crew travelled on the M30 supply vehicle, which was an M12 without the gun and its mounting carrying an additional 40 rounds of ammunition and the other four men of the gun crew under a canvas cover.

ABOVE LEFT: **An American battery of M12 vehicles has been placed into the sustained fire position. The guns have been driven up and on to a raised ramp which helps increase the elevation of the gun.**
ABOVE: **The open nature of the fighting compartment of this vehicle can clearly be seen. The travel lock for the gun barrel is lying on the glacis plate between the driver's and co-driver's position.**

June 1944 saw 74 of these vehicles arrive in Europe and they made a big difference instantly. They were used as "door knockers" by the Americans during their attacks on the Siegfried Line. One of these guns would be brought forward and the Germans inside the defensive position were offered the options of surrender or having their bunker blown apart around them.

LEFT: **An American M12 being readied to fire. The target cannot be far away as the gunner is checking the visual sight and the barrel is flat. The gun might be about to be used as a "door knocker" on a fixed-defence structure.**

M12 155mm Gun Motor Carriage

Country: USA
Entered service: 1944
Crew: 6
Weight: 29,464kg/29 tons
Dimensions: Length – 6.73m/22ft 1in
　Height – 2.69m/8ft 10in
　Width – 2.67m/8ft 9in
Armament: Main – 155mm/6.1in M1918M1 gun
　Secondary – 12.7mm/0.5in Browning machine-gun
Armour: Maximum – 50mm/1.97in
Powerplant: Continental R-975 Radial
　263kW/353hp petrol engine
Performance: Speed – 39kph/24mph
　Range – 225km/140 miles

M15 Multiple Gun Motor Carriage

The M15 was developed to provide an improved anti-aircraft capability for the American armoured formations as the M13 and M14 were not producing the desired results. Using the M3 chassis, the rear fighting compartment was removed and replaced by a flat bed on which the M42 multiple gun-mount was placed in a turret. The gun turret had a 360-degree traverse while its armament consisted of a fully automatic 37mm/1.46in gun and two 12.7mm/50cal machine-guns, with storage for 240 37mm/1.46in and 3,400 12.7mm/50cal rounds. It was designed to engage both ground and aerial targets, the 37mm/1.46in gun having a rate of fire of 40 rounds per minute and the 12.7mm/50cal 500 rounds per minute, giving the vehicle enough ammunition for six minutes firing. Autocar produced the

initial order of 600 vehicles between February and April 1943 and they entered service in May 1943. The M15 proved to be very effective in action and consequently a new order was placed for more vehicles, but this could not be fulfilled as there were no more M42 gun mounts and so a new mount was required for this development.

The new vehicle was the M15A1 which used the M54 gun mount. There was very little difference between the two vehicles except that in the M15, the 12.7mm/50cal machine-guns are mounted above the 37mm/1.46in gun, and in the M15A1 it is the other way round. Autocar again were the producers of the vehicle, with production starting in October 1943 and finishing in February 1944 during which time a total of 1,652 vehicles were built. To give the gun crew

ABOVE LEFT: **A prototype T28E1 vehicle dug in beside a fortress in Tunisia, North Africa, in 1943. These early vehicles had no crew protection and were fitted with water-cooled machine-guns.** ABOVE: **A M15A1 which has been fitted with a roller on the front of the vehicle. To give the gun crew some protection a three-sided turret was fitted around the gun mounting.**

more room to operate, the ammunition storage in the turret was reduced to enough for just five minutes firing time.

The M15 would see action in Sicily, Italy and northern Europe, while the M15A1 would only see service in Italy and northern Europe. These vehicles were greatly valued by the infantry as close-support guns, but one major weakness was the lack of protection for the crew. They would also see service in the Korean War and would remain in American service until late in the 1950s.

RIGHT: **A T28 prototype vehicle on test at the Aberdeen Proving Ground in 1942. The men standing beside the gun mount are the machine-gun magazine changers. The very exposed position of the crew can be clearly seen.**

M15 Multiple Gun Motor Carriage

Country: USA
Entered service: 1943
Crew: 7
Weight: 10,160kg/10 tons
Dimensions: Length – 6.14m/20ft 3in
   Height – 2.44m/8ft
   Width – 2.49m/8ft 2in
Armament: Main – 37mm/1.46in M1A2 automatic gun
   Secondary – 2 x 12.7mm/0.5in Browning machine-guns
Armour: Maximum – 12.7mm/0.5in
Powerplant: White 160AX 6-cylinder 95kW/128hp petrol engine
Performance: Speed – 64kph/45mph
   Range – 280km/200 miles

LEFT: One of the prototype vehicles on test at the Aberdeen Proving Ground in the USA. When they were used in the ground-support role these vehicles were called "Meat Choppers".
BELOW: The gun mount for the M16 is the M45D. The low height of this mount required the sides and back of the rear compartment to be capable of folding down.

M16 Multiple Gun Motor Carriage

Development started in December 1942 on a new vehicle as a replacement for the M13 which mounted the under-powered twin 12.7mm/50cal M33 gun. The improved version, known as the M16, carried the M45 gun mount.

The White Motor Company started production of the M16 in May 1943 and continued until March 1944, with a total production of 2,877 vehicles. The gun mount was placed in the rear fighting area which had been cleared of all the internal fittings. The rear area had no rear door and the tops of the sides were hinged so the guns could fire over the sides and rear of the vehicle. The new turret for the M16 was fitted with four 12.7mm/50cal machine-guns and had to be raised by 152mm/6in so that the guns could clear the sides of the vehicle. The

M16 could carry enough ammunition for eight minutes firing of the M45 gun mount. White were also given a contract to convert 677 M13 vehicles up to M16 standard, while a further 60 vehicles were converted by Diebold Incorporated, bringing total production of the M16 to 3,614 vehicles in all.

The M17 was similar to the M16, the only difference being the chassis, for while the M16 used the M3, the M17 used the M5. International Harvester produced a total of 1,000 M17s between December 1943 and March 1944, and all were sent to the Soviet Union under the Lend-Lease programme.

The M16 would see service on most fronts during World War II. They proved extremely valuable to the Marines in the Pacific as they could bring a large amount of firepower into a concentrated area. These vehicles would remain in service with the American Army until 1958 but the M45 gun mount would

remain in service until 1970. The chassis had changed but the M45 would find widespread use during the Vietnam War mounted on M54 5,080kg/5-ton supply trucks. In 1980 these vehicles were still in service with 12 different countries.

LEFT: The M16 had very little storage room for ammunition so most of these vehicles had a small ammunition trailer which was pulled behind the vehicle. Some of these systems would remain in active service for 40 years.

M16 Multiple Gun Motor Carriage

Country: USA
Entered service: 1943
Crew: 5
Weight: 10,160kg/10 tons
Dimensions: Length – 6.14m/20ft 3in
Height – 2.62m/8ft 7in
Width – 2m/6ft 6in
Armament: Main – 4 x 12.7mm/0.5in Browning machine-guns
Secondary – Small arms
Armour: Maximum – 12.7mm/0.5in
Powerplant: White 160AX 6-cylinder 95kW/128hp petrol engine
Performance: Speed – 64kph/45mph
Range – 280km/200 miles

M40 155mm Gun Motor Carriage

At the end of 1943, the American Army decided to standardize their AFV chassis into the Light Weight Combat Team based on the M24 light tank, and the Medium Weight Combat Team based on the M4A3 Sherman tank. The main idea behind this was to make production, the supply of spares and servicing quicker and easier for the troops in the field. Development of this new weapon started in January 1944, following the decision to send the M12 to Europe.
The American Army Armoured Force Board still firmly believed that they did not require the M40 but the success of the M12 in active service forced them to change their minds.

The M40 fell into the Medium Weight Combat Team, as it was designed around the M4A3 chassis. This was widened and Horizontal Volute Spring Suspension (HVSS) was fitted. The general layout was the same as the M12 with the driver located in a crew compartment in the front of the vehicle, the engine in the middle and the gun in the rear area. An escape hatch was also fitted into the floor of the driver's compartment just behind the co-driver's position. The fighting compartment was open, as in the M12, because this vehicle was never intended to be deployed in the front line but several miles behind supporting the front-line troops. Like the M12 there was a recoil spade

ABOVE: **The M40 used the same chassis as the M4A3 Sherman tank, which helped to make the supply of spares easier. The gun is fitted with a shield but this gives the gun crew very little protection. The travel-lock for the gun barrel is in the raised position.**

attached to the rear of the vehicle and operated by a hand winch. The M40 would carry a new gun, as supplies of the M1918 had finished, and this would be the 155mm/6.1in M1 or the 203mm/8in howitzer, both very successful towed weapons that had proved themselves in combat. In March 1944, five pilot models were ordered from the Pressed Steel Car Company, with production starting in February 1945 and not finishing until late 1945. Total production for the M40 was 418 vehicles. The upper hull was made of 12.7mm/0.5in homogeneous armour plate, but gave the crew no protection at all as the sides were too low. Development of an armoured cover for the crew area of the M40 was under way but with the ending of World War II, the need for this shelter also ended. The vehicle could not carry a lot of ammunition in the fighting compartment so it was intended to convert some as cargo carriers. These would carry extra ammunition and also the other crew members for the gun. They were never developed because there was a shortage of vehicle chassis as they were urgently needed in northern Europe.

The Americans had problems in breaching the concrete bunkers during the fighting along the Siegfried Line as they had no AFV that could do this, unlike the British who had developed the Churchill AVRE. They got over this by bringing up the M12 to point-blank range (732m/2,400ft), calling on the German defenders inside to surrender and if they failed to do so, then blasting the bunker open. Due to the success of the M12 in breaching these bunkers, a larger weapon was developed to go on the M40 chassis to be used as a siege gun. This carried a 250mm/9.84in short-range mortar, but development was stopped in August 1945 as the war had finished.

The M43, the vehicle carrying the 203mm/8in howitzer, was developed at the same time as the M40, but was not put into production until August 1945. An order for 576 of these weapons had been placed but by the cessation of hostilities, only 48 had been built before the order was cancelled.

The M40s arrived in Europe in time to take part in the final battles in Germany, their first action being the bombardment of Cologne. They would remain in service with the American Army until the late 1950s, having proved their worth during the Korean War. The British Army bought a number of M40 and M43 vehicles from the Americans after the war and these would remain in service until the early 1960s. The M40 proved to be a very reliable and well-liked vehicle, and the men who manned this weapon were known as "long-range snipers" due to the accuracy of the gun.

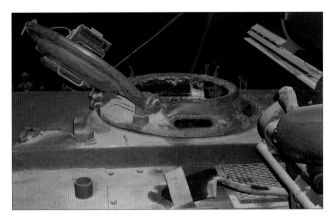

TOP AND ABOVE: **The driver's hatch was changed to an all-round vision cupola on the M40. There is a periscope through the top of the hatch. The lower picture shows the working end of the gun, the breach of which is an interrupted screw breach.**

ABOVE RIGHT: **Three fire extinguishers were attached to each side of the gun shield.**

ABOVE LEFT AND LEFT: **Inside the driver's position. The hand controls are in the middle of the picture with the foot pedals at the bottom. The recoil spade is in the lowered position and just requires the vehicle to reverse to push it into the ground.**

M40 155mm Gun Motor Carriage

Country: USA
Entered service: 1945
Crew: 8
Weight: 40,640kg/40 tons
Dimensions: Length – 9.04m/29ft 9in including gun barrel
Height – 2.69m/8ft 10in
Width – 3.15m/10ft 4in
Armament: Main – 155mm/6.1in M1A1 gun
Secondary – Small arms
Armour: Maximum – 12mm/0.47in
Powerplant: Continental 9-cylinder 295kW/395hp radial petrol engine
Performance: Speed – 38.6kph/24mph
Range – 161km/100 miles

LEFT: **The first version of the Marder III was this vehicle, which is armed with the Soviet 76.2mm/3in gun. Both the high position of the gun and the very exposed crew position can be clearly seen. This was very much a makeshift vehicle with everything piled on top of the chassis. A total of 344 of these vehicles were produced between April and October 1942.**

Marder III Self-Propelled Anti-Tank Gun

The Marder, the German name for the marten – a vicious little animal of the weasel family, was a series of three different vehicles built on several different chassis. Production of all three variants started in 1942 with three different manufacturers and in three different countries. They would remain in active service with the German Army until the end of World War II.

The Marder I was built on the captured French Lorraine Schlepper using the PaK40 anti-tank gun as main armament. The conversions were undertaken by a factory in Paris and all vehicles were to be issued to German units based in France. The Germans had captured over 300 of these old vehicles, most of which were converted into self-propelled artillery, but 84 were converted into Marder I anti-tank vehicles. The fighting compartment was at the rear and was surrounded by a sloped superstructure. The PaK40 retained its own gun-shield as a

form of mantle, but the main weakness was the open top to the fighting compartment which was a serious grenade trap.

The Marder II was built on the chassis of the Panzer II, but the German Army was by now questioning whether or not the Panzer II was still capable of combat. The driver's compartment was at the front, the fighting compartment in the middle and the engine at the rear. The main armament was again the excellent PaK40 anti-tank gun. Production started in 1942 and finished in June 1943, with a total of 671 Marder II vehicles being produced. As all Panzer II chassis were being switched to production of the Wespe SPG, production of the Marder II terminated prematurely. However, due to the success of the vehicle more were required, and so between July 1943 and March 1944 a further 73 were built. The fighting compartment was open-topped and open-backed but the

RIGHT: **A mid-production Marder III in Italy in 1944. This vehicle has the gun and fighting compartment in the middle of the vehicle, but a much larger armoured shield has been placed around this compartment. The compact size of the Marder can be clearly seen.**

LEFT: **The driver's position is forward and under the main gun, and has very limited vision. This vehicle has been hit in the engine and destroyed by fire.**
ABOVE: **The very open fighting compartment of this early Marder shows up well here. The basket on top of the engine deck was used to store personal kit and ammunition.**

front was closed by the gun-shield of the main armament. The Marder II was both very agile and very reliable, and proved to be a very useful combat vehicle. It would see service on all fronts and remained in active service until the end of the war.

The Marder III, based on the PzKpfw 38(t) tank chassis, was built in two versions. By late 1941, the 38(t) was considered both obsolete as a main battle tank and too slow for the reconnaissance role, so all production was changed to the SPG chassis. The first version was very much a makeshift temporary vehicle, using the captured Russian 76.2mm/3in gun. Production started in March 1942 with 24 units per month being built, moving up to 30 units per month by July 1942, with a total production of 344 vehicles. Most were sent to the Eastern Front, but 66 went to join the *Afrika Korps* in North Africa. The gun crew were very exposed in this vehicle and the Russian gun put considerable strain on the 38(t) tank chassis.

The Germans had realized that the first version of the Marder III was wasteful and unsatisfactory but now that the initial

pressing needs of the army had been dealt with, it could be redesigned and improved. The new vehicle was very different to the original with the successful PaK40 gun for its main armament. The driver's compartment in the front was improved with the engine moved to the middle of the vehicle behind the driver and the fighting compartment moved to the rear. These alterations made for a more balanced vehicle and gave the crew better protection, but it was still open-topped. It was built by BMM (*Böhmisch-Mährische Maschinenfabrik*). The original company designation had to be changed as it had a Jewish name in the title, but after the war the company reverted to its original name. Production stopped in May 1944 when the manufacturing facilities were switched to the Hetzer Tank Destroyer, by which time a total of 975 vehicles had been produced.

All the Marder vehicles performed well above their expected level and were a real problem to the Allied troops that came across them. They proved to be very reliable and by January 1945 some 300 were still in action in the German Army.

LEFT: **This is a late-production version of the Marder III. The gun position has been moved to the rear of the vehicle and the front has been completely redesigned. This Marder has a full load of ammunition in the gun position but has been damaged in an air raid.**

Marder III Self-Propelled Anti-Tank Gun

Country: Germany
Entered service: 1943
Crew: 4
Weight: 10,668kg/10.5 tons
Dimensions: Length – 4.95m/16ft 3in
    Height – 2.5m/8ft 2in
    Width – 2.15m/7ft 1in
Armament: Main – 7.5cm/2.95in PaK40/3 gun
    Secondary – 7.92mm/0.312in MG34
    machine-gun
Armour: Maximum – 15mm/0.59in
Powerplant: Praga EPA 6-cylinder 112kW/150hp
    petrol engine
Performance: Speed – 42kph/26mph
    Range – 190km/120 miles

Marmon-Herrington Armoured Cars

South Africa had never produced an AFV until development started on the Marmon-Herrington armoured car. Progress was slow at first but once war was declared this speeded up dramatically. The chassis was made by Ford and imported from Canada, the four-wheel drive was imported from Marmon-Herrington in America and all the armament came from Britain. The armour plate was supplied by local factories and the assembly plants were old railway workshops.

The Mk 1 was only two-wheel drive and this was discovered to have poor cross-country ability. At first the vehicle had a riveted construction but this was quickly changed to an all-welded fabrication. Total production of the Mk 1 was 135 vehicles.

The Mk 2 was very similar in layout to the Mk 1 but was now fitted with four-wheel drive which improved its performance. The hull of the vehicle was quite spacious for the crew of four and had twin doors at the rear. The Mk 2 came in two variations: the Middle East (ME) and the Mobile Field Force (MFF). The ME had a Boys anti-tank rifle in the turret and two mounts on the turret for Bren guns, one being anti-aircraft. There were also flaps on each side of the vehicle for additional Bren guns. The MFF had a 7.7mm/0.303in Vickers machine-gun in the turret and another one in a ball mount on the near side of the vehicle. Total production of these vehicles was 549 MFF and 338 ME, and in the early days of the North African campaign they were the main armoured car used by British forces. A number of Mk 2s were converted with captured Italian and German weapons. The armour was a little thin so on the Mk 3 this was increased.

ABOVE LEFT: **This car has been fitted with a captured German 37mm/1.46in AT gun, which is mounted over the driver's position. A Vickers machine-gun is fitted in the rear.** ABOVE: **This column of cars is being prepared for a patrol in East Africa. Some of these cars have had additional Vickers machine-guns fitted to the rear of the turret.**

The Mk 2 was to see extensive service with British forces in several theatres of war. Some were even captured by the Japanese and used by them. Others were sent to East Africa and the West Indies. These cars were to prove surprisingly effective and easy to operate, with some remaining in service after the war.

LEFT: **These Marmon cars have been fitted with different turrets. The first vehicle has a heavy and a light machine-gun in the turret, while the following cars have been fitted with a single machine-gun.**

Marmon-Herrington Mk 2 ME Armoured Car

Country: South Africa
Entered service: 1941
Crew: 4
Weight: 6,096kg/6 tons
Dimensions: Length – 5.18m/17ft
  Height – 2.67m/8ft 9in
  Width – 2m/6ft 6in
Armament: Main – Boys 14mm/0.55in
  anti-tank rifle
  Secondary – 2 x Bren 7.7mm/0.303in
  machine-guns
Armour: Maximum – 12mm/0.47in
Powerplant: Ford V8 63kW/85hp petrol engine
Performance: Speed – 80kph/50mph
  Range – 322km/200 miles

LEFT: **A crew member is standing in the roof-mounted reloading hatch next to the 10-round Nebelwerfer. The elevation and rotation of the unit was done from inside the vehicle.** BELOW: **A design picture for the mounting of the 8cm R-Vielfachwerfer. This fired 24 fin-stabilized rockets and was adopted by the Waffen SS.**

Maultier Nebelwerfer 15cm Panzerwerfer

The Maultier (Mule) was developed following the German experiences in Russia when ordinary wheeled vehicles became immobilized by mud and snow. The original Maultier half-track was built by the SS Division *Das Reich*, who fitted a Carden-Loyd track system to a Ford V8 truck. This proved so very successful that an order came down from high command to develop the idea further. Some 20,000 of these vehicles were built by three manufacturers.

In late 1942 Opel were asked to develop a spacious armoured body for the Maultier. Some 289 of these were to be used as ammunition carriers and 300 others were to be fitted with the Nebelwerfer 15cm/5.91in rocket launcher. The body of the vehicle was

an all-welded construction and its simple design made mass production easy. The front wheels retained normal brakes operated by a foot pedal while the tracks were braked by two hand-operated leavers beside the driver. The engine was in the front of the vehicle with the driver's compartment behind. The driver and commander sat side by side with a third crew member behind them. The reload rocket storage was in the body of the vehicle, with a large hatch in the roof for the crew to reload the launch tubes in safety. When the Nebelwerfer fired it left great smoke trails behind pinpointing the battery position but by fitting the weapon to a half-track vehicle, the rockets could be fired then the vehicle could quickly move to a new position.

The ten-barrelled Nebelwerfer 42 was subsequently developed with five tubes layered in two rows mounted on a 360-degree mount fitted to the rear of the vehicle. To fire all ten rockets took just 10 seconds and a reload was completed in 90 seconds. These vehicles were organized into companies with each company having eight vehicles carrying 80 launch tubes.

The Nebelwerfer was nicknamed "Moaning Minnie" by Allied troops, due to the noise the rocket made in flight. These Panzerwerfer units were deployed mainly on the Eastern Front and in France.

RIGHT: **Under the rocket tubes can be seen the small sighting window, which has two manual sliding shutters. The large rear doors give access into the ammunition storage area which is at the rear. This half-track is well equipped with storage lockers down each side of the vehicle.**

Maultier 15cm Panzerwerfer

Country: Germany
Entered service: 1943
Crew: 3
Weight: 8,636kg/8.5 tons
Dimensions: Length – 6m/19ft 6in
 Height – 3.05m/10ft
 Width – 2.2m/7ft 3in
Armament: Main – 10 x 15cm/5.91in Nebelwerfer
 Secondary – 7.92mm/0.312in MG34 machine-gun
Armour: Maximum – 10mm/0.394in
Powerplant: Opel 3.6-litre 6-cylinder 51kW/68hp petrol engine
Performance: Speed – 40kph/25mph
 Range – 130km/81 miles

Minerva Armoured Car

ABOVE LEFT: **One of the early Minerva cars. The armoured doors in front of the radiator are half-open and the driver's visor is fully open. Extra storage boxes have been fitted to the car.** ABOVE: **The three-man crew of this car pose for a picture. The headlight has been moved on to the frontal plate of the vehicle next to the driver. The gun crew have very little protection when operating the gun.**

The Belgians were the progenitors of armoured car warfare and would demonstrate to the world how flexible and useful the armoured car could be, yet in spite of this, Minerva armoured cars are not well known outside Belgium. Lieutenant Charles Henkart allowed two of his cars to be converted into armoured cars at the Cockerill Works in Hoboken and these cars were soon in action gathering intelligence and causing disruption among the German cavalry at the beginning of World War I.

The Minerva armoured car was based on the chassis of a 28kW/38hp touring car while the engine was a Knight-type four-cylinder double-sleeve valve which had proved itself in racing. The body of the car was covered in 4mm/0.16in armour plate, with the fighting compartment protected by two layers of armour spaced 3mm/0.12in apart. However, this armour was only just about bullet- and shell-splash-proof. The fighting compartment was in the middle of the vehicle and was open-topped, with a large single light fitted to the front next to the driver. The normal armament was a single Hotchkiss machine-gun on a pintle mount with an armoured shield, but some vehicles had a single 37mm/1.46in Puteaux cannon fitted. In 1918 the Belgians modified the Minerva by placing a basic open-backed turret over the machine-gun to give the gunner better protection.

The Belgians converted several more cars in 1914 and used them very much in the guerrilla role, harassing the German advanced troops. They also gave a lot of support to local troops during the withdrawal of forces in front of the German advance of 1914. By October 1914 the trench line had reached the coast and ended the mobile armoured car war. Like the British, the Belgians sent an armoured car section to help the Russians in their fight against the Germans, and these were shipped home in early 1918 and refurbished, following the Revolution and Russia's withdrawal from the war.

The Minerva armoured cars were to remain in service until the early 1930s. Some were even passed to the Gendarmerie and these would remain in police service until 1937.

Minerva Armoured Car

Country: Belgium
Entered service: 1914
Crew: 3
Weight: 4,064kg/4 tons
Dimensions: Length – 4.9m/16ft 1in
              Height – 2.3m/7ft 6in
              Width – 1.75m/5ft 9in
Armament: Main – 8mm/0.315in Hotchkiss machine-gun
              Secondary – Small arms
Armour: Maximum – 11mm/0.43in
Powerplant: Minerva 4-cylinder sleeve valve 30kW/40hp petrol engine
Performance: Speed – 40kph/25mph
              Range – 240km/150 miles

ABOVE: **A column of late-production Minerva cars. Some of the vehicles are carrying an extra crew member. The RNAS heard about these cars and very quickly copied the idea, and so the armoured car was born.**

Model 93 Sumida Armoured Car

The Sumida was designed by Japanese engineers to be able to run equally well on roads or railways, as it was intended to be used to police large areas. Development started in 1931; the vehicle went into production in 1933 and entered service in the same year.

It was a standard 6x4 chassis but with a few novel modifications to enable the car to carry out its dual role. The vehicle had one set of six wheels for road use and another for rails. These were easily interchangeable using four jacks built into the underside of the car, the spare set of six wheels being mounted in clips on the side of the fighting compartment. The driver and commander sat in the front of the vehicle with the other four crew members behind. There was a one-man turret mounted on the top of the fighting compartment with small arms firing slits in the sides. These vehicles were mainly operational in Manchuria, covering vast areas. These cars would always operate in pairs.

LEFT: **This Model 93 is being used as a railway patrol vehicle. It has its railway wheels fitted while its rubber road wheels are stored on the side of the vehicle. The radiator armoured doors are in the open position.**

Model 93 Sumida Armoured Car

Country: Japan
Entered service: 1933
Crew: 6
Weight: 7,620kg/7.5 tons
Dimensions: Length – 6.55m/21ft 6in
   Height – 2.97m/9ft 8in
   Width – 1.9m/6ft 3in
Armament: Main – 6.5mm/0.256in machine-gun
   Secondary – Small arms
Armour: Maximum – 16mm/0.63in
Powerplant: 6-cylinder 75kW/100hp petrol engine
Performance: Speed – 60kph/37mph
   Range – 240km/150 miles

Morris CS9/LAC Armoured Car Reconnaissance

Between 1935 and 1936 the Royal Ordnance Factory at Woolwich built two prototype armoured cars using the Morris 762kg/15cwt as the chassis, but both were turned down by the British Army. The third one was much better as the chassis was lengthened by 457mm/18in, engine power was increased and the turret design was changed. The new turret was open-topped and was now armed with a Boys anti-tank rifle and a Bren gun, while between the two guns was a smoke discharger. The Morris CS9 entered service with the British Army in 1938 with a total production run of only 100 vehicles.

The BEF took 38 of these vehicles to France in 1939 and all were lost in the withdrawal to the Channel Ports. In North Africa the CS9 would remain in service until 1941, but by fitting a radio it became a troop leader's car, while some of these vehicles were converted to command cars. However, the steering and suspension did not hold up well over rough terrain or in the deserts of North Africa.

LEFT: **This is a troop commander's vehicle in the deserts of North Africa in 1942. The crew have found some additional shade. The Boys AT rifle is fitted in the front of the turret while the Bren gun is fitted to the rear.**

Morris CS9/LAC Armoured Car Reconnaissance

Country: UK
Entered service: 1938
Crew: 4
Weight: 4,267kg/4.2 tons
Dimensions: Length – 4.78m/15ft 8in
   Height – 2.21m/7ft 3in
   Width – 2.06m/6ft 9in
Armament: Main – Boys 14mm/0.55in
   anti-tank rifle
   Secondary – 1 x Bren 7.7mm/0.303 machine-gun, and 1 x 51mm/2in smoke discharger
Armour: Maximum – 7mm/0.27in
Powerplant: Morris Commercial 4-cylinder 52kW/70hp petrol engine
Performance: Speed – 72kph/45mph
   Range – 386km/240 miles

LEFT AND BELOW: **This Morris armoured car seen here in Normandy has a cut-down turret, and the other gunner's hatches are in the open position. The car below has a full-size turret, but this afforded the gunner a very limited view, so in combat the crews cut the turret down as a field modification.**

Morris Mk 1 Light Reconnaissance Car

The Morris Mk 1 was one of the better British designs of a number of armoured cars produced during 1940 and 1941. Morris was subsequently given a contract to produce 1,000 of these Light Reconnaissance cars, with the first entering service in 1941.

The body of the car was a monocoque design of all-welded armour plate construction. The vehicle had a solid rear axle with independent suspension on the front wheels, but it was only two-wheel drive which would prove to be a problem in the cross-country role. The engine was mounted in the rear of the vehicle with the crew compartment in the front, while there were two large doors, one on each side, for the crew to enter and exit.

The driver sat in the middle of the crew compartment on the centreline of the vehicle with the turret gunner on the right side and the vehicle commander on the left. The vehicle commander would also operate the Boys anti-tank rifle, which could be fired to the front and rear only. The machine-gun turret had all-round traverse and a 51mm/2in smoke discharger mounted on its side.

Morris produced the Mk 2 version in 1942 and received an order for 1,050 of these new vehicles. The main improvements were that the vehicle was made into a 4x4 and the suspension was changed to leaf spring. The Boys anti-tank rifle was done away with and replaced with a second machine-gun. Large numbers of these armoured cars

were passed over to the RAF to be used as airfield defence vehicles. Some were also converted to turretless observation vehicles and a number of these would be taken to France by the RAF in 1944. When being used by the RAF as a Forward Observation Vehicle the gun turret was retained but the vehicle commander's position was converted to a radio position.

These armoured cars proved to be very serviceable and reliable and would remain in service in secondary roles until the end of the war.

LEFT: **The side door into the crew compartment is small, making access difficult. The crew compartment itself is compact with no space for the storage of personal kit. The turret on this vehicle has been fitted with a smoke discharger and is armed with a Bren gun.**

Morris Mk 1 Light Reconnaissance Car

Country: UK
Entered service: 1941
Crew: 3
Weight: 3,759kg/3.7 tons
Dimensions: Length – 4.06m/13ft 4in
Height – 1.88m/6ft 2in
Width – 2.03m/6ft 8in
Armament: Main – 14mm/0.55in Boys anti-tank rifle
Secondary – Bren 7.7mm/0.303in machine-gun
Armour: Maximum – 14mm/0.55in
Powerplant: Morris 4-cylinder 53kW/71hp petrol engine
Performance: Speed – 72kph/45mph
Range – 233km/145 miles

Ole Bill Bus

The name for this unusual AFV comes from a World War I cartoon character. The bus was a B-Type built by AEC for the London General Omnibus Company (LGOC) that had entered service on the streets of London in 1911.

The LGOC allocated 300 B-Type buses to the British Army for use in France from October 1914 and they would remain on active service until 1918 when they helped bring the British Army home.

The first buses manned by volunteer crews arrived in France just in time to help move men forward during the First Battle of Ypres (October 19–November 22, 1914). They turned up painted in London red and cream livery with all the advertising still in place but were soon painted khaki and the windows were removed and boarded up. Wooden planking 51mm/2in

thick was attached as armour but this was only effective against small shell splinters. Each bus could carry 25 fully armed men; the first unit carried being a London Scottish battalion. Some 900 buses would serve in France.

LEFT: **The first London buses sent out to France were required to enter service immediately so were seen moving behind the British lines in their full London livery.**

Ole Bill Bus B-Type	
Country: UK	
Entered service: 1914 Military service	
Crew: 2	
Weight: 4,064kg/4 tons	
Dimensions: Length – 6.86m/22ft 6in	
Height – 3.79m/12ft 5in	
Width – 2.11m/6ft 11in	
Armament: Main – None	
Secondary – None	
Armour: Maximum – 51mm/2in wooden planking	
Powerplant: AEC 4-cylinder 22kW/30hp petrol engine	
Performance: Speed – 32km/20mph	
Range – 241km/150 miles	

Otter Light Reconnaissance Car

The Otter, intended as a Canadian replacement for the British Humber Scout Car, was designed in early 1942 and went into production soon after. The vehicle turned out to be under-powered and had very poor visibility for the driver and crew, but despite these shortcomings, it was still placed into production. The vehicle had an all-welded construction with four-wheel drive and had a fair cross-country performance

but, due to its height, a high centre of gravity. Total production of these vehicles was 1,761, with manufacturing finishing in 1943.

The Otter entered service with Canadian and British forces in late 1942, seeing action in Italy and northern Europe. The vehicle was very popular with its crews as it proved to be very reliable and was an easy vehicle to maintain in the field. The RAF regiment also used it as there was room in the body of the vehicle

to carry extra radio equipment. The RAF increased the armament on its Otters including, among other weapons, an anti-aircraft machine-gun.

Otter Light Reconnaissance Car	
Country: Canada	
Entered service: 1942	
Crew: 3	
Weight: 4,877kg/4.8 tons	
Dimensions: Length – 4.5m/14ft 9in	
Height – 2.44m/8ft	
Width – 2.13m/7ft	
Armament: Main – 14mm/0.55in Boys anti-tank rifle	
Secondary – 1 x Bren 7.7mm/0.303in light machine-gun, and 1 x 101.6mm/4in smoke discharger	
Armour: Maximum – 12mm/0.47in	
Powerplant: GMC 6-cylinder 79kW/106hp petrol engine	
Performance: Speed – 72kph/45mph	
Range – 402km/250 miles	

LEFT: **The Boys AT rifle has its own port in the front of the vehicle, while above this is a smoke discharger. This vehicle is covered in personal kit as there is no space for it inside the car.**

PA-III Armoured Car

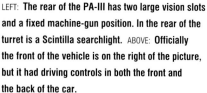

LEFT: **The rear of the PA-III has two large vision slots and a fixed machine-gun position. In the rear of the turret is a Scintilla searchlight.** ABOVE: **Officially the front of the vehicle is on the right of the picture, but it had driving controls in both the front and the back of the car.**

In the 1920s Czechoslovakia was a very poor country but was in need of modern armoured vehicles to bring its army up to date. Skoda started to develop the PA-III in 1924 while still manufacturing the PA-II. They kept the same chassis that had been used since the PA-I. This chassis was four-wheel drive and four-wheel steering and could be driven in both directions at the same speed as there were driving controls in both the front and the back of the vehicle's crew compartment.

The PA-III was a big improvement on the PA-II. The new car was lighter, smaller, more mobile and above all less

expensive. The army kept changing its mind about what was required in the new car and this slowed up development. The original body was made up of beautifully curved armour plates, but these were replaced by short angled straight armour plates. This would speed up production and reduce costs, but would still give the same ballistic protection to the crew. In 1925 a single prototype was produced which immediately went for extensive testing by the army. In December 1927 the Czechoslovak Army accepted the PA-III as fit for service and placed an order for 12 cars with Skoda providing an extra three free of charge due to

three PA-II armoured cars being sold to the police in Vienna. Production started in 1929 and 16 cars were built. The engine was in the front of the vehicle with the fighting compartment in the middle, a turret fitted with two machine-guns mounted on the top and a single machine-gun in the rear.

The PA-III was easy to maintain, robust and well-liked by its crews, but by the time of the outbreak of World War II it was showing its age. The armoured cars were placed into three armoured regiments in 1937 to act as reconnaissance vehicles for the tanks and in 1938 they took part in the fighting for the Sudeten region. By 1939 nearly all of the cars had been captured by the German or Romanian forces, and only one survived the war.

LEFT: **This is the rear of the PA-III and has a tow-hitch fitted to the lower body work. The turret has been rotated so the front machine-gun is facing the rear of the vehicle. The main doors into the vehicle are on either side below the turret.**

PA-III Armoured Car

Country: Czechoslovakia
Entered service: 1929
Crew: 5
Weight: 6,706kg/6.6 tons
Dimensions: Length – 5.35m/17ft 7in
  Height – 2.66m/8ft 9in
  Width – 1.95m/6ft 5in
Armament: Main – 2 x vz.7/24 7.92mm/0.312in
  machine-guns
  Secondary – ZB vz.26 7.92mm/0.312in
  machine-gun
Armour: Maximum – 5.5mm/0.22in
Powerplant: Skoda 4-cylinder 44.3kW/60hp
  petrol engine
Performance: Speed – 35kph/22mph
  Range – 250km/155 miles

FAR LEFT: **This car is in post-World War II service with the French Army. The driver's side hatch is in the open position. The coaxial machine-gun is not fitted to the turret of this car.** LEFT: **This side view of the Panhard, in French camouflage colours, shows the main entrance and exit** door in the side of the vehicle below the turret. The design of this car would influence many designs in the 1950s. TOP: A French Panhard in German service in Russia, 1943. The extensive use of rivets in the construction of the vehicle can be clearly seen. The rear of the crew compartment below the turret can be raised to improve ventilation and give better vision.

Panhard AMD Type 178 Armoured Car

The AMD (*Automitrailleuse de Découverte*) was conceived as a replacement for some of the ageing French armoured cars of World War I. The prototype appeared in 1933 but development was very slow as money was in short supply. It entered service with the French Army in 1935 and was issued to both infantry and cavalry units. The AMD 178 was a very good clean design, with the interior divided into fighting/driving and engine compartments. The armour was sloped and the construction was all riveted. The car was a 4x4 vehicle and had good cross-country performance due to the engine being mounted in the rear.

Only 360 were in service when the Germans invaded France in 1940 but the French had distributed these vehicles among so many units in "penny packets" that the Germans were able to capture over 200 of the AMD 178s intact and, as it performed well, they were taken into German service. However,

the French managed to rescue 46 of these cars and had them repaired after which they were then sent to the new unoccupied Vichy territory and hidden from the Germans.

The Germans replaced the 25mm/ 0.98in gun with their 37mm/1.46in anti-tank gun. Some were also modified to run on railway track by replacing the road wheels with railway wheels. A number of these cars were also converted into command radio cars by fitting a large frame aerial over the top of the vehicle. Many of these converted vehicles as well as standard AMD 178s were sent to the Eastern Front to support the anti-partisan war that was taking place behind the German lines. When the Germans overran Vichy they captured the remaining 46 AMD 178 cars that were in French hands. These were converted into a wheeled tank by installing a larger turret on the vehicle and arming it with a 50mm/1.97in gun. Most of these remained in France.

The AMD 178 was the most advanced medium armoured car in French service in 1940, and was soon back in production when the Renault factory was restored to French control in August 1944. It would remain in French service for many years after World War II.

Panhard AMD Type 178 Armoured Car

Country: France
Entered service: 1935
Crew: 3
Weight: 8,636kg/8.5 tons
Dimensions: Length – 4.79m/15ft 8in
  Height – 2.31m/7ft 7in
  Width – 2.01m/6ft 7in
Armament: Main – 1 x 25mm/0.98in gun, and
  1 x 7.5mm/0.295in MG31 coaxial machine-gun
  Secondary – None
Armour: Maximum – 26mm/1.02in
Powerplant: Panhard SK 6.33-litre 4-cylinder
  78kW/105hp petrol engine
Performance: Speed – 72kph/45mph
  Range – 300km/186 miles

LEFT: **An improved version of the Flakpanzer called the "Wirbelwind". This vehicle mounted the 2cm/0.79in Flakvierling 38 in an armoured rotating turret, and provided good crew protection. The slow rotational speed of this new turret was the one drawback of the design.** BELOW: **The first Flakpanzer to be issued to the Panzer formations was called the "Möbelwagen" (Furniture Van). To operate the gun you had to drop the sides of the vehicle.**

Panzer IV Flakpanzer

The problem of supplying the German Army with mobile anti-aircraft guns for protection from fighter bombers first came to light during the campaign in North Africa in 1942, when the RAF Desert Air Force destroyed large numbers of vehicles. To give the army convoys basic protection a number of very ad hoc conversions were made to allow some vehicles to carry a single 2cm/0.79in flak gun. However, this problem was passed back to the German High Command for a permanent solution to be found.

The first vehicle to based on the Panzer IV chassis was the Möbelwagen (Furniture Van) which was shown to Hitler on May 14, 1943, but he rejected it on the grounds that it was too expensive and that fighter bombers were not currently a great problem. The Möbelwagen was a basic Panzer IV chassis with

the flak gun mounted in a box structure fixed to the top of the vehicle. When the gun went into action, the sides of the box were lowered exposing the gun and crew. The gun was the quadruple 2cm/0.79in Flakvierling 38, which had a high rate of fire but was magazine-fed. The vehicle was again shown to Hitler in October 1943 and was yet again rejected, this time due to its overall height being over 3m/9ft 10in and reservations that the crew had very little protection.

As the situation deteriorated on the Eastern Front and in Italy, an interim order was placed for the Möbelwagen, now armed with the 3.7cm/1.46in Flak 43. From February 1944, 20 of these vehicles were produced per month. The vehicle had a crew of seven, though in service this was often reduced to five, and could carry 416 rounds which gave three minutes firing time for the Flak 43. The first of these vehicles entered service in April 1944 and total production by the end of the war was 240 Möbelwagens.

The first true Flakpanzer was the Wirbelwind, which had been shown to General Guderian in May 1944. He requested that it be put into production straight away. These vehicles were built using old Panzer IV chassis returned from the front, with a total of 105 conversions being completed. There was a

ABOVE: **The Flakpanzer Wirbelwind was seen as a stop-gap solution, allowing a quick conversion of the Panzer IV chassis. With this vehicle the driver could remain at his position for a fast response.**

LEFT: The "Ostwind" version of the Flakpanzer IV which mounted a single 3.7cm/1.46in Flak 36. This vehicle could also be used against ground targets.
ABOVE: Inside the driver's position of a Flakpanzer IV. The driver's vision block is top centre, the track control arms are in the middle, with the gear lever and other controls to the right of the seat.

crew of five; four were in the turret manning the gun, while the driver remained at his post. The turret was made from angled 16mm/0.63in armour plates welded into position, the angle of the plates helping to close the open top a little. The vehicle was armed with the quadruple 2cm/0.79in Flakvierling 38, which was enclosed in the armoured, but still open-topped, turret. The Wirbelwind entered production in July 1944, but the gun was not delivering the results required and so production stopped in November 1944.

The Ostwind was to replace the Wirbelwind, still using the Panzer IV chassis but with a new gun fitted. The new gun was the 3.7cm/1.46in Flak 43 as used on the Möbelwagen which was fitted into the same turret as had been used on the Wirbelwind. The Ostwind II had the same body and turret as the Ostwind, but with the armament changed to a twin 3cm/1.18in Flakzwilling 44 guns, with the twin barrels mounted side by side. This vehicle only reached the prototype stage before the war ended.

On April 20, 1944 Hitler ordered that the twin 3cm/1.18in Doppelflak 303 that was just going into production for the U-Boat service should be fitted to a Panzer IV chassis. This new vehicle would be called the Kugelblitz Anti-Aircraft Tank and would replace all the other flak vehicles in production. By February 1945 when production stopped only two full vehicles and five chassis had been built. Other chassis were also being considered for the new flak tanks and these included the PzKpfw 38(t) and the Panther.

In 1944 Flakpanzer Platoons were formed and were assigned to Panzer regiments. These were normally formed of 8 Möbelwagen or 4 Möbelwagen and 4 Wirbelwind per platoon. The vast majority of these Flak vehicles were sent to France in an attempt to protect the German tanks from the virtually unchallenged Allied air force. Most of these vehicles were either destroyed or captured in the Falaise Pocket in Normandy. The rest were abandoned during the retreat across the Seine.

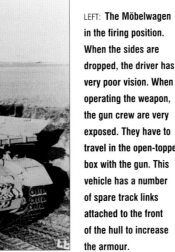

LEFT: The Möbelwagen in the firing position. When the sides are dropped, the driver has very poor vision. When operating the weapon, the gun crew are very exposed. They have to travel in the open-topped box with the gun. This vehicle has a number of spare track links attached to the front of the hull to increase the armour.

Möbelwagen

Country: Germany
Entered service: 1944
Crew: 5
Weight: 24,384kg/24 tons
Dimensions: Length – 5.92m/19ft 5in
  Height – 2.73m/8ft 11in
  Width – 2.95m/9ft 8in
Armament: Main – 3.7cm/1.46in Flak 43
  Secondary – 7.92mm/0.312in MG34 machine-gun
Armour: Maximum – 50mm/1.97in
Powerplant: Maybach HL 120 TRM 112 203kW/272hp 12-cylinder petrol engine
Performance: Speed – 38kph/24mph
  Range – 200km/124 miles

LEFT: **This Priest of the 1st Armoured Division in North Africa is being readied for action. The lack of storage provision can be clearly seen as the vehicle is covered with personal kit, camouflage netting and bedding.** BELOW: **An American M7 on trial in America. When these vehicles went overseas, the large white star was made smaller. The crews very quickly found that the star was an aiming point for the Germans, so either painted it out or covered it in mud.**

Priest 105mm Self-Propelled Gun

Reports coming out of North Africa in 1940 had shown the Americans the urgent need for an SPG and as an interim solution the T19 half-track was introduced into service. In early 1941, an alternative solution of mounting the 105mm/4.13in howitzer on the M3 tank chassis was proposed. The weapon was mounted in an open fighting compartment and was offset to the right to give room for the driver. Trials of the vehicle proved to be very successful and reliable, and the British Tank Mission in America placed orders immediately it was shown to them. Known to the US Forces as the M7, the British named it the "Priest" as the AA machine-gun was mounted in what looked like a pulpit and all Royal Artillery SPGs were given ecclesiastical names.

American Loco started production in April 1942 and by the end of the year had produced 2,028 vehicles of a total M7 production of 3,490 vehicles. The first British order was

for 2,500 in the first year and 3,000 by the end of 1943, but this was never met as the American forces were armed with the new weapon first. The Priest had identical chassis and automotive parts as the M3 tank but, just as the M4 Sherman tank was replacing the M3 Grant in service, so from late 1943 the M4 chassis replaced the M3 chassis in Priest production. In American service, this new vehicle using M4 chassis and automotive parts was known as the M7B1. The height of the fighting compartment sides was raised by the fitting of hinged plates to give the ammunition better protection as there was storage for 69 rounds in open bins. Nine hundred and fifty-three of these vehicles were built from March 1944 to March 1945.

LEFT: **This British Priest is being unloaded from an LCT (Landing Craft Tank). The driver's visor is in the open position but because of the poor vision, the "pulpit" gunner is helping direct the vehicle off the craft.**

LEFT: **The driver has good forward vision on his side of the main gun, but can see nothing on the machine-gunner's side of the vehicle. Here you can see the high driving position in the vehicle which has the effect of making the vehicle tall.** ABOVE: **The storage boxes on the front of the vehicle are for spare track links. The running gear and chassis for these vehicles came from the M4 Sherman. The machine-gun position has a circular swivel mount on the top of it.**

In September 1942, 90 Priest SPGs were sent to the British 8th Army in North Africa and took part in the second Battle of El Alamein. From this time onwards it became the standard issue to British medium SP batteries. The British units equipped with the Priest that landed in Normandy during June 1944 soon had their vehicles replaced by the Sexton SPG, but the Priest remained in service with the 8th Army for the remainder of the war as it fought all the way up Italy. One problem encountered there was that the howitzer could not be elevated enough to reach targets high up in the mountains, so the vehicle would be driven up on to a log ramp to increase the angle of elevation. This same problem would arise again during the Korean War and at first was solved in the same way as in Italy until a modification was made raising the gun by 155mm/6in, so creating the M7B2.

The Canadians, like the British, stopped using their M7 Priests soon after D-Day as they were replaced by the new 25pdr Sexton. However, General Simonds, commander of the Canadian II Corps, got permission to keep the M7 chassis for troop-carrying purposes, so at the end of July these chassis were sent to the Canadian field workshop codenamed "Kangaroo" for conversion. The main armament and all its internal fittings were removed and the aperture for the gun was plated over, but the "pulpit" with its machine-gun was kept to give covering fire to the troops as they debussed, and the side plates were raised to give the men more protection. These vehicles could carry 20 fully armed infantry and had a crew of two; they were a great success and would lead to a whole new type of infantry vehicle. The Canadians used a number of these "Unfrocked Priests" to drive their infantry through the German lines during Operation "Totalize". By August 6, 1944, 75 "Priest Kangaroos", as they were later named, were ready and the infantry had just one day to learn how to use them, the drivers for the new vehicle being taken from the artillery units that had used the Priest. This conversion proved very popular and more Priests were converted into Kangaroos in Italy. In addition, a number of redundant Priests were converted to artillery observation vehicles by removing the gun and putting extra radios, telephones and map tables into the resulting space.

LEFT: **A battery of Priest SPGs camouflaged up in Normandy on June 6, 1944. The sides of the vehicle have been increased in height by the fitting of the deep-water wading gear. The front of the vehicle is covered in spares for the running gear.**

Priest 105mm SPG

Country: USA
Entered service: 1942
Crew: 7
Weight: 26,010kg/25.6 tons
Dimensions: Length – 6.02m/19ft 9in
    Height – 2.54m/8ft 4in
    Width – 2.88m/9ft 5in
Armament: Main – 105mm/4.13in M1A2 howitzer
    Secondary – 12.7mm/0.5in machine-gun
Armour: Maximum – 62mm/2.44in
Powerplant: Continental 9-cylinder radial
    280kW/375hp petrol engine
Performance: Speed – 41.8kph/26mph
    Range – 201km/125 miles

Renault and Peugeot Armoured Cars

The French formed their armoured car units in 1914. At first these used touring cars but they were soon replaced by rudimentary armoured cars such as the Renault and Peugeot. At the start of World War I, Renault was the largest car construction company in France. By November 1914 they had produced 100 AM Renault 20CV mod.E1 armoured cars which entered service in December 1914 crewed by French marines. At first the armour was poor but this was very quickly upgraded to 5mm/0.2in, while the famous Renault engine cover was retained and armoured. The vehicle was open-topped with an 8mm/0.315in Hotchkiss machine-gun mounted on a pintle mount. A heavier 37mm/1.46in Puteaux gun was carried by some Renault cars and these would be used in many actions as close-support vehicles especially during the retreat and advances of 1918.

The Peugeot 18CV was the other main French armoured car in 1914. They were designed by Captain Reynauld who made both the machine-gun car and the heavy gun car the same so armament could be interchangeable in these open-topped vehicles. The first ones were armed with an 8mm/0.315in machine-

gun, but this was soon supplemented by fitting a 37mm/1.46in gun to some of the cars. These vehicles were built on the Peugeot 146 chassis at first and later the 148 chassis was used, giving a total production run of 150 of these armoured cars. The Peugeot cars initially saw active service in January 1915 when the first cars were sent to join the 7th Cavalry Division and formed the 6th and 7th Armoured Car Groups. There was a crew of three on the machine-gun car and four on the 37mm/1.46in heavy gun car. They could also carry five infantry if required and during the great German retreat of

1918 they were used to great effect in harassing the German infantry. By the end of World War I, the French had only 28 Peugeot armoured cars still fit for service. Poland bought 18 of these in 1918 and some were still in Polish service when the Germans invaded in 1939.

ABOVE: **This Renault armoured car has a crew of four and is armed with a single 37mm/1.46in gun, which has an armoured shield around it. This car has its starting handle in place in the front of the vehicle between the wheels.** LEFT: **Five Peugeot machine-gun armed armoured cars at Magnicourt in May 1915. The third car in is armed with a 47mm/1.85in gun. The large single door is mounted in the side of the vehicle behind the driver and in front of the gun.**

Peugeot 18CV Armoured Car

Country: France
Entered service: 1915
Crew: 3 plus 5 infantry
Weight: 5,000kg/4.9 tons
Dimensions: Length – 4.8m/16ft
    Height – 2.8m/9ft 2in
    Width – 1.8m/5ft 11in
Armament: Main – 8mm/0.315in Hotchkiss
    Mle 14 machine-gun
    Secondary – Small arms
Armour: Maximum – 5mm/0.2in
Powerplant: Peugeot 146 4-cylinder 34kW/45hp
    petrol engine
Performance: Speed – 40kph/25mph
    Range – 140km/87 miles

LEFT: **The driver is in his position and all his hatches are open. The hatch is split in two parts with the dome part folding backwards. The other crew position is all "buttoned up".** BELOW: **This UE is pulling a small four-wheel trailer, which has been fitted with cross-country tracks. Behind this is the Hotchkiss 25mm/0.98in AT gun.**

Renault UE Infantry Tractor

Production of these light tractors had started in 1931 at Renault and in 1936 at AMX, and by 1940 the French had some 6,000 in service. These vehicles were not designed for combat but to act as an armoured supply vehicle, the hardship of Verdun having shown the necessity for such a design. Some of these vehicles were produced with a machine-gun for the co-driver but these were far and few between.

Renault based these vehicles on the Carden-Loyd Mk VI carrier design. It was of a riveted construction, with a Renault engine. The crew were fully protected as they sat in the main body of the vehicle with the engine between them and only had their heads protruding. These were protected by armoured domes that were

hinged in the middle so that the front part could lift like a knight's visor. Behind the crew was a storage box for supplies but it was very small and could not carry more than 150kg/331lb. The vehicle was always designed to pull an armoured trailer, which was open-topped. These four-wheeled trailers were capable of carrying 500kg/1,102lb and for extreme conditions could be fitted with caterpillar tracks to improve their overall cross-country performance.

The Germans captured so many of these vehicles that they would see service in many areas and in many forms. A large number were converted into light Panzerjager, armed at first with a 37mm/1.46in PaK35/36, and many of these were used by garrison forces in

France. When Rommel took over the coastal defences in France, he instructed that a lot of the Renault UEs should be converted into rocket carriers. They were fitted with four Wurfrahmen 40 rockets mounted in either of two ways on the vehicle. One method was to put side-skirts on the vehicle with two rockets placed on each side, while the other means was a box structure built over the rear supply box and again capable of carrying and firing four rockets. These were first encounter by the Allies in Normandy, but later more widely throughout the European theatre.

LEFT: **This UE is being inspected by a group of British soldiers in France in 1944. The short exhaust can be seen. This was the cause of a few problems with fumes going into the crew compartments.**

Renault UE Infantry Tractor

Country: France
Entered service: 1931
Crew: 2
Weight: 2,032kg/2 tons
Dimensions: Length – 2.69m/8ft 10in
  Height – 1.03m/3ft 5in
  Width – 1.7m/5ft 7in
Armament: Main – None
  Secondary – Small arms
Armour: Maximum – 7mm/0.27in
Powerplant: Renault 4-cylinder 63kW/85hp petrol engine
Performance: Speed – 30kph/19mph
  Range – 180km/112 miles

LEFT: Dominion troops in Palestine during World War I. The car has an open-topped turret allowing for much-needed additional ventilation in the hot climate. The desert was very hard on tyres, hence all the spares carried on the side of the car.
ABOVE: A column of Rolls-Royce cars stopped in a village behind the Western Front. The rear wheels have been fitted with chains to improve traction in the mud. The cars are covered in personal kit.

Rolls-Royce Armoured Car

When the Royal Naval Air Service (RNAS) was sent to France in 1914, it went with a very mixed array of aircraft and vehicles. After observing the Belgian Army using their armoured cars and how they were harassing the advancing German forces, the RNAS decided to join in, sending two Rolls-Royce Silver Ghost cars to a depot in Dunkirk for conversion into armoured cars. These were covered in boiler plate and armed with a machine-gun. This proved to be so successful that the Royal Navy agreed to develop the design into a proper armoured car using the Rolls-Royce Silver Ghost tourer as the chassis.

The chassis had its suspension strengthened and was fitted with 9mm/0.354in armour and a new large single turret. This turret was referred to as the "Admiralty Pattern" and would be fitted to all but the last model. It was shaped like a bishop's mitre and was fitted with a single heavy machine-gun, either a Vickers or a Maxim belt-fed 7.7mm/0.303in. In very hot weather the top could be removed to give better ventilation. The radiator had armoured doors and a large open space

was left behind the turret for the carriage of stores or another machine-gun. The first of these new cars arrived in France in late 1914 and were issued to the RNAS.

Once the "Race for the Sea" had reached the North Sea coast and the Western Front trench line was established, there was very little for the RNAS armoured cars to do. In 1915 the Navy handed over most of their cars to the British Army, which did not really want them initially as it had no idea how to use them. Some officers, like the Duke of Westminster and Colonel Lawrence (Lawrence of Arabia), took to these new weapons and, using them with dash and flair in the deserts of the Middle East, demonstrated to the army how to get the best from these machines. Seeing the potential but faced with several types of armoured car, the army decided to standardize on the Rolls-Royce and formed them into Light Armoured Motor (LAM) batteries of the Motor Machine-gun Corps. The Rolls-Royce armoured car was then sent to several other fronts during World War I, such as the North West Frontier in India, German South West Africa and Persia (later Iran). These 1914 Pattern

LEFT: A Rolls-Royce car bogged down in the mud of the Western Front. The car has been camouflaged in typical British World War I scheme. Note that the machine-gun has been removed. RIGHT: A Rolls-Royce 1924 Pattern Mk 1, with a modified turret, patrolling the border in Egypt in 1940.

LEFT: **This was originally a 1924 Pattern Rolls-Royce armoured car. By 1940 the chassis of these cars were worn out, so in August 1940 a number of Rolls-Royce cars were fitted with a Fordson chassis in Cairo, Egypt. These cars were armed with a Boys AT rifle, a Vickers machine-gun in the turret and a pair of Vickers K guns on the top of the turret.**

cars would remain in service officially until replaced by the Rolls-Royce 1920 Pattern.

This new car was placed into production after World War I and a number of the 1914 type were modernized to the 1920 Pattern. The wire-spoked wheels became disc-type, while the turret sides were made higher and louver doors were fitted to the radiator. The Air Ministry also produced these new 1920 Pattern cars for the RAF, but with wider tyres as they were operating in the deserts of Persia and Iraq. They would see service in many parts of the British Empire, being used to "police the Empire".

In 1924 a new pattern car went into production with a number of small changes and improvements. The body of the car was altered: a cupola for the vehicle commander was fitted to the turret and a new gun mounting was fitted to help close a weakness. A number of the 1920 cars were brought up to this

new pattern. Others were sold to various countries around the world and would see service in World War II.

There were a few problems with the Rolls-Royce, one being that there was a small fuel tank fitted in the dashboard and another that brakes were only fitted to the rear wheels, so stopping was a problem at times. These cars were still in active service with the British Army when war was declared in 1939 and in some parts of the Empire there were even a few 1914 Pattern cars in military use. In all, there was a total of 83 Rolls-Royce armoured cars remaining, most of them in Egypt. These were fitted with a new open-topped turret carrying a Boys anti-tank rifle instead of the machine-gun. A twin Lewis gun was mounted on a pintle mount on the back of the vehicle in an anti-aircraft role. These vehicles would, however, only remain in service for a few more years.

LEFT: **A Rolls-Royce Admiralty Pattern turreted car at a Forward Aid Station in France in 1915. The front of this car has been fitted with a pivoted hook to pull away barbed wire entanglements.**

Rolls-Royce 1920 Pattern Armoured Car

Country: UK
Entered service: 1920
Crew: 3
Weight: 3,861kg/3.8 tons
Dimensions: Length – 5.18m/17ft
    Height – 2.33m/7ft 5in
    Width – 1.9m/6ft 3in
Armament: Main – 7.7mm/0.303in Vickers
    machine-gun
    Secondary – Small arms
Armour: Maximum – 9mm/0.354in
Powerplant: Rolls-Royce 6-cylinder 60kW/80hp
    petrol engine
Performance: Speed – 80kph/50mph
    Range – 240km/150 miles

Sd Kfz 7/1 8-ton Half-Track

The design of these vehicles goes back to 1926 and was personally championed by Ernst Kniepkamp, head of the *Heereswaffenamt*. During 1932, it was decided to standardize the half-tracks into light (5,080kg/5-ton), medium (8,128kg/8-ton), and heavy (12,193kg/12-ton), while in 1934 two more half-tracks, a 1,016kg/1-ton and a 3,048kg/3-ton, were added to the list. The last one to be developed was the giant 18,289kg/18-ton half-track in 1936. The first of these vehicles to go into production and enter service with the German Army was the Sd Kfz 7 8-ton half-track. The army used the *Zugkraftwagen* (Towing Tractor) as their main artillery towing vehicle, but this half-track went on to be used for many other purposes for which it was never originally designed during World War II.

Development and design of the Sd Kfz 7 was undertaken by Krauss-Maffei (KM) based in Munich-Allach. They would be the largest single producer, building 6,129 of these vehicles with the remaining 5,880 being built by various other manufacturers. Production continued to the end of World War II. The vehicle had an 8-ton trailer-towing capacity, and the suspension was leaf-spring on the early models but by 1940 this had been changed to torsion bar which was much more satisfactory. The engine would not change from the original Maybach throughout the entire production run, but the horsepower it developed would increase from

89kW/120hp to 119kW/160hp. The tracks were made up of metal plates with rubber inserts, which had sealed lubricated needle-roller bearings in them. This helped to give the vehicle long track life and ensured low rolling resistance.

Some of the KM production run were converted into supply vehicles by removing the rear crew area and replacing this with a wooden flat bed. Another significant conversion of 442 units into Flakvierling vehicles started in late 1943. In this case the driver's bench seat was retained with a second one placed back to back and an anti-aircraft gun, either the quadruple 2cm/0.79in Flak 38 or the 3.7cm/1.46in Flak 36, mounted on the flat-bed. As the fighter bomber threat increased, armoured cabs were fitted to the vehicle to give the crew better protection while travelling, though not for the gun crew while the vehicle was in action.

TOP: **The first of the Flak half-tracks was the 1,016kg/1-ton Sd Kfz 10 which entered service in 1938. The single gun required a crew of seven men.** ABOVE: **The Sd Kfz 10 in action against a ground target. The exposed crew position can be clearly seen.**

LEFT: **The Sd Kfz 7 Flak half-track in action in Russia. These vehicles still had a very exposed crew position but with the introduction of the Flakvierling 38 the fire-power was quadrupled. These half-tracks proved to be deadly against both aircraft and ground targets.**

Sd Kfz 7/1 8-ton Half-Track

Country: Germany
Entered service: 1943
Crew: 10
Weight: 11,786kg/11.6 tons
Dimensions: Length – 6.85m/22ft 6in
 Height – 2.62m/8ft 7in
 Width – 2.4m/7ft 10in
Armament: Main – 4 x 2cm/0.79in Flak 38
 Secondary – Small arms
Armour: Maximum – 8mm/0.315in
Powerplant: Maybach HL 62 6-cylinder TUK 104kW/140hp petrol engine
Performance: Speed – 50kph/31mph
 Range – 250km/155 miles

Sd Kfz 8 and 9 Heavy Half-Tracks

These were two of the largest half-tracks produced by the Germans. In 1931, development was started by Daimler-Benz on the Sd Kfz 8, a 12,193kg/12-ton half-track. It was designed to be a heavy tractor for heavy artillery such as the 21cm/8.25in and the 10.5cm/4.13in Flak gun. The first 12-ton tractors were built by Krupp and Skoda from 1932 and between them they produced 315 of these vehicles. Daimler took over production from 1934, initially using the DB 7 chassis, and these vehicles would remain in production until late 1944 with the final mark of chassis used being the DB 11. In total, 3,973 of these half-tracks were built. In 1939, Krupp converted ten of these 12-ton half-tracks into self-propelled gun mounts by placing the 8.8cm/3.46in Flak 18 on the flat bed of the vehicle. The normal cab was done away with

and replaced with an armoured cupola for the driver, with ammunition stacked on the rear of the vehicle and the eight-man crew sitting unprotected under the gun. These weapons were built to destroy fortifications, as the gun had restricted movement and tended to destabilize the vehicle when fired.

The Sd Kfz 9 was an 18,289kg/18-ton heavy half-track; it was designed as a heavy tank recovery vehicle and as a prime mover for 24,385kg/24-ton recovery trailers. Four different models were built during the production run of 2,334 vehicles which would finish in late 1944. These vehicles were also used by the German engineers working for the bridging section. In 1940, 15 of these 18-ton half-tracks were converted into heavy self-propelled gun mounts for the 8.8cm/3.46in Flak 18. These guns were more manoeuvrable and stable on this

ABOVE: The Sd Kfz 9 was the largest of the half-tracks produced by the Germans. These vehicles proved to be very good and stable firing platforms. The crew cab has been armoured, but when the crew operate the gun they have no protection. The wire-mesh sides of the vehicle have to be folded down before the gun can go into action.

platform than on the Sd Kfz 8 and could be used for many tasks including anti-aircraft work. However, the main task of this vehicle, like the earlier 12-ton half-track version, was to destroy fortified positions. The engine and driver's position were covered in armour, with ammunition carried in a locker on the rear deck. There were also side-screens that were lowered when the gun was in action, increasing the rear deck area.

Sd Kfz 9 8.8cm SPG Half-Track

Country: Germany
Entered service: 1940
Crew: 9
Weight: 25,400kg/25 tons
Dimensions: Length – 9.32m/30ft 7in
  Height – 3.67m/12ft
  Width – 2.65m/8ft 8in
Armament: Main – 8.8cm/3.46in Flak 18
  Secondary – Small arms
Armour: Maximum – 14.5mm/0.57in
Powerplant: Maybach HL 108 TUKRM
  186kW/250hp 12-cylinder petrol engine
Performance: Speed – 50kph/31mph
  Range – 260km/162 miles

LEFT: This version of the Sd Kfz 8 half-track was produced in 1939 and was designed to be a fortress-buster and heavy AT gun. The vehicles were very tall and the gun crew were very exposed on the rear of the vehicle.

LEFT: **A 2.8cm/1.12in armed Sd Kfz 221 armoured car. The front of the turret has been cut away so the gun could be fitted on to the turret ring. The gunner has to stand high up in the turret to operate the gun.**
ABOVE: **An Sd Kfz 221 armoured car fitted with a 2.8cm/1.12in tapered-bore anti-tank gun. This vehicle has been fitted with wire-mesh anti-grenade screens. The gun was phased out of service due to the shortage of tungsten for the ammunition.**

Sd Kfz 221 Armoured Car

Development of this vehicle was started by the firm of Weserhütte in 1934 as a replacement for the Kfz 13. It entered service in 1936 with the reconnaissance forces of the German Army. Total production was 339 vehicles in two batches, the first of which comprised 143 vehicles.

The Sd Kfz 221 was built on the Horch 801 heavy passenger car chassis and had a crew of two. The driver sat in the front, while the turret was in the middle and the engine in the rear. The suspension was of independent coil spring type, with 4x4 drive and front-wheel steering. The construction was of rolled armour plate that was welded together at sharp angles, which made production slow and difficult. The armour

was little more than bullet-proof. The turret was a seven-sided truncated pyramid in which was mounted a single machine-gun. It had an open top but this could be covered by an anti-grenade screen. The first production run had very complicated vision ports that were cut from rolled armour plate but the second batch of vehicles had cast vision ports. No radio equipment was fitted to the vehicle as there was insufficient space in the main compartment and so communication was by semaphore flags.

In 1941 the PzB 39 anti-tank rifle was fitted in the turret alongside the machine-gun to improve the armament of the vehicle, but only a few of these conversions were carried out. In 1942 the machine-gun and the front of the turret

were removed so that a new larger gun, the 2.8cm/1.12in sPzB41 tapered-bore, light anti-tank gun, could be fitted. The gun was fixed above the driver's position forward of the turret and extended back into the modified turret as the new gun was breech-loaded.

The Sd Kfz 221 was used as a commander's vehicle and would be accompanied into action by radio cars and heavy armoured cars armed with a 2cm/0.79in gun. The combat life of this vehicle was extended to the end of World War II as a result of the 2.8cm/1.12in gun being fitted.

Sd Kfz 221 Armoured Car

Country: Germany
Entered service: 1936
Crew: 2
Weight: 4,064kg/4 tons
Dimensions: Length – 4.8m/14ft 7in
Height – 1.7m/5ft 6in
Width – 1.95m/6ft 4in
Armament: Main – 7.92mm/0.312in MG34 machine-gun
Secondary – Small arms
Armour: Maximum – 14mm/0.55in
Powerplant: Horch V8-108 8-cylinder 56kW/75hp petrol engine
Performance: Speed – 80kph/50mph
Range – 320km/200 miles

RIGHT: **The armoured body and turret were mounted on a standard German passenger car. Between the wheels is a large storage chest of vehicle tools. The turret is seven-sided and was normally fitted with wire-mesh anti-grenade screens.**

Sd Kfz 222 Armoured Car

The Germans started developing a new armoured car in 1934 with several criteria in mind: that the vehicle was reliable, that it could run off various grades of fuel, that it was a simple construction and that it had a good cross-country ability. The first of these new cars was the Sd Kfz 221, but this proved to be too small and lightly armed, so in 1937 development started on the Sd Kfz 222. Two standard chassis for four-wheeled armoured cars had been developed during 1936–7, the first of which had the engine mounted in the rear while the second had the engine mounted in the front. The latter type was used in the Sd Kfz 222.

The Sd Kfz 222 would become the standard light armoured car of the German Army until the end of World War II. This car entered service in 1938 and had heavier armament and a larger turret than the Sd Kfz 221. However, the new turret was still very small and cramped. It was open-topped but included a wire mesh screen that could be pulled over to protect the crew. This screen was divided in the middle and would hang over each side of the turret when open. When the screen was in the closed position, use of the main armament was even more difficult. The Sd Kfz 222 mounted one 2cm/0.79in cannon and a coaxial machine-gun, both of which could be elevated to 87 degrees so that the car could engage enemy aircraft. The cannon was mounted on a pintle which incorporated the elevation and traverse mechanism and had a firing button on the floor. At the rear of the vehicle the engine deck was sharply sloped to improve the driver's vision when reversing.

The Sd Kfz 222 suffered from a number of problems, particularly the poor cross-country performance and short range of the vehicle, which would lead to the car being removed from front-line service during the invasion of the Soviet Union in 1941. Production stopped in 1943 after 989 vehicles had been built.

TOP: **This Sd Kfz 222 armoured car has been caught in the open during an air attack. The turret has been removed from this vehicle and a larger wire mesh has been fitted.** ABOVE: **A mixed group of German armoured cars on exercise in 1938. The Sd Kfz 222 is on the right and has the turret-mounted screens in the raised position.**

Sd Kfz 222 Light Armoured Car

Country: Germany
Entered service: 1938
Crew: 3
Weight: 4,877kg/4.8 tons
Dimensions: Length – 4.8m/14ft 9in
Height – 2m/6ft 7in
Width – 1.95m/6ft 5in
Armament: Main – 2cm/0.79in KwK38
Secondary – 7.92mm/0.312in MG34 machine-gun
Armour: Maximum – 30mm/1.18in
Powerplant: Horch/Auto Union 108 8-cylinder 60kW/81hp petrol engine
Performance: Speed – 80kph/50mph
Range – 300km/187 miles

RIGHT: **This is the Sd Kfz 223 long-range radio car. This car uses the chassis, engine and the body of the Sd Kfz 222. The frame aerial folds back towards the rear of the vehicle and this aerial is in the down position.**

LEFT: **A standard Sd Kfz 231 coming down a slope. The long bonnet of the vehicle, which caused a number of problems for the driver, can clearly be seen. This car has the secondary hull machine-gun fitted.** ABOVE: **A heavy 6 Rad (six-wheeled) radio car. The frame aerial is fixed to the body of the vehicle at the rear and to two fixed uprights on the turret. The turret supports were quickly changed to a form that allowed the turret to rotate.**

Sd Kfz 231 Heavy Armoured Car 6 Rad

This German heavy armoured car was developed at the Kazan test centre in the Soviet Union in the 1920s. The first heavy car chassis to be developed were 8x8 and 10x10 but these were too expensive to be put into production. As a result the Germans decided to select a truck chassis already in production and fit an armoured body. The chassis selected was the Daimler-Benz 6x4, but other manufacturers' chassis were also used in production.

The Sd Kfz 231 had a front-mounted engine and the chassis was strengthened to take the extra weight of the armour. A second driving position was constructed in the rear of the fighting compartment so the vehicle could be driven in reverse. During trials it was discovered that the front axle needed strengthening and the radiators

needed to be improved. With these improvements, the car entered service with the German Army in 1932 and remained in production until 1935. Initially the armament was a single machine-gun in the turret, but this was quickly upgraded to a 2cm/0.79in KwK30 and coaxial MG34 machine-gun while there was provision for an anti-aircraft machine-gun on the roof of the turret. These vehicles did not perform particularly well as they were too heavy for the chassis, were underpowered, and had very poor cross-country ability. However, the car did provide the German Army with a very good training vehicle, as on hard roads the vehicle was as good as any of its contemporaries.

These armoured cars were used during the occupation of Austria in 1938 and of Czechoslovakia in 1939. They

would see combat during the invasion of Poland, and were used during the Blitzkrieg operations (the invasion of the Low Countries and France) in 1940. This vehicle looked very impressive in action and was used extensively in propaganda, receiving a lot of media coverage.

The Sd Kfz 232 was a long-range radio vehicle variant of the Sd Kfz 231. A basic Sd Kfz 231 was fitted with a large frame aerial fixed to the top of the vehicle and extra radio sets were installed in the fighting compartment.

Sd Kfz 231 Heavy Armoured Car 6 Rad

Country: Germany
Entered service: 1932
Crew: 4
Weight: 5,791kg/5.7 tons
Dimensions: Length – 5.61m/18ft 4in
　　　　　Height – 2.24m/7ft 4in
　　　　　Width – 1.85m/6ft 1in
Armament: Main – 2cm/0.79in KwK30 gun, and
　　　　　coaxial 7.92mm/0.312in MG34 machine-gun
　　　　　Secondary – 7.92mm/0.312in MG34
　　　　　machine-gun
Armour: Maximum – 8mm/0.315in
Powerplant: Daimler-Benz M09 6-cylinder
　　　　　48kW/65hp petrol engine
Performance: Speed – 65kph/40mph
　　　　　Range – 250km/150 miles

LEFT: **Behind the front wheel is an engine grill and beside that is a small hull hatch which gives access to the hull gunner's position. The spare wheel is carried on the rear of the car.**

Sd Kfz 231 Heavy Armoured Car 8 Rad

Almost as soon as the first six-wheeled armoured cars entered service, the expanding German Army realized that a better vehicle was needed and so development started in 1935. The new vehicle was to have eight wheels and a more powerful engine, based on the chassis of the Bussing-NAG 8x8 truck. The new car was given the same designation as the six-wheeled car except that 8 Rad (8-wheel) was added after the name.

This new armoured car was the most advanced cross-country vehicle at the time with a good road speed. However, the vehicle was very complex, the chassis was very complicated and the vehicle was very expensive and slow to produce. The eight-wheel drive and steering proved to be of great benefit in areas such as the Eastern Front and it was well able to cope with the Russian mud. In combat, the vehicle's most significant drawback was its height, which made it easier to observe from a distance. The engine was mounted in the rear of the vehicle and the rear deck was sloped to give a clear view from the rear driving position, allowing the car to be driven easily in reverse. Combat reports led to a number of changes to the design

in 1940, the main one being increased armour. Production started in 1937 and finished in 1942, by which time 1,235 had been built. It remained in service until the end of World War II.

The Sd Kfz 232 was the long-range radio version with extra radios fitted. A large frame aerial was fixed above the rear of the vehicle, while a small frame was fitted to the top of the turret with a pivot which allowed the turret freedom to traverse with the aerial attached.

The Sd Kfz 263 was a special command vehicle that had a fixed superstructure in place of the turret, extra radio sets and a large frame aerial, as in the Sd Kfz 232, attached to the top of the vehicle.

These vehicles came to prominence during the fighting in North Africa when they could range far and wide in the open expanses of the desert environment.

ABOVE: **A late production Sd Kfz 232 heavy radio car. This Sd Kfz 232 is fitted with a star aerial, which replaced the fixed frame aerial, attached to the rear of the car. The Sd Kfz 232 was fitted internally with extra radio equipment. The small rods at the front and rear of the vehicle help the driver judge the vehicle width.** BELOW: **A standard heavy Sd Kfz 231 armoured car. This car is fitted with an armoured shield on the front of the car, which had a secondary role as a storage bin. The hatch on the front of the vehicle gives access to the driver's controls.** BOTTOM LEFT: **This is a fixed-frame Sd Kfz 232 radio car on active service in Poland in 1939. The additional armoured shield has not as yet been fitted to the vehicle. The white cross has been smeared with mud.**

Sd Kfz 231 Heavy Armoured Car 8 Rad

Country: Germany
Entered service: 1937
Crew: 4
Weight: 8,433kg/8.3 tons
Dimensions: Length – 5.85m/19ft 2in
  Height – 2.34m/7ft 8in
  Width – 2.2m/7ft 3in
Armament: Main – 2cm/0.79in KwK38 gun and
  coaxial 7.92mm/0.312in MG34 machine-gun
  Secondary – Small arms
Armour: Maximum – 30mm/1.18in
Powerplant: Bussing-NAG L8V-GS 8-cylinder
  112kW/150hp petrol engine
Performance: Speed – 85kph/53mph
  Range – 150km/95 miles

LEFT AND ABOVE: **The main gun is offset to the right of the vehicle and there is a large cut-out next to the driver to allow the weapon to fire directly forwards. The gunsight periscope can be seen above the gun shield on the driver's side.**

Sd Kfz 233 7.5cm Heavy Armoured Car 8 Rad

The Sd Kfz 233 was manufactured by F. Schichau in Elbing from December 1942 to October 1943 with a total production run of 119 vehicles. These vehicles were issued to armoured reconnaissance units of the German Army to increase the offensive power of the unit and to act as a close-support weapon.

The basic chassis of this vehicle was the same as the Sd Kfz 231 8 Rad heavy armoured car, but otherwise there were substantial differences between the two. The Sd Kfz 233 had the turret removed while the roof of the fighting compartment was cut away to allow the gun crew to man the main weapon, but they were very exposed as the sides of the vehicle gave them little protection

when standing up. On later models the height of the side walls of the fighting compartment were raised by 20mm/ 0.79in which gave the crew better protection, but the interior of the fighting compartment was very cramped as, apart from the gun and mount, there were 55 rounds of ammunition for the main armament. The front right-hand side of the original Sd Kfz 231 design was cut away to make room for the 7.5cm/2.95in KwK37 short-barrelled, low-velocity tank gun. This weapon was salvaged from Panzer III and Panzer IV tanks when both types had their main armament upgraded to a longer gun. It had very limited traverse, an elevation of only 12 degrees in every plane, and could fire

high-explosive and armour-piercing ammunition. The driver remained in the front of the vehicle, but was offset to the left-hand side to create space for the gun mount while the rear driving position was retained as before. The frontal armour of the vehicle was upgraded to 30mm/1.18in as a result of feedback from combat reports of early operations with the basic armoured car.

These vehicles first saw action with the *Afrika Korps* during the campaign in North Africa and were well-liked by their crews for their reliability and ruggedness. The Sd Kfz 233 served on all fronts during World War II.

Sd Kfz 233 7.5cm Heavy Armoured Car 8 Rad

Country: Germany
Entered service: 1942
Crew: 3
Weight: 8,839kg/8.7 tons
Dimensions: Length – 5.85m/19ft 2in
  Height – 2.25m/7ft 5in
  Width – 2.2m/7ft 2in
Armament: Main – 7.5cm/2.95in KwK37
  low-velocity gun
  Secondary – 7.92mm/0.312in MG34
  machine-gun
Armour: Maximum – 30mm/1.18in
Powerplant: Bussing-NAG L8V-GS 8-cylinder
  134kW/180hp petrol engine
Performance: Speed – 85kph/53mph
  Range – 300km/190 miles

ABOVE: **The top of this vehicle has been covered with a canvas sheet, which is supported on two curved frames. This vehicle is also fitted front and back with width indicators.**

Sd Kfz 234/2 Puma Heavy Armoured Car

In August 1940, the German Army issued a requirement for a new heavy armoured car. This was to have a monocoque hull, i.e. no chassis, the wheels and suspension being attached directly to the hull of the vehicle. The car was also to be fitted with a Tatra diesel engine that would be both more powerful and more suited to operating in hot climates. The new vehicle would have increased armoured protection, increased internal fuel capacity, and in general better performance than previous armoured cars. The new body design was given the designation ARK and production lasted from September 1943 to September 1944. The original order was for 1,500 vehicles but this was reduced to 100 when the Sd Kfz 234/1 (earlier number but later into production) came into service. The first Puma cars had a range of 600km/373 miles but by improving the fuel capacity this was increased to 1,000km/621 miles. These changes would make this car the best all-round vehicle in its class during World War II.

The turret of the Puma was originally designed for the cancelled Leopard light tank. It was of an oval design with

ABOVE: **This is an Sd Kfz 234/1 armoured car and uses the same chassis as the 234/2. In 1943 an order was given that 50 per cent of Sd Kfz 234 production was to be armed with the 2cm/0.79in KwK38. The top of the turret has been fitted with the wire-mesh anti-grenade screen.**

steeply sloping sides, giving it an excellent ballistic shape, and there were two hatches in the roof. The main armament was fitted with a semi-automatic sliding breach and a hydro-pneumatic recoil system mounted above the gun. The barrel was terminated with a muzzle brake and the mantlet was a single piece casting known as a "*Saukopf*" (Sow's Head). The Puma was very similar in design to the Sd Kfz 231 but it had large single-piece side fenders with four built in storage boxes on each side.

The 100 Pumas were divided up into four units of 25 cars and sent to join four armoured regiments, with which they would see service on both the Eastern and Western Fronts. The superb Sd Kfz 234 series of cars were the only reconnaissance vehicles kept in production after March 1945 with 100 of the various marks being produced each month until the end of the war.

ABOVE: **This vehicle is fitted with a Saukopf gun mantlet, and there are three smoke dischargers on each side of the turret. The side panniers are now made in one piece and give more storage space.**

LEFT: **The exhaust for the car is mounted on the rear of the side pannier, just above the rear wheel. This car belonged to a Panzer Grenadier regiment in Normandy.**

Sd Kfz 234/2 5cm Puma Heavy Armoured Car

Country: Germany
Entered service: 1943
Crew: 4
Weight: 11,928kg/11.74 tons
Dimensions: Length – 6.8m/22ft 4in
 Height – 2.28m/7ft 6in
 Width – 2.4m/7ft 10in
Armament: Main – 5cm/1.97in KwK39/1 anti-tank gun and coaxial 7.92mm/0.312in MG42 machine-gun
 Secondary – Small arms
Armour: Maximum – 30mm/1.18in
Powerplant: Tatra 103 12-cylinder 164kW/220hp diesel engine
Performance: Speed – 85kph/53mph
 Range – 1,000km/621 miles

Sd Kfz 234 7.5cm Heavy Support Armoured Cars

ABOVE LEFT: **The driver's position is now in the middle of the front of the car and the gun is mounted above the driver. The height of the armour has been increased to give the crew better protection.** ABOVE: **An Sd Kfz 234/4 armoured car armed with the PaK40 AT gun which went into production in December 1944.**

In September 1943, half of all the new Sd Kfz 234 chassis produced were ordered to be converted into support vehicles for the reconnaissance forces. These cars were to mount the 7.5cm/2.95in KwK37 to enable them to act as close-support vehicles. The KwK37 had been removed from the Panzer IV in 1942 when the tank was upgunned and these weapons had been placed into store until required, so this seemed a quick and easy way to give the reconnaissance force some real hitting power on the new chassis.

From June 1944, it was decided that only one in four vehicles would be converted in this way. Then in November 1944, Hitler ordered that the PaK40 should be fitted to these vehicles, turning them into self-propelled anti-tank

mounts. It was consequently often called the PaK-Wagen by the troops. In December 1944, production of the Sd Kfz 234/3 was stopped in favour of the new vehicle, the Sd Kfz 234/4, which would remain in production until March 1945. The Germans produced 88 of the Sd Kfz 234/3 and 89 of the Sd Kfz 234/4. The fighting compartment of both vehicles was open-topped but the sides were raised to give the crew some protection from small arms fire and shell splinters. The PaK40 was mounted on a pedestal mount and had limited traverse. It was raised up in the fighting compartment so that the driver could remain in his position under the gun in the centre of the front of the vehicle. One significant shortcoming with the Sd Kfz 234/4 was that it could only

carry 12 rounds of ammunition; the Sd Kfz 234/3 on the other hand carried 50 rounds of ammunition. The crew in both vehicles was increased from three to four, so that the driver was not necessary as part of the gun crew and could remain in position.

These heavy-support armoured cars were mainly issued to units in the West, but not always to the Panzer divisions. A number of these vehicles were sent to Normandy to help in attempting to stop the Allied invasion of France, but were easy prey for Allied aircraft.

Sd Kfz 234/3 7.5cm Heavy Support Armoured Car

Country: Germany
Entered service: 1944
Crew: 4
Weight: 11,684kg/11.5 tons
Dimensions: Length – 6m/19ft 8in
　　Height – 2.21m/7ft 3in
　　Width – 2.4m/7ft 10in
Armament: Main – 7.5cm/2.95in KwK37 gun
　　Secondary – 7.92mm/0.312in MG34 or
　　MG42 machine-gun
Armour: Maximum – 30mm/1.2in
Powerplant: Tatra 103 12-cylinder 164kW/220hp
　　diesel engine
Performance: Speed – 85kph/53mph
　　Range – 1,000km/621 miles

LEFT: **The PaK40 takes up most of the room in the fighting compartment. It is mounted on a pedestal mount behind the driver and retains its original gun shield. The gun crew were very exposed when operating the gun.**

Sd Kfz 250 Half-Track Armoured Personnel Carrier

This vehicle had its roots in the operational requirements of the German Army in the mid-1930s which led to the manufacture of the Sd Kfz 251 3,048kg/3-ton half-track. The Sd Kfz 250 was produced by two companies; the Demag AG Company of Wetter in the Ruhr built the chassis while Bussing-NAG built the body of the vehicle. There was a total production run of 5,930 of these carriers, which were designed to transport a half-section of infantry in support of the reconnaissance units. Trials started in 1939 and although delays held up production until 1940, a number of these vehicles were in service with the German Army by the time of the invasion of France.

The Sd Kfz 250 was an open-topped vehicle which could carry five men and a driver. In the rear of the vehicle was a single door, which made debussing slow. The front wheels were not powered and so made steering heavy. When a sharp turn was made using the steering

wheel, this action would automatically engage the required track-brake and so help the vehicle make the sharp turn. Two other variations were being built at the same time as the basic vehicle. The first was an ammunition carrier for the StuG batteries while the other vehicle was a signals car that could carry two large radios and had a large frame aerial over the top. In 1943, the Sd Kfz 250 was completely redesigned to make production simpler and faster. The angled sides of the crew compartment were now flattened and made from a single piece of armour plate.

These half-tracks were built in 15 official variants and many other modifications were carried out by vehicle crews in the field. In one variant, an armoured cover was fitted over the crew compartment and a turret placed on top. These vehicles replaced the 4x4 Sd Kfz 222 armoured car in front-line service. Among the other variants there were a mortar carrier, a telephone

exchange, an ammunition carrier, a command car and a self-propelled gun mount. These vehicles would remain in service until the end of World War II.

ABOVE: **This Sd Kfz 250 is "under new ownership" as it is being driven by British soldiers. Half the gun shield is missing along with the machine-gun. The half-track is passing over a pontoon bridge.**

LEFT: **This Sd Kfz 250 half-track is on active service in the desert of North Africa. It has had its forward firepower increased by the fitting of a PaK35/36.**

RIGHT: **This vehicle replaced the Sd Kfz 222 wheeled armoured car in service. The rear of the vehicle was roofed over and the turret from the armoured car was placed into the roof of the half-track. This vehicle has a crew of three and would remain in service until 1945.**

Sd Kfz 250/1 Half-Track Armoured Personnel Carrier

Country: Germany
Entered service: 1940
Crew: 1 plus 5 infantry
Weight: 5,893kg/5.8 tons
Dimensions: Length – 4.56m/15ft
  Height – 1.98m/6ft 6in
  Width – 1.95m/6ft 5in
Armament: Main – 2 x 7.92mm/0.312in MG34
  machine-gun
  Secondary – Small arms
Armour: Maximum – 14.5mm/0.57in
Powerplant: Maybach HL42 6-cylinder
  74.6kW/100hp petrol engine
Performance: Speed – 59.5kph/37mph
  Range – 299km/186 miles

LEFT AND ABOVE: **The Sd Kfz 251 on the left has the normal frontal armament of a single machine-gun, while the vehicle above has had the PaK35/36 fitted to increase the fire power of the half-track.**

Sd Kfz 251 Medium Half-Track

During the development of the Panzer Division in Germany throughout the 1930s it was very quickly realized that an armoured personnel carrier would be required and that this would have to have good cross-country ability to keep pace with the tanks. Development of a suitable vehicle started in 1937 with Hanomag producing the chassis and Bussing-NAG building the body. Production started in 1939 and initially three marks, A, B, and C, were built with 4,650 vehicles produced in total, but by far the largest production run was of the Ausf D of which 10,602 were built. This mark would remain in production until the end of World War II. General Guderian was unhappy with the original design as he anticipated that the Panzer Grenadiers would occasionally have to fight from inside their vehicles making the large open top a great weakness.

The chassis of the Sd Kfz 251 was very strong and well-protected and this gave the whole vehicle great strength. The body of the vehicle was bolted to the chassis in the early marks and was made in two sections with each section being bolted together just behind the driver's position. The body of Ausf A, B and C had a good ballistic shape but were very difficult and slow to produce. Hanomag and Bussing-NAG could not keep up with demand so other manufacturers were brought in to speed up production. The engine was at the front with the driver and commander's position behind and this area had an armoured roof on which a machine-gun was mounted. The platoon commander's vehicle would have a 3.7cm/1.46in anti-tank gun mounted on the roof instead of the machine-gun. The infantry section sat in the back on two benches running the length of the rear area with the men facing inwards. Two large doors giving easy accessibility for the infantry section were positioned at the rear, and above these was a mount for an anti-aircraft machine-gun. There were no brakes fitted to the front wheels; these were fitted instead to the driving sprockets of the track section. The tracks were light and lubricated, and each track shoe was fitted with a rubber pad which helped prolong the track life of the vehicle. Each road wheel had a rubber tyre and was grouped in a pair, being supported on a torsion bar type suspension system.

The last type of the Sd Kfz 251 was the Ausf D. This went into production in 1944 and was a major redesign of the basic vehicle. The Ausf D had a greatly simplified construction with the use of larger flat armour plates to build the body, which was now of an all-welded construction. The rear door was built with a reverse slope and the storage boxes along the sides had become part of the main body of the vehicle.

ABOVE: **This knocked-out Sd Kfz 251 Ausf D is a late version and has its engine covers in the open position.**

LEFT: **This German vehicle is symbolic of Blitzkrieg and would remain in service with other countries for many years after the war. The Sd Kfz 251 Ausf A has a large number of angled plates and this made production slow. Three storage bins are fitted on each side of the vehicle between the top of the tracks and the body of the vehicle.**

There were no less than 22 official variations of the basic half-track design. Many were simply changes in the armament fitted to the vehicle while others included command, communications, ambulance and observation types. The most powerful variant of these vehicles was the Sd Kfz 251/1 *Stuka zum Fuss* (Dive-bomber on Foot) which was more commonly known as the Infantry Stuka. Racks were fitted to the sides of the vehicle and three 28cm/11in or 32cm/12.6in rockets, which could be fitted with either high-explosive or incendiary warheads, could be mounted on each side. They were used to demolish strongpoints or large structures and also to give support to an attack on an enemy position. The last version was the Sd Kfz 251/22 which mounted the PaK40 7.5cm/2.95in anti-tank gun. However, the sheer weight of the weapon overloaded the half-track and firing the gun also put a great strain on the suspension of the vehicle.

Skoda in Czechoslovakia was one of the manufacturers of the Sd Kfz 251 and it was decided after World War II to keep it in production for the Czechoslovakian Army as the firm was tooled up to build this vehicle. With this second lease of life the vehicle would remain in service until 1980.

ABOVE: **This picture clearly shows the low profile of the Sd Kfz 251 Ausf A. To increase the frontal armour of the vehicle a common practice was to attach spare track-link to the front.** LEFT: **This is the post-war version of the Sd Kfz 251 that continued to be made in Czechoslovakia after World War II. This vehicle was known as the OT-810 and would remain in service for many years.**

Sd Kfz 251/1 Ausf A Medium Half-Track

Country: Germany
Entered service: 1939
Crew: 2 plus 10 infantry
Weight: 7,935kg/7.81 tons
Dimensions: Length – 5.8m/19ft
    Height – 1.75m/5ft 9in
    Width – 2.1m/6ft 10in
Armament: Main – 2 x 7.92mm/0.312in MG34
    machine-guns
    Secondary – Small arms
Armour: Maximum – 15mm/0.59in
Powerplant: Maybach HL42 TUKRM 6-cylinder
    89kW/120hp petrol engine
Performance: Speed – 53kph/33mph
    Range – 300km/185 miles

Sd Kfz 251 Support Vehicles

The Sd Kfz 251 went through many conversions into various close-support vehicles for the German Army and Luftwaffe. Some of these conversions were undertaken in a great hurry and proved less than satisfactory such as the Sd Kfz 251/17 Flak conversion, that was modified in the field and turned out to be of little use.

In March 1942 Bussing-NAG were instructed to develop a close-support version of their half-track, as the German infantry required better support in their attacks particularly if StuGs were unavailable. Two test vehicles were sent to the Eastern Front in June 1942 and proved to be very good, resulting in an order being placed that month for another 150 Sd Kfz 251/9s. These vehicles mounted the short 7.5cm/2.95in KwK40 gun from the old Panzer III and

Panzer IV. The co-driver's position was dispensed with as the weapon was mounted in this space and the roof and front vision port were removed so the gun could sit next to the driver. However, this was a very complicated conversion so the gun mount was redesigned in early 1944 so it could also be fitted to other vehicles such as the Sd Kfz 250. The new mount sat on top of the existing body of the vehicle and gave the crew extra protection.

The Sd Kfz 251/16 was a flamethrower vehicle. It was fitted with two flame guns and carried 700 litres/154 gallons of flame fuel. The rear door was fixed in the closed position as one of the fuel tanks was positioned in front of it. The vehicle carried enough fuel for 80 two-second bursts from the flame gun which had a range of 35m/115ft. These entered service

ABOVE LEFT: **The exhaust system for the vehicle is mounted between the front wheel and the tracks. As there was only a crew of three, there was a lot of room for ammunition and equipment storage in the rear of the vehicle.** ABOVE: **Guns from old Panzer IV tanks were used to arm vehicles such as this.**

in January 1943 and most were sent to the Eastern Front. They proved to be very useful in street fighting. Other conversions produced command, radio, ambulance, engineering and ammunition carriers. The Sd Kfz 251 was a vehicle that was well-liked by its crews and crucially was capable of being adapted to many uses on the battlefield.

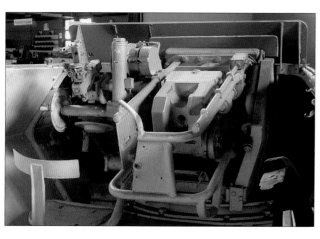

LEFT: **This is the working end of the 7.5cm/2.95in KwK L/24 gun. The gun was taken from the PzKpfw IV when these tanks were upgunned. It was placed on a simple cradle in the half-track, making for a fast and easy conversion.**

Sd Kfz 251/9 Close Support Vehicle

Country: Germany
Entered service: 1942
Crew: 3
Weight: 8,738kg/8.6 tons
Dimensions: Length – 5.98m/19ft 7in
  Height – 2.07m/6ft 9in
  Width –2.1m/6ft 11in
Armament: Main – 7.5cm/2.95in KwK37 L/24 gun
  Secondary – 2 x 7.92mm/0.312in MG34 machine-guns
Armour: Maximum – 15mm/0.59in
Powerplant: Maybach HL42 TUKRM 6-cylinder 89kW/120hp petrol engine
Performance: Speed – 53kph/33mph
  Range – 300km/186 miles

LEFT: **This vehicle uses the M40 chassis which was the first type used. The main visual difference between the two chassis is that the track-guard does not run the length of the vehicle in the M40.** ABOVE: **This SPG uses the M42 chassis and was the final version of this vehicle. The gun has a very distinctive "pepper-pot" muzzle brake.**

Semovente M42 DA 75/18 Self-Propelled Gun

This was an excellent self-propelled gun/howitzer and was the first Italian vehicle to be produced as part of a series during World War II. The M42 was tested in early 1941 and went into production the same year with the first vehicles being issued to service units later that year. The first unit to receive these new vehicles was the Ariete Division who initially used it in North Africa in early 1942. Originally intended to fulfil a self-propelled artillery role within the armoured division, they were more often deployed in an anti-tank role. At this time, these vehicles were the best armed self-propelled guns in North Africa and could easily outgun any British or German tank.

The first vehicles in this series were built on the M13/40 tank chassis, but later the chassis of the M14/41 was used, with production being stopped in 1943. The first order was for 200 vehicles and this was met in full, with a further order for 500 being placed in 1943. These new vehicles were to be equipped with the 75/34, a longer gun. The M42 could carry 100 rounds of 75mm/2.95in ammunition.

However, delays in putting the new P40 tank into production resulted in the unused guns being fitted to the M42, which then became the M42M. None of these vehicles were issued to the Italian Army before Italy's surrender but they were captured and used by the Germans.

Each M42 battery was given a command vehicle built on the M13/40 chassis. This was basically a turretless tank chassis that was initially armed with twin 8mm/0.315in machine-guns mounted on the right-hand side of the vehicle. The twin guns were later replaced by a single 13.5mm/0.53in heavy machine-gun.

When Italy surrendered in 1943, the Germans took over the production facilities for the M42 as they had found this vehicle to be very good. They also took 292 of them into German service, common practice with captured weapons they admired. These vehicles would see constant service during 1944 in Italy and the Balkans and by January 1945 only 93 were left in action after months of heavy fighting.

ABOVE: **The driver's position in the Semovente M42. The side of the main armament sits beside the driver's head. The large lever in the picture is the firing handle.**

Semovente M42 DA 75/18 SPG

Country: Italy
Entered service: 1942
Crew: 3
Weight: 15,240kg/15 tons
Dimensions: Length – 5.04m/16ft 6in
  Height – 1.85m/6ft 1in
  Width – 2.23m/7ft 4in
Armament: Main – 75mm/2.95in model 35 gun/howitzer
  Secondary – 8mm/0.315in Breda model 38
Armour: Maximum – 50mm/1.97in
Powerplant: Spa 15 TM41 8-cylinder 138kW/185hp petrol engine
Performance: Speed – 38kph/24mph
  Range – 230km/143 miles

LEFT: **The Canadian Ram tank was used for this conversion. The Ram was a right-hand-drive vehicle and so the British crews took to it quickly. The driver's hatch on this vehicle is in the open position. The fighting compartment is covered with a canvas roof giving the crew some protection from the weather.**

Sexton 25pdr Self-Propelled Gun

In 1942, the Americans attempted to improve the M7 Priest by replacing the existing armament with a British 25pdr gun. The "pulpit" was retained to give the vehicle some close-quarter protection, and the gun was mounted well over on the right-hand side of the fighting compartment. There were a number of delays in the development programme when the first live-firing of the gun destroyed the gun mount. By the time the vehicle was ready for a second test firing, the Canadians had come up with the Sexton and so in March 1943 the British cancelled the American project in favour of the simpler Canadian vehicle.

The Canadian Department of National Defence selected the Ram tank to act as a chassis for the 25pdr gun to meet the British Army requirement for a self-propelled gun. The pilot model was finished in late 1942 and it proved to be very successful in tests. Production started at the Montreal Locomotive Works in early 1943 and continued until 1945, by which time 2,150 had been built. Originally designated the "25-pounder Ram Carrier", it was renamed following Royal Artillery tradition and given the religious name "Sexton". The 25pdr was mounted just off the centreline to the left-hand side of the fighting compartment. The driver's position was on the right-

LEFT AND RIGHT: **The driver's position in the vehicle is very cramped and yet very light, as it is open at the top into the fighting compartment. The dashboard has the minimum of gauges, and in the centre are the track control levers. The large doors on the rear of the vehicle give access to the radial engine.**

hand side of the fighting compartment down in the bottom of the tank chassis, the driver being below the level of the gun. The fighting compartment was constructed out of 12mm/0.47in armour plate, with an open back and low sides extending to just above waist height. It was also open-topped and exposed to the elements. However, a number of Sexton batteries had steel loops made in field workshops so that a canvas cover or tent could be placed over the fighting compartment. The front of the fighting compartment was protected by 25mm/0.98in armour plate with the final drive housing being in three pieces that were bolted together.

The 25pdr gun had a traverse of 25 degrees to the left and 15 degrees to the right, while the elevation range was plus 40 degrees to minus 9 degrees. The recoil of the gun was also restricted to 51cm/1ft 8in compared with 91cm/3ft of the standard 25pdr. The main ammunition storage was under the floor of the fighting compartment and held 112 rounds, but there was also one small ready-to-use locker on the rear wall of the fighting compartment. On a later version of the Sexton this housing was changed to a single casting and the running gear was modified. The suspension system was also changed on the Sexton II from an M3 style to an M4 trailing arm type, and the Canadian dry pin track was used. The rear deck of the vehicle carried box structures in each corner for batteries and an auxiliary generator.

The first 124 vehicles produced were designated Sexton I, but following a number of modifications the improved vehicle became the Sexton II. The Sexton I had no provision for anti-aircraft machine-guns on the vehicle and this was addressed with the Sexton II with the addition of two Bren light machine-guns. A number of Sextons also had a 12.7mm/50cal machine-gun fitted to the front left-hand corner of the fighting compartment as a field modification.

Some Sextons were converted to Gun Position Officers (GPO) vehicles with one of these being issued to each Sexton battery. This conversion involved the removal of the gun and most of the internal fittings to provide space for a map table, extra field telephones, and radios.

The Sexton would become the standard medium self-propelled gun used by the British and Canadian armies in World War II. It first saw action with the 8th Army in Italy and was used throughout the campaign in northern Europe. Some British units that were converted from the Priest to the Sexton had very few days to practise with their new equipment before going into action on June 6, 1944. A number of Sexton units were allocated "run-in shooting" missions (firing at shore targets from the landing craft bringing them in) as they landed on the D-Day beaches. This was intended to aid in the suppression of the German beach defences but, perhaps not surprisingly, was not very accurate.

ABOVE: **This Sexton has had an additional machine-gun fitted to the front of the fighting compartment above the driver. The front of the vehicle is three separate pieces bolted together. This gun has been assigned to the 11th Armoured Division.** BELOW: **The main weapon of the Sexton is the British 25pdr gun. The breach of this weapon slides vertically and the red wheels are the elevation and traverse controls.**

Sexton 25pdr SPG

Country: Canada
Entered service: 1942
Crew: 6
Weight: 25,908kg/25.5 tons
Dimensions: Length – 6.12m/20ft 1in
Height – 2.43m/8ft
Width – 2.71m/8ft 11in
Armament: Main – 11kg/25pdr C Mk II or III
Secondary – 2 x 7.7mm/0.303in Bren light machine-gun
Armour: Maximum – 32mm/1.26in
Powerplant: Continental 9-cylinder 298kW/400hp radial petrol engine
Performance: Speed – 38kph/24mph
Range – 200km/125 miles

LEFT: **The height of this vehicle is very apparent and led to a number of problems during combat. The driver's position is on the left-hand side of the vehicle. These SPGs were issued to six Panzer divisions in 1940.** BELOW: **The gun and its unaltered carriage were placed on to the top of the Panzer I. The open rear and open top of the gun shield give the crew very little protection from either the weather or small-arms fire.**

slG33 15cm Infantry Support Self-Propelled Gun

This was the first self-propelled gun to see service in the German Army of World War II, and valuable experience was gained from its combat performance. It was an improvised vehicle manufactured to an army specification for a fully tracked vehicle that could give close support to the infantry. These vehicles were built by Alkett in 1939 and entered service in time to take part in the Blitzkrieg operation throughout northern France and the Low Countries in 1940. While it represented a great step forward for the military, it had significant faults and only 38 of these vehicles were built.

The chassis was that of the Panzer I Ausf B with the turret removed and the superstructure left in place. At this time,

the Panzer I was already being replaced by bigger and better tanks thus providing the chassis to mount the slG33. A large box structure, 1.83m/6ft in height constructed of 10mm/0.394in armour was built on the vehicle. This box was open-topped, with two small doors on the rear which did not meet in the middle but only partially closed the opening. The gun, which retained its wheels and box trail, was mounted inside the box on the top of the tank superstructure.

This SPG could be brought into action very quickly and open fire instantly. It also proved to be very efficient in service. However, it is worth considering that all infantry guns were horse-drawn until this vehicle made its appearance, and so it did not have any equivalent competition.

The vehicle was not designated an Sd Kfz number and had a number of major faults. At over 2.74m/9ft high, the vehicle was very tall which gave it a high centre of gravity. It was also overloaded which placed a great strain on the suspension and contributed to the poor cross-country ability.

These guns were issued to Heavy Infantry Gun Companies 701–706, in early 1940. They would remain in service until 1943 when the last unit, the 704th of the 5th Panzer Division, was refitted.

---

slG33 15cm Infantry Support SPG

Country: Germany
Entered service: 1940
Crew: 4
Weight: 8,636kg/8.5 tons
Dimensions: Length – 4.42m/14ft 6in
Height – 3.35m/11ft
Width – 2.6m/8ft 6in
Armament: Main – 15cm/5.91in slG33 L/11 gun
Secondary – Small arms
Armour: Maximum – 13mm/0.51in
Powerplant: Maybach NL38 TKRM 6-cylinder
75kW/100hp petrol engine
Performance: Speed – 40kph/25mph
Range – 140km/87 miles

LEFT: **An improved mount for the slG 15cm was built using the Panzer II chassis. An extra road wheel had to be fitted to each side of the vehicle, which had been widened and lengthened. Only 12 of these vehicles were built and all were sent to the *Afrika Korps* in North Africa.**

Staghound Armoured Car

The Staghound was an American designed and built vehicle that was destined never to be used by the US Army. All the cars of this type that were produced were sent to the British and Commonwealth armies. The design had its origins in a US Army requirement for a heavy armoured car, which was developed in two forms – one with six wheels (T17) and one with four wheels (T17E1). The British Tank Mission to America saw the two cars, which had been heavily influenced by British experience in battle, selected the T17E1 and placed an initial order for 300 vehicles. Production started in early 1942 with the first vehicles entering service in later the same year. In British service, the vehicle was called the Staghound Mk I.

The Staghound was a large well-armoured vehicle having a 37mm/

1.46in gun and coaxial 7.62mm/0.3in machine-gun in the turret. In combat it proved to be very reliable, easy to maintain and had good cross-country ability. It had a fully automatic hydraulic transmission with two engines mounted side by side in the rear of the vehicle, and two 173-litre/38-gallon jettison fuel tanks to increase the vehicle's range. The vehicle had no chassis with the suspension parts attaching directly to the hull. Two further machine-guns were fitted to the vehicle, one in the front next to the driver and one on a pintle mount on the rear of the turret for anti-aircraft use. However, the Staghound was found to be too large, heavy and unwieldy for fighting in northern Europe and Italy compared to the British Daimler armoured car and was not well-liked by its British and Commonwealth crews.

The British were to produce three more versions of the Staghound. The Mk II was a close-support version with a short 75mm/ 2.95in gun mounted in a new turret. The Mk III was an attempt to upgun the Staghound by fitting the Crusader III 75mm/2.95in gun turret to the vehicle, turning it into a wheeled tank. The last conversion was the Staghound AA vehicle, armed with two 12.7mm/0.5in machine-guns in a small open-topped turret. None of these conversions was produced in large numbers.

Staghound Mk I Armoured Car

Country: USA
Entered service: 1942
Crew: 5
Weight: 14,122kg/13.9 tons
Dimensions: Length – 5.49m/18ft
　　　　Height – 2.36m/7ft 9in
　　　　Width – 2.69m/8ft 10in
Armament: Main – 37mm/1.46in ATG,
　　　　and coaxial 7.62mm/0.3in machine-gun
　　　　Secondary – 2 x 7.62mm/0.3in machine-guns
Armour: Maximum – 22mm/0.866in
Powerplant: 2 x GMC 270 6-cylinder 72kW/97hp petrol engine
Performance: Speed – 89kph/55mph
　　　　Range – 724km/450 miles

Sturmgeschutz III Self-Propelled Gun

The Sturmgeschutz III (StuG III) was an excellent vehicle performing well as a close-support weapon and, with its ability to take larger guns, would remain in service for most of World War II. It was relatively cheap and easy to produce when compared with a tank and this proved to be important in wartime Germany. Towards the end of the war, the StuG III would also have to fill gaps left by the shortage of tanks in the Panzer divisions – a role for which it was never designed – and was without doubt one of the most important vehicles the Germans produced in World War II.

The order to develop a close-support vehicle was given in June 1937 and by January 1940 the resulting vehicle was placed into production and given the designation of StuG III Ausf A. Two companies, Alkett and MIAG, undertook most of the production but these would be joined by MAN at times when extra output capacity was required. It used the same chassis, suspension and engine as the Panzer III Ausf F. The upper hull and turret were removed and replaced with a thick carapace of armour. A short 7.5cm/2.95in gun was mounted in the front of the vehicle and offset to the right providing space for the driver who sat on the left next to the main armament. These basic positions would not change throughout its career, even after a number of improvements. The Ausf B had improvements to the engine while Ausf C and D had improvements to the superstructure of the fighting compartment. The Ausf E was the last of the short-barrelled StuG IIIs and it was the first model to have a close-support machine-gun fitted to the upper hull. The standard gun up until then had been the 7.5cm/2.95in L/24 gun (the length of the barrel was 24 times the calibre).

TOP: **This was the most numerous StuG produced during World War II. The vehicle was made up of the Panzer III chassis and running gear. The superstructure was in two parts, with the main armament trunnioned between. The shield on the roof of the vehicle is for the close-support machine-gun.**
ABOVE: **The travel lock is mounted on the front of the vehicle under the gun barrel. When the vehicle was travelling any distance the barrel would be locked in place to save the gun mounting from damage.**

From April 1942 onwards when the Ausf F entered service, the gun length increased to L/43, and this was further improved in June when the gun was changed to the L/48. This gave the StuG III a very potent anti-tank capability that would serve the vehicle well for the remainder of the war.

The last version of the StuG III was the Ausf G that entered service in January 1943 and would remain in production and active service until the end of the war. The Ausf G had a number of improvements to the superstructure, such as the addition of a commander's cupola with periscopes and sloping of the side plates. Other modifications were the introduction of the *Saukopf* (Sow's Head) gun mantlet in late 1943, and

LEFT: **The front of the fighting compartment had extra armour bolted to it, as on the left-hand side of the picture. In the middle is the gun mantlet and on the right is the driver's vision slit.** ABOVE: **This StuG III has had several bolt-on plates added to the front of the vehicle to increase its armour thickness.**

LEFT: **Two British soldiers are looking at the hits on this StuG III which has been struck four times on the lower front hull plate. The gun mantlet has collapsed into the vehicle.**

the addition of a coaxial machine-gun in early 1944 as these vehicles were now engaging enemy infantry at close-quarters.

Variants of the StuG III included an assault howitzer which mounted a 10.5cm/4.13in gun for close-support duties. Alkett manufactured a total of 1,211 of these vehicles from October 1942 to March 1945.

From 1943 onwards, the StuG III was fitted with two further defensive measures. February 1943 saw the introduction of *Schürzen* (skirts). Made from wire mesh or metal plates, these helped stop anti-tank shells from penetrating the side of the vehicle where the armour was thin. However, the procurement of wire mesh proved difficult and so side-skirts of this type were not produced in great numbers. The second defensive measure was the introduction of *Zimmerit*. This was

a protective coating, 3–5mm/0.1–0.2in thick, that covered the hull and superstructure and was intended to prevent Russian troops from attaching magnetic mines or shaped charges to the hull of the vehicle. Initially this coating was to be made of tar but AFV crews rejected this due to the fire hazard, so a thin layer of cement paste was put on the vehicle instead, giving it a very distinctive finish.

During World War II, 74 StuG units were formed and these saw active service on all fronts. Total war production was 10,306 Sturmgeschutz III vehicles.

ABOVE: **This is one of the first StuG III prototype vehicles to enter service and has an open-topped fighting compartment. The vehicle is armed with the short 75cm/2.95in gun.**

Sturmgeschutz III SPG Ausf G

Country: Germany
Entered service: January 1943
Crew: 4
Weight: 24,282kg/23.9 tons
Dimensions: Length – 6.77m/22ft 3in
　　　　　Height – 2.16m/7ft 1in
　　　　　Width – 2.95m/9ft 8in
Armament: Main – 7.5cm/2.95in StuK40
　　　　　L/48 gun
　　　　　Secondary – 2 x 7.92mm/0.312in MG42
　　　　　machine-guns
Armour: Maximum – 80mm/3.15in
Powerplant: Maybach HL 120 TRM 12-cylinder
　　　　　197.6kW/265hp petrol engine
Performance: Speed – 40kph/24.9mph
　　　　　Range – 165km/102 miles

Sturmgeschutz IV Self-Propelled Gun

In February 1943, the Krupp company was asked to look at a proposal for mounting the StuG III superstructure on the Panzer IV chassis (8 BW). However, instead of using a basic Panzer IV chassis Krupp used a new development, the 9 BW chassis, which would have sloped frontal armour and much thicker side armour. These alterations would cause great disruption to StuG and Panzer IV production lines and resulted in no great saving in either the weight or the materials used in the new vehicle. These disruptions were deemed intolerable at this time, the spring of 1943, as the war was showing signs of turning against Germany.

In late November 1943, the Alkett factory was badly damaged during a bombing raid and production of the StuG III suffered. Hitler insisted that the shortfall must be made up and therefore some of the Panzer IV facilities at the Krupp factory in Magdeburg were reassigned to the production of a StuG IV using StuG III superstructures. The new StuG IV was

ABOVE LEFT: **A column of StuG IVs stopped in the road. The vehicles are all fitted with the Saukopf mantle, and are carrying spare road wheels on the side of the vehicle.** ABOVE: **The front of this StuG has been covered with various lengths of spare track.**

shown to Hitler on December 16, 1943, and he approved the vehicle, insisting that it was put into production immediately. An additional impetus was provided by combat reports stating that the Panzer IV was having a hard time on the battlefield, and the losses from battles such as Kursk also had to be made up as quickly as possible.

The Panzer IV chassis was combined with the super-structure of the StuG III G but due to the greater length of the tank, the driver's compartment was positioned forward of the superstructure and a special armoured cupola was built for the driver. This box-shaped structure was situated on the left-hand side at the front of the vehicle, with two periscopes

LEFT: **This vehicle has been fitted with rails for the side-skirt armour. The body of the SPG has been covered in anti-magnetic** *Zimmerit* **paste. On the roof of the vehicle is a remote-controlled close-support machine-gun which is operated from inside the vehicle by one of the gun crew. The rail on the hull front is for spare track.**

mounted on top of the cupola along with an escape hatch. The Panzer IV escape hatch was in the belly of the vehicle for use by the driver and radio operator, but in the StuG IV this was welded shut as it was not required. Ammunition storage was 87 rounds; an additional 12-round bin was planned for the engine bay utilizing vacant space left by the unfitted turret motors. However, this caused problems and at times great confusion at the chassis production plants so the idea was dropped. The StuG IV was also to be fitted with concrete armour. The concrete was to be applied some 100mm/3.9in thick, mainly to the driver's position and the flat front on the right-hand side of the superstructure, but tests revealed that this did not help deflect incoming munitions and it added considerable weight to the vehicle. The modification was therefore stopped by the manufacturers, who simply put a coat of *Zimmerit* on the vehicle. However, the troops in the field thought it was a good idea and so added the concrete and extra armour plate to what they felt were weak areas. The driver's seat was adjustable and the back rest could be folded down so that the driver could escape into the fighting compartment if necessary. A 2,032kg/ 2-ton crane could be attached to the hull of the vehicle to ease the removal of the gun and could also be used for basic engine maintenance. The StuG IV was also fitted with the new Rundum-Feuer machine-gun, which could be operated from inside the vehicle and give all-round defence against attacking enemy infantry. Like with the StuG III, the StuG IV was fitted with *Schürzen* (skirts). These had been inspected by Hitler in March 1943 and were placed in to production immediately with the first field modification kits going out in early June 1943 to be fitted by field workshops.

The Sturmgeschutz was intended to act as close support for the infantry, but this was one role that the StuG IV would not perform as the bulk of these vehicles went either to Panzerjager units to act as tank destroyers or to Panzer Divisions as replacements for knocked-out tanks. In total, 1,141 StuG IVs were built by Krupp.

ABOVE: **This StuG IV has the side-skirts fitted. These acted as a form of spaced armour. The driver's position on the StuG IV was moved forward of the superstructure.** BELOW: **A close-up of the driver's cupola: the driver's hatch is in the open position. The vehicle commander's hatch is also open and the cut-out for the commander's periscope can be seen. The front of the driver's position has a thick layer of concrete which acts as additional armour.**

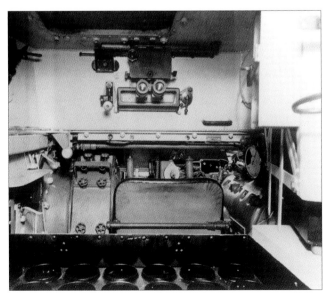

LEFT: **The driver's position inside a StuG IV. The periscope can be seen in front of the driver's seat. Above in the roof is the driver's hatch. The driving instruments are mounted on the right-hand side. In the front of the picture is one of the ammunition containers.**

Sturmgeschutz IV SPG

Country: Germany
Entered service: 1944
Crew: 4
Weight: 23,368kg/23 tons
Dimensions: Length – 6.7m/22ft
 Height – 2.2m/7ft 3in
 Width – 2.95m/9ft 8in
Armament: Main – 7.5cm/2.95in StuK40 L/48 gun
 Secondary – 2 x 7.92mm/0.312in MG42
 machine-guns
Armour: Maximum – 80mm/3.15in
Powerplant: Maybach HL 120 TRM 12-cylinder
 198kW/265hp petrol engine
Performance: Speed – 38kph/24mph
 Range – 210km/131 miles

LEFT: **The hull of this Sturmmörser Tiger has been covered in** *Zimmerit*, **while the new superstructure and glacis are in painted bare metal. The crane on the rear of the fighting compartment is for loading the ammunition.** ABOVE: **Inside the rear of the fighting compartment is the ammunition storage. Six rounds were stored on each side of the loading tray. Due to the weight of the rounds, they were placed on the loading tray before being pushed up and into the weapon.**

Sturmmörser Tiger Assault Rocket Mortar

The Sturm Tiger was the largest of the German heavy self-propelled guns produced during World War II. Officially these vehicles were known as *38cm Raketenwerfer 61 auf Sturmmörser Tiger* (38cm Rocket Launcher 61 on Assault Mortar Tiger). They were never issued with an Sd Kfz number and only 18 of them were built by their manufacturer, Alkett.

The project originally arose out of a requirement from Hitler in August 1943 to mount the 21cm heavy-support gun, but this was changed when the 38cm launcher became available and could be mounted on a Tiger 1 chassis. Hitler felt that there would be a great demand from the troops in the front line for these vehicles. The inspiration came from battle experience gained at Stalingrad and Leningrad, where there was a requirement for heavy close-support vehicles. Hitler and Guderian agreed for one prototype to be built, with, if successful, a production run of ten vehicles per month. The prototype was demonstrated to Hitler in October 1943, and in April 1944 it was decided to start a limited production run of a dozen vehicles, launchers and superstructures.

The vehicle conversions were carried out by Alkett at their Berlin/Spandau works. By September 1944, the first seven vehicles had been finished with the total rising to 18 vehicles by the end of the year. The monthly output of 38cm rockets was envisaged to be 300 rounds, this weapon having originally been developed for the German Navy as an anti-submarine warfare system. Two different warheads were available, one being high-explosive and the other being a hollow charge. The complete round which weighed 329kg/726lb was 1.5m/5ft long, and was loaded on to the vehicle using a hand-operated crane mounted on the rear of the superstructure. The ceiling

ABOVE: **A German Bergepanther is being used to move this Sturmmörser Tiger. The enormous size of the vehicle can be seen from the two British officers standing next to the vehicle.**

of the vehicle was fitted with an overhead hoist to move the ammunition from its racks and on to a loading tray, a ram was used to load the weapon and then the loading tray was folded away so the weapon could be fired. There was storage for 12 rounds in the fighting compartment and a thirteenth was carried loaded in the mortar.

The conversion of the vehicle consisted of removing the turret and hull top of the Tiger from the engine compartment forward. The new fighting compartment made from sloping armour plate was placed over the open space. The front glacis plate was sloped at 45 degrees and was 150mm/5.91in thick, with the driver's vision block on the left side with a sighting

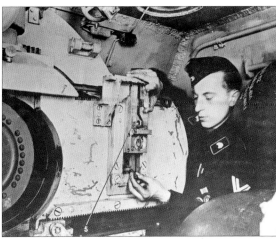

LEFT: On the left of the picture is the close-support machine-gun blister. Above the driver's vision slit is the sighting aperture for the main weapon.
ABOVE: Inside the fighting compartment. A round has been placed in the weapon and the breach is about to be closed. The circle of small holes on the rear of the round is the rocket motor exhausts.

aperture above it and a close-support machine-gun on the right. The side and rear plates were made of 80mm/3.15in armour with a circular hatch in the rear wall of the fighting compartment and a large loading door for the ammunition in the roof.

The rocket launcher was the most interesting part of this vehicle. It was breech-loaded and the barrel was rifled with a right-hand twist to induce spin into the munitions as they left the weapon. As the munitions were rocket-propelled, a way had to be found of stopping the rockets' exhaust from entering the fighting compartment. The exhaust gases operated a bypass valve in the breech which allowed the gases to escape forwards as the round left the barrel. The vehicle had to carry out "shoot and scoot" operations as the exhaust from the weapon was a give-away of the position of the vehicle even at the maximum range of 6km/3.7 miles.

As these vehicles could only carry a few rounds, each gun vehicle had to be supported by a tracked ammunition carrier built on Tiger 1 chassis that would carry an extra 40 rounds. Only one vehicle was ever produced before the Alkett factory was overrun by the Soviet Army.

Eighteen chassis were completed but only 12 of these vehicles were finished to be used in combat and these were formed into three companies of four vehicles each. The companies were 1001, 1002 and 1003, and were all used in the defence of the homeland, a task for which they were ill-suited. Some of them were used during the destruction of Warsaw and in fighting in other large cities.

ABOVE: The small square blocks on the end of the barrel are for the attachment of a counterweight. On the top of the fighting compartment is a dome-shaped fume extractor.

Sturmmörser Tiger Assault Rocket Mortar

Country: Germany
Entered service: 1944
Crew: 5
Weight: 66,040kg/65 tons
Dimensions: Length – 6.28m/20ft 7in
Height – 2.85m/9ft 4in
Width – 3.57m/11ft 9in
Armament: Main – 38cm/14.96in Stu M RW61 L/5.4 rocket motar
Secondary – 7.92mm/0.312in MG42 machine-gun
Armour: Maximum – 150mm/5.91in
Powerplant: Maybach HL 230 P45 12-cylinder 522kW/700hp petrol engine
Performance: Speed – 40kph/25mph
Range – 120km/75 miles

LEFT: **Several batteries of SU-76 vehicles drawn up for inspection. Part of the exhaust system can be seen below the vehicle number. This vehicle has had at least one tank kill, as it is painted on the side of the fighting compartment.** BELOW: **The very small fighting compartment can be clearly seen. The gunner is on the left, loader in the middle and vehicle commander on the right. The driver remained in his position in the front of the vehicle.**

SU-76 Self-Propelled Gun

In 1942, the task of developing a new self-propelled gun was given to the Kolomenskiy Locomotive Works in Kirov. They were instructed to mount the ZiS 3 76.2mm/3in gun on a suitable chassis. Initially the T-60 was selected for this project but this proved to be far too small. In the spring of 1942 it was decided that the longer, T-70 chassis was more suitable for the ZiS 3, and the improved new vehicle was called the SU-76. The T-70 was becoming available at this time because it was being phased out as a tank as it was too lightly armoured and the twin-engine layout, one for each track, was not reliable.

Trials were conducted in the summer of 1942 and the new vehicle went into production in December, 26 of these being built in that month and issued to the army, who found it to be unusable.

In early 1943 the vehicle was passed to a new design bureau, which made several changes. They placed the engines in-line so that power from both was fed to both tracks and consequently if an engine broke down the vehicle would not simply go round in circles. The new engine layout also required the front of the vehicle to be redesigned, and the fighting compartment was improved. This new vehicle was called the SU-76M.

Even in its improved version the SU-76 was never liked by the crews who had to use the vehicle. The fighting compartment was open-topped and gave the gun crew very little protection from small arms fire and no protection from the weather. The driver had to sit with the engines as there was no bulkhead separating the two compartments and the noise was horrendous, added to

which the heat was very hard to work with in the summer. These SPGs were originally designed as anti-tank vehicles but were soon relegated to an infantry-support role. Nevertheless, they would serve on into the 1960s, seeing action on the Chinese side during the Korean War. The nickname of the vehicle was "Suka" meaning Bitch.

LEFT: **This SU-76 has been painted up in a disruptive winter pattern with whitewash. The large driver's hatch in the centre of the glacis is in the open position. The exhaust system was inadequate on this vehicle and resulted in some of the fumes entering the fighting compartment.**

SU-76 SPG

Country: USSR
Entered service: 1942
Crew: 4
Weight: 11,176kg/11 tons
Dimensions: Length – 5m/16ft 5in
  Height – 2.20m/7ft 3in
  Width – 2.74m/9ft
Armament: Main – 76.2mm/3in 1942 ZiS 3 gun
  Secondary – Small arms
Armour: Maximum – 35mm/1.38in
Powerplant: 2 x GAZ 6-cylinder 52.2kW/70hp petrol engine
Performance: Speed – 45kph/28mph
  Range – 450km/280 miles

LEFT: **The short barrel of the SU-122 is clearly seen along with the very large gun mantle. These vehicles were copied from the German StuG III but never had the same success.**
ABOVE: **An SU-100 vehicle which replaced most of the SU-122 and SU-85 vehicles in combat. One problem the SU-100 had was that it was not as manoeuvrable in narrow lanes or woods due to the long gun barrel.**

SU-122 Medium Self-Propelled Gun

This was the first self-propelled weapon to be mounted on the T-34 chassis and would lead the way to a whole family of guns based on this very famous tank.

The Soviet Army had been very impressed by the success of the German StuG vehicles, so in April 1942 the Main Artillery Directorate (GAU – *Glavniy Artilleriskoye Upravleniye)* issued a requirement for a self-propelled close-support gun. SPGs were a lot cheaper and quicker to produce than a tank mainly due to the tank's turret and turret-ring bearing race that were complicated to manufacture and required the use of specialist engineering equipment. Several vehicles were put forward by a

number of different design bureaux in consultation with the Commissariat for the Tank Industry (NKTP), but none of these passed the trials stage.

In October 1942 the State Defence Committee (GKO) ordered the design bureaux to have another look at an SPG design, but this time only using the T-34 chassis. The Uralmash plant in Sverdlovsk came up with the winning design. They removed the front and turret area of the T-34 chassis and mounted an all-welded box structure on the top of the opening. The glacis plate was made from one piece of sloped armour, and the sides of the fighting compartment were sloped as well. The new vehicle was designated the SU-35

and mounted the M-30 Model 1938 122mm/4.8in howitzer. On the successful completion of trials it was ordered into production in December 1942. GKO changed the name of the vehicle to SU-122 as it entered service in January 1943. Production finished in the summer of 1944, by which time 1,100 vehicles had been made.

It was intended to mix the SU-76 and the SU-122 in the same assault gun units, but due to the technical problems of the SU-76 this never worked. Each SU-122 regiment consisted of 16 vehicles divided into four batteries. These vehicles were slowly replaced by the SU-100, but some could still be found in service into the 1950s.

ABOVE: **The extended range fuel tanks on the rear of the vehicle can be seen, as well as the very short barrel length. A two-man tree saw is fitted as standard to the hull of the vehicle: this item was fitted to all Soviet armoured vehicles.**

SU-122 Medium SPG

Country: USSR
Entered service: 1943
Crew: 4
Weight: 30,480kg/30 tons
Dimensions: Length – 6.95m/22ft 10in
　　Height – 2.45m/8ft
　　Width – 3m/9ft 10in
Armament: Main – 122mm/4.8in M-30 howitzer
　　Secondary – 12.7mm/0.5in machine-gun
Armour: Maximum – 45mm/1.77in
Powerplant: V-2-34M 12-cylinder 375kW/500hp diesel engine
Performance: Speed – 55kph/34mph
　　Range – 271km/168 miles

Somua MCG Half-Track

LEFT: **This Somua has been fitted with an armoured roof on which an eight-tube Nebelwerfer rocket launcher has been mounted. One weakness of this vehicle was that the front wheels were very easily damaged.** ABOVE: **This U304 (f) half-track has been turned into an armoured ambulance by the Germans. The front of the vehicle is fitted with an unditching roller. This vehicle used the same chassis and track as the larger Somua.**

In the 1920s, the French led the world in the development of the half-track, especially using the Kegresse-type suspension. This system with its rubber tracks was even bought by the Germans and built under licence. In 1935, the Somua Company produced the MCG-type half-track, with production lasting until the invasion of France by the Germans in 1940. A year later they would produce an improved version, the MCL. In total 2,543 of both types of vehicle were built.

These vehicles were originally built for the French artillery as tractors for the 155mm/6.1in gun, and, using a heavy duty trailer, as general towing tractors for tank recovery. Most of these half-tracks were fitted with a jib with block and tackle for lifting the rear of the gun carriage up and on to the towing hook. They were not armoured and there was a standard wooden cargo bed behind the driver's cab.

The Germans captured over 2,000 of these vehicles and put them back into service with their own artillery units where they acted as tractors and supply vehicles. The MCL was redesignated the Le Zgkw S303 (f) while the MCG was given the designation of Le Zgkw S307 (f). In 1944, the Germans started to convert a number of these vehicles into self-propelled weapon carriers. All of these conversions were fitted with an armoured body and crew compartment, while 16 of them were converted into self-propelled anti-tank gun vehicles by the fitting of a 7.5cm/2.95in PaK40. Another conversion was the installation of sixteen 81mm/3.2in French mortars mounted in two rows of eight on the back of the half-track. The mortars would be preloaded and fired electrically from inside the armoured cab when the S307 had been driven to the desired position in the combat area. Other vehicles were fitted with various types of rocket launchers such as the Nebelwerfer.

These converted vehicles were issued to German units based in France, while some of the basic half-tracks remained in France and others were sent to Italy or the Eastern Front.

LEFT: **This Somua half-track has been converted to carry the German PaK40 AT gun. The gun and fighting compartment were placed at the rear of the vehicle. The driver's position was located in front of the gun.**

Somua MCG Half-Track

Country: France
Entered service: 1935
Crew: 3
Weight: 8,636kg/8.5 tons
Dimensions: Length – 5.3m/17ft 4in
    Height – 1.95m/6ft 4in
    Width – 1.88m/6ft 2in
Armament: Main – None
    Secondary – Small arms
Armour: None
Powerplant: Somua 4-cylinder 45kW/60hp petrol engine
Performance: Speed – 36kph/22mph
    Range – 170km/106 miles

LEFT AND BELOW: **This vehicle has been given the name of "Darlington" by its crew. The gun has been placed on a platform between the driver's and the brakeman's armoured cabins. The wheels for the gun have been stowed on the side of the vehicle, and the ammunition for the gun has been stored in the gap between the vehicle's brakeman's cabin and the engine compartment.**

The Gun Carrier

The Gun Carrier was a vehicle well ahead of its time and if it had been deployed more appropriately could have had a great impact on the outcome of World War I. These vehicles should have been able to take guns forward very quickly to help bolster the gains made by British infantry and help hold off the subsequent German counter-attack. They were ordered in October 1916 and were delivered to the army in France in July 1917.

The Gun Carrier used the engine and transmission of the Mk I tank, the basic vehicle being made up of six boxes. The tracks ran around two boxes 457mm/18in wide, 9.1m/30ft long and 1.5m/5ft high that made up the sides of the

vehicle. Above the tracks at the front of the vehicle were two one-man boxes; the one on the right was for the driver, the one on the left was for the brake man. Between the tracks was a platform open at one end while at the other was a box structure with a crew compartment, ammunition storage and the engine room. The open platform extended between the tracks and acted as a loading ramp which could be raised or lowered to mount a gun. A loading trolley which was housed on the platform could be run out in front of the vehicle and the gun would then be positioned over it. Its wheels were removed and the gun winched back on to the platform on the trolley. The wheels of the gun were then

placed on the side of the carrier. Guns such as the 152mm/5.98in howitzer could be fired from the carrier, making this vehicle the first true SPG.

These vehicles were first used at the Third Battle of Ypres in 1917, when they carried forward a number of 60pdr guns and several hundred tons of ammunition. They also carried out a limited number of night shoot missions on the German positions and some gas attacks. However, their main task was to carry supplies forward as each vehicle could do the work of 300 men. Well-suited to the conditions of the Western Front, they would remain in use as supply vehicles for the rest of the war.

The Gun Carrier	
Country: UK	
Entered service: 1917	
Crew: 4 plus gun crew	
Weight: 34,544kg/34 tons	
Dimensions: Length – 9.14m/30ft	
Height – 2.85m/9ft 4in	
Width – 2.49m/8ft 2in	
Armament: Main – None	
Secondary – Small arms	
Armour: Maximum – 8mm/0.315in	
Powerplant: Daimler 6-cylinder 78kW/105hp petrol engine	
Performance: Speed – 5.96kph/3.7mph	
Range – 56km/35 miles	

ABOVE: **The large box structure at the rear of the vehicle housed the engine in the front and a crew compartment in the rear. At the rear of the carrier are the Mk I steering wheels.**

LEFT: **The vehicle is fitted with four out-riggers and each one has a jack on it. The driver and vehicle commander's positions are very exposed as it that of the gun crew who also had to ride on the open back of the truck.** ABOVE: **The driver's position in the Thornycroft. In front of the steering wheel is the fuel tank, while on the outside of the vehicle is the large hand brake and a rubber bulb horn. The gear selector is under the steering wheel.**

Thornycroft "J" Type 13pdr Self-Propelled AA Gun

The Basingstoke firm of John Thornycroft had a long history of producing trucks to meet a military standard. The design and development of the "J" Type 3-ton General Service truck started in 1912 and it was ready and in production for the Government Subsidy Trials that were held during 1913–14. The British government introduced a subsidy scheme that allowed private companies to buy lorries suitable for military service and, in return for a grant of 110 pounds towards the purchase price of the vehicle, to place

them at the disposal of the government in times of national emergency. The "J" Type won most of its classes in the trials and it was also the lightest vehicle in the 3-ton class. The British Army were supplied with 5,000 of these vehicles between 1914–18, and by the end of World War I it would be the most highly mechanized force in the world. These vehicles would remain in production until 1926 and stay in service with the British Army until 1930. They were also used in a number of specialist roles providing the chassis for variants such as mobile anti-aircraft guns and mobile field workshops.

At the start of the World War I, the British Army had no anti-aircraft guns. This led to a stopgap solution where guns were mounted on vehicles to provide a mobile defensive capacity. Thornycroft built 183 of these vehicles between November 1915 and September 1916. The gun selected was the British

LEFT: **The armament for the vehicle was the QF (quick-firing) 13pdr 9cwt Mk 1. The pedestal was kept to a very basic design and was fitted with an 18pdr mounting for the gun. A number of these guns remained in service in Canada until 1930.**

13pdr, which was removed from its normal carriage and mounted on a high-angle pedestal on the rear of the vehicle to improve its elevation. The standard 13pdr munitions were not powerful enough to reach higher flying aircraft so the 13pdr shell was fitted to the 18pdr propellant cartridge. The new gun was called the 13pdr 9cwt anti-aircraft gun.

These vehicles were well-liked by their crews and were very reliable. They would see service on the Western Front until the end of the war even if they were originally intended as a stopgap weapon. The "J" Type did have one failing however and that was a very poor cross-country ability.

Thornycroft "J" Type 13pdr SPAAG	

Country: UK
Entered service: 1915
Crew: 8
Weight: 3,302kg /2.3 tons
Dimensions: Length – 6.7m/22ft 2in
  Height – 3.2m/10ft 5 in
  Width – 2.2m/7ft 2 in
Armament: Main – 5.9kg/13pdr, 457kg/9cwt
  Mk 1 AA gun
  Secondary – Small arms
Armour: None
Powerplant: Thornycroft 4-cylinder, side valve,
  30kW/40hp petrol engine
Performance: Speed – 27.4kph/14.5mph
  Range – 201km/125 miles

Troop Carrier/Supply Mk IX Tank

LEFT: **Next to the driver's visor is a ball-mounting for a machine-gun. The twin set of rails passing over the top of the vehicle is for an unditching beam that was carried by all British tanks.**
BELOW: **The screw-like device at the front of the track sponson is the track-tensioning device and was used to take up the slack in the track.**

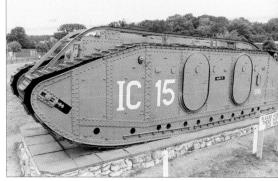

The development of supply tanks was a major step towards the full mechanization of the British Army, these vehicles making their appearance in the summer of 1917. Two supply vehicles would appear at the same time: the Gun Carrier and a converted version of the Mk I gun tank, both having a large impact on the battlefield. In the case of the Mk I conversion, the gun sponsons were removed and replaced with 91cm/3ft mild steel sponsons that had a tendency to dig into the ground and slow the tank down. The handling was terrible on both vehicles. However, the significant issue was that these new vehicles could each free up 300 men from the job of moving supplies, and this meant that 300 trained infantry could be used in other

roles. The next tank to be converted was the Mk IV gun tank and some 200 of these were freed up from combat duties for conversion into supply tanks.

The Mk IX was the first purposed built supply tank to be designed from scratch rather than being converted from a combat tank. Designed by Lieutenant G. J. Rackham in September 1917, it would enter service in France in October 1918, but only 35 of these vehicles were built by the end of the war. To give extra space in the vehicle, the engine was located in a position just behind the driver, and two machine-guns were fitted, one in the front beside the driver and the other in the rear. This vehicle was designed to carry 30 fully armed men across No Man's Land and into the

German position, thus making it the first APC. The Mk IX could alternatively carry 10,160kg/10 tons of supplies, loading and unloading being carried out through four oval doors, two on each side of the vehicle and opposite to each other.

The load capacity of the vehicle was further increased by towing a specially designed sledge, which was developed by the tank workshop in France and allowed an additional 10,160kg/10 tons of supplies to be moved. Sadly, the Mk IX proved to be underpowered, slow, and very cumbersome to drive and handle.

RIGHT: **This vehicle has been painted in a standard World War I camouflage pattern. The large entrance and exit oval doors can be clearly seen. Opposite these on the other side of the vehicle were two more doors.**

Troop Carrier Mk IX

Country: UK
Entered service: 1918
Crew: 4
Weight: 37,592kg/37 tons
Dimensions: Length – 9.70m/31ft 10in
Height – 2.57m/8ft 5in
Width – 2.46m/8ft 1in
Armament: Main – 2 x Hotchkiss 8mm/0.315in machine-guns
Secondary – None
Armour: Maximum – 10mm/0.394in
Powerplant: Ricardo 6-cylinder 112kW/150hp petrol engine
Performance: Speed – 6kph/4mph
Range – 193km/120 miles

LEFT: **A Universal Carrier towing a 6pdr AT gun. The crew of the gun are perched on the top of the carrier as there is no room for them to sit inside. The carrier is also piled high with personal kit. The Germans captured a number of these and pressed them into service as Panzerjager Bren. This was just one amongst a wide variety of uses they made of them.**

Universal Carriers

The original role of an infantry carrier was as a fast, lightly armoured vehicle to transport a light machine-gun section into battle and to support an infantry section attack. Each infantry section would be issued with one carrier. By 1939 there were four different types of carrier in service with the British Army, but it was decided at this point that the cavalry carrier was no longer required and to simplify production by standardizing on one universal design for all purposes. The first production contract was issued in April 1939 and with a few modifications it would remain in production for the whole of World War II, with some 35,000 vehicles being produced in Britain alone.

The Universal Carrier No.1 Mk I was the first version to be placed into production and entered service in 1940. It had a riveted hull, which was made of armour plate and provided some protection for the bodies of the crew when sitting down, but none for their heads and shoulders. The engine, a Ford V8

48.5kW/65hp, had a large fan fitted to it to draw cooling air into the radiator and this made it extremely noisy. As it was mounted in the middle of the crew compartment, which was divided into two equal parts, conversation between the crew of the carrier was impossible. The driver was located on the right in the front of the carrier with the gunner, who manned the machine-gun, sitting next to him. Steering was controlled by a simple steering wheel that connected to the braking system on the tracks. When moved firmly left or right this would turn the vehicle sharply, but if it was only moved a few degrees the carrier used track-warp to turn the vehicle in a wide circle. This gave the carrier great manoeuvrability and good cross-country ability.

The Mk II had an improved engine, the Ford V8 63.4kW/85hp, and better stowage, while the Mk III was of all-welded construction and again had improvements to the engine and stowage.

ABOVE: **A Universal Carrier that has been converted into the amphibious flamethrower called the "Dragonfly". The flotation screen is in the folded-down position. When in the water, the screen comes above the height of the vehicle.**
RIGHT: **This Universal Carrier has got water in the engine and has stalled before reaching dry land. The vehicle is covered in personal equipment.**

LEFT: **This Universal Carrier has been issued to African troops in East Africa. The Carrier is armed with a single Boys AT rifle.** BELOW: **This Carrier has just landed in France on June 6, 1944. The vehicle is fitted with the deep-wading screens, which helped stop water entering the engine. The Carrier has equipment piled up in the rear.**

A large number of infantry sections would carry out field modifications to their carrier by fitting more and heavier machine-guns such as the 7.62mm/30cal or the 12.7mm/50cal. In some cases, until the supply of tanks had improved, the carrier would act as a substitute in the jungles of the Far East.

The Carrier Armoured Observation Post, No.1 Mk II, was one of many conversions of the Universal Carrier. The OP Carrier was fitted with cable drums for field telephones and a No.19 radio set. This vehicle carried a crew of four. The machine-gun aperture in the gunner's position was covered over and the Bren gun was mounted on a pintle in the rear. Some 5,400 of these vehicles were produced, mainly for the artillery. Other conversions included the mounting of the 2pdr anti-tank gun on some 200 Carrier chassis. This proved to be very successful and would remain in British service until 1946. The Carrier was also used to tow the 6pdr (57mm) anti-tank gun. In 1942, a special Universal Carrier was designed to carry a 76.2mm/3in mortar and its crew, along with 30 rounds of ammunition. These were mainly produced by the Wolseley Motor Company, who had built some 14,000 of this type of carrier by the end of World War II.

One of the most successful conversions of the Universal Carrier carried a flamethrower and was known as the Wasp. Production of these vehicles started in 1942 and an order for 1,000 of them was placed in September that year. The Wasp Mk I had two large fuel tanks for the flame gun fitted in the crew compartments. The pipe work then passed over the top of the vehicle and down into the gunner's position in the front of the vehicle. The Mk I was deemed unsuitable for action by 1943 and was replaced by the Wasp Mk II. This carried 273 litres/60 gallons of fuel for the flame gun and had a range of 91.4m/300ft.

The Universal Carrier was inevitably used in many roles for which it was never originally intended, and would carry a great diversity of weapons. It was to serve on all fronts with British and Commonwealth troops throughout World War II. The Germans captured a number of British carriers and pressed them into service, calling them "Panzerjager Bren".

Universal Carrier No.1 Mk II	
Country: UK	
Entered service: 1942	
Crew: 3	
Weight: 4,064kg/4 tons	
Dimensions: Length – 3.76m/12ft 4in	
Height – 1.63m/5ft 4in	
Width – 2.11m/6ft 11in	
Armament: Main – Bren 7.7mm/0.303in light machine-gun	
Secondary – Small arms	
Armour: Maximum – 12mm/0.47in	
Powerplant: Ford V8 8-cylinder 63.4kW/85hp petrol engine	
Performance: Speed – 52kph/32mph	
Range – 258km/160 miles	

RIGHT: **This Universal Carrier has been fitted with a Vickers machine-gun, and has a crew of four. The rear of the vehicle has extra jerry cans fitted to it, and canvas covers are rolled up and stored on the carrier.**

Wespe 10.5cm Self-Propelled Gun

LEFT: **This is an ammunition carrier for the Wespe, basically a Wespe without the gun. The driver's top hatch and front visor are in the fully open position. This particular vehicle has been captured from the Germans by the French Maquis.** ABOVE: **This is one of the prototype Wespe vehicles and is being finished off by a small team of men from the manufacturer, FAMO.** BELOW: **The engine is mounted under the gun, with the air intakes built into the side of the fighting compartment. The crew area at the rear of the vehicle is very small.**

When the Panzer II was withdrawn from front-line service in early 1942 and relegated to second-line duties, a number of these chassis were made available for conversion into SPG mounts. A design competition was run between the Panzer II, III and IV chassis to find a suitable mounting of the 10.5cm/ 4.13in le FH18/2 howitzer, and the Panzer II Alkett design was chosen.

The vehicle that won was the Wespe (Wasp) which was built on a modified Panzer II chassis. The first of these new vehicles were produced by Famo in March 1943 and entered service with the German Army in May 1943. The initial construction contract was for 1,000 vehicles but this was later reduced to 835, of which 150 were munitions carriers. The munitions carriers were the same specification as the gun vehicle except that the gun was not mounted; it could carry 90 rounds of ammunition. The Wespe had the main gun mounted in the rear of the vehicle in an open-topped fighting compartment. The

sides of this were made of 10mm/0.394in sloped armour and it had storage for 32 rounds of ammunition. The engine was placed in the middle of the vehicle, with the engine cooling-system louvers completely redesigned from the Panzer II and placed in the sides of the vehicle. The driver sat at the front in a separate compartment and the only contact he had with the rear of the vehicle was by intercom. The crew consisted of five men: the driver, commander, and three gun crew. The first versions of the Wespe were built on standard Panzer II chassis but this made the fighting compartment very small and cramped. The modified chassis was extended by 254mm/10in which resulted in an increased space between the road wheels and rear idler, but this did not improve the cramped conditions in the rear fighting compartment. The suspension system had to be strengthened to absorb the recoil of the gun, with bump-stop springs being added to the first, second and fifth road wheel. The production run was completed in August 1944 when it was intended to replace the vehicle with a Waffenträger (Weapon Carrier) with a turret-mounted 10.5cm/4.13in gun.

Several critical reports were written about the Wespe by the German units using it as it had several severe mechanical problems. The steering gear wore out very quickly in France and (especially) in Italy due to the narrow roads and tight turns. The brakes became covered in oil due to the leaking final drive, a fault that was never properly cured. It caused problems in convoy due to its slow speed and it did not cope well with the mud of the Russian spring and autumn, due to its narrow tracks which caused it to sink.

The combat debut for the Wespe was the great tank battle of Kursk, where it had been issued to six Panzer Divisions especially for the battle. The Wespe was intended to be deployed several miles behind the main action, rather than in the front line, but at Kursk this was not to be the case. However, due to its small size all but two of the Wespe managed to escape, having accounted for several Soviet tanks. Twelve Wespe were sent to the 17th Panzer Division on the Eastern Front where they fired off 18,000 rounds at the Soviet forces during the fighting around Orel and the withdrawal to the river Dnieper in August 1943. Another detachment of 12 Wespe vehicles was sent to Italy to join the 26th Panzer Division in November 1943, but in just four weeks none was left in service due to mechanical breakdowns. It had also been discovered that the vehicles could not be used in battery formations due to the nature of the Italian landscape and they were more often used on their own as single guns in the "shoot and scoot" role. It was therefore decided that the bulk of the Wespe production would be sent to the Eastern Front where its mechanical problems were not such a handicap.

The Wespe was disliked by its crews, as there was very little working space in the cramped crew compartment and nowhere for their personal kit. In addition, the vehicle was not reliable and there was no protection from the weather due to the low silhouette of the vehicle.

TOP: **This Wespe is taking part in the Battle of the Bulge in the winter of 1944. Ammunition has been laid out on the rear door of the vehicle to keep it clean, ready for a bombardment. The small size of the fighting compartment is very clear in this picture.** ABOVE: **This Wespe has had the muzzle brake removed from the end of the barrel. The air intakes for the engine can be seen between the two American soldiers. The driver's top hatch is in the open position.**

ABOVE: **The Panzer II chassis and running gear can be clearly seen, but the vehicle is missing its exhaust. This should be mounted on the lower rear hull of the Wespe.**

Wespe 10.5cm SPG

Country: Germany
Entered service: 1943
Crew: 5
Weight: 11,176kg/11 tons
Dimensions: Length – 4.82m/15ft 10in
　　Height – 2.31m/7ft 7in
　　Width – 2.28m/7ft 6in
Armament: Main – 10.5cm/4.13in le FH18 howitzer
　　Secondary – 7.92mm/0.312in MG34 machine-gun
Armour: Maximum – 30mm/1.18in
Powerplant: Maybach HL62TR 6-cylinder 104kW/140hp petrol engine
Performance: Speed – 40kph/25mph
　　Range – 140km/87 miles

A–Z of Modern Armoured Fighting Vehicles 1945 to the Present Day

With the beginning of the Cold War, an arms race started all around the world. Various weapons were rushed into development as military theory changed – such as the suggestion that the tank would become obsolete and would be replaced by the missile carrier. The armoured car remained a firm military favourite until 1970 when a number of armies replaced them with light tanks. Now, however, the armoured car has been revived and functions again as the eyes of armoured and infantry divisions. The self-propelled gun was developed further and has now become a very sophisticated weapons system with extremely long ranges that can reach far into the enemy's rear. Its modern mobility means the guns can use "shoot and scoot" tactics.

The infantry carrier has undergone the greatest metamorphosis of any vehicle type. In the early 1950s, carriers were open-topped vehicles with a single machine-gun. They then became "battlefield taxis" carrying the infantry to the front line in fully armoured vehicles with overhead protection. The latest infantry fighting vehicles take troops into the heart of the fighting while providing them with close support.

LEFT: **Boxer Mechanised Infantry Vehicle (MIV).**

LEFT: **A 2S1 in a two-tone camouflage scheme. The driver and vehicle commander are in their positions with their hatches open. The driver has no physical contact with the turret crew. On the barrel behind the muzzle brake is the fume extractor.**
ABOVE: **A battery of 2S1 SPGs taking part in a parade to commemorate the November Revolution. The 2S1 was given the name "Gvozdika" (Carnation) by the Soviet Army. When it entered service, the 2S1 was first issued to BMP-equipped units.**

2S1 122mm Self-Propelled Gun

During the period when Khrushchev was in power in the Soviet Union from 1955–64, the armed forces were forced in the direction of nuclear weapons resulting in the demise of a number of basic weapon systems such as the SPG. When Leonid Brezhnev took over as the Soviet leader following Khrushchev's removal, it was realized that basic weapons development was lagging far behind those that NATO (the North Atlantic Treaty Organization) could deploy. In 1965, the GRAU (Gun Development Department) laid down a requirement for new conventionally tubed artillery, both towed and self-propelled. At this time NATO could field three main types of SPG, the M109, M110 and the Abbot, and had developed an excellent counter-battery fire technique based around these guns. With the development of improved artillery location radars the NATO guns could target the Soviet artillery very quickly, and with the new and improved ammunition at NATO's disposal, Soviet towed gun crews were very vulnerable.

The Soviet ground forces received several new guns in the 1960s. One was the D-30 122mm/4.8in towed gun and this was later mounted on a tracked chassis. Development of this vehicle started in the late 1960s and it was given the codename of "izdeliye 26". The chassis was developed by the GAVTU (Main Auto-transport Directorate) and was based on the MT-LB armoured transporter that was developed to replace the AT-P light artillery tractor. Production started in 1971 at the Karkov Tractor Plant, under the designation 2S1 Gvozdika (Carnation). The gun itself was a development of the 122mm/4.8in D-30, the main difference being the muzzle brake which on the 2S1 had a double baffle. The vehicle normally has a crew of four but when emplaced for a sustained fire role the crew is increased to six with the addition of two extra ammunition handlers. The gun can fire the full range of Soviet 122mm/4.8in ammunition to a maximum range of 15.2km/9.4 miles. The 2S1 carries 40 rounds of ammunition in the fighting compartment.

The 2S1 is fully amphibious and only takes a few minutes to be made ready to enter the water. The hull is boat-shaped and is very large, the bulky hull being necessary to provide enough buoyancy to allow the 2S1 to float. The vehicle uses its tracks to propel it through the water and a set of swim vanes are attached at the rear of the tracks to provide some form of steering. The driver is positioned right at the front of the vehicle on the left-hand side and his only contact with the fighting compartment is by internal intercom. The engine is placed alongside the driver, while the main air intake for the engine

LEFT: **A group of 2S1 vehicles demonstrating its amphibious capability. The vehicle commander is acting as the eyes for the driver who can see nothing from his position.**

LEFT: **A 2S1 in an artillery scrape and under a camouflage net. The driver's front visor is in the open position. Next to the driver's position is the access hatch to the clutch and compressed air system.** ABOVE: **A cut-away view of the 2S1. In the front of the vehicle is the compressed air unit and clutch, next is the driver's compartment, then the engine, followed by the main turret area and finally ammunition storage.**

is behind him. The gun is mounted in a turret at the rear of the vehicle and has a very low profile that has the appearance of an upside-down frying pan. The turret can be traversed through 360 degrees and is electrically powered or may be manually turned if necessary. The suspension is pneumatic and can be raised or lowered depending on the terrain that the vehicle is traversing. The vehicle is normally fitted with 400mm/15.7in wide tracks, but these can be replaced by 670mm/26.4in tracks to allow for better operation in snow or over soft ground.

The 2S1 chassis was used for a number of command vehicles, designated ACRV (Armoured Command and Reconnaissance Vehicle) and were attached to a number of SPG batteries. The ACRV-1 had a taller body, with the driver

at the front and the vehicle commander next to him and accommodation in the rear for four men. There was a fixed circular cupola on the roof with a single large hatch which was fitted with a 12.7mm/0.5in machine-gun. All versions of the 2S1 and the gun vehicle were equipped with a full NBC system.

The 2S1 was first seen in 1974 at a military parade in Poland, but had been in service for at least a year before this sighting. It was issued to Motor Rifle and Tank Divisions to replace the towed 122mm/4.8in guns. Each division had six 2S1 batteries attached to it, and each battalion had eighteen guns, divided between three batteries. Not surprisingly, given its adaptability and performance, it is still in service in many parts of the world today.

LEFT: **The engine grill can be seen in front of the turret. The grill on the back of the turret is for the air filtration unit that is mounted in the rear of the turret.**

2S1 122mm SPG

Country: USSR
Entered service: Approximately 1973
Crew: 4 plus 2 extra loaders
Weight: 15,951kg/15.7 tons
Dimensions: Length – 7.26m/23ft 10in
　　Height – 2.73m/8ft 11in
　　Width – 2.85m/9ft 4in
Armament: Main – 2A31 122mm/4.8in gun
　　Secondary – Small arms
Armour: Maximum – 20mm/0.79in
Powerplant: YaMZ 238N V8 220kW/300hp
　　diesel engine
Performance: Speed – Road 61kph/38mph;
　　Water 4.5kph/2.8mph
　　Range – 500km/311 miles

LEFT: **The muzzle brake has been covered by a canvas bag to stop dust and debris from entering the barrel while on the move. These vehicles belong to the East German Army, here seen in the Berlin area. This vehicle is fitted with an entrenching blade on the front of its hull.**

2S3 152mm Self-Propelled Gun

The development of this vehicle can be traced back to the end of World War II and the programmes of the Gorlitskiy design bureau based at the Uraltransmash plant at Sverdlovsk (now called Ekaterinberg) in 1949. Surprisingly, these designs were simply shelved and never went in to production. In 1965, some of the designs were resurrected and the first of these was the Obiekt 120 or SU-152. This was first modified in the early 1960s as the Obiekt 123 which became the SA-4 Ganef air defence missile system and was based on a 1949 chassis design. The Obiekt 120 was developed into a turreted self-propelled gun using the M-69 152mm/5.98in gun. This vehicle had a fully automatic loading system. A small number of these vehicles were built and put on trial but they were not accepted for service. In the late 1960s the Obiekt 303 was developed. This was another turreted self-propelled gun but used the 2A33 152mm/5.98in howitzer which was a development of the D-20 152mm/5.98in towed gun. In 1971 the Obiekt 303 was accepted for service in the Soviet Army and was renamed the 2S3 Akatsiya (Acacia).

The 2S3 is of an all-welded construction with thin armour that just about provides bullet and shrapnel protection to the crew (though not at close quarters) and is equipped with a dozer blade on the front for making its own field scrape. The driver has a compartment in the front of the vehicle with no direct contact with the rest of the crew in the fighting compartment. The engine is mounted next to the driver, and is a multi-fuel engine that normally uses diesel fuel but can in an emergency use other fuels for a short time. The vehicle is fitted with a full NBC system. Behind the engine and driver is the fighting compartment which takes up half the space in the vehicle. The turret can be traversed through 360 degrees, and the commander's cupola can be fitted with an anti-aircraft heavy machine-gun.

ABOVE: **These 2S3 vehicles have just finished firing as evidenced by the dust created from the back-blast that is still settling. These vehicles were known as "Akatsiya" (Acacia) and they became the mainstay of Soviet mobile artillery.**

The gun was modernized twice during its production. The first improvement, known as the 2S3M, came out in 1975 when the design of the autoloader was improved, which increased the rate of fire of the vehicle. A second improvement, the 2S3M1, came out in 1987, with better communications and new sighting equipment for the gun. Normally there is a crew of four men on the 2S3, but in a sustained fire role two extra loaders can be placed outside the vehicle to load ammunition through two small hatches in the rear of the vehicle. The gun can fire all the Soviet types of 152mm/5.98in ammunition including nuclear shells, rocket-propelled shells (which give the gun a range of 30km/18.6 miles) and precision-guided rounds such as the Krasnapol laser projectile. The normal rate of fire for this weapon is between three and four rounds per minute, but this cannot be sustained for long. The normal rate of fire in a sustained role is one round per minute, which means that the gun carries less than one hour's worth of ammunition, there being 46 rounds stored in the vehicle.

The 2S3 replaced the towed D-1 152mm/5.98in howitzer regiments in Motor Rifle Divisions. The new self-propelled 2S3 regiments consisted of eighteen vehicles divided into three batteries of six guns. In the tank regiments, the 2S3 replaced one battalion of 122mm/4.8in guns and gave the tank regiments greater firepower in the close-support role. This vehicle also replaced a number of guns in the artillery divisions. The 2S3 was the second most common gun in the Soviet Army after the 2S1 and there were 2,012 in service in the western Soviet bloc in 1991, just prior to the break up of the Soviet Union. The 2S3 came to be considered outdated due to its range compared to more modern self-propelled artillery. That said, an updated variant – the 2SM2 – was developed in the 2000s and equipped two Russian Army gun battalions from 2006. The 2S3 was largely replaced in Russian Army Service by the new 2S19, but the 2S3 can still be found in service with numerous countries around the world. Czechoslovakia were the only Soviet bloc country not to take the 2S3 as they had developed the wheeled 152mm/5.98in DANA self-propelled gun.

ABOVE: **Two East German 2S3 SPGs taking part in a November Parade in East Berlin. On the end of the barrel is a large double-baffle muzzle brake. There is also a fume extractor on the barrel.** BELOW LEFT: **When the 2S3 is being used in the sustained fire role then an ammunition vehicle can be parked at its rear and, using the two hatches in the lower rear hull, ammunition can be passed into the gun.**

ABOVE: **This vehicle has been painted up in a two-tone camouflage pattern. The commander's cupola has been fitted with a machine-gun.**
BELOW LEFT: **An entrenching blade is fitted under the front of the 2S3, which allows the vehicle to dig its own firing scrape. The driver and vehicle commander are in their positions.**

2S3 152mm SPG

Country: USSR
Entered service: 1972
Crew: 4 plus 2 extra loaders
Weight: 27,940kg/27.5 tons
Dimensions: Length – 8.4m/27ft 7in
    Height – 3.05m/10ft
    Width – 3.25m/10ft 8in
Armament: Main – 2A33 152mm/5.98in howitzer
    Secondary – 7.62mm/0.3in PKT machine-gun
Armour: Maximum – 20mm/0.79in
Powerplant: V-59 12-cylinder 382kW/520hp
    multi-fuel engine
Performance: Speed – 60kph/37mph
    Range – 500km/311 miles

LEFT: The 2S5 uses the same hull and chassis as the 2S3. The travel lock is mounted on the top of the driver's cupola. When operating the gun, the crew are very exposed. This vehicle was developed to improve the mobility of the towed 2A36.

2S5 152mm Self-Propelled Gun

One of the last self-propelled guns of the first generation of mechanized artillery vehicles to enter service with the Soviet Army was the 2S5 Giatsint (Hyacinth). Development commenced in the early 1970s and the vehicle started life as the Obiekt 307, being a marriage of the Uraltransmash chassis as used for the 2S3 and the 2A36 towed 152mm/5.98in gun.

The 2S5 is of an all-welded construction, and the main body of the vehicle has just 15mm/0.59in of armour. The crew of five are very exposed when operating the weapon as they are out in the open behind the gun except for the gun layer, who is seated on the left, again in the open but with a small shield in front of him. The driver sits in the front on the left of the vehicle, while behind the driver is the vehicle and gun commander,

whose cupola is fitted with a machine-gun. Alongside them on the right of the vehicle is the compartment for the diesel and multi-fuel engine. The gun crew travel in a small compartment in the rear of the vehicle which is fitted with roof hatches for them. The gun is mounted on the roof at the rear of the vehicle, while to the left of the gun is storage for 30 warheads mounted on a carousel and on the other side of the vehicle are the 30 propellant charges. Crew fatigue is kept to a minimum by the use of a semi-automatic loading system. There is a large recoil spade on the rear of the vehicle and a small dozer blade is fitted to the front for removing small obstacles and making gun scrapes.

The 2S5 entered service in 1974, but was not identified by NATO until 1981. It

ABOVE: The recoil spade on the rear of the 2S5 is in the raised position. The gun crew are entering the crew compartment in the middle of the vehicle, with the driver up front.

replaced a number of towed guns in the heavy artillery brigades at army level. The 2S5 can be brought into action in just three minutes and a battery of six guns can put 40 rounds of ammunition in the air before the first one has landed. A number of them were still in front-line use in 2022.

RIGHT: The entrenching spade can be seen under the front of the vehicle. The slotted muzzle brake of the gun can also be clearly seen. Mounted in the open like this, the gun is susceptible to damage.

2S5 152mm SPG

Country: USSR
Entered service: 1974
Crew: 5 plus 2 extra loaders
Weight: 28,956kg/28.5 tons
Dimensions: Length – 8.33m/27ft 4in
    Height – 2.76m/9ft 1in
    Width – 3.25m/10ft 8in
Armament: Main – 2A37 152mm/5.98in gun
    Secondary – 7.62mm/0.3in PKT machine-gun
Armour: Maximum – 15mm/0.59in
Powerplant: V-59 12-cylinder 382kW/520hp
    multi-fuel diesel engine
Performance: Speed – 63kph/39mph
    Range – 500km/311 miles

2S19 152mm Self-Propelled Gun

In 1985 work started on a replacement weapon for the 2S3 and the 2S5 self-propelled guns. The new vehicle would use parts from both the T-72 and T-80 tanks, and a new gun was to be developed as the 2A33 had been in use since 1955. The 2S19 was accepted for service with the Soviet Army in 1989 and given the name of Msta-S. This was a departure from the previous practice of naming SPGs after flowers or plants as the Msta was a river in the Ilmen district of Russia.

The 2S19 uses the hull and suspension of the T-80 tank, but the tried and tested 12-cylinder diesel engine of the T-72. The first, second and sixth road wheels are equipped with regulated telescopic shock absorbers which are controlled when firing the gun so the vehicle does not require a recoil spade on the rear. The driver's compartment is the same as that in the T-80 and has no connection with the crew in the turret except by internal intercom. The turret sits on the top of the chassis and can traverse through 360 degrees. It is equipped with two loading systems: a fully automatic loader for the warheads, and a semi-automatic loader for the propulsion charges. These two systems allow the 2S19 to maintain a high rate of sustained accurate fire and it can hit 38 out of 40 targets at a range of 15km/9.3 miles. The auto-loaders can reload the gun at any angle so the gun does not have to return to the horizontal position

between rounds. The turret has an independent power supply from the main vehicle and this allows the diesel engine to be switched off during combat to suppress its heat signature. This is essential on the modern battlefield as the latest guided weapons can be targeted on to a heat source such as a hot engine or exhaust vents.

Like most Soviet weaponry, this vehicle was widely exported. It remains in use with a number of nations including Ruusia, Azerbaijan, Belarus, Ethiopia, Georgia, Morocco, Ukraine and Venezuela.

TOP: **This vehicle has an extremely long barrel, which shows up well in this picture. The very robust travel lock can be seen at the rear end of the barrel. On the front of the turret are six smoke dischargers and the vehicle commander's cupola has been fitted with a machine-gun.**

ABOVE: **The very large turret covers the top of the T-80 tank hull and chassis. On the end of the barrel is a double-baffle muzzle brake.**

LEFT: **A rear view of the 2S19. Under the rear of the turret are the engine grills. On the back of the turret is a large conveyor, which is used for resupplying ammunition into the turret. Towards the front of the turret on each side are large access hatches for the crew.**

2S19 152mm SPG

Country: USSR
Entered service: 1989
Crew: 5 plus 2 extra loaders
Weight: 41,961kg/41.3 tons
Dimensions: Length – 11.92m/39ft 1in
Height – 2.99m/9ft 10in
Width – 3.38m/11ft 1in
Armament: Main – 2A64 152mm/5.98in howitzer
Secondary – 12.7mm/0.5in NSVT machine-gun
Armour: Classified
Powerplant: V-84A 12-cylinder 626kW/840hp multi-fuel diesel engine
Performance: Speed – 60kph/37mph
Range – 500km/311 miles

LEFT: **This Abbot is on a live-firing exercise. The additional ammunition supply has been dropped at the rear of the vehicle; the rounds are delivered in plastic cases. The large rear door is used for passing ammunition through to the gun crew. The small hatch above the main door is for communication.**
ABOVE: **The compact size of the Abbot can be clearly seen. The chassis is the same as the FV 432 armoured personnel carrier. Running along the side of the vehicle above the track is the exhaust system for the vehicle.**

Abbot 105mm Self-Propelled Gun

In the late 1950s NATO decided that the 105mm/4.13in calibre would be adopted as the standard close-support shell size. As a result, Britain had to retire the 25pdr gun and design a new weapon. The first Abbot prototype was produced in 1961, with the first vehicle being issued for service in 1965. It would remain in service until replaced by the AS90 in 1995.

The main production line was located at the Vickers Armstrong works in Newcastle-upon-Tyne. The Abbot was the field artillery version of the FV 432 family but the Abbot only used the engine and suspension of the FV 432. The vehicle was an all-welded construction. The driver was located on the right at the front of the vehicle with the engine next to him on the left. Mounted at the rear of the vehicle was a large spacious turret, which housed the three remaining members of the crew and had storage for 40 rounds of ammunition although only 38 were normally carried. The turret had a power-operated traverse but gun-elevation was performed by hand. A power rammer was installed to aid ramming the shells into the gun and a semi-automatic vertical sliding breach was also fitted. The gun had a maximum range of 17,000m/55,775ft and a maximum rate of fire of 12 rounds per minute, but this could not be sustained for long. Access to the fighting compartment was via a single large door in the rear of the vehicle and this was also used to pass

ammunition to the gun when tasked with a sustained fire mission. Six of the rounds carried in the turret were HESH (High-Explosive Squash-Head); this was an anti-tank round that was provided for use in the event of an engagement with enemy tanks. The Abbot was permanently fitted with a flotation screen to allow river-crossing and could be erected by the crew in 15 minutes.

Vickers also produced a simplified version for export but the only customer was India. An Abbot regiment consisted of three batteries, each with two troops of three guns supported in the field by the Stalwart 6x6 high-mobility load carrier.

LEFT: **The barrel of this Abbot is at maximum elevation. On the front of the turret are two clusters of smoke dischargers. There is a bank of four headlights on the hull front. The travel lock for the gun barrel is in the upright position.**

Abbot 105mm SPG	

Country: UK
Entered service: 1965
Crew: 4
Weight: 17,475kg/17.2 tons
Dimensions: Length – 5.84m/19ft 2in
   Height – 2.48m/8ft 2in
   Width – 2.64m/8ft 8in
Armament: Main – 105mm/4.13in L13A1 gun
   Secondary – 7.62mm/0.3in L4A4 machine-gun
Armour: Maximum – 12mm/0.47in
Powerplant: Rolls-Royce K60 6-cylinder
   179kW/240hp multi-fuel diesel engine
Performance: Speed – 50kph/30mph
   Range – 395km/245 miles

AMX-10P Mechanized Infantry Combat Vehicle

The AMX (*Atelier de Construction d'Issy les Moulineaux*) company started development on this vehicle in 1965 to meet a requirement from the French Army for a replacement for the AMX VCI infantry vehicle. The first prototype was finished in 1968 and proved to be unacceptable to the army, so major changes were made to the design, and new prototypes were produced. The resulting new vehicle was higher, wider and had a two-man 20mm/0.79in turret. The trials were completed successfully and the revised vehicle entered service with the French Army in 1973 as the AMX-10P.

The hull of the vehicle is made of all-welded construction with the driver's compartment at the front of the vehicle on the left-hand side. To the right of the driver is the main engine compartment which houses the Hispano-Suiza super-charged diesel engine. The engine compartment is fitted with aircraft engine-style fire-extinguishing equipment and the engine pack can be changed in just two hours. The AMX-10P is fully amphibious and has two water jets fitted to the rear of the vehicle to propel it when in the water. The two-man Toucan II turret is mounted in the centre of the vehicle, offset slightly to the left. The 20mm/0.79in cannon is mounted on the outside of the turret and has a dual-feed ammunition system which allows the gunner to select either HE (High-Explosive) or AP (Armour-Piercing) ammunition. The turret carries 325

rounds which are made up of 260 rounds HE in one belt and 65 AP rounds in the other and the gunner can switch between belts while firing. The infantry compartment in the rear of the vehicle has accommodation for eight men, and is accessed via an electrically operated ramp at the back.

The basic AMX-10P has been developed into a complete family of vehicles numbering some 15 different types. A close-support version known as "Marine" has been produced for amphibious operations and is armed with a 90mm/3.54in gun. The French Army took delivery of over 2,500, and between 2006–08 just over 100 AMX-10Ps in French Army service underwent extensive overhauls to improve armour and mobility with new gearboxes and suspension. Now retired from French military service, it remains in use with export customers including Iraq and Saudi Arabia.

TOP: **The 20mm/0.79in turret is mounted in the middle of the vehicle, while around the front of the turret is a bank of smoke dischargers. Down the side of this vehicle is a series of equipment attachment points.** ABOVE: **The large hydraulic ramp can clearly be seen. The men leaving the vehicle are carrying AT missiles. On each corner at the rear of the vehicle are two twin smoke dischargers. This vehicle is fitted with a MILAN AT system.**

LEFT: **The trim vane is in the down position on the front of the vehicle. Under the gun turret is a large cupola that is fitted with all-round vision blocks. The driver's periscopes are also clearly visible. The external equipment attachment points have been removed here.**

AMX-10P MICV

Country: France
Entered service: 1973
Crew: 3 plus 8 infantry
Weight: 13,818kg/13.6 tons
Dimensions: Length – 5.82m/18ft 1in
  Height – 2.54m/8ft 4in
  Width – 2.78m/9ft 2in
Armament: Main 1 x 20mm/0.79in M693 cannon, and 1 x coaxial 7.62mm/0.3in machine-gun
  Secondary – Small arms
Armour: Classified
Powerplant: Hispano-Suiza HS-115 8-cylinder 194kW/260hp super-charged diesel engine
Performance: Speed – 65kph/40mph
  Range – 600km/370 miles

AMX-10RC Armoured Car

ABOVE: The boat-shaped hull of the AMX-10RC can be clearly seen in this picture. The gun barrel of this vehicle has a very long overhang.

Development on the AMX-10RC started in September 1970 to meet a French Army requirement for a replacement for the Panhard EBR heavy armoured car. The first three prototypes were built in June 1971 and then a six-year trials and development period started which ended when the car was accepted for service in 1977. The AMX-10RC entered service in 1978 and by the time the production run was finished in 1987, the French Army had taken delivery of 207 cars, while the largest export contract (for 108 vehicles) was to Morocco, North Africa.

The all-welded aluminium hull and turret provide bullet and shell-splinter protection for the crew. The driver is positioned in the front of the vehicle on the left-hand side, with the main fighting compartment in the middle and the turret on the top. The engine is in the rear of the vehicle and is the same as that fitted to the AMX-10P MICV. The gearbox has two functions: one is to drive the vehicle in both directions using a pre-selection through four gears in both directions, and the other is to supply power to the two water-jets that are mounted on the rear of the car to propel it through water. None of the wheels on the vehicle turns as the car uses the same skid-steering system as a tracked vehicle. The suspension is hydro-pneumatic and allows the vehicle to change its ride height depending on the terrain encountered. The vehicle is fitted with a full NBC system and night-fighting optics.

The AMX-10RC has a three-man turret with the commander and gunner on the right and the loader/radio operator on the left. The COTAC fire-control system is composed of a number of sensors that provide the computer with the following data: target range, speed, angle of cant and wind speed, while altitude and outside temperature are fed into the computer by the gunner. A laser is used for measuring the distance to the target and is effective from 400–10,000m/1,312–32,808ft. The vehicle commander can override the gunner and take over the aiming of the gun. Although gradually replaced in French service, it remains in service with export customers.

ABOVE: The grill behind the rear wheel is the intake for the water-jet propulsion system. The trim vane is folded down on the top of the glacis plate.

AMX-10RC Armoured Car

Country: France
Entered service: 1978
Crew: 4
Weight: 15,850kg/15.6 tons
Dimensions: Length – 9.15m/30ft
    Height – 2.69m/8ft 10in
    Width – 2.95m/9ft 8in
Armament: Main – 1 x 105mm/4.13in gun, and
    1 x 7.62mm/0.3in coaxial machine-gun
    Secondary – None
Armour: classified
Powerplant: Hispano-Suiza HS-115 8-cylinder
    194kW/260hp supercharged diesel engine
Performance: Speed – Road 85kph/53mph;
    Water 7.2kph/4.5mph
    Range – 1,000km/621 miles

AMX-13 DCA SPAAG

The first prototypes of the AMX DCA were completed in 1960, but were not fitted with the guidance radar as it was not yet ready. The first radar-equipped prototype was built in 1964 and was tested by the French Army until 1966, when an order was placed for 60 vehicles that were to be delivered and in service by 1969.

The AMX DCA system was mounted on the AMX-13 light tank chassis in a very similar way to that of the 105mm/4.13in SPG vehicle conversion. The driver was seated in the front of the vehicle on the left with the engine next to him on the right. The SAMM turret with positions for the other two members of the crew was mounted on the rear of the vehicle. The vehicle commander sat on the left with the gunner on the right, and between them were the twin 30mm/1.18in cannon, while mounted on the top rear of the turret was a pulse-Doppler DR-VC-1A radar dish. When the vehicle was moving, this was stowed in a lightly armoured box. Both the commander and gunner could traverse the turret. Each gun could be selected either independently of the other or both

together while the gunner could select single-shot, bursts of 5 or 15 rounds or fully automatic fire. The turret carried 600 rounds of belt-fed ammunition, 300 rounds per gun. The rate of fire of the guns per barrel was 600 rounds per minute, which gave the turret a 30-second supply of ammunition. The maximum range of the guns was 3,000m/9,842ft and all the empty cartridges and links were ejected to the outside of the turret. The turret also carried all the optical, electrical and hydraulic systems for the guns.

In the late 1960s the French took the DCA turret and mounted it on the AMX-30 tank chassis, but the improvement in mobility did not impress the French Army and so the project was dropped. In 1975, Saudi Arabia asked for the system but with an improved ammunition supply to 1,200 rounds, and subsequently placed an order for 56 vehicles.

ABOVE: **This is an early version of the AMX-13 DCA. The vehicle uses the chassis of the AMX-13 light tank. The guns are at 45 degrees of elevation. Two further 300-round belts of ammunition are carried below the turret in the body of the vehicle.**

ABOVE: **The vents for the exhaust system can be seen running down the side of the vehicle. On each side of the turret is a pair of smoke dischargers. The turret crew have remote gun-control boxes in front of them.** LEFT: **This is one of the prototype vehicles as it has no fittings on the turret. The three crew positions can be clearly seen on this vehicle.**

AMX-13 DCA SPAAG

Country: France
Entered service: 1968
Crew: 3
Weight: 15,037kg/14.8 tons
Dimensions: Length – 5.4m/17ft 9in
　　Height – 3.8m/12ft 6in (radar operating)
　　Width – 2.5m/8ft 2in
Armament: Main – 2 x 30mm/1.18in HSS-831A
　　automatic cannon
　　Secondary – None
Armour: Maximum – 30mm/1.18in
Powerplant: SOFAM 8-cylinder 201kW/270hp
　　petrol engine
Performance: Speed – 60kph/37mph
　　Range – 350km/215 miles

LEFT: **The extremely long gun barrel of this SPG is clearly visible. The GCT does not require any outriggers to stabilize the vehicle when firing due to the hydraulic shock absorbers. The extra long recuperators can be seen mounted under and over the gun barrel.**

AMX GCT 155mm Self-Propelled Gun

In the late 1960s, the French Army required a replacement for the ageing 105mm/4.13in Mk 61 and the 155mm/6.1in Mk F3 self-propelled guns, both of which used the AMX-13 light tank chassis. Development of the new vehicle started in 1969. The first prototype was completed in 1972 and went on public display the next year. Between 1974 and 1975 ten vehicles were built for trials with the French Army. The AMX GCT (*Grande Cadence de Tir*) finally entered production in 1977, with the first vehicles being sold to Saudi Arabia. It was accepted for service in the French Army in July 1979.

The chassis used was the AMX-30 MBT (Main Battle Tank). The engine and suspension were untouched in this conversion; the main area affected being the turret. This was removed together with all the ammunition storage in the body of the tank and was replaced by a generator and ventilator, which fed fresh air to the new 155mm/6.1in gun turret. The driver sits in the front of the vehicle on the left-hand side and has three periscopes in front of him, the central one of which can be

replaced by an infrared or image-intensifier periscope for night driving. The engine is at the rear of the vehicle and is a Hispano-Suiza HS 110 supercharged multi-fuel unit. The complete engine pack can be removed by a three-man team in as little as 45 minutes. The gearbox is mechanically operated and has just five gears for both forward and reverse, and is combined with the steering mechanism. The suspension system uses torsion bars and the first and last road wheels are fitted with hydraulic shock absorbers.

The turret is of all-welded construction with the commander and gunner stationed on the right of the turret and the loader on the left. The commander's cupola is fixed but has periscopes mounted all around it to give 360 degrees of sight. The loader has a hatch as he operates the anti-aircraft machine-gun that can be either a 7.62mm/0.3in or 12.7mm/0.5in weapon. The gun crew enter the turret through two side doors, the door on the left opening towards the front while the door on the right opens towards the rear. The turret and the breech are hydraulically operated. The breech is a vertically sliding wedge breech block which is hermetically sealed by a blanking plate. There are manual controls for use in the event of the vehicle losing hydraulic power. The gun takes just two minutes to bring into action and, in case of counter-battery fire, just one minute to take out of action and start to move the vehicle. The average rate of fire using the automatic loader is eight rounds per minute, while with manual loading the rate of fire falls to just three rounds per minute. The gun is capable of firing six rounds in just 45 seconds in what is called "burst firing". The ammunition is stored in the rear of the turret in two separate sections; in one box are

LEFT: **A night-firing exercise. The sheer size of the turret can be seen when compared to the hull of the AMX-30. This gives the vehicle a high centre of gravity.**

42 projectiles and in the other are 42 cartridge cases with propellant. A further 40 propellant charges can be stored in a fixed container under the turret. The turret is resupplied with ammunition through two large doors in the rear which fold down and form a platform for the reloading crew. The gun can be reloaded while still firing and a full reload will take a crew of four men 15 minutes or two men 20 minutes. The normal maximum range of the gun is 18,000m/59,055ft, but using rocket-assisted ammunition, this can be increased to 30,500m/100,065ft. Both the vehicle and the turret are fitted with a full NBC system and there is no recoil spade attached to the rear.

The turret can be adapted to fit many different MBT chassis including the German Leopard and the Russian T-72 and it is in service with three other countries in addition to France. In 2005, the French upgraded the engine to the Renault E9 diesel. The French Army had 190 AMX GCTs in service but have now withdrawn the vehicle from front-line use, although export versions continue in service.

ABOVE LEFT: **This GCT turret has been fitted to the T-72 hull and chassis. This is an Egyptian vehicle. The turret has also been developed to fit the German Leopard hull and chassis.** ABOVE: **The gun is at maximum elevation. The barrel is fitted with a large double-baffle muzzle brake. The lower front of the turret has two clusters of three smoke dischargers fitted.**

ABOVE: **A GCT on exercise. This vehicle has been fitted with a 12.7mm/0.5in heavy machine-gun on the top of the turret.** RIGHT: **The rear of the turret opens downward and exposes the ammunition racks. The gun can continue to fire even with the back down. Full reloading takes the crew of the vehicle just 15 minutes.**

AMX 155mm GCT SPG

Country: France
Entered service: 1980
Crew: 4
Weight: 41,961kg/41.3 tons
Dimensions: Length – 10.4m/34ft 1in
　　　Height – 3.25m/10ft 8in
　　　Width – 3.15m/10ft 4in
Armament: Main – 155mm/6.1in howitzer
　　　Secondary – 1 x 7.62mm/0.3in or 1 x 12.7mm/ 0.5in machine-gun
Armour: Maximum – 30mm/1.18in (estimated)
Powerplant: Hispano-Suiza HS 110 537kW/720hp multi-fuel engine
Performance: Speed – 60kph/37mph
　　　Range – 450km/280 miles

AMX VCI Infantry Combat Vehicle

The AMX VCI (*Véhicule de Combat d'Infanterie*) was developed in the early 1950s to meet a requirement for the French Army following the cancellation of the Hotchkiss TT6 and TT9 APCs. The first prototype was completed in 1955 with production starting in 1957.

The AMX VCI used the chassis and the front of the hull up to and including the driver's compartment of the AMX-13 tank. The hull behind the driver was increased in height to allow for troops to be seated in the rear of the vehicle. The infantry compartment in the rear held ten men seated back to back, five on each side. There were four firing ports in the side and two in the rear doors, which opened outwards. The vehicle had no NBC equipment at first but this was later fitted as an upgrade to all vehicles. The driver was in the front of the vehicle on the left, with the engine compartment on the right. Behind and above the driver was the vehicle gunner and the vehicle commander was next to him. When this vehicle originally came into service the gunner used a 7.5mm/0.295in machine-gun. This was quickly improved to a

12.7mm/0.5in heavy machine-gun, which was subsequently modified to a CAFL 38 turret armed with a 7.62mm/0.3in machine-gun which could be aimed and fired from inside the vehicle. The French then went on to develop a number of turrets that could be fitted to the vehicle ranging from a twin 7.62mm/0.3in Creusot-Loire TLiG to a CB20 20mm/0.79in turret. The AMX VCI was not amphibious but could ford

ABOVE: **The hatches above the rear crew area are in the open position. The turret gunner is in his turret, with the vehicle commander next to him. The compact size of the vehicle can be seen clearly in this picture.**

shallow water and a splash board was mounted on the glacis plate at the front of the vehicle to facilitate this.

The AMX VCI was developed into a family of vehicles with ten different variations. In total, 15,000 of this family of vehicles were built, of which 3,000 were the VCI version, and some remain in service with export customers. It was replaced in French service by the AMX-10P from 1977.

RIGHT: **The small square hatches in the top rear of the crew compartment are the firing ports. The dome under the turret is part of the air filter system.**

LEFT: **The turret of the AMX is armed with a single 12.7mm/0.5in machine-gun. The large driver's visor can be seen on the left of the vehicle. The gap between the tracks has been closed by a splash plate. The headlights are mounted halfway up the glacis plate.**

AMX VCI Infantry Combat Vehicle

Country: France
Entered service: 1958
Crew: 3 plus 10 infantry
Weight: 14,021kg/13.8 tons
Dimensions: Length – 5.54m/18ft 2in
  Height – 2.32m/7ft 7in
  Width – 2.51m/8ft 3in
Armament: Main 1 x 12.7mm/0.5in machine-gun
  or 1 x 7.62mm/0.3in machine-gun, basic fit
  Secondary – Small arms
Armour: Maximum – 30mm/1.18in
Powerplant: SOFAM 8 GXB, 8-cylinder
  186kW/250hp petrol engine
Performance: Speed – 65kph/40mph
  Range – 400km/250 miles

LEFT: **This is the six-wheeled Fuchs NBC vehicle. The commander's door is open, and a machine-gun has been mounted above his position. The rear of the vehicle is covered in personal kit.** BELOW: **This is the 4x4 version of the Fuchs. The exhaust system can be seen on the hull side; it exits the vehicle under the main armament and runs back along the length of the vehicle. This Fuchs is armed with a single 2cm/0.79in cannon.**

APC Transportpanzer 1 Fuchs

The development of this vehicle dates back to 1964, when the German Army were looking for a family of vehicles that would be capable of covering most of their future non-tank AFV requirements. This new generation of vehicles was to be developed using three new chassis, a 4x4, a 6x6 and an 8x8, for tactical trucks, reconnaissance vehicles and APCs. MAN won the contract to deliver the new trucks and Rheinmetall won the contract to supply the 6x6 armoured amphibious load carriers that became the Transportpanzer 1.

The Transportpanzer 1 is an all-welded steel construction and protects the crew from bullets and shell-splinters. The hull also has spaced armour in a number of critical places. The driver sits on the left in the front of the vehicle with the commander next to him on the right. Both the driver and the commander have their own access doors in the front of the vehicle and both doors have large windows that can be covered by an armoured shutter. The vehicle has a large single windscreen for both the driver and commander and gives an excellent field of vision. This is a bullet-proof screen but can be covered by an armoured shutter that folds down from the top of the vehicle. The engine compartment is behind the driver on the left of the vehicle with a small passageway linking the front to the rear crew compartment. The engine compartment is fitted with an automatic fire-extinguishing system and the complete engine pack can be removed in just ten minutes. The troop cargo area in the rear holds ten men in two rows of five sitting facing each other. The vehicle is fitted with a full NBC system and night-driving equipment.

The German Army began to take delivery of their vehicles in 1979 with the last batch delivered in 1986; in total 996 were supplied. Britain, Holland and the USA all bought special contamination-measuring versions fitted for NBC and electronic warfare. Upgraded and original versions remain in service with a number of armies around the world.

LEFT: **The four-wheel steering can be clearly seen on this vehicle. The large trim vane is folded back on the front of the vehicle. The armoured shutter above the screen is half deployed.**

APC Transportpanzer 1 Fuchs

Country: Germany
Entered service: 1979
Crew: 2 plus 10 infantry
Weight: 16,967kg/16.7 tons
Dimensions: Length – 6.83m/22ft 5in
　　Height – 2.3m/7ft 7in
　　Width – 2.98m/9ft 9in
Armament: Main – None
　　Secondary – None
Armour: Classified
Powerplant: Mercedes-Benz V8 8-cylinder 239kW/320hp diesel engine
Performance: Speed – 105kph/65mph
　　Range – 800km/500 miles

AS90 155mm Self-Propelled Gun

In the late 1960s, the British Army started to look for a replacement for the 105mm/4.13in Abbot and the American 155mm/6.1in M109. It was to be built by a consortium of firms from three countries: Britain, Germany and Italy. Britain was to produce the turret and sights, Germany would produce the engine, the hull and the main gun, and Italy would produce the recoil, fuel and loading systems. This new weapon system was due to go into service in 1980 but the project disintegrated with each of the participating countries going their own way, resulting in the joint venture being finally wound up in 1986. Vickers, the British firm in the consortium, decided to go it alone and produce a private venture vehicle using the FH70 gun that they had developed along with the German and Italian companies. The new vehicle they built was designated the GBT 155 and

ABOVE: **The soldier at the rear of the vehicle is standing under the auxiliary power unit which is fitted to the rear of the turret. A wire-mesh storage box has been fitted to the top of the turret for the storage of camouflage netting and tents.** BELOW LEFT: **The vehicle commander in his cupola is giving directions to the driver. The hatch in the side of the turret is folded back to give increased ventilation to the turret.** BELOW: **The gun barrel is locked into the travel lock, which when not in use folds back on to the glacis plate. On the front of the turret is one of the two clusters of smoke dischargers.**

this would become the prototype for the AS90. It was ready for testing in 1982, while the second prototype was ready to join the test programme in 1986. This new vehicle entered the competition for the replacement for the Abbot in 1989 and won, with the result that the army placed a fixed-price contract of

300 million pounds for 179 AS90 units. The first AS90 vehicles entered service in 1993 with the final deliveries to the British Army being made in 1995, replacing all its other self-propelled guns.

The AS90 uses a specially developed turret and chassis, but is otherwise constructed using a large number of standard parts from other vehicles in service with the British Army. It is of all-welded steel construction, which is bullet and shell-splinter proof. The driver sits in the front of the vehicle on the left-hand side, while alongside is the main power pack, consisting of a Cummins diesel engine. The turret houses the other four men in the crew, with the gunner and the vehicle commander, stationed on the right and the shell loader and the charge loader, on the left. Above the loaders is a hatch with an anti-aircraft 7.62mm/0.3in or 12.7mm/0.5in pintle-mounted machine-gun. The commander has a cupola with all-round vision. The turret houses all the targeting computers, direct sights and fully automatic gun-laying equipment, and also has an ammunition management system and a fully automatic loading system. Thirty-one warheads are stored in the turret bustle, with a further seventeen stored under the turret, which has a full 360-degree traverse. The normal maximum range of the FH70 155mm/6.1in 39-calibre gun is 24,700m/81,036ft but by using

rocket-assisted ammunition the range can be extended to 30,000m/98,425ft. The gun can elevate to maximum of 70 degrees, and has a minimum range of 2,500m/8,200ft. It can fire three rounds in less than 10 seconds and has a sustained rate of fire of two rounds per minute. The suspension is hydro-pneumatic which not only gives the vehicle excellent cross-country ability but also ensures a comfortable ride for the crew.

In 2008 and 2009, an AS-90 capability enhancement programme primarily upgraded the vehicle's electronics system including the laser inertial artillery pointing system (LINAPS) digital gun sight.

Around 100 remain in British Army service equipping three field regiments of the Royal Horse Artillery and Royal Artillery, supporting armoured infantry brigades for the foreseeable future. The AS-90 is expected to remain in British Army service until 2032 with a hoped-for replacement entering service from 2029.

Polish interest in the AS-90 led to the Krab variant for Polish Army service. This has a licence-built turret mounted on a South Korean K9 Thunder SPG chassis and the latest Azalia Battle Management System.

A total of 120 are to be provided to the Polish Army.

ABOVE: **This AS90 has had a machine-gun fitted to the commander's position. Behind the fume extractor on the barrel of the gun is a rubber protective sleeve which helps keep dirt from entering the turret.** BELOW: **The crew of this AS90 are about to break camp. The vehicle would be placed in this type of hide each time it is stationary for long periods of time. Vehicles on the modern battlefield have to hide to survive.**

ABOVE: **The large storage boxes on the side of the turret can be clearly seen, along with the empty wire-mesh bin on the roof of the vehicle. The large door in the rear of the vehicle is in the open position; this is the main entrance and exit from the vehicle. The AS90 turret has also been fitted to the Indian T-72 MBT chassis for trials with the Indian Army.**

AS90 155mm SPG

Country: UK
Entered service: 1993
Crew: 5
Weight: 45,000kg/44.3 tons
Dimensions: Length – 9.9m/32ft 6in
　Height – 3m/9ft 10in
　Width – 3.4m/11ft 4in
Armament: Main – FH70 155mm/6.1in howitzer
　Secondary – 7.62mm/0.3in machine-gun
Armour: Maximum – 17mm/0.67in
Powerplant: Cummins VTA 903T 660T-660
　8-cylinder 492kW/660hp diesel engine
Performance: Speed – 55kph/34mph
　Range – 370km/230 miles

LEFT: This BMD is taking part in a November Parade in Moscow in 1981. The top of the commander's hatch has the badge of the Soviet Airborne Forces painted on it. The six men of the infantry section carried in the vehicle can be seen sitting on the rear of the BMD. BELOW: A side view of a BMD during a parade in Moscow. A Sagger AT missile is in place on its launcher on the top of the gun barrel.

BMD Airborne Combat Vehicles

When the Soviet Union was forced into a humiliating climb down after the Cuban Missile Crisis in 1963, it was decided to expand and upgrade the Soviet Airborne Forces (VDV). It was very quickly realized that the paratroopers required some form of mechanization to combat anti-personnel weapons and to give them better mobility once on the ground. Development started on the BMD in about 1965. The first production vehicles were issued for service in 1969, and it was first seen by the West in 1970.

The BMD is the only airborne infantry vehicle in service anywhere in the world and it was initially thought by NATO to be an airborne tank. The driver/mechanic is seated in the centre-front of the vehicle with the gun barrel just above his head, while the vehicle commander and radio operator is to the left and slightly to the rear. To the right of the driver is the bow machine-gunner, and behind them is the turret with a single gunner in it. This is the same turret as fitted to the BMP and can fire Sagger wire-guided anti-tank missiles. Behind this is an infantry compartment that was originally designed to accommodate six men, but this has been reduced to five as the vehicle is very small and cramped for the crew. The vehicle is fully amphibious and has two water jets mounted on the rear for propulsion. A protective splash board is fitted on the glacis plate and this is raised when the vehicle enters the water. The turret is fitted with a low-pressure 73mm/2.87in gun fed by a 40-round magazine. The gun fires fin-stabilized HEAT (High-Explosive Anti-Tank) or HE-FRAG (High-Explosive Fragmentation) rounds. Once the round leaves the barrel,

a rocket motor fires in its rear and increases the speed of the round and its range to 1,300m/4,265ft, but this system is adversely affected by the weather and wind, reducing its accuracy greatly.

The Soviet Army realized that the three cargo parachutes that were required to drop the vehicle safely from an aircraft were very heavy, but that they could reduce this to a single parachute by fitting rockets to the PRSM-915 pallet used for air-launching the vehicle. As the pallet leaves the aircraft, four wires with ground contact sensors fitted to their ends are released under the pallet. When one of these sensors strikes the ground, the rockets are fired and these slow the vehicle down for a safe landing. They also realized that dropping the vehicle without its driver and gunner made it very vulnerable,

LEFT: This vehicle is the improved BMD-2. It is armed with a 30mm/1.18in cannon in the turret. The chassis has five road wheels, with the drive wheel at the rear of the vehicle. The air intake for the engine can be seen in the middle of the glacis. BELOW: These two BMDs are on exercise. When the driver is in his raised driving position then the gun barrel has to be at maximum elevation.

so at first the driver and gunner descended in the vehicle. The idea was that they could very quickly dispose of the parachutes, drive the vehicle off the pallet and go to find the rest of the crew. The vehicle would be dropped from a maximum height of 457.2m/1,500ft and the descent takes less than one minute. A great deal of courage was required by the crew to be in the vehicle when it leaves the aircraft especially as a number of accidents occurred in the development of this system, killing the crew. A new system has subsequently been developed where radio beacons are fitted to each vehicle, each one having a different signal, so that the crew can drop separately yet find their vehicle very quickly and move off into action.

Development of the BMD-2 was started in 1983 as an interim solution to combat reports from Afghanistan that showed a number of faults with the BMDs, which were the first vehicles into the country. In particular the 73mm/2.87in gun was shown to be very poor and so the turret was replaced in the BMD-2 with a new one armed with a 30mm/1.18in cannon. Production

started in 1985 and it entered service the same year. BMD-2s were employed by Russian airborne troops in the Russo-Georgian War in 2008, and more recently in the 2022 Russian invasion of Ukraine, where unconfirmed reports suggest the loss of Russian 190 BMD-2s in the first eight months of combat.

The BMD-3 was developed to overcome problems with the track and suspension in the earlier version, and the engine was also upgraded to a more powerful diesel. This new vehicle was due to go into service by 1990 but this was delayed by a year. Ongoing financial issues resulted in limited numbers entering service for only a comparatively short period.

RIGHT: This **BMD-2** is taking part in an informal parade. The turret has an infrared light fitted to the side. At the rear of the turret is a pintle mount for a Spigot or Spandrel AT missile. This is the same turret as mounted on the BMP-2.

BMD-1 Airborne Combat Vehicle

Country: USSR
Entered service: 1969
Crew: 2 plus 5 infantry
Weight: 6,807kg/6.7 tons
Dimensions: Length – 5.4m/17ft 9in
 Height – 1.77m/5ft 10in
 Width –2.55m/8ft 4in
Armament: Main – 1 x 2A28 73mm/2.87in gun,
 and 1 x coaxial 7.62mm/0.3in machine-gun
 Secondary – 2 x 7.62mm/0.3in machine-guns,
 and 1 x Sagger launch rail
Armour: Maximum – 23mm/0.91in
Powerplant: 5D20 6-cylinder 216kW/290hp
 diesel engine
Performance: Speed – Road 80kph/50mph;
 Water 10kph/6mph
 Range – 320km/199 miles

LEFT: **The low profile of the BMP-1 turret can be clearly seen. The chassis is made up of six road wheels with the driving wheel at the front. The upper part of the track is covered by a skirt.** ABOVE: **A BMP-1 leaving the water, with the trim vane in the raised position. The crew are in the closed-down position. The transition to amphibious vehicle only takes a few minutes.**

BMP-1 Infantry Fighting Vehicle

The BMP (*Boevaya Mashina Pekhota*) was the world's first infantry combat vehicle and was the most significant innovation in infantry combat tactics of the late 20th century. It was also the first Soviet military vehicle to be designed with the needs of the nuclear battlefield in mind. This new vehicle provided the infantry with unprecedented firepower, mobility and protection that could be taken into the heart of the enemy position and the idea would be copied in vehicles such as the American Bradley, the German Marder and the British Warrior.

Development started in the 1960s and prototypes were ready for testing in 1964. In 1966 the BMP-1 was accepted for service and placed into production, but, due to a number of problems that subsequently came to light, mass production was not started until 1970. The BMP-1 is of an all-welded steel construction which offers protection from bullets and shell-

splinters; the front is even proof against 12.7mm/0.5in anti-tank rounds. The glacis plate is distinctively ribbed with the driver located behind the ribbed area on the left-hand side of the vehicle and the commander seated behind. The engine is mounted on the right-hand side of the vehicle next to the driver and commander while the air intakes and outlets are on the top of the vehicle. Two forms of starting the main engine are fitted; either compressed air or battery. The compressed air system is normally used in very cold winter temperatures.

Behind the commander and the engine is a one-man turret which is equipped with the 73mm/2.87in smooth-bore low-pressure gun, fed from a 40-round magazine. On leaving the barrel, a rocket motor in the tail of each round is ignited, but these munitions are badly affected by the wind and the weather. The maximum rate of fire is eight rounds per minute.

RIGHT: **The driver of this BMP-1 is standing in front of his vehicle in Afghanistan. The vehicle has been fitted with additional storage on the rear of the turret. The three pistol ports are open on the rear. The ribbed glacis plate can be clearly seen here. A large searchlight has been fitted in front of the commander's hatch but behind the driver's position.**

Mounted coaxially to the main gun is a 7.62mm/0.3in PKT machine-gun which is fed by a 2,000-round belt housed in a box under the turret, while mounted over the main armament is a rail for a Sagger wire guided anti-tank missile. The Sagger has a minimum range of 500m/1,640ft and a maximum of 3,000m/9,842ft. One missile is carried on the rail in the ready-to-use position, while two others are stored in the turret. Reloading takes 50 seconds. The missile controls are stored under the gunner's seat and these are pulled out and locked in position between his legs when required. After firing, the gunner watches the missile through a scope while controlling its flight using a joystick. This missile system can only be used in daylight as there is no other way of tracking it.

The BMP-1 has a full NBC air-filtration system. The troop compartment in the rear holds eight men, four down each side sitting back to back facing the outside of the vehicle. The main fuel tank is positioned between the backs of these men, while the rear doors of the vehicle are also fuel tanks, giving a total fuel capacity of 460 litres/101 gallons. This fuel storage system poses considerable risks to both vehicle and occupants on the battlefield. In the roof of the troop compartment are four hatches for the infantry to use and each man also has a firing port in front of his position in the rear of the vehicle. Apart from the men's own personal weapons an RPG-7 anti-tank grenade launcher is also carried. It has been found that the vehicle is very cramped under service conditions due to the low height of the roof and several countries using the BMP-1 have reduced the number of troops in the infantry section in the rear to six men. The vehicle also has a very poor ventilation system so the rear compartment becomes unbearably hot.

The BMP-1 is fully amphibious and is propelled through the water by the vehicle's own tracks. Just before entering the water, a trim vane is attached to the front of the vehicle, the bilge pumps are switched on and the splash plate is raised. Over a thousand BMP-1s remain in service with Russia, India, Poland and the People's Republic of China.

TOP: The rear of a BMP-1 with all its doors and hatches open. The bulbous rear doors doubled as fuel tanks for the vehicle. The four large hatches are fully open, each hatch acting as an exit for two men. The pistol ports just above the track skirt are in the closed position. On the rear of the door is storage for two metal track chocks. ABOVE: The full complement of the vehicle can be clearly seen. On the left is the driver, behind him is the vehicle commander, in the turret is the gunner, and in the rear of the vehicle is the eight-man infantry section. LEFT: A close-up of the Sagger AT missile. The loading hatch is just large enough for the missile to be pushed up and on to its launching rail.

BMP-1 Infantry Fighting Vehicle

Country: USSR
Entered service: 1966
Crew: 3 plus 8 infantry
Weight: 12,802kg/12.6 tons
Dimensions: Length – 6.74m/22ft 1in
  Height – 2.15m/7ft 1in
  Width – 2.94m/9ft 8in
Armament: Main – 1 x 2A28 Grom 73mm/ 2.87in gun, 1 x coaxial 7.62mm/0.3in PKT machine-gun
  Secondary – Sagger launch rail and small arms
Armour: Maximum – 33mm/1.3in
Powerplant: UTD-20 6-cylinder 224kW/300hp diesel engine
Performance: Speed – Road 80kph/50mph; Water 6–8kph/4–5mph
  Range – 500km/311 miles

BMP-2 Infantry Fighting Vehicle

The BMP-2 amphibious infantry fighting vehicle was a development of the BMP-1 and was first seen in public and by the NATO allies in the Moscow Parade of 1982. Development work had begun in 1972 and several steps were taken to improve on the BMP-1, specifically its main armament which had become obsolete. While the BMP-2 is heavier than the earlier design, it has a more powerful engine which endows the IFV with similar road performance.

The new vehicle had a larger, two-man welded and armoured steel turret, each position having its own hatch, and the turret can traverse 360 degrees in 10.28 seconds. The infantry section in the rear was reduced from eight to seven troops, and rear infantry roof hatches were reduced from four

ABOVE: **A Russian Army BMP-2 pictured during a 2016 demonstration. Main armament is the 2A42 turret-mounted 30mm/1.18in cannon. The 223kW/300hp diesel engine gives a top road speed of 65kph /40mph. The turret is fitted with two clusters of three smoke dischargers. On the rear of the vehicle is a snorkel tube in the stored position. The mounting for the Spandrel AT-5 ATGW is situated on the roof of the turret at the rear.** BELOW LEFT: **Ukrainian BMP-2 infantry fighting vehicles on parade in Kiev, 2008. Fourteen years later, sources reported that during the 2022 invasion of Ukraine, Russia lost around 700 BMP-2s.**

to two. Troops sit back to back, along the vehicle centreline and each side of the troop compartment has three firing ports with periscopes. Main access to the troop compartment is by two rear doors, which contain integral periscopes as well as diesel fuel tanks which are drained before combat.

The vehicle commander position was moved from behind the driver's position into the turret to the right of the gunner to give better all-round vision. The commander has three day-vision periscopes, specifically a 1PZ-3 day-sight designed for anti-aircraft use with up to x 4 magnification, an OU-3GA2 infra-red searchlight, a TNP-165A designator together with a TKN-3B binocular sight with x 4.75 day magnification and x 4 night-sight magnification.

The gunner position has a rectangular hatch in the roof and is equipped with three day periscopes facing forward and left, as well as a rearward-facing day periscope. The gunner's BPK-1-42 binocular sight has a moon/starlight vision range of 650m/2,132ft, or 350m/1,148ft using the vehicle's infra-red searchlight mounted coaxially to the 30mm/1.18in cannon.

LEFT: Indian Army BMP-2 Saraths (chariot of victory) pictured during a 2009 military exercise on the firing range at Camp Bundela, Rajasthan, India. Indian BMP-2s were initially locally assembled using provided components but by 1999, 90 per cent of the vehicle was of Indian manufacture. An estimated 2,500 Indian Saraths have been produced. BELOW LEFT: Cadets of the Ukraine Military Academy (Odessa) demonstrate the amphibious capabilities of the BMP-2, 2016.

The driver sits in the vehicle's front left with the radio operator behind, and the engine is located in a separate compartment to their right. The driver also has his own entry hatch in the roof as well as three day periscopes. The centre periscope can be replaced with either an extended periscope for amphibious operations, or a night-vision scope. Drivers of the BMP-1 were especially vulnerable to anti-tank land mines so the BMP-2 driver has an armoured seat as well as additional belly armour in the lower front portion of the vehicle.

Overall, the BMP-2 armour was similar to that of the BMP-1 but it has been improved through its service life and in light of combat experience in theatres such as Afghanistan – this included fitting spaced armour, a second layer of "stand-off" armour made of, for example, ballistic rubber-like material, to act as spaced armour to the hull sides.

The vehicle can become amphibious with some preparation with in-water propulsion coming from water jets produced by moving of the vehicle tracks. The vehicle is however not totally watertight and is not equipped with an anchor. The hull can withstand 7.62mm/0.3in AP ammunition and the front will cope with hits from 23mm/0.9in AP shells.

The BMP-2 has seen extensive combat use, from the Soviet-Afghan war, Gulf War, Chechen War, Invasion of Iraq, and the 2022 Russian invasion of Ukraine.

The type remains in widespread use with over thirty nations around the world and it is expected to remain in frontline use for some time.

The BMP-2's main armament is a stabilized 30mm/1.18in 2A42 automatic cannon, which has two rates of fire: slow at 200 rounds per minute and fast at 550 rounds per minute. However, the turret extractor fan cannot remove the gun fumes fast enough when faster speed firing takes place, impeding the crew's performance. Maximum effective range is 1,500m/4,921ft against armour, 2,500m/8,202ft against air targets and 4,000m/13,123ft against ground targets.

The cannon's high elevation of 74 degrees make it effective against helicopters and slower, low-flying fixed-wing aircraft. The addition of the roof-mounted 9P135M ATGM launcher enabled firing of the 9M111 AT-4 Spigot, 9M113 AT-5 Spandrel and 9M113 Konkurs-M AT-5B Spandrel anti-tank missiles.

BMP-2 Infantry Fighting Vehicle

Country: USSR
Entered service: 1981
Crew: 3 plus 6 infantry
Weight: 14,224kg/14 tons
Dimensions: Length – 6.74m/22ft 1in
Height – 2.45m/8ft
Width – 3.15m/10ft 4in
Armament: Main – 2A42 30mm/1.18in cannon, and coaxial 7.62mm/0.3in machine-gun
Secondary – Spandrel launcher and small arms
Armour: 33mm/1.3in maximum
Powerplant: UTD-20 6-cylinder 224kW/300hp diesel engine
Performance: Speed – Road 65kph/40mph;
Water 7kph/4mph
Range – 600km/373 miles

BMP-3 Infantry Fighting Vehicle

Whole hen the BMP-3 IFV was first seen in 1990, it was considered to be a radical and unconventional new design, intended to be the successor to the BMP-1 and BMP-2.

The design of the BMP-3 has its origins in the Obyekt 685 light tank prototype dating back to 1975. This in turn led to the next-generation infantry combat vehicle the Obyekt 688, that ultimately became the BMP-3 that officially entered Soviet Army service in 1987, and was first seen in public at the 1990 Moscow Victory Day parade. In the course of the BMP's production, the vehicle's design underwent 1,500 changes and "improvements" which delayed production and delivery.

ABOVE: **United Arab Emirates (UAE) BMP-3 being unloaded in Kuwait from an Elbahia L62 landing craft, 2003.** BELOW LEFT: **BMP-3 based self-propelled anti-aircraft gun variant, 2018.**

Unlike most other IFVs, the BMP-3 was designed with an all-new diesel engine positioned under the floor and the hull, in the rear of the vehicle together with some of the fuel cells. This is why the driver is seated in the front centre, under the main gun, and flanked by an infantryman position on each side. The other five infantrymen are carried seated behind the two-man turret.

Early versions had the 450hp UTD-29 engine but most BMP-3s now have the 500hp UTD-29M liquid-cooled diesel engine which bestows a land range of 600km/373m. Like its predecessors, the vehicle is amphibious and it is propelled at up to 10kph/0.6pmh whilst in the water by two water jets mounted at the rear.

The BMP-3 is one of the most heavily armed ICVs currently in service and the initial version carries a turret-mounted low-velocity 2A70 100mm/3.93in rifled gun which can fire both conventional shells (40 rounds carried) or 9M117 Bastion anti-tank guided missiles, eight of which were carried on board. A turret-mounted 30mm autocannon and a 7.62mm/0.3in machine-gun with 2,000 rounds, together with two bow-mounted 7.62mm machine-guns add to the impressive firepower. The vehicle has five firing ports and features including radiation and chemical agent detector, an automatic fire extinguisher and six 81mm/3.2in smoke grenade launchers.

LEFT: The BMP-3 hull and turret are made of high-strength aluminium alloy. The front of the hull is also provided with an extra steel plate welded to it. Manufacturers claim the vehicle can withstand 30mm/1.18in gun rounds at 200m/219yd range. The internal self-sealing fuel tank is designed to provide additional protection to crew should any autocannon rounds penetrate the vehicle's front armour.

BELOW LEFT: Abandoned Russian BMP-3 during the 2022 Russian invasion of Ukraine.

In May 2015, the Russian Defence Ministry ordered "hundreds" more BMP-3 vehicles to keep its armoured vehicle force at strength while development of the BMP-3's proposed replacement, the Kurganets-25, is completed. Experience has also shown that the vehicle has low battlefield survivability – at least 200 Russian BMP-3s were destroyed during the first six months following Russia's invasion of Ukraine.

The BMP-3 is in service with a number of nations including Algeria, Azerbaijan, Cyprus, Indonesia, Kuwait, Libya, Morocco, Syria, Sri Lanka, South Korea, United Arab Emirates and Venezuela. Ukraine captured at least 60 Russian examples during the first six months of the Russian invasion.

Through its production, the BMP-3 was updated with improved fire control systems in which the main gunsight had an integrated laser rangefinder and missile guidance function,

thermal imaging camera and a ballistic computer. From 2018, some Russian BMP-3s were fitted with the AU-220M combat module comprising a 57mm/2.2in cannon that can carry and fire 80 rounds per minute of air burst, high-explosive, fragmentation and armour-piercing ammunition, as well as guided munitions. This, reportedly, gives the BMP-3 the ability to penetrate main battle tank side armour.

The improved BMP-3M version is equipped with the better-armoured Bakhcha-U turret, which mounts similar weapons to the original BMP-3 turret but also features two-axis stabilization for the main gun, a Forward Looking Infra Red gunner sight, panoramic thermal imaging equipment in the commander position, new ammunition autoloader, and a new sighting system. The -3M can also carry two 9M120 Ataka AT-9 anti-tank missiles on the turret.

BMP-3 Infantry Fighting Vehicle

Country: USSR
Entered service: 1989
Crew: 3 plus 7 infantry
Weight: 19,304kg/19 tons
Dimensions: Length – 7.14m/23ft 5in
  Height – 2.3m/7ft 7in
  Width – 3.15m/10ft 4in
Armament: Main – 1 x 2A70 100mm/3.94in gun,
  1 x 2A72 30mm/1.18in cannon, and
  1 x 7.62mm/0.3in machine-gun
  Secondary – Small arms
Armour: Alluminium alloy and steel, 35mm/1.4in front
Powerplant: UTD-29M 10-cylinder multi-fuel 373kW/500hp engine
Performance: Speed – Road 70kph/44mph;
  Water 10kph/6mph
  Range – 600km/373 miles

LEFT: **A Boxer pictured during Australian trials in 2016 – note the 30mm/1.18in main gun. Australia has committed to acquiring 211 Boxer Combat Reconnaissance Vehicles (CRVs), 12 mission modules and associated support systems. The majority of these vehicles will be built in Australia.**

Boxer Multi-role AFV

The ARTEC Boxer multi-role AFV started life in 1993 as a joint venture design project between France and Germany, which was joined by the UK in 1996. The idea from the outset was that a number of missions could be effectively executed through the use of the same base vehicle mounting a wide variety of interchangeable, installable mission modules.

By 1999, prototypes were ordered and France had left the project to be replaced two years later by the Netherlands. The design, known variously by its participants as GTK/MRAV/PWV, was unveiled in late 2002 and the Boxer name was announced soon after. By mid-2003 the UK had withdrawn from the project. Orders were placed by the Netherlands and then Germany who received the first production example in 2009. Three production facilities were established for Boxer, two in Germany and one in the Netherlands.

The Boxer drive module (sometimes referred to as platform or drive-line module) contains the wheels and the engine, an MTU 8V199 TE20 diesel engine, a militarized version of the Mercedes-Benz OM 500 truck engine. The engine installation was designed so it can be changed, impressively, in around 20 minutes. More powerful versions of the same engine can be selected depending on mission profile. A total of 562 litres/148 gallons of fuel can be carried by a Boxer, supplied by the front 280 litre/74 gallon tank, a rear 238 litre/63 gallon tank and a reserve tank with a 44 litre/11 gallon capacity. The vehicle has a central tyre inflation system and each wheel has run-flat inserts providing a "get-out-of-trouble" capability of 30k/18.6m of travel at up to 50kph/31mph if a tyre is punctured.

It is the Boxer's unique and innovative interchangeable pod-like mission module that determines the vehicle role and contains mission-specific elements e.g. specialist equipment, armament etc. The mission modules are attached to the drive module by just four points and can be replaced or swapped in under an hour.

The Boxer's manufacturers Artec, who justifiably describe the vehicle as having "unique modularity" have identified more than twenty different modules for Boxer, including Armoured Personnel Carrier, Command Post, Ambulance, Combat Reconnaissance Vehicle, Cargo, Driver Training Vehicle, Repair and Recovery, Counter UAV, Joint Fire Support Team and Heavy Weapon Carrier.

While the modules are designed with in-built driver and passenger protection as a key consideration, additional

LEFT: **This Dutch boxer is the command post variant and is shown with its access ramp down and protective collapsible "porch" deployed.**

LEFT: **A German Army Boxer base vehicle pictured from behind with its mission module dismounted showing the basic vehicle on which all versions are based.** ABOVE: **TA FLW (Fernbedienbare Leichte Waffenstation – remotely operated, light weapon station) 200 system mounted on top of a German Boxer AFV. To the left is the system's optronics, enabling the operator within the vehicle to operate the gun using a computer screen. Ammunition is held in the box on the right, obscured by smoke grenade launchers.** BELOW LEFT: **A Lithuanian Land Forces IFV Vilkas (wolf) pictured at a military parade, Vilnius, 2018. Note this example is fitted with the Israeli-designed Samson Mk2 unmanned turret armed with a 30mm/1.18in Bushmaster automatic cannon.**

modular armour can be applied if mission requirements demand. The manufacturers claim the Boxer will withstand anti-personnel and large anti-tank mines and the vehicle and module's standard armour is resistant to 14.5mm/0.57in armour-piercing rounds. The crew compartment interior is also completely covered by a spall liner to minimise injury from armour and projectile fragments should the hull be breached.

The Boxer can be fitted with an array of armament options depending on mission and preferences of the operating force but these typically include a remote operated 7.62mm/0.3in light machine-gun to a 30mm/1.18in cannon in a turret. Dutch Boxers have 12.7mm/0.5in heavy machine-guns while German vehicles have the FLW-200 remotely operated, light weapon station system. The Lithuanian Vilkas version has a turret-mounted 30mm dual-feed cannon while Australian Boxer CRVs also have a 30mm cannon and coaxial 7.62mm machine-gun in a two-man turret.

Britain rejoined the Boxer programme in 2018 to meet the British Army's Mechanised Infantry Vehicle (MIV) requirement. A £2.3 billion deal was signed to acquire 623 vehicles in

a number of versions – infantry carriers, engineer section vehicles, recce/fire support vehicles, mortar carriers, repair vehicles, command-and-control, utility vehicles observation post vehicles, beyond-line-of-sight observation platforms, electronic warfare and signals/intelligence gathering vehicles, and ambulances.

Lithuanian Land Force are committed to deploying over 200 Boxers in a variety of IFV configurations, as well as some examples of the all-important driver training versions which most customers also purchase. In Lithuanian service the Boxer is known as the IFV Vilkas (vilkas is Lithuanian for wolf).

Boxer Multi-Role AFV

Country: Germany, The Netherlands
Entered service: 2009
Crew: Driver plus up to 8 infantry in module
Weight: 36,500 kg/40.2 tons
Dimensions: Length – 7.93m/26ft
    Height – 2.37m/7ft 9in
    Width – 2.99m/9ft 10in
Armament: various, but 30mm/1.18in cannon
    typical
    Secondary – 7.62 mm/0.3in machine-gun
Armour: Classified
Powerplant: MTU 8V199 TE20 diesel
    engine, 530–600kW/711-805hp depending
    on variant
Performance: Speed – 103kph/64mph;
    Range – 1100km/684 miles

Bradley M2 Infantry Fighting Vehicle

In the mid-1960s, the US Army required a new infantry vehicle, capable of outperforming the Soviet BMP-1, to replace the M113. Until 1977 no development vehicle had been produced which proved to be adequate and so the projects were dropped. In that year, two new vehicles were developed – the XM2 (Bradley Infantry Fighting Vehicle) and the XM3 (Bradley Cavalry Vehicle). However, in 1978 both of these vehicles were condemned by the General Accounting Office as being too slow, too high, having a poor engine and insufficient armour. Some of these problems, but not all, were rectified in further development and in 1981 the first M2 Bradley production vehicles were handed over to the US Army. Initially, the US Army had a requirement for 6,800 Bradley M2s, but this was later reduced.

The M2 was the first production model, had a 447kW/600hp Cummins VT903 engine and was amphibious thanks to a permanently fitted swim barrier or flotation screen. It was designed to be transportable by US Air Force C-141 Starlifter and C-5 Galaxy aircraft. The vehicle's turret was offset to the right to maximize room for six troops in the passenger compartment. Three periscopes in the roof enabled the troops to see outside, together with two periscopes on each side of the vehicle's hull above the side firing ports. Up to five TOW or Dragon missiles can also be stored in the passenger compartment. The vehicle's NBC system is limited to the three-man crew and does not provide protection for the infantry in the rear.

M2 armour was designed to protect the vehicle through 360

ABOVE: **Digital modifications introduced by the M2A3 included the Improved Bradley Acquisition Subsystem (IBAS), fire control and navigation as well as situational awareness. Armour was improved together with fire-suppression systems and improved NBC equipment. The Commander's Independent Viewer (CIV) enables the commander to safely search for targets and maintain situational awareness independent of the gunner and their activity. This M2A3 Bradley operating near Fallujah, Iraq, 2004 shows the Commander's Independent Viewer (CIV) at the right rear of the turret.**

degrees against 14.55mm/0.57in armour-piercing incendiary (API) ammunition. The hull top, bottom, and front is made of all-welded military-grade 5083 aluminium armour, with 9.1mm/0.36in of steel armour added to the front third of the hull bottom to increase protection against mines, IEDs etc. The hull's side and rear armour consisted of spaced laminated armour of two 6.4mm/0.25in steel plates separated by 25mm/0.98in, mounted 89mm/3.5in away from the inner face of the aluminium armour.

The driver of the vehicle sits at the front on the left-hand side, with the engine on the right-hand side. The top-mounted turret has the commander position on the right and the gunner on the left. The main armament is the 25mm/0.98in M242 chain gun with a coaxial M240 7.62mm/0.3in machine-gun. The gunner can select a single shot or two different burst rates and it is fully stabilized in all planes enabling it to be fired on the move. Two TOW missiles, with a range of 3,750m/12,300ft, are mounted on the outside of the turret.

Bradley M2 Infantry Fighting Vehicle

Country: USA
Entered service: 1981
Crew: 3 plus 6 infantry
Weight: 22,260 kg/22 tons
Dimensions: Length – 6.47m/21ft 3in
Height – 3m/9ft 10in
Width – 3.28m/10ft 9in
Armament: Main – M242 25mm/0.98in
cannon, and coaxial M240 7.62 mm/0.3in
machine-gun
Secondary – Small arms
Armour: Classified
Powerplant: Cummins VTA-903T
turbocharged 8-cylinder 373kW/500hp
diesel engine
Performance: Speed – Road 61kph/38mph;
Water 6.4kph/4mph
Range – 400km/249 miles

In the M2A1 variant introduced in 1986, in addition to a Gas Particulate Filter Units (GPFU) NBC system, an additional position for a seventh infantryman was added immediately behind the turret.

Based on combat experience during the first Gulf War, the M2A2 ODS/ODS-E (Operation Desert Storm/Operation Desert Storm-Engineer) version introduced improvements including an eye-safe laser rangefinder (ELRF), a tactical navigation system, a missile countermeasure device to counter wire-guided missiles, and the Force XXI Battle Command Brigade and Below (FBCB2) Battlefield Command Information System. Internal stowage was improved, troop carrying capacity was increased back to seven and the driver's position received a thermal imaging system. Importantly an MRE (Meal, Ready-to-Eat) heater was added to the vehicle interior to provide hot foot for the crew in the field.

The M2A3 variant introduced in 2000, brought upgrades that made the Bradley fully digital through upgraded or improved electronics systems throughout.

Following combat experience in Iraq, the US Army were keen to revisit the basic design of the Bradley in light of the impact on performance caused by the addition of armour and equipment in-theatre. Extra equipment and armour add to weight, reduce mobility and manoeuvrability and make IFVs sit lower to the ground, making them more vulnerable to landmines and IEDs. The resulting M2A4 variant saw the inclusion of lighter tracks, improved shock absorbers, a new suspension support system, larger engine, improved transmission, and a smart-power management system to improve current and future-proof against future demands on the vehicle's electrical system.

In 2018, BAE Systems Land and Armaments was contracted to produce M2A4 Bradleys using existing M2A3, M7A3 and M2A2 ODS-SA Bradleys vehicles and the first completed vehicles appeared in 2022.

ABOVE: **M2 Bradley Fighting Vehicles from the US Army's 1st Battalion, 68th Armor Regiment, 3rd Armored Brigade Combat Team, 4th Infantry Division on exercise in Poland, 2022.** BELOW: **The M2A2 introduced in 1988 has a 447 kW/ 600hp, improved armour as standard and the ability to mount explosive reactive armour (ERA). The new armour fit provides the vehicle with protection against 30mm APDS rounds and RPGs. Soldiers from the US Army 3rd Armored Cavalry Regiment load into the rear of an M2, February 2006.**

BRDM-2 Armoured Car

The same team that designed the original BRDM-1 (Boyevaya Razvedyvatelnaya Dozornaya Mashina – Combat Reconnaissance Patrol Vehicle) armoured car were used to develop the improved and better-armed BRDM-2 amphibious armoured scout car for use by the states that made up the Soviet Union, and for widespread export to its allies. It has also been known by the designations BTR-40PB, BTR-40P-2 and GAZ 41-08. The development process started in 1962, using the team's experience and the basic BRDM-1 as a starting point. Visually, the -2 has a larger, more box-like hull but retained the boat-like bow of the earlier vehicle. The new design had to incorporate several improvements such as better road and cross-country performance, full amphibious capability and heavier, turret-mounted armament.

ABOVE: **Two Bulgarian Army BRDM-2-based anti-tank vehicles, 2006.**

The crew compartment (for driver, co-driver, commander, and gunner) was moved further forward and a new GAZ-41 V8 petrol engine was located to the rear, within an armoured compartment to better protect it from frontal enemy fire. The crew enter and leave the vehicle through two hatches over the driver/commander positions.

The vehicle has an innovative centralized tyre pressure regulation system which enables the driver to increase or decrease the pressure of all four or individual tyres while the vehicle is in motion, to best suit the ground conditions encountered. Between the main wheels are two pairs of smaller chain-driven belly wheels which drop down when lowered by the

LEFT: **A radiological-chemical reconnaissance BRDM-2 car. The boxes at the rear of the car carry a number of pennants that are used to mark a safe lane through contaminated ground.**

driver, for operating on soft ground or for trench-crossing.

The BRDM-2 is an all-welded steel construction, with the driver and commander sitting side by side – left and right respectively – in the front of the vehicle, behind a bulletproof windscreen which can be augmented by twin armoured shutters in combat situations.

Both commander and driver positions have periscopes, enabling them to monitor surrounding terrain. The commander has six periscopes – five in the front and one on the vehicle's side – as well as day and night sights, while the driver has four front-mounted periscopes, as well as night-vision facility.

The gunner sits in the turret for combat, otherwise sits inside the hull. The manually-operated turret is the same as that fitted to the BTR-60PB, BTR-70 and the OT-64 model 2A, and is armed with a 14.55mm/0.57in heavy machine-gun and a coaxial 7.62mm/0.3in machine-gun.

In amphibious mode, the engine supplies power to a circular water-jet, equipped with a four-bladed propeller at the vehicle's rear, protected by an armoured shutter when not in water. The water-jet bestows an in-water speed of 10kph/6.2pmh for up to 19 hours. A trim board, stowed under the front of the hull (and providing additional armour protection) when travelling on land, is raised at the front of the vehicle to keep the vehicle stable in water and to prevent water from inundating the bow of the craft.

There are six variations of the basic vehicle, the most common being the BRDM-2, armed with Sagger ATGWs, which was first used in combat during the 1973 Middle East campaigns. In this variant, the turret and the hull top are removed and replaced by a six-rail Sagger launcher in which the armoured cover, missile rails, missiles and firing mechanism are all one unit. When travelling, the missiles are stored in the body of the vehicle but in action the entire unit is raised into the firing position. Other vehicle variants include a command version, radiological-chemical reconnaissance car, Swatter-B and Spandrel ATGW vehicles and the SA-9 Gaskin AA system. The

ABOVE: **This thoroughly updated Georgian BRDM-2, pictured in 2014, has a front-mounted day and night vision camera, remote controlled weapon station, enhanced armour, front-mounted foldable wire-cutter, a door on each side and smoke dischargers.** BOTTOM LEFT: **The armoured triangular cover for the water-jet on the rear of this BRDM-2 has been opened to prepare for water-jet propulsion.**

BRDM-2 has proved to be a very rugged and reliable design and is expected to be in service for many more years with a number of countries.

The BRDM-2 entered production in 1963 and was first seen in a public parade in 1966. Production finished in 1989 but it is still in service with the Russian Army and the armed forces of almost 40 other countries.

BRDM-2 Armoured Car

Country: USSR
Entered service: 1964
Crew: 4
Weight: 7,000kg/6.9 tons
Dimensions: Length – 5.75m/18ft 10in
 Height – 2.31m/7ft 7in
 Width – 2.35m/7ft 9in
Armament: Main – 14.55mm/0.57in KPVT
 machine-gun, and coaxial 7.62mm/0.3in PKT
 machine-gun
 Secondary – Small arms
Armour: Maximum – 14mm/0.55in
Powerplant: GAZ 41 8-cylinder 105kw/140hp
 petrol engine
Performance: Speed – Road 100kph/62mph;
 Water 10kph/6mph
 Range – 750km/466 miles

BTR-60 Armoured Personnel Carrier

The BTR-60 was developed in the late 1950s to replace the BTR-152 and was the first in a related series of eight-wheeled armoured personnel carriers produced by the former Soviet Union. It entered service in 1960 with the Motorized Rifle Divisions and was first seen by the West during the Moscow Parade of November 1961. At the height of its Soviet Army use, each Rifle Division was equipped with 417 of these vehicles which were in turn replaced by the BMP-1. Despite the fact that open-topped troop carriers had already been shown to be vulnerable in combat, the open-top (for the troops, not crew who were in a covered compartment) BTR-60P was the first model of the new vehicle to be released as it was comparatively cheap and easy to mass-produce. This version, which could carry 16 troops, was only in service for a few years and was quickly relegated to a training role.

ABOVE: **A former East German Army BTR-60PB displayed at the Museum of Military History, Dresden, Germany. Note the open steel hatch covers at the driver and commander positions and the trim vane beneath the hull front, raised in amphibious mode to improve stability.** BELOW LEFT: **The driver and vehicle commander's front hatches are open. The hatch halfway down the vehicle can be used as an exit point.**

It was followed into service by the new BTR-60PA which had a covered, armoured roof and could carry 14 troops, but this was in turn soon improved upon by the BTR-60PAI which entered service in 1965. The 60PAI, developed as a result of German turreted APC development, only differed from the PA version by having the same turret as the BRDM-2 and mounting a single 14.55mm/0.57in KPV heavy machine-gun and a 7.62mm/0.3in machine-gun. The BTR-60PB introduced a new sighting system for the vehicle's machine-guns.

The hull of the BTR-60 is an all-welded steel construction providing protection against small arms fire and shrapnel – the thicker front armour can withstand 7.62mm bullets from any range while the rest of the armour can withstand 7.62mm bullets from 100m/328ft range.

Within the hull, the driver sits on the left and the vehicle commander on the right in the front of the vehicle, while behind them is the one-man turret. In the BTR-60P, access for the crew was through the vehicle sides ,whilst for the BTR-60PA, two hatches on top of the vehicle provided access to their positions. The arrangement became the standard for

subsequent production variants and the BTR-60B introduced a door on the vehicle's right side for the gunner. Firing ports were also provided for the driver and commander, and a further two for the gunner, one on each side of the vehicle. The driver and commander can see ahead through bulletproof windscreens, both of which have steel covers which can be lowered as required for additional protection, but with vision slots. Periscopes were also provided and later production models had infra-red searchlights and night-vision capability.

Behind the turret area is the infantry accommodation which seats 14 men on bench seats. These troops, when debussing under fire, are extremely exposed as they have to emerge from hatches in the top of the vehicle or through two small hatches, one on either side.

At the rear of the vehicle is the engine area, which houses the twin engines of the vehicle. The engine on the right side drives the second and the fourth axles while the left-hand engine propels the first and the third axles. The twin-engine set-up offers a primitive form of system redundancy in that if one engine is damaged in combat, the other would not be affected and could still drive the vehicle, even if at a reduced speed. The negative aspect of this arrangement is its complexity and

ABOVE LEFT: **A captured enemy BTR-60PB on display at the Yad la-Shiryon Museum, Israel. Note the exposed amphibious-mode water-jet with its lids open.** ABOVE RIGHT: **Interior of a Soviet BTR-60B showing the very basic driver's position. Note the numerous periscopes with padding.** BELOW LEFT: **The first vehicle on the flat car is a BTR-60PU command car. This is a conversion of the basic BTR-60PB. The PU version is fitted with several radios and a 10m/32ft 10in aerial, which on this vehicle is folded down and stored on the top of the vehicle.**

associated high maintenance compared to that of a single powerplant. The BTR-60 is fully amphibious, propelled by a water-jet centrally mounted in the vehicle's rear.

The BTR-60 is an 8-wheel drive. The forward four wheels are steerable and each tyre is attached to a central tyre pressure system that is controlled by the driver to optimise performance in different driving environments, adding to the vehicle's good cross-country ability.

The BTR-60 was slowly phased out of service to be replaced by the BTR-70 from 1979 onwards. Total production was about 25,000 new vehicles, excluding the upgrades carried out on the early models to bring them up to BTR-60PB standard. Many versions of these vehicles can still be found in service with export customers and former Soviet bloc countries.

BTR-60PB APC

Country: USSR
Entered service: 1960
Crew: 2 plus 14 infantry
Weight: 10,300kg/10.1 tons
Dimensions: Length – 7.56m/24ft 10in
    Height – 2.31m/7ft 7in
    Width – 2.83m/9ft 3in
Armament: Main – 14.55mm/0.57in KPV
    machine-gun
    Secondary – Small arms
Armour: Maximum – 9mm/0.354in
Powerplant: 2 x GAZ 49B 6-cylinder 67kW/90hp
    petrol engines
Performance: Speed – Road 80kph/50mph;
    Water 10kph/6.2mph
    Range – 500km/311 miles

BTR-70 Armoured Personnel Carrier

While the BMP was perhaps the most revolutionary armoured vehicle developed by the Soviet Union, the BTR-70 was the least radical as it was developed as a replacement for, but was a straight evolution of, the BTR-60 and retained most of its shortcomings. These issues, including the flammable petrol-powered engines, were brought into sharp focus when the vehicle was combat-tested during the Soviet-Afghan war.

Development started in 1971 with production commencing in 1972. It entered service in 1976, but was not seen by the West until 1980 when it was spotted in the November Moscow Parade. The delays in production of the vehicle were a result of a catastrophic fire at the engine factory.

The BTR-70 is a fully amphibious vehicle and is propelled in the water by a single water-jet mounted at the rear of the hull. To prepare the vehicle for water deployment, the driver has to deploy the trim vane mounted on the vehicle's front upper hull and activate the vehicle's bilge pumps. This preparation can all be done from within the vehicle.

The slightly thicker and heavier all-welded steel hull of the vehicle is longer than the BTR-60, while the front and rear were widened to give the wheels better protection.

Driver and commander sit in the front, and behind them two infantrymen who could use the forward-facing pistol ports to cover the front of the vehicle and the debussing infantry as they left the vehicle. Driver equipment includes three vision blocks, day and night vision devices. The

ABOVE: **A Russian Army BTR-70 pictured during a parade in Donetsk, 2015. Note the trim vane stowed flush to the top of the vehicle's front, the front windscreen protective plates shown open and the small vision blocks offering additional views from within the crew area. Between the second and third wheels is a small hatch which troops can use to exit the vehicle, but only when stopped. The pistol ports in the side of the crew compartment can also be seen.**

commander position is similarly equipped and also has an infra-red searchlight. Behind them was the turret area which was the same as that fitted to the BTR-60 and was operated by one of the infantrymen. There were plans to fit the BMP turret to the vehicle but this proved to be too expensive and would have required a major redesign. Main armament is typically a 14.5mm/0.57in or 12.7mm/0.5in heavy machine-gun complemented by a 7.62mm/0.3in machine-gun.

Behind the turret are two bench seats for six infantry who sit in two rows of three facing outwards so they could use the pistol ports in the side of the vehicle. Behind the infantry area is the engine compartment.

The BTR-70 retained the eight wheel and twin-engine layout of the BTR-60 except that one engine powered the first and third wheels while the other powered the second and fourth wheels, so that if the vehicle lost an engine at least it could still limp off the battlefield. Between the second and third wheels on each side of the vehicle's lower hull is a small crew hatch for the infantry to debus, but the vehicle has to stop for this to happen otherwise the soldiers would be crushed by the

wheels. The vehicle features the proven Soviet central tyre-pressure regulation system that allows the driver to adjust the tyre-pressure to suit different terrain encountered.

During the fighting in Afghanistan the BTR-70 was shown to be very vulnerable to attack from the side by heavy machine guns and rocket launchers, such as the RPG7. A number of field modifications were carried out to increase the vehicle's armour and extra weapons were fitted such as the AGS-17 grenade launcher.

Compared to the earlier BTR-60PB, relatively small numbers were manufactured, but large numbers of the vehicle were also produced under licence in Romania as the TAB-77. The

ABOVE: **Romania built the BTR-70 under licence and also developed its own, improved TAB-77 diesel-engined version. Romanian TAB-77 APCs are pictured on patrol in Afghanistan during Operation Enduring Freedom, 2002.** BELOW LEFT: **The experimental GAZ-50 vehicle, preserved in the tank museum at Kubinka, Russia, was the prototype that proved the concept of the BTR-70 design.**

BTR-70 was only exported to four other nations – Afghanistan, German Democratic Republic, Hungary, and Romania. Many were however inherited by the armies of various post-Soviet republics or were re-exported and, at the time of writing, over 1,500 remain in service with over 20 nations. Russian BTR-70s took part in the 2022 invasion of Ukraine.

BTR-70 APC

Country: USSR
Entered service: 1976
Crew: 2 plus 9 infantry
Weight: 11,481kg/11.3 tons
Dimensions: Length – 7.54m/24ft 9in
Height – 2.23m/7ft 4in
Width – 2.8m/9ft 2in
Armament: Main – 14.55mm/0.57in KPVT machine-gun, and coaxial 7.62mm/0.3in PKT machine-gun
Secondary – Small arms
Armour: Maximum – 10mm/0.394in
Powerplant: 2 x ZMZ-4905 6-cylinder 172kW/230hp petrol engines
Performance: Speed – 80kph/50mph
Range – 600km/370 miles

BTR-80 Armoured Personnel Carrier

The BTR-70 did not cure all the deficiencies of the BTR-60, which had become evident during the fighting in Afghanistan – it simply displayed the shortcomings of the reliance on the conservative development of armoured vehicles. The replacement for the BTR-70, initially called the GAZ 5903, started development in 1982. Having passed its trials it was renamed the BTR-80, with production starting in 1984. Once it began to enter service in the Soviet Army, it largely replaced the earlier BTR-60 and BTR-70.

ABOVE: **A Russian Army Russian BTR-80 pictured during Victory Day celebrations, Moscow, 2011.** BELOW LEFT: **The trim vane is in its new stored position lying flat on the glacis plate. The vehicle commander is standing in his position with his hatch opening to the front of the vehicle. The exhaust system on the BTR-80 now runs almost horizontal along the rear of the raised engine compartment.**

The three main differences between the fully amphibious BTR-80 APC and the earlier BTR-70 were the engine, the crew exit doors and the turret. The twin petrol engine configuration was dropped in favour of a single large 194kW/260hp V8 turbocharged water-cooled diesel engine, which simplified the automotive train and made maintenance easier. The new engine arrangement resulted in a change to the design of the vehicle's back end and engine compartment.

Clam-shell doors split horizontally were fitted to the sides of the vehicle instead of small hatches. When the doors are opened, the bottom one forms a step which drops down between the second and third road-wheels. The BTR-80 does not have to halt to allow the infantry to debus – the clam-shell doors are opened and the men leap off the step one at a time hoping to miss the wheels. As a result it is known as the "death step". Additional protection can be provided via turret-mounted smoke grenade projectors.

The last major change was the vehicle's manually operated turret. The 30mm/1.18in gun was designed to allow elevation

to 60 degrees, as it had been found in Afghanistan that guns could not be elevated high enough to sweep the hills where attackers rained down fire. This also gives the vehicle some anti-aircraft ability to deal with helicopters or slow moving low-flying aircraft. Increased gun elevation is also vital in urban fighting situations.

The BTR-80 has two firing ports in the front and three down each side for the infantry on board to use, and is fully amphibious with a single water-jet mounted in the rear. The steering is applied to the front four wheels and the vehicle is fitted with a full NBC system as well as night-vision equipment.

One version of the BTR-80 is the BREM-80 (Bronirovannaya Remontno-Evakuatsionnaya Mashina) Armoured Recovery Vehicle, which was developed to recover damaged wheeled vehicles from the battlefield. As well as towbars, there is a nose-mounted spade to secure the vehicle during winching operations, a small jib crane on the roof and a large "A" frame that can be fitted to the front of the BREM for engine changes. Welding equipment is carried as standard.

The improved BTR-80A has a 30mm/1.18in dual-feed cannon firing High Explosive Fragmentation (HE-FRAG) and Armour-Piercing Tracer (AP-T) rounds with an effective range of 2km/1.24m by day and 800m/2.624ft by night. This version of the APC is known to have been used by the Russian Army

ABOVE LEFT: **The BREM-K Armoured Recovery Vehicle version - note the "A" frame on the top side of the vehicle, winches and spotlight.** ABOVE RIGHT: **The rather spartan BTR-80 interior showing the driver and commander positions. Note the numerous vision blocks and sighting equipment.** BELOW LEFT: **Ukrainian BTR-80 APC during a live fire exercise, 2013. Note bank of smoke dischargers fitted to the rear of the turret. At the rear can be seen the hydro water-jet hatch for in-water propulsion.**

during the Second Chechen War and export customers included Sudan, Hungary, Indonesia, North Korea and Venezuela amongst others.

With a crew of three, this APC can carry seven infantry, each of whom has a firing port and periscope for aiming and firing from within the comparatively lightly-armoured hull.

The central tyre inflation system was retained and the vehicle can also be fitted with run-flat tyres that can sustain direct hits from bullets but continue to carry the vehicle over large distances. Impressively, this version can continue to move effectively with any two of its wheels totally missing.

The BTR-80 remains in service with over 30 countries. Large numbers of the BTR-80 and the derived BTR-82A took part in the 2022 Russian invasion of Ukraine, and around 350 were confirmed as destroyed within just the first eight months of action, underlining the vulnerability of these types of vehicles on the sophisticated 21st-century battlefield.

BTR-80 APC

Country: USSR
Entered service: 1984
Crew: 3 plus 7 infantry
Weight: 13,614kg/13.4 tons
Dimensions: Length – 7.5m/24ft 7in
  Height – 2.45m/8ft
  Width – 2.9m/9ft 6in
Armament: Main – 14.55mm/0.57in KPVT
  machine-gun, and coaxial 7.62mm/0.3in
  PKT machine-gun
  Secondary – Small arms
Armour: Maximum – 10mm/0.394in
Powerplant: KAMAZ 7403 8-cylinder
  194kW/260hp diesel engine
Performance: Speed – 80kph/50mph
  Range – 600km/370 miles

Buffalo MPCV

The Buffalo, developed and manufactured by US company Force Protection – a division of General Dynamics – is a six-wheeled heavily armoured Mine Protected Clearance Vehicle (MPCV) developed as a specialist hostile route clearance system. Considered to be the world's most advanced mine resistant vehicle, the Buffalo is operated by the US Army, US Marine Corps, Canada, UK, France and Italy. The route clearance version uses infrared technology to detect the presence of dangerous ordnance and is equipped with a hydraulically-actuated interrogation or robot arm, located over the vehicle's front right, that can safely investigate and dispose of any suspicious item or other ordnance, making routes safe. In simple terms the Buffalo protects convoys from the threat of mines and Improvized Explosive Devices (IEDs). The vehicle enables engineers to inspect suspect objects from a safe distance, operating the robotic arm and video cameras from the relative safety of the well-armoured crew cabin.

The vehicle design was based on the successful and innovative South African Casspir four-wheeled mine-protected vehicle and retains the original vehicle's V-shaped monohull, a proven design that directs the force of a mine or IED blast up, around and away from the vehicle's occupants.

BAE Systems LROD lightweight cage armour, developed very quickly to provide protection against RPG-7 anti-tank rounds in Afghanistan, was added to the Buffalo to provide additional protection. The vehicle's armoured glass is six inches thick to optimize passenger protection. All six of the Buffalo wheels have run-flat capability.

Power for this very large, 8.2m/27ft long vehicle comes from a 330kW/450hp Mack ASET AI-400 I6 diesel engine. It has an operational range of 483km/ 300m and a top speed of 105kph/65mph.

Specialist operators control the Buffalo's 9.14m/30ft long robotic arm and claw from safe inside the vehicle's armoured hull, via a mounted camera and sensory equipment, to safely dispose of mines and IEDs. The crew compartment has the driver/co-driver at the front and up to four other troops can also be seated inside with their full gear. There are six hatches in the roof but crew access to the vehicle is via a ladder and door to the rear. A platform also at the rear is used for additional stowage and equipment. Typically the vehicle carries no armament.

LEFT: **Buffalos (foreground) were used extensively and effectively during deployments in Iraq and Afghanistan. Buffalos sustained hundreds of direct hits from IEDs and detonated mines without loss of life. This convoy is in Helmand Province, Afghanistan, 2012.** BELOW: **The reach of the Buffalo's extended mechanical arm can be seen in this image of a pre-deployment US Army training exercise taking place in Germany, 2013.**

An upgrade known as the Super Buffalo was developed to counter an increasing threat of IEDs in Afghanistan. The vehicle's front axle was strengthened to enable greater weight-carrying capacity as a result of a ground penetrating radar installation that bestowed a multi-function capacity on the vehicle. Appropriate weight distribution led to the interrogation arm's removal to the vehicle's rear.

Ongoing improvements include increased engine power and greater cross-force compatibility, increased range, increased fording and slope angle performance, enhanced HVAC (heating, ventilation and air conditioning) and a common spare for all six tyres. Enhanced safety features include larger roof hatches for crew egress and both crew and engine compartment Automatic Fire Extinguishing Systems (AFES). The vehicles were used extensively and effectively during

deployments in Iraq and Afghanistan. Buffalos sustained hundreds of direct hits from IEDs and detonated mines without loss of life. In 2008, the US Army took delivery of its 200th Buffalo vehicle and the 795th and final example was completed in June 2014.

RIGHT: **Italian Army Buffalo, Afghanistan, 2010, showing the sheer size of the vehicle. Once suspect devices have been positively identified they are either moved to a safe position to be made safe or safely denoted. In the event a device is unsafe to move, sharpshooters will fire upon the device to detonate it.**

Buffalo MPCV

Country: USA
Entered service: 2003
Crew: 2–6
Weight: 25,000kg/27.5 tons
Dimensions: Length – 8.2m/27ft
    Height – 4m/13ft   Width –2.6m/8ft 5in
Armament: N/A
Armour: Resistant to 7.62mm/0.3in standard
    ammunition, also equipped with BAE Systems
    L-ROD aluminium armour and 15cm/6in
    armoured window glass
Powerplant: 330kW/450hp Mack ASET AI-400 I6
    diesel engine
Performance: Speed – 105kph/65mph
    Range – 483km/300 miles

BTR-152V1 Armoured Personnel Carrier

The BTR-152 was the first Soviet APC to be developed after World War II. The process started at the end of World War II and the vehicle entered service in 1950, but was not seen by the West until the 1951 Moscow Victory Parade.

Initially the BTR-152 was developed using the ZIL-151 2.5-ton truck as its basis but this was later changed to the ZIL-157 truck.

The BTR-152 has the engine located at the front of the vehicle and behind this is an open-topped compartment with accommodation for two crew and 17 infantry. The infantry in the rear of the vehicle sit on bench seats behind the crew compartment, while the driver and commander sit in the front with the driver on the left. There are eight firing ports, three down each side and one in each of the rear doors. The early vehicles had no NBC equipment, night-driving equipment or amphibious capability but some of the later variants,

such as the BTR-152V3, were fitted with a central tyre pressure system, and a night-driving infrared driving light.

The BTR-152K version came into service from 1961. This has a full armoured roof with two large hatches, one in the front and one in the rear, each with a machine-gun mount. All the other improvements from the early variants were fitted to this version, but still no NBC system. There were three machine-gun mounts in total, one over the driver and commander's position which would take a heavy 12.7mm/0.5in machine-gun and one 7.62mm/0.3in SGMB machine-gun mounted on each side of the vehicle.

In addition to being used as an infantry carrier, the BTR-152 was also used as an artillery tractor, mortar carrier and a basic load carrier. One command vehicle version of the BTR-152 was produced as well as three anti-aircraft versions. The first of

ABOVE: **The truck origins of the vehicle chassis can be clearly seen. The driver is entering his position in the vehicle. The pistol ports in the side of the crew compartment are visible. The main 12.7mm/0.5in heavy machine-gun mount is sited above the driver's position.**

these mounted a twin 14.55mm/0.57in machine-gun turret, the second had a quadruple 12.7mm/0.5in machine-gun turret and the last version had twin 23mm/0.91in cannon. The Egyptians fitted the Czechoslovak M53 turret to some of their BTR-152s. The BTR-152 has been long replaced in the Russian Army but a variety of often locally modified examples still remain in service with many countries from Cuba to Syria.

LEFT: **A BTR-40 APC. This was the second vehicle type to be built by the Soviet Union after World War II. It had a crew of two and could carry eight men in the back. There is a 12.7mm/0.5in machine-gun mount above the driver's cab.**

BTR-152V1 APC

Country: USSR
Entered service: 1950
Crew: 2 plus 17 infantry
Weight: 8,738kg/8.6 tons
Dimensions: Length – 6.55m/21ft 6in
 Height – 2.36m/7ft 9in
 Width – 2.32m/7ft 7in
Armament: Main – 12.7mm/0.5in DShKM machine-gun, and 2 x 7.62mm/0.3in SGMB machine-guns
 Secondary – Small arms
Armour: Maximum – 14mm/0.55in
Powerplant: ZIL-123 6-cylinder 82kW/110hp petrol engine
Performance: Speed – 75kph/47mph
 Range – 600km/373 miles

Cascavel EE-9 Mk IV Armoured Car

The Cascavel was designed by ENGESA to meet the requirements of the Brazilian Army, with design work starting in July 1970. The first prototype was completed in 1970 and a pre-production order for ten vehicles was placed and delivered between 1972 and 1973. Production began in 1974 with the vehicle entering Brazilian Army service in the same year. These early vehicles (Mk I) were fitted with M3 37mm/1.46in turrets taken from the now-redundant American light tanks used by the Brazilian Army. The second version (Mk II) of the vehicle was fitted with the Hispano-Suiza H90 turret. The EE-9 and the EE-11 APC have many parts in common and a lot of these are standard commercial parts.

The hull of the vehicle is made from spaced armour with the outer layer having dual hardness. This outer layer is constructed of a hardened steel sheet and a softer steel rolled together to form one single dual-hardened steel sheet.

The driver sits in the front on the left-hand side with the two-man turret behind him and the engine in the rear. The rear wheels are mounted on an ENGESA Boomerang walking beam suspension arm that allows the vehicle to have all four wheels in contact with the ground at all times. The vehicle is a 6x6 and is fitted with run-flat tyres. Even after being fully deflated, the EE-9 can travel on them for 100km/62m before they have to be replaced.

Anticipating the finite supply of M3 turrets, ENGESA started to manufacture their own turrets and guns. These ENGESA ET-90 turrets and EC-90 guns were fitted to the EE-9 once the M3 turrets had run out, creating the Mk III.

The Mk IV, produced from 1979, saw significant improvements with the installation of a new engine and a Soviet-style central tyre pressure system controlling all wheels. The Mk V variant is powered by a German Mercedes-Benz diesel rather than the American engine of

ABOVE LEFT: **This is a Cascavel on parade in Venezuela. Both the vehicle commander and the turret gunner are standing in the top of their turret position. The commander's cupola is fitted with a machine-gun.** ABOVE: **The Cascavel climbing a steep slope. The very flat rear of the vehicle and turret sides can be seen.**

the Mk IV. The VI is a Mk V derivative with a Mercedes-Benz OM352A diesel engine while the Cascavel Mk VII is a Mk V with the MT-643 gearbox of the Mk IV.

A new version, the Novo Cascavel, is a modernised version ordered by the Brazilian Army in 2022 with a new engine, digital optics, air conditioning, anti-tank missile capability and a new fire control computer.

Cascavel EE-9 Mk IV Armoured Car

Country: Brazil
Entered service: 1979
Crew: 3
Weight: 13,411kg/13.2 tons
Dimensions: Length – 6.2m/20ft 4in
    Height – 2.68m/9ft 9in
    Width – 2.64m/8ft 8in
Armament: Main – EC-90 90mm/3.54in gun,
    and coaxial 7.62mm/0.3in machine-gun
    Secondary – 12.7mm/0.5in anti-aircraft
    machine-gun
Armour: Maximum – 16mm/0.63in
Powerplant: Detroit Diesel model 6V-53N
    6-cylinder 158kW/212hp diesel engine
Performance: Speed – 100kph/62mph
    Range – 880km/547 miles

LEFT: **The vehicle commander's position has been fitted with a 7.62mm/0.3in machine-gun and the vehicle is fitted with two whip aerials. At the rear of the turret on each side is a cluster of smoke dischargers, one set of which is visible here.**

Commando V-150 Armoured Personnel Carrier

The Cadillac Gage Company started development of the Commando in 1962 as a private venture, with the first prototype being finished in March 1963. The first production vehicles entered service in 1964. The Commando saw extensive service with the American Army and with the American Air Force during the Vietnam War. It was deployed as a convoy escort for both services and also as an airfield defence vehicle.

The Commando is very much a mix-and-match vehicle: the customer can chose one of several bodies and one of about 14 different turrets. Its American designation is the M706. The first type of vehicle was the V-100, which was followed very shortly by the V-200 and finally the V-150 which came into service in 1971 and replaced both the V-100 and V-200. The V-150S entered production in 1985. The V-100 is very similar to the V-150 except that the V-100 has a petrol engine while the V-150's engine is a diesel. The V-200 was a beefed-up version, much larger than ether of the other two vehicles.

The V-150 is an all-welded steel construction and provides the crew with protection from up to 7.62mm/0.3in bullets and shrapnel. The driver sits at the front on the left-hand side and, depending on the version, the vehicle commander's seat is next to the driver. Behind them is the main crew compartment that can be fitted with a variety of turrets and can even have an open top. The one-man turrets have a single hatch in the top and are armed with a variety of machine-guns up to 20mm/0.79in, either mounted in pairs or singly. The two-man turret has two hatches and the armament ranges from 20mm/0.79in up to 90mm/3.54in guns. There are three doors in the main hull, one on each side and one in the rear. The top half of the door folds back flush with the vehicle while the bottom folds down and forms a step for the infantry to clear the vehicle and its wheels. There are eight pistol ports fitted to the vehicle, two in the front and three down each side. The maximum number of infantry that can be carried in the vehicle is 12 but this does vary depending on the version. The engine is mounted in

LEFT: **The rear of the Commando prototype vehicle showing the large rear exit door. The top of the door flips up and the bottom drops down to form a step.**

LEFT: **The good ground clearance can be clearly seen. This turret can be fitted with either a single or twin 7.62mm/0.3in machine-gun.** ABOVE: **This Commando is being used as a reconnaissance vehicle. It is armed with a single machine-gun.** BELOW: **The V-200 was an enlarged version designed specifically for the Singapore Armed Forces, entering service in 1968. The fleet was upgraded in the early 2000s and some were equipped with surface to air missiles for airfield defence. This V-200 Commando with 20mm/0.8in gun is at the Singapore Army Museum, Singapore.**

the rear of the V-150 on the left-hand side with a corridor on the right leading to the rear door. In this corridor are two seating positions while above the corridor is a small circular hatch that opens towards the front of the vehicle and has a pintle mount for a 7.62mm/0.3in machine-gun to cover the rear of the vehicle.

The mortar vehicle and the TOW missile vehicle have a raised section added to the roof in place of the turret. This is fitted with two folding hatches that run the length of the raised area and fold to the sides of the vehicle. The 81mm/3.19in mortar is mounted in the middle of the crew compartment on a turntable and can be traversed through 360 degrees. Its minimum range is 150m/492ft with a maximum range of 4,400m/14,435ft. There are also four pintle mounts for 7.62mm/0.3in machine-guns. The vehicle has a crew of five and also carries 62 mortar bombs. The hatches for the TOW vehicle open front and back; it can carry seven missiles and has a crew of four. There is also a command version built using this

basic type of hull and a police riot vehicle has also been developed for several American police departments. An armoured recovery version of the V-150 has also been developed and it is designed for the recovery of broken down or damaged light armoured vehicles. This is fitted with a heavy duty winch and "A" frame that is attached to the front of the vehicle and folds back across the top of the crew compartment when not required. A large number of these vehicles are still in service.

The HMV-150 upgraded variant was produced by Thailand in 2017, modified to provide greater internal accommodation for up to ten troops. Some 4,000 V-150s were built in total and several hundred remain in service with a number of countries.

RIGHT: **The driver's and vehicle commander's vision ports are protected by armoured covers. The vehicle also has a number of vision ports in the side of the vehicle. The open fixed turret of this vehicle has been improved and turned into a command turret.**

Commando V-150 APC

Country: USA
Entered service: 1971
Crew: 2 crew plus 10 infantry
Weight: 9,550kg/9.4 tons
Dimensions: Length – 5.68m/19ft 8in
  Height – 2.43m/8ft
  Width – 2.26m/7ft 5in
Armament: Main – Various
  Secondary – Small arms
Armour: Classified
Powerplant: Chrysler V-504 8-cylinder
  151kW/202hp diesel engine
Performance: Speed – 88kph/55mph
  Range – 950km/600 miles

Cougar MRAP

Force Protection, a US company that became part of General Dynamics, specialized in developing vehicles that could operate with resistance to mines and improvized explosive devices. One of their most successful designs was the Cougar mine resistant ambush protected (MRAP) vehicle that saw extensive action in Iraq, Libya and Afghanistan. The Cougar, in production since 2002, was developed in two forms – the 4x4 Cougar H and the 6x6 Cougar HE. The 4x4 can transport up to four passengers plus equipment, while the larger 6x6 version can carry up to eight passengers with equipment. The vehicle's conventional layout has its 246kW/330hp Caterpillar C7 diesel engine in the front, crew cab in the middle with armoured glass, and a troop compartment at the rear. The crew access their cab through doors on either side of the cab while a double door at the rear provides access to the troop compartment which has its own armoured observation windows.

ABOVE: **As well as ex-British Army Wolfhounds, in 2022 the British government supplied Ukraine with a number of Mastiff vehicles. This image shows Ukrainian marines training with one of the supplied Mastiffs, June 2022.** BELOW LEFT: **US Marines Cougar H vehicle, Al Taqaddum Air Base, Iraq, 2007, deployed in support of Operation Iraqi Freedom. Note the large engine exhaust running along the edge of the roof. Both the 4x4 and 6x6 variants are powered by the same 253.5Kw/30hp Caterpillar C7 diesel engine.**

Building on the success of South African mine-protected vehicles, the Cougar has a v-shaped monohull that extends to the engine bay and directs the force of a mine or IED blast up, around and away from the vehicle's occupants. The Cougar is known to have great resistance to direct blasts as the Cougar H 4x4 was designed to withstand a 13kg TNT blast to its front and rear axles and a 7kg blast to the centre section of the vehicle. This vehicle has proven combat survivability and thanks to its advanced ballistic and blast protection, the Cougar boasts an outstanding occupant survival rate. In 2004, the US Marine Corps reported that no troops had died in more than 300 IED attacks on Cougars.

The Cougar was a workhorse for the US Marine Corps combat engineers in Iraq from 2004. The Cougar achieved almost legendary status among troop transports in Iraq and Afghanistan, where it withstood literally thousands of IED/landmine attacks. The Cougar is built to drive into danger and its reparability typically allows it to return to service within just a matter of hours. As well as the several thousand in US military service, the Cougar's consistent performance in harsh combat

LEFT: **US Navy 6x6 Cougars. Cougars are typically armed with roof-mounted protected 7.62mm/0.3in machine-guns but remote-controlled weapon stations can also be fitted to the roof for protection. All Cougars are fitted with run-flat tyres so the Cougar could still get itself out of trouble if required.** BELOW: **Ukrainian marines pictured in the troop compartment of a British-supplied Mastiff, 2022. Note the roof hatches above the troop and the spall liner on the roof and sides to minimize injury from armour and projectile fragments should the hull be breached.** BELOW LEFT: **A British Army Mastiff from 5 Armoured Engineer Squadron, Royal Engineers fitted with Choker Mine Rollers on exercise in Jordan, 2012. Mine rollers are designed to detonate anti-tank mines and allow engineers to clear a route through a minefield, even under fire.**

environments earned it export sales with nations including Canada, Iraq, Italy, Poland and the UK. The British Army acquired an early version of the Cougar and operated it as the Tempest MPV.

The British Army also operated the Ridgback PPV (Protected Patrol Vehicle). This was a British version of the Cougar 4x4 fitted with British armour package and electronics, and remote weapon stations on some vehicles. This vehicle was acquired for better mobility in Afghanistan villages. The British Army Mastiff PPV was a heavily-armoured version of the Cougar 6×6 and was first deployed to Afghanistan in late 2006. It is armed with a 7.62mm/0.3in machine-gun, 12.7mm/0.5in heavy machine-gun or a 40mm/1.57in grenade machine-gun. The British Army Wolfhound is a Heavy Tactical Support Vehicle (HTSV) 6x6 variant with a rear loading area for bearing vital combat supplies such as ammunition to front lines. The versatile vehicle can also tow a 105mm/4.1in field

gun and mount a 7.62mm or 12.7mm machine gun on its roof. Of the 130 examples acquired for the British Army, 80 of them were donated to Ukraine to aid their fight against invading Russian forces.

Cougar MRAP 6x6

Country: USA
Entered service: 2002
Crew: 2 plus 8 infantry
Weight: 22,226kg/24.5 tons
Dimensions: Length – 7.08m/23ft 3in
  Height – 2.64m/8ft 6in
  Width – 2.74m/9ft
Armament: Remotely operated weapon station
Armour: 7.62mm/0.3in resistant
Powerplant: 246kW/330hp Caterpillar C7 diesel engine
Performance: Speed 105kph/65mph
Range – 966km/600 miles

LEFT: The hatches over the troop compartment have been folded back against the hull of the vehicle, with the men sitting in the raised position. The vehicle commander is operating the machine-gun over his position.

DAF YP-408 Armoured Personnel Carrier

DAF (*Van Doorne's Automobielfabrieken*) started development of the YP-408 carrier in 1956 to meet a Dutch Army requirement. The first prototypes were finished in 1958 and were powered by an American Hercules JXLD petrol engine, but this was changed in the production model. The vehicle went through a number of modifications and finally an order was placed for 750 vehicles with the first carriers being delivered to the Dutch Army in 1964. By 1988, the YP-408 had been phased out of service with the Dutch being replaced by the YPR-765.

The hull is an all-welded construction with the engine, transmission and radiator in the front. The driver and the commander/gunner are placed side by side behind the engine with the driver on the left. The gunner's hatch cover is in two parts that only open to the vertical position and so provide some protection when manning the machine-gun. The troop compartment is in the rear of the vehicle and holds ten men, who sit down the sides of the vehicle facing each other with their legs interlocking. Entry and exit from the crew compartment is by twin doors in the rear, each door having a single firing port in it.

The YP-408 uses many of the same components as the YP-328 (6x6) truck, but this vehicle is an 8x6 layout. It has power steering and steers using the front two axles, the second axle being unpowered. The YP-408 is fitted with dual air and hydraulic brakes, and the tyres can be driven on for 50km/31 miles when punctured. The vehicle is not fitted with an NBC system and is not amphibious, but it can be fitted with infrared night-driving equipment.

There were several variations on the basic vehicle including command post, ambulance, armoured supply carrier, mortar tractor and anti-tank versions. Following their retirement from Dutch Army service in 1987, 28 examples were supplied to the Portuguese Air Force in 1992 for use in the airbase security role.

MIDDLE LEFT: A Dutch Army YP-408 in United Nations colours. The troop compartment roof has six large hatches recessed into it, shown open here. LEFT: The second axle from the front can be raised and locked into position clear of the ground. This is so the wheels can be used as spares for the other wheel positions.

DAF YP-408 APC

Country: Netherlands
Entered service: 1964
Crew: 2 plus 10 infantry
Weight: 11,989kg/11.8 tons
Dimensions: Length – 6.2m/20ft 4in
  Height – 1.55m/5ft 11in
  Width – 2.4m/7ft 9in
Armament: Main – 12.7mm/0.5in heavy
  machine-gun
  Secondary – Small arms
Armour: Maximum – 15mm/0.59in
Powerplant: DAF Model DS-575 6-cylinder
  123kW/165hp diesel engine
Performance: Speed – 80kph/50mph
  Range – 500km/310 miles

LEFT: The left rear of the turret houses the hydraulic motor for the elevation and traversing of the turret. This vehicle has been sheeted up as it is not operational. ABOVE: The armoured cab of the DANA houses the driver and vehicle commander. Their armoured hatches are in the open position. All the wheels are connected to a central tyre pressure system operated by the driver. The gun layer sits behind the large hatch on the left of the turret.

DANA 152mm Self-Propelled Howitzer

The DANA 152mm/5.98in SPG was first seen in 1980 but development had been taking place during the 1970s, using an extensively modified Tatra 815 (8x8) chassis. A wheeled chassis was selected rather the normal tracked chassis as maintenance is easier and the vehicle is significantly cheaper to produce. Czechoslovakia also has a very good road network making the cross-country capability less important. However, the DANA has a more than adequate cross-country ability for medium-range artillery support for infantry and armour.

By 1994, 750 DANA vehicles had been built, and it has been sold to Poland, Russia and Libya, besides being supplied to the

Czechoslovak and, after the break-up of Czechoslovakia, Slovak armies.

The engine on the original Tatra 815 is in the front but on the DANA it was moved to the rear of the vehicle. The lightly armoured cab is protected by armour just 7.62mm/0.3in thick, making it only bullet and light shell-splinter proof. It is situated very low down on the chassis at the front of the vehicle. The driver and one other crew member sit side by side in the cab along with the main radio. The driver and co-driver have large individual toughened glass windscreens that are protected in action by large steel shutters that fold down and cover them. The turret has a crew of three including the vehicle commander together with a gunner and loader. It is

divided into two parts; the left-hand side contains all the optics and fire control systems with the ammunition handler on the right-hand side. Access to the turret is via two doors, one on each side, and it can traverse through 225 degrees to each side being restricted due to internal cables. The turret holds 60 rounds of ammunition and the gun has a fully automatic loading system.

DANAs have seen action in a number of conflicts including use by Georgia in the 2008 Russo-Georgian war, and the Czech Republic is known to have supplied a number of DANAs to Ukraine during the 2022 Russian invasion. Improved versions continue to appear in both the Czech Republic and Slovakia.

LEFT: The gun barrel on this vehicle is at maximum elevation. Between the second and third axle is a stabilizer on each side of the vehicle with a third one at the rear of the vehicle. Five countries operate the DANA, four of which are at present upgrading to the ZUZANA.

DANA 152mm SPG

Country: Czechoslovakia
Entered service: 1980
Crew: 5
Weight: 29,261kg/28.8 tons
Dimensions: Length – 11.15m/36ft 7in
  Height – 2.85m/9ft 4in
  Width – 3m/9ft 10in
Armament: Main – 152mm/5.98in howitzer
  Secondary – 12.7mm/0.5in DshKM machine-gun
Armour: Maximum – 12.7mm/0.5in
Powerplant: Tatra 2-939-34 12-cylinder 257kW/345hp diesel engine
Performance: Speed – 80kph/50mph
  Range – 700km/435 miles

LEFT: **This is a prototype vehicle of the Urutu. The hull sides of the car are vertical until halfway up the vehicle from which point they slope slightly inwards. There is a large single door in the rear.**

ENGESA EE-11 Urutu Armoured Personnel Carrier

The EE-11 was designed and developed by ENGESA in January 1970 and the first prototype was delivered in July 1970. Once the vehicle had passed its trials, an order was placed in 1974 by the Brazilian Army for the Brazilian Marines.

The EE-11 shares many of the automotive components of the EE-9 armoured car which was developed at the same time. The hull of the vehicle is made from spaced armour with the outer layer having a dual hardness. The outer layer is made up of a hardened steel sheet and a softer steel rolled together to form one single dual-hardened steel sheet. The driver sits in the front on the left-hand side with the engine on the right. The air inlet louvers are on the top of the vehicle next to the driver, with the exhaust on the right-hand side. This amphibious vehicle has been upgraded seven times and each improvement has been to the engine. From the Mk VI onwards, the propellers that propel the EE-11 in the water have been removed as the wheels of the vehicle work well enough in the water to move it forward. There is also a trim vane, hydraulically operated by the driver, fitted to the glacis plate.

The vehicle can be fitted with a range of turrets, but the basic Urutu has a pintle mount for either a 7.62mm/0.3in or a 12.7mm/0.5in machine-gun, and five firing ports down each side and one in the rear door. When fitted with any turret from the ET-20 up to the ET-90, the number of firing ports each side of the vehicle is reduced to two with one in the rear door. The crew compartment is behind the gun position and in the basic form carries 12 crew although when larger turrets are mounted only four crew can be carried. The crew sit down the sides of the vehicle, five a side, and a two-man bench across the top. The rear door can be operated by the driver from his position, to make pick-up quicker and safer for the infantry. Two side doors are used for debussing or loading in a peaceful area. Many remain in service in South America, Africa and the Middle East.

LEFT: **The exhaust system is fitted to the right-hand side of the vehicle above the side door. The trim vane is folded back against the glacis plate, and the headlights are recessed into the hull front. There are several pistol ports down the side of the vehicle. The travel in the suspension system can be clearly seen.**

EE-11 Urutu APC Mk VII

Country: Brazil
Entered service: 1974
Crew: 1 plus 12 infantry
Weight: 14,000kg/13.8 tons
Dimensions: Length – 6.1m/20ft
　　Height – 2.9m/9ft 6in
　　Width – 2.69m/8ft 10in
Armament: Main – 12.7mm/0.5in machine-gun
　　Secondary – Small arms
Armour: Classified
Powerplant: Detroit Diesel 6V-53T 6-cylinder 194kW/260hp diesel engine
Performance: Speed – Road 105kph/65mph;
　　Water 8kph/5mph
　　Range – 850km/528 miles

LEFT: **This Ferret Mk 1 has a large storage basket fitted to the rear hull above the engine. Behind the storage bin between the wheels is an escape hatch. When opened, the hatch and storage bin drop away from the vehicle.** ABOVE: **The driver's position in this Ferret armoured car. The dashboard is split into two with the steering wheel in the middle. The handbrake is just in front of the driver's seat. The driver has one large vision block above the steering wheel with smaller ones to the side.**

Ferret Mk 1 Scout Car

In 1947, the British Army issued a requirement for a replacement for the Daimler Dingo scout car. Daimler consequently started development of the Mk 1 Ferret Scout Car in 1948 with the first prototype being produced in December 1949. The first production Mk 1 Ferrets were delivered in October 1952 and the type would remain in production for 20 years, the final Ferret being produced in 1971. Total production was 4,409 vehicles of which 1,200 were Mk 1s. The Ferret proved to be extremely popular with the men using it and could be found in almost every British Army unit, even units that were

not issued with them. It would remain in service with the British Army until 1994.

The Mk 1 Ferret is a monocoque design made from 30 separate flat plates and is an all-welded construction. The driver is seated in the front with the crew compartment in the middle and the engine in the rear. The crew compartment is open-topped but can be covered by a canvas tilt. The vehicle is a 4x4 layout with steering on the front axle which is not power-assisted. A spare wheel is carried on the left side of the vehicle with storage boxes on the right. The Daimler pre-selective gearbox has five forward and five reverse gears. The

Ferret Mk 1 does not carry night-driving infrared lights or NBC system. It can be fitted with deep wading gear but this was a later development that appeared on the Mk 1/3.

The Ferret Mk 1 went through some modifications, the first being in 1959 when the Mk 1/1 came into service. This had increased armour protection, and the open top was covered by a fixed turret, which had a split hatch that folded towards the rear of the vehicle. The Mk 1/3 deep wading gear attaches over the top of the opening or turret area and is a canvas screen that can be raised like an inflated bellows, allowing the vehicle to be submerged (including the driver) with the commander standing in the top of the turret giving directions.

LEFT: **The last combat service for the Ferret was the Gulf War of 1991. This Mk 1 has had a fixed turret placed on the top of the crew area. On each side of the front of the vehicle is a cluster of three smoke dischargers. The storage basket on the rear of the vehicle has been raised.**

Ferret Mk 1 Scout Car

Country: UK
Entered service: 1952
Crew: 2–3
Weight: 4,369kg/4.3 tons
Dimensions: Length – 3.84m/12ft 9in
　　Height – 1.45m/4ft 9in
　　Width – 1.9m/6ft 3in
Armament: Main – 7.62mm/0.3in light
　　machine-gun
　　Secondary – Small arms
Armour: Maximum – 16mm/0.63in
Powerplant: Rolls-Royce B60 6-cylinder
　　87kW/116hp petrol engine
Performance: Speed – 93kph/58mph
　　Range – 300km/185 miles

LEFT: **The Ferret Mk 2 is fitted with a fully rotating turret armed with a single machine-gun as standard. The exhaust system is fitted on the rear mudguard.**
BELOW: **This Ferret Mk 2/6 has been fitted with the Vigilante AT missile system. This type of vehicle entered service in 1963. The missile boxes increase the overall width of the car. An additional storage box has also been fitted to the side of the vehicle.**

Ferret Mk 2 Scout Car

The AFV offers an incredible variety of possibilities to the military. It is therefore not surprising that when the British Army issued a requirement for a replacement for the Daimler Dingo in 1947, Daimler developed two variants of the same basic type and both were adopted. Development of the Mk 2 Ferret Scout Car was started in 1948, the first prototype being produced in December 1949. The first production Mk 2 Ferrets were delivered in July 1952, entering service before the Mk 1 Ferrets. It remained in production for 20 years, the final Ferret being produced in 1971. Of the total production of 4,409 vehicles, 1,850 were Mk 2s.

The Mk 2 Ferret is a monocoque design made from 30 separate flat plates and is an all-welded construction. The driver is seated in the front with the turret in the middle and the engine in the rear. The driver has three hatches. The one to the front can be folded down so it lies on the glacis plate and can

then be replaced by a splinter-proof windscreen. There are also hatches on each side of his position, each fitted with a periscope. The turret is very small and cramped and was heavily modified during the trials as it was found that the gunner could accidentally catch his clothing in the trigger and fire the machine-gun. The turret is manually operated as it is small and light and so does not require power. It has two hatches; one in the top that opens forward and gives the gunner some protection as it does not fold flat, and one at the rear of the turret which also folds down to form a seat that the gunner can use. A sighting periscope is fitted in the top of the turret for the gunner to use when in the closed-down position. There are two escape hatches in the Ferret; one behind the spare wheel and the other behind the storage bin on the right-hand side of the vehicle.

LEFT: **The rear vision visors are all open to give the driver a better rear view from the vehicle. Beside the jerry-can on the rear of the car is a fire extinguisher. The small compact size of the vehicle can be clearly seen.**

LEFT: **This Ferret Mk 2/3 has two unditching channels fitted to the front of the car. The aerial on this car is mounted behind one of the clusters of smoke dischargers fitted to the vehicle. A large single searchlight has also been fitted to the side of the turret.** ABOVE: **The driver's and vehicle commander's positions inside the car. The steering wheel is set in a reversed–raked position. The gear selector box is under the steering wheel.**

The engine is fully waterproofed and drive is transmitted to all four wheels by a fluid coupling, five speed pre-selecting epicyclic gearbox and a transfer box, incorporating a forward and reverse mechanism, thus giving the vehicle five forward and five reverse gears and so allowing the vehicle to travel at the same speed in each direction. The Ferret is fully air-transportable and can be delivered by parachute cluster. As a result of this, a lightweight recovery vehicle had to be developed and a number of Ferrets were converted to the role. The Armoured Recovery Vehicle (ARV) conversion came as a kit and could be quickly fitted to a vehicle in the field. This was not an official conversion and remained classified as a local workshop conversion. Another modification that started off as a field modification was the introduction of a storage basket, which was mounted above the engine and was hinged so it could be tilted out of the way to give access to the engine. The basket was fitted to improve the storage of personal equipment which was always a problem.

The Ferret Mk 2 was produced in six different versions. The Mk 2/2 was a local conversion carried out on vehicles in the Far East and consisted of an extension collar fitted between the hull and the turret. The Mk 2/3 was an uparmoured version of the basic Mk 2 and was converted to carry the 7.62mm/0.3in GPMG (General Purpose Machine-Gun). The Mk 2/4 was an uparmoured version of the Mk 2/3 and was fitted with a new fire-fighting system in the crew compartment. The Mk 2/5 was the basic Mk 2 brought up to Mk 2/4 standard. The Ferret Mk 2/6 was fitted with two Vigilante anti-tank missiles, one on each side of the turret, with two spare missiles being carried instead of the spare wheel. The missiles were fired from inside the turret by the vehicle commander.

The Ferret proved to be extremely popular with the men using it and could be found in almost every British Army unit, including units that were not officially issued with them. It would remain in service with the British Army until 1994, some 20 years after it was supposed to retire.

LEFT: **The extra-large storage bin on the side of the vehicle carried two spare missiles. The vehicle commander guides the missiles from this position by a combined sight. The wire guidance box is situated on the top of the turret. Reloading of the missile launchers could be undertaken in less than five minutes.**

Ferret Mk 2 Scout Car

Country: UK
Entered service: 1952
Crew: 2
Weight: 4,369kg/4.3 tons
Dimensions: Length – 3.84m/12ft 9in
  Height – 1.88m/6ft 2in
  Width – 1.9m/6ft 3in
Armament: Main – 7.62mm/0.3in machine-gun
  Secondary – Small arms
Armour: Maximum – 16mm/0.63in
Powerplant: Rolls-Royce B60 6-cylinder
  87kW/116hp petrol engine
Performance: Speed – 93kph/58mph
  Range – 300km/185 miles

LEFT: **This is the Ferret Mk 5 armed with two Swingfire AT missiles. Spare missiles are carried in storage bins fitted to the vehicle's sides under the turret. The missile boxes are in the maximum elevation firing position.** ABOVE: **This prototype Ferret Mk 4 has the flotation screen fixed in a box structure around the edge of the vehicle. The new water-tight glass-fibre storage box can be seen clearly.**

Ferret Mk 4 Big Wheeled Scout Car

In 1963 work began on improving the Ferret's automotive and amphibious capabilities, and on providing better storage facilities for the crew's personal equipment. The first six prototypes were converted from Mk 1 vehicles; the basic hull was unchanged but larger tyres were fitted and a flotation screen was carried around the top of the hull. The Mk 4 entered service with the British Army in 1967. None of these vehicles were brand new but were converted Mk 2/3 cars. The last of these conversions were carried out in 1976.

The Mk 4 Ferret is a monocoque design made from 30 separate flat plates and is an all-welded construction. The driver is seated in the front with the turret in the middle and the engine in the rear. The driver's hatch is in the front of the vehicle and can be folded down so it lies on the glacis plate and can then be replaced by a splinter-proof windscreen. During development the larger wheels caused a number of problems with the steering due to the increased weight of the vehicle as the steering was not power-assisted. This would remain a problem with this mark of Ferret. Other improvements on the Mk 4 were enlarged disc brakes and improved suspension. The vehicle was also extended by 38cm/15in to incorporate the flotation screen.

The Mk 5 was a development of the Mk 4, the main difference being the design of the turret. The Mk 5 was to have been built in large numbers but in fact only 50 of these vehicles were made. The new turret had a very flat design and carried four BAC Swingfire anti-tank missiles, two on each side of the centreline. The maximum range of the Swingfire was 4,000m/13,123ft and the missiles were wire-guided and controlled from inside the vehicle by the gunner using a combined sight and controller. Two spare missiles were carried on the vehicle. The turret was made from aluminium armour and could be traversed through 360 degrees but it was not power operated. A 7.62mm/0.3in machine-gun was mounted in the front of it for close protection.

LEFT: **The basic Mk 2/3 was used to produce the Mk 4. The 2/3 was fitted with new brakes, suspension and wheels which gave it a wider track. To make the Mk 5, the suspension changes were made to the 2/6 and a new turret was fitted.**

Ferret Mk 4 Scout Car

Country: UK
Entered service: 1967
Crew: 2
Weight: 5,400kg/5.3 tons
Dimensions: Length – 4.1m/13ft 5in
　　Height – 2.34m/7ft 8in
　　Width – 2.13m/7ft
Armament: Main – 7.62mm/0.3in light
　　machine-gun
　　Secondary – Small arms
Armour: Maximum – 16mm/0.63in
Powerplant: Rolls-Royce B60 6-cylinder
　　87kW/116hp petrol engine
Performance: Speed – 80kph/50mph
　　Range – 300km/185 miles

Fox Light Armoured Car

LEFT: The exhaust is mounted on the rear of the vehicle. There are two side hatches, one on each side of the vehicle below the large two-man turret. These vehicles had a high centre of gravity.

BELOW: When the flotation screen is raised, the driver has no vision from his position and so relies on the vehicle commander giving him directions. Transparent screens were fitted to the flotation screen on later models.

In the 1960s the Fighting Vehicles Research and Development Establishment (FVRDE) developed two vehicles; one was the Combat Vehicle Reconnaissance (Tracked) (CVR(T)) Scorpion and the other the CVR (Wheeled) Fox. Both used the same Jaguar engine. Development started in 1965 and a development contract for 15 prototypes was given to Daimler in 1966. The first vehicle was finished in November 1967 and the last in 1969. Production began in 1972 and the first vehicles entered service in 1973, but this was not to be a replacement for the Ferret. This was the projected role of the Vixen, which was cancelled in 1974.

The Fox was a further development of the late-production Ferret scout car. The vehicle has an-all welded aluminium hull and turret which gives the crew protection against light and heavy machine-guns and shell splinters. The driver sits in the front of the vehicle with his hatch opening to the right, while the two-man turret is positioned in the middle of the vehicle and is fitted with a 30mm/1.18in RARDEN cannon and a coaxial 7.62mm/0.3in machine-gun. The 4.2-litre Jaguar XK engine is positioned in the rear of the vehicle, where there are also two radiators, and a Ki-gas cold-weather starter is fitted. The Fox has the same fluid coupling, five speed pre-selecting epicyclic gearbox, and transfer box as the Ferret, giving the vehicle five forward gears and another five in reverse. It can ford to a depth of 1m/3ft 3in with no preparation. If the water is deeper, the flotation screen can be raised into position in just two minutes and then the vehicle becomes amphibious and is driven in the water by the wheels of the car. The Fox is fully air-transportable and three can be carried at once by a C130 Hercules transport aircraft. It can also be deployed by parachute. The vehicle is fitted with night-fighting and night-driving equipment, but no NBC system is installed.

The Fox was not a successful vehicle and did not remain in service for long. Its turrets were removed and fitted to the Scorpion and the FV 432.

RIGHT: The smoke dischargers have been moved from the hull and on to the front of the turret. The turret has a large overhang and so the driver's hatch was designed to fold to the side. The flotation screen is attached around the side of the hull of this vehicle.

Fox Light Armoured Car

Country: UK
Entered service: 1973
Crew: 3
Weight: 6,120kg/6 tons
Dimensions: Length – 5.08m/16ft 8in
    Height – 2.2m/7ft 3in
    Width – 2.13m/7ft
Armament: Main – 30mm/1.18in RARDEN
    cannon, and coaxial 7.62mm/0.3in machine-
    gun
    Secondary – Small arms
Armour: Classified
Powerplant: Jaguar XK 4.2-litre 6-cylinder
    142kW/190hp petrol engine
Performance: Speed – Road 104kph/65mph;
    Water 5.2kph/3mph
    Range – 434km/270 miles

Foxhound LPPV

ABOVE: **A British Army Foxhound. The vehicle has proven high levels of survivability if attacked, due in part to its v-shaped hull, clearly visible in this image.** BELOW LEFT: **A Foxhound Light Protected Patrol Vehicle, Camp Bastion, Helmand, Afghanistan, 2012. Comparatively light for vehicles in its class, it has a top speed of 112kph/70mph and can do 0-80kph/0-50mph in just 19 seconds. Its size and agility allows troops to carry out a wide range of tasks in environments that may restrict larger, heavier vehicles.**

In service since 2012, the Foxhound Light Protected Patrol Vehicle (LPPV) was specifically designed and built in the UK to protect against the threats faced by British troops in Afghanistan. It was a direct replacement of the comparatively much more vulnerable Snatch Land Rover that had served with British forces for some time and was demonstrably ill-suited to counter-insurgency operations in Iraq and Afghanistan. The only replacement vehicles available to acquire at the time that offered acceptable levels of crew and passenger safety were either too heavy or lacked the manoeuvrability that was essential for operating in walled compounds and the twisting streets of Afghanistan villages.

Developed from the US-designed Force Protection Ocelo, it was designed as a smaller, lighter alternative to the large and heavy Buffalo and Cougar. After its procurement the vehicle was named Foxhound in UK service, in keeping with the tradition of giving dog names to British Army wheeled armoured vehicles. 400 vehicles have been delivered to the British Army, and in its first decade of service the Foxhound has covered more than 1 million km/621,371 miles on operations. Having proved itself in the most demanding environments, this modular-by-design, agile and versatile vehicle will be a mainstay of the British Army for years to come.

Foxhound is one of the finest examples of protected patrol vehicle technology in service and, for its size and weight, the vehicle provides its crew and occupants with unprecedented levels of blast protection. Early examples of these patrol vehicles underwent rigorous final testing in the dusty and hot conditions of the Helmand desert in Afghanistan before being deployed on operations there. The vehicles, equipped to Theatre Entry Standard (TES), arrived at Camp Bastion in Afghanistan in June 2012. In what must be something of a record for UK military procurement, the Foxhound had been the subject of an Urgent Operational Requirement (UOR) that saw the vehicle go from the drawing board to front-line service in just two years.

Featuring v-shaped hull blast-protection technology with a modular demountable protected crew pod made of glass reinforced plastic composite, the Foxhound is powered by a Steyr M16-Monoblock diesel engine and has a top speed of 112kph/70mph despite being a highly-armoured vehicle. This is due in part to the involvement of UK automotive engineering company Ricardo who built all the British Foxhounds having had experience of Formula 1 racing car design and construction. The protective pod can be changed with ease to change the vehicle role from troop carrier to supply vehicle to ambulance and back again. While a landmine detonation under a Foxhound might blow off a wheel, the V-shaped hull design would deflect the blast outwards, up and away from the vehicle's occupants. For extra safety, passengers sit on blast-attenuated seats inside the vehicle pod to reduce the impact and disrupt the transfer of energy from the vehicle directly to the person in the seat.

ABOVE: **A soldier from the Royal Irish fires his GPMG (General Purpose Machine Gun) from his Foxhound vehicle during a NATO exercise, 2018. Note the torsion bar suspension bars running along the lower hull on the side of the drive module.** BELOW LEFT: **A Foxhound traverses the arid terrain of the Oman desert as part of an exercise, 2021. Note the very large hinges which allow the mission pod to be hinged up, away and clear of the drive module to enable maintenance.**

The Foxhound interior layout is pretty standard for light tactical vehicles in that it has its engine at the front, the crew compartment in the middle and the troop area at the rear. With a crew of two (commander and driver) troops sit on individual seats facing inwards. Driver and commander are provided with two large bulletproof windows at the front, and another small one each side of the hull. Two doors are fitted at the rear of the troop compartment allowing troops to enter and leave the vehicle quickly.

Foxhound LPPV

Country: UK
Entered service: 2012
Crew: 2
Weight: 7,500kg/8.26 tons
Dimensions: Length – 5.32m/17ft 5in
 Height – 2.35m/7ft 6in   Width – 2.1m/6ft 11in
Armament: N/A
Armour: Protection against small arms fire and grenades
Powerplant: 164kW/210hp Steyr M16-Monoblock diesel engine
Performance: Speed – 112kph/70mph

LEFT: **The large size of this vehicle can be seen from the crew member standing at the rear of the vehicle. The reloading crane can be seen under the missile launching rail. On the rear of the TEL are two stabilizers that have to be put in place before the missile can be elevated on its rail.**

Frog-7 Battlefield Missile System

The Frog (Free Range Over Ground) missile system was designed and built to deliver nuclear warheads on to the battlefield, just like the American Honest John system. The first in the series was the Filin (Eagle Owl), which has the NATO codename Frog-1. This entered service in 1955 but was not seen by the Western allies until the Moscow November Parade in 1987. The launching vehicle for this system was the 2P4, which was based on the IS-2 heavy tank. Not very many of these rocket systems were deployed as the whole system was very large and unwieldy and the missile was powered by seven separate solid-fuel rockets which did not always fire at the same time, making it inherently unstable. The Frog-2 (NATO codename Mars), using the 2P2 modified PT-76 amphibious tank as its carrier, came into service in the same year as the

Frog-1, but only 25 of these vehicles were built and it was more of a propaganda tool than a useful battlefield system.

The Frog-3 used the Luna-1 (NATO codename Moon-1) rocket and appeared in 1957. This was the first true battlefield tactical missile system and was mounted on 2P16 vehicles, some 200 of these being produced for the Soviet Army and a further 100 for export. The vehicle was very similar to the 2P2 and was based on the PT-76 tank. It had a road speed of 44kph/27.3mph and could fire its first rocket within 15 minutes of parking, but reloading could take up to 60 minutes. The same vehicle was used for the Frog-3, Frog-4 and Frog-5 and remained in service for several years.

The final version of the Frog family was the Frog-7 which used the Luna-M rocket (NATO codename Moon-3) and the

RIGHT: **This is a reload vehicle for the Frog-7 system. The same chassis as the TEL is used, except that the crane and launching rail have been removed and replaced with three fixed transport ramps. The official designation of this vehicle was 9T29.**

LEFT: **This Frog-7 system is ready for firing. Behind the TEL on the road is a column of tanks. Each Frog battery consisted of four TEL vehicles and 170 personnel. Each battery carries seven missiles for each TEL.** ABOVE: **The cab of the TEL has its blast screen folded down on to the glacis of the vehicle. The engine compartment is mounted behind the cab of the vehicle. The crews for the two TEL vehicles are being briefed by their officer.**

9P113 TEL (Transporter, Erector and Launcher). This was based on the ZIL-135LM 8x8 heavy truck that was used for several rocket and transport duties. The ZIL-135LM was built at the Bryansk Automobile Plant near Moscow and was designated BAZ-135 but the Soviet Army still referred to the vehicle as the ZIL-135LM. The crew cab is at the front of the vehicle and holds four men. Before the missile is fired, an armoured cover which normally lies on the top of the front sub-nose of the vehicle is put in place by the crew to protect the windscreen from the rocket blast. Behind the cab is the engine bay. The engine area has two ZIL-135 8-cylinder petrol engines, with one engine for each side of the vehicle powering all four wheels on that side. Power steering was fitted on the front and rear axle and a central tyre pressure system was fitted as standard. Mounted behind the front axle and on the rear of the vehicle are four stabilizing jacks. In the middle of the vehicle are cable reels which are used for sending signals to the missile from a remote firing position some 25m/82ft away. On the right-hand side between the third and fourth axle is a 4,064kg/4-ton crane which is used for reloading. The hydraulically operated missile

erecting mechanism is at the rear of the vehicle, while the sighting and elevation controls are on the left-hand side. There is also a small platform that folds down to allow the operator to reach the sighting controls.

These vehicles were relatively cheap at just 25,000 US dollars when they came into service with the Soviet Army in 1965 and were the last unguided nuclear weapon in service with the Soviet Union and other Warsaw Pact members. The Bryansk plant produced 750 of these vehicles of which 380 have been exported and it is estimated that in 1999, Russia still had 1,450 nuclear warheads in stock for the Frog-7. The Frog is no longer in service with the Russian Army but is still in service with a number of countries including former Soviet satellites.

The Luna-M missile is capable of carrying nuclear, high-explosive, chemical and sub munitions warheads. It has a minimum range of 15km/9.3 miles and a maximum of 65km/40.4 miles, but is not very accurate as it has a circular error of probability of between 500–700m/1,640–2,297ft, which means you could aim at an airfield and definitely hit it but not a target the size of a bridge.

ABOVE: **These vehicles are taking part in a victory parade. Between the first and second wheels is the forward stabilizer, one on each side of the vehicle. The reload crane can be clearly seen in this picture.**

Frog-7 Missile System

Country: USSR
Entered service: 1965
Crew: 4
Weight: 20,411kg/20.1 tons
Dimensions: Length – 10.69m/35ft 1in
    Height – With missile 3.35m/11ft
    Width – 2.8m/9ft 2in
Armament: Main – 1 x Luna-M missile
    Secondary – Small arms
Armour: None
Powerplant: 2 x ZIL 135 8-cylinder 132kW/180hp
    petrol engine
Performance: Speed – 40kph/25mph
    Range – 650km/400 miles

209

FV432 Armoured Personnel Carrier

The first prototype for the FV432 was completed in 1961, the first vehicle of this series being the earlier FV431 which did not enter production as there was no need for an armoured load carrier. In 1962, GKN Sankey was given a contract to mass-produce the FV432 or "Trojan" as it was called when it first entered service, but this name was dropped to avoid confusion with the Trojan car company. The first production vehicles were completed in 1963 and the FV432 entered service with the British Army replacing the Humber "Pig" and Saracen APC over a period of time. The FV432 was due to be replaced in the mid-1980s by the Warrior, but this has not happened due to defence cutbacks and the FV432 is expected to remain in service for some years yet. These vehicles are currently undergoing a refurbishment programme to extend their service life.

The FV432 is basically box-shaped and is an all-steel welded construction. The armour of the vehicle is proof against small arms fire and shell splinters. The driver sits in the front of the vehicle on the left-hand side and has a wide-angle periscope mounted in his hatch. The vehicle commander/gunner is situated behind the driver and has a cupola that can be rotated through 360 degrees with a mount for a single 7.62mm/0.3in GPMG mounted on the front of it. The driver's and commander's positions are open inside the vehicle and the commander can communicate with the driver by hitting him

TOP: **This British FV432 is on exercise in Germany. All the hatches on this vehicle are in the open position. The driver's and vehicle commander's positions are at the top of the picture. The large circular hatch above the crew compartment is in the open position, and a section of British troops are debussing.** ABOVE: **A side view of an FV432 showing the exhaust system running the length of the vehicle. The exhaust stopped just by the rear exit, so at times when the vehicle was stopped, exhaust gases would enter the infantry compartment.**

in the shoulders to indicate any desired changes of direction. Unfortunately this can be very painful after a while! Next to them on the right-hand side of the vehicle is the engine bay. Behind this is the infantry compartment which extends to the rear of the vehicle. This compartment can hold ten fully armed troops who sit on bench seats, five down each side of the vehicle facing each other. Above them is a large single circular hatch that is divided in the middle and, when opened, folds flush with the top of the vehicle on each side. Each half-hatch is hinged in the middle making opening easier. The bench seats can be folded up when not in use so the vehicle can then be used as a cargo carrier. At the rear of the vehicle is a single large door that opens outwards and to the right allowing the troops to debus very quickly, with the open rear door acting as a shield. The exhaust system is mounted on the left-hand side of the vehicle with the NBC system fitted to the right-hand side. All marks of the vehicle are fitted with a full NBC system.

The FV432 was usually fitted with the Peak Engineering 7.62mm/0.3in turret, but the 30mm/1.18in turret from the Fox armoured car was mounted on a few vehicles of the Berlin Brigade. The turret was fitted behind the commander's position and into the upper hatch, which was now fixed in the closed position, and had a full 360-degree traverse, while behind the turret was a small circular hatch. The FV432 is not amphibious but the Mk 1 was at first fitted with a flotation screen that could be raised in ten minutes, with the vehicle using its tracks to power it in the water. The flotation screen was not installed in the Mk 2 variant.

The FV432 has been produced in three main marks. The Mk 1 was powered by a Rolls-Royce B81 8-cylinder 179kW/ 240hp petrol engine. The Mk 2 started to appear in 1966 and was fitted with a diesel engine that had a multi-fuel capability that improved reliability and range. The last mark was the 2/1 and this had improvements to the exhaust system and the engine area. The vehicle commander is extremely vulnerable in the FV432 and has no protection when manning the machine-gun with the hatch open. By 1967, many were slating the vehicle because it lacked heavy armament like that of the new Soviet BMP-1. However, no NATO APC could match the BMP for firepower.

ABOVE: **An FV432 mine plough developed by the British Army but never seriously put into service. The glacis plate of the vehicle has several control boxes for the plough fitted to it. The plough blade is constructed in sections, so if one section is damaged it can be replaced quickly.** BELOW: **Another mine-clearing device fitted and tested on the FV432 was the flail. The vehicle was called the Aardvark. The large box on the rear of the vehicle holds the lane-marking equipment. This device did not enter service with the British Army.**

MIDDLE LEFT: **The vehicle commander has a 7.62mm/0.3in machine-gun fitted to his cupola. The large boxes either side of the rear door are for storage. There was never enough storage space in or on the FV 432; many units fitted wire-mesh storage bins to the rear of the vehicle.**

LEFT: **A 432 Mk 1 fitted with a RARDEN turret from the cancelled Fox armoured car. This vehicle is also fitted with a flotation screen around the top of the FV432. On the front of the vehicle is a trim vane. The 432 is moved through the water by its tracks.**

FV432 Armoured Personnel Carrier	

Country: UK
Entered service: 1963
Crew: 2 plus 10 infantry
Weight: 15,240kg/15.1 tons
Dimensions: Length – 5.25m/17ft 7in
   Height – 2.29m/7ft 6in
   Width – 2.8m/9ft 2in
Armament: Main – 7.62mm/0.3in General
   Purpose machine-gun
   Secondary – Small arms
Armour: Maximum – 12mm/0.47in
Powerplant: Rolls-Royce K60 No.4 Mk 4F
   6-cylinder 170kW/240hp diesel/multi-fuel
   engine
Performance: Speed – 52kph/32mph
   Range – 483km/300 miles

FV430 Mk 3 Bulldog

As the implications of the British military fighting counter-insurgency ground campaigns in both Iraq and Afghanistan crystallized, it became clear that there was a need for more armoured vehicles in both theatres to, amongst other needs, relieve the pressure on the British Army Warrior fleet. Based on this urgent need, the UK Ministry of Defence (MOD) decided to explore an immediate upgrade of the venerable FV432 APC to further extend its already long service life. This led the MOD to commission BAE Systems Land Systems to update, at a cost of £85m, more than 1,000 FV432s APCs to FV430 Mark 3 standard.

In keeping with allocating dog breed names to British Army wheeled armoured vehicles, this version of the FV432 was named Bulldog Mk 3. The FV432, conceived in the Cold War, has an impressive heritage having entered service with the British Army four decades before this counter-insurgency mission, in the 1960s.

To make the Bulldog a viable, survivable vehicle in such harsh combat settings, it featured an applique, explosive reactive armour package provided by Israeli company Rafael. This enhanced safety for driver, commander and troops meant it could withstand 12.7mm/0.5in ammunition and hollow charge warheads like the deadly RPG-7 rocket propelled grenades favoured by the insurgents British troops faced in both Iraq and Afghanistan.

The Bulldog received a new, more powerful engine (a 179kW/240hp Rolls-Royce K60 multi-fuel engine), and steering

ABOVE: **The upgraded FV430 Mk3 Bulldog is a version of the veteran FV430, given extra armour and a turret. This is a Bulldog operated by the British Army's Royal Green Jackets (RGJ), the first to use them on operations in late 2006.**

and braking system which provided better mobility and manoeuvrability. Other improvements were air conditioning and a top-mounted gun station fitted with a remote-controlled 7.62mm/0.3in machine-gun that could be operated from inside the vehicle. Some areas of the vehicle were fitted with slat-armour for protection against the ever-present threat of anti-tank rockets. Kevlar-lined plates were added to the bottom of the vehicle's hull to provide improved protection against improvized explosive devices.

Nine hundred FV430s were modified like this, ready for service in Iraq and Afghanistan alongside the British Mastiff PPV. The specified modifications bestowed an impressive performance on the Bulldog so it not only matched the Warrior's level of protection but also had a new top speed of 72kph/45mph. The first 500 "new" vehicles were handed over to the British Army and arrived in Iraq at the end of 2006. However, such was the urgency of the need for the vehicles in the war zones that the Bulldogs arrived unfinished and had to be made ready for combat in-theatre. The British Army's Royal Green Jackets (RGJ) were the first to use the vehicle on operations and it became the regiment's vehicle of choice when carrying out patrols in Basra City.

The FV430 chassis is a conventional tracked AFV design with its engine at the front and the driver's position on the vehicle's right-hand side. A hatch for the vehicle commander can be found directly behind the driver's hatch while a side-hinged door in the rear of the vehicle allows for loading and unloading of both troops and supplies. Although there are no firing ports for the troops carried onboard the Bulldog, a pintle mount next to the top hatches can mount a machine-gun.

A number of Bulldogs were among the military equipment aid package pledged by the UK government to Ukraine following the 2022 Russian invasion. According to the UK Ministry of

ABOVE: **A British Army Bulldog on patrol in Iraq. Note the additional reactive armour applied to the vehicle sides and slatted armoured on the front of its hull. With a standard wading screen fitted, the vehicle can also be converted for use in water with a speed of around 6kph/3.7mph.** BELOW LEFT: **The Bulldog has two crew members and is capable of carrying up to ten passengers. Bulldog variants are in service with the infantry as command vehicles, 81mm/3.1in mortar carriers, ambulances, and recovery vehicles.**

Defence, it is planned that the Bulldog will be out of service by 2030, a remarkable seven decades after the FV430 family of vehicles first entered British Army service.

FV430 Mk 3 Bulldog

Country: UK
Entered service: 2006
Crew: 2, plus 10 infantry
Weight: 15,300kg/16.8 tons
Dimensions: Length – 5.25m/17ft 3in
   Height – 2.28m/7ft 6in
   Width – 2.8m/9ft 2in
Armament: 7.62mm/0.3in machine-gun
Armour: Applique, explosive reactive armour
   to withstand 12.7mm/0.5in ammunition and
   RPG-7s
Powerplant: 179kW/240hp Rollls-Royce K60
   multi-fuel engine
Performance: Speed – 52kph/32mph
   Range – 580km/360 miles

LEFT: **This German Gepard has the rear surveillance radar in the raised position. When the vehicle is moving, the surveillance radar folds back into the horizontal position. The vehicle commander is using a manual sight, attached to his cupola.** ABOVE: **Both radar dishes on this Gepard are in the raised active position. A bank of four smoke dischargers is fitted to each side of the bottom of the turret.**

Gepard Self-Propelled Anti-Aircraft Gun

In 1961, contracts were issued to two companies for the development of a new Self-Propelled Anti-Aircraft Gun (SPAAG) for the *Bundeswehr* (German Army) as a replacement for the American M42. However, the whole project was cancelled in 1964 as the projected main chassis was considered to be too small and the tracking radar was not fully developed. In 1965, it was decided that a new all-weather design based on the Leopard 1 MBT chassis was required. Two development contracts were issued in 1966 for two vehicles armed with 3cm/1.18in guns and two vehicles armed with 3.5cm/1.38in guns. In 1970, following the decision to concentrate on the 3.5cm/1.38in vehicle, an order for 420 Gepards was placed, with the first vehicles entering service in 1976. The Belgian Army placed a contract for 55 Gepards that was fulfilled between 1977 and 1980, while the Dutch Army order for 95 vehicles was completed over the same period. In 1998 the German Government donated 43 Gepard vehicles to the Romanian Army along with training and maintenance equipment. The first of these were delivered in 1999.

The all-welded hull of the Gepard is slightly longer than the Leopard MBT while the armour on the vehicle has been reduced in thickness. The driver is located in the front of the vehicle on the right-hand side due to the tracking radar being mounted on the front of the turret. Next to the driver is the auxiliary power unit which is a Daimler-Benz OM314 70.8kW/95hp engine. The exhaust pipe for this runs along the left-hand side of the hull to the rear of the vehicle. The vehicle is fitted with a full NBC system.

The two-man turret is positioned in the middle of the vehicle; the commander is on the left with the gunner on the right and both are provided with their own hatch which is mounted in the roof of the turret. Both the gunner and commander have

ABOVE: **On the front of the turret is the tracking radar. Targets are acquired by the surveillance radar and then the most prominent threat is worked out by computer and the target information passed to the tracking radar, which then locks the guns on to the target.**

a fully stabilized panoramic telescope sight which is mounted on the roof of the turret and is used for optically tracking aerial targets and for use against ground targets. The optical sights can be linked to the radar and computer, and a Siemens laser rangefinder is also fitted for engaging ground targets. Mounted on the rear of the turret is the pulse-Doppler search radar, which has a 360-degree traverse, a range of 15km/9.3 miles, and an IFF (Identification Friend or Foe) capability. Once a target has been acquired the information is passed to the tracking radar which is mounted at the front of the turret between the guns. The computer and radar systems

are capable of dealing with several targets at once. The main armament is two Oerlikon 35mm/1.38in KDA cannon. Each gun barrel has a firing rate of 550 rounds per minute and the vehicle carries 660 rounds in total, with 310 anti-aircraft shells and 20 rounds of armour-piercing ammunition for each barrel. A normal burst of fire lasts for a fraction of a second and can be up to a maximum of 40 rounds. The guns normally open fire when the target is at a distance of between 3,000m/9,842ft and 4,000m/13,123ft with the rounds reaching the target at a range of between 2,000m/6,561ft and 3,000m/9,842ft, the computer calculating the predicted position of the target. The guns are mounted externally on the sides of the turret with the ammunition being fed in on hermetically sealed chutes, which keeps the gun fumes away from the crew.

Upgrade programmes to fire-control systems and ammunition ensured the Gepard remained a viable deterrent well into the 2000s. As part of this project, the German and Dutch vehicles were data-linked so they could exchange

ABOVE LEFT: This is a Dutch Gepard. The Dutch fitted different surveillance radar to that installed by the Germans; it is shaped like a large letter "T" which rotates at 60 revolutions per minute. The Dutch also fitted banks of six smoke dischargers to each side of the bottom of the turret. ABOVE: The barrels of this Gepard have been covered in camouflage netting. The turret can complete a full rotation of 360 degrees in just 4 seconds. The fumes from the gun barrels and the empty cases are ejected directly to the outside of the vehicle.

information. The upgrade programme was finished in 2002 and the German upgraded version, known as the Gepard Flakpanzer, continued in front-line use until 2010.

Around forty of these ex-German Gepards were supplied to Ukraine to aid their defence against the 2022 Russian invasion. Ukrainian forces claim the Gepards proved especially effective against Russian loitering munitions (suicide drones) which the vehicle's radar can detect up to 16km/10m away and bring down with an average of 6 rounds. The Gepard was also used to great effect destroying incoming cruise missiles.

LEFT: This Gepard is in travelling mode. The tracking radar dish has been folded forward to protect the dish from damage. With the surveillance radar folded down, the height of the vehicle is lowered by 1m/39in. Acquisition speed of the radar is 56 degrees per second, with a full traverse of the turret taking just four seconds.

Gepard SPAAG

Country: West Germany
Entered service: 1976
Crew: 3
Weight: 45,009kg/44.3 tons
Dimensions: Length – 7.68m/25ft 2in
  Height – 3.01m/9ft 9in to top of turret
  Width – 3.27m/10ft 7in
Armament: Main – 2 x 35mm/1.38in Oerlikon KDA guns
  Secondary – None
Armour: Maximum – 70mm/2.76in
Powerplant: MTU MB 838 Ca M500 10-cylinder 619kW/830hp multi-fuel engine
Performance: Speed – 64kph/40.5mph
  Range – 550km/340 miles

LEFT: **The vehicle is fitted with three stabilizing jacks. One is mounted in front of the rear wheels on each side of the vehicle and a single jack is mounted at the rear of the vehicle in the centre.**
ABOVE: **A British Honest John during a live-firing exercise. The missile could be fitted with two 20 or 40 kiloton W31 nuclear warheads. It could also be fitted with a 680kg/1,500lb high-explosive or 564kg/1,243lb chemical warhead.**

Honest John Missile System

Development of the M31 started at Redstone Arsenal, USA, in May 1950. The Douglas Aircraft Company was appointed to assist with development and later to carry out production, the first production contract being for 2,000 rockets. The M31 was deployed in Europe in June 1954 and it remained in service until 1961 when the improved M50 Honest John, which was lighter and had an increased range, replaced it. In July 1982, the Honest John system was declared obsolete as the Lance nuclear system came into service.

The rocket was a solid-fuel system and therefore required no countdown time and could remain in storage for several years with no maintenance. The M31 had a maximum range of 19.3km/ 12 miles, which meant that when firing a 20-kilotonne/19,684-ton nuclear warhead the fallout area would have been greater than the range of the missile, whereas the M50 missile, with its range of 48.3km/30 miles, would have been safer for the crew to use. The missile was unguided and required the whole vehicle to be pointed at the target area. The missile could be fitted with either a conventional high-explosive or a nuclear warhead and was never used in action.

The Transporter, Erector and Launcher (TEL) was built by the International Harvester Company and used the M139 5,080kg/5-ton truck, a stretched version of the M54 5,080kg/5-ton truck, as the base vehicle for the conversion. The TEL was designated M289 and was a 6x6 configuration which gave it excellent cross-country ability. The vehicle had the engine located at the front, the three-man soft-top crew cab behind it and the missile erector at the rear. The first version of the TEL had an "A" frame supporting the launch rail and this was pivoted in the middle of the vehicle above the two centrally mounted stabilizers while the launch rail protruded over the front of the TEL by 1.8m/6ft, restricting the driver's vision. The improved TEL had a much shorter launch rail, the front of which could be folded back on itself while travelling. The elevation controls were at the rear of the vehicle on the left-hand side.

ABOVE: **A control wire is run from the vehicle to a command position a safe distance away from the back-blast of the missile. The three-man crew of this vehicle are getting instructions from an officer before firing the missile.**

M289 TEL

Country: USA
Entered service: 1954
Crew: 3
Weight: 16,400kg/16.1 tons
Dimensions: Length – 9.89m/32ft 5in
Height – 2.9m/9ft 5in
Width – 2.67m/8ft 8in
Armament: Main – M31 Honest John Missile
Secondary – Small arms
Armour: None
Powerplant: Continental R6602 6-cylinder 146kW/196hp petrol engine
Performance: Speed – 90kph/56mph
Range – 480km/300 miles

LEFT: **The launching arm on this vehicle is retracted for travelling and the driver's and vehicle commander/gunner's hatches are in the open position. Above the gunner's position is a domed armoured sight.** ABOVE: **The launching arm of this Hornet Is In the raised firing position. This vehicle and missile system was specifically designed to be dropped by parachute.**

Hornet Malkara Anti-Tank Missile System

The Hornet was developed from the Humber "Pig" 1-ton APC, and was originally designed to give the armoured divisions of the British Army a long-range anti-tank capability. This was intended to replace the Conqueror heavy tank with a guided missile system as it was felt that the tank no longer had a role on the modern battlefield.

The Hornet was based on the Humber 1,016kg/1-ton 4x4 vehicle and while it used the same chassis and engine as the standard vehicle, the crew compartment and the rear of the vehicle were modified to take the Malkara wire-guided missile system. The engine was located at the front, with the crew compartment behind and the missile launching arm fitted to the rear of the vehicle. The crew compartment was configured with the driver on the right, the commander/gunner on the left and the radio operator in the middle. The driver and radio operator also doubled as reload crew for the vehicle.

The superstructure at the rear of the 1,016kg/1-ton APC vehicle was removed and replaced by two storage boxes for two Malkara missiles and the launcher hydraulic arm. When travelling the launching arm was stowed in a lowered position below the top of the crew compartment. When the vehicle reached its firing location it halted and the launching arm was raised to the firing position, some 90cm/3ft above the crew compartment, so that the missiles had a clear flight to the target. The commander/gunner had an optical sight that was mounted in the roof of the crew compartment and controlled the missile using a joystick. Each missile had two flares attached at the rear which helped the gunner to track it to the target. The missile weighed 91kg/200lb of which the warhead was 27kg/60lb; this represented the largest warhead carried by any anti-tank missile at the time.

The Malkara missile was a joint British and Australian development, but was never very successful and the Hornet Malkara was replaced in service with the British Army from 1965 onwards by the Ferret Mk 2/6 armed with Vigilant ATGW missiles. The Hornet could rightly be described as a very expensive white elephant when compared with the economic Ferret.

LEFT: **The rear storage area of the Hornet, where two reload missiles are carried. The rear hatch splits in two with the bottom part folding downwards to form a shelf, while the top half of the hatch folds flat on the top of the storage box. The wings are stored separately from the missiles in the rear of the vehicle.**

Hornet Malkara ATGM

Country: UK
Entered service: 1958
Crew: 3
Weight: 5,893kg/5.8 tons
Dimensions: Length – 5.05m/16ft 7in
   Height – 2.34m/7ft 8in
   Width – 2.22m/7ft 3in
Armament: Main – 4 x Malkara ATGM
   Secondary – 7.62mm/0.3in General Purpose
   machine-gun
Armour: Maximum – 10mm/0.394in
Powerplant: Rolls-Royce B60 Mk 5A 6-cylinder
   89kW/120hp petrol engine
Performance: Speed – 64kph/40mph
   Range – 402km/250 miles

LEFT: **This Humber Pig is fitted with a grill for pushing road blocks such as burning cars out of the way of the vehicle. An armoured plate has been fitted to the rear of the vehicle to stop fire-bombs or other objects being thrown under the vehicle.**

ABOVE: **The inside of the vehicle commander's door. Mounted in the door is an armoured vision port. The clear plastic tank in front of the commander's position is a screen-wash bottle. The bottle is filled with a chemical that can remove paint and other liquid that might be thrown at the vehicle.**

Humber "Pig" 1-Ton Armoured Personnel Carrier

In the late 1940s and early 1950s, the Humber/Rootes Group developed a range of 1,016kg/1-ton armoured vehicles for the British Army. The Saracen APC was also under development at the same time but production proved to be slow and so the Humber "Pig" APC was developed as an interim solution. It was designed as a battlefield taxi and not as a combat vehicle; troops would debus away from the action and attack on foot. This interim vehicle entered production in 1954 and came into service in 1955. It was originally intended to produce only a few vehicles but the total quickly mounted to 1,700. This vehicle was so successful and adaptable that it is still in service with the British Army in 2005.

Humber took the basic 1,016kg/1-ton 4x4 cargo vehicle and added an armoured roof and rear doors to make a very basic APC for the army. The exact derivation of the vehicle's label

"Pig" is not known for certain, but it is certainly difficult to drive and lives up to its name.

The Pig is an all-welded construction with the engine at the front and the crew compartment behind. The driver and vehicle commander sit side by side in the front of the crew compartment behind the engine. Each of them has a windscreen to their front that can be covered when in action by an armoured shutter that folds down from the roof of the vehicle. Both also have an access door in the side of the vehicle and above them in the roof are two circular hatches. There are two firing ports in each side of the crew compartment with a further two mounted in the rear doors of the vehicle.

In the early 1960s it was thought that there were enough Saracen APCs in service and as the FV 432 was also just coming into service, it was decided to sell off the now-redundant Pigs. However, when the "Troubles" started in Northern Ireland in 1969, the army was asked to step in to help the police in maintaining the peace. The Pig was chosen to give the troops some mobility and protection without further arousing passions in a situation of civil unrest, being relatively small and innocuous and not having the aggressive appearance of a tank. Unfortunately, only a few of these vehicles had been kept in reserve, the majority having been scrapped or sold off to private collectors and the Belgian armed forces. These were bought back at an inflated price

LEFT: **The driver's position inside the Humber Pig. The gear stick is between the seats with the handbrake next to the driver's seat. The dashboard is in the centre of the vehicle so both the driver and commander can see it.**

LEFT: This Humber Pig has been fitted with a six-barrel smoke and CS gas discharger. Under the rear of the vehicle, the armoured plate to stop bombs being thrown under the vehicle can be clearly seen.

BELOW: The inside of a Humber Pig command vehicle. One set of seats has been removed and replaced with a map table. Two wooden boards separate the driver and vehicle commander's cab from the troop compartment of the vehicle. The rear doors of the vehicle are held open by a simple metal hook and eye.

and refurbished, and some 500 Pigs were sent to Northern Ireland. In 1972 it was discovered that the IRA had acquired armour-piercing ammunition that could damage the vehicle and cause casualties inside. As a result, Operation "Bracelet" was launched to upgrade the armour of the Pig and fit vision blocks to the open firing ports. The vehicle's suspension was also strengthened to accommodate the additional weight, and an extra armoured shutter was added to the rear of the vehicle which would fall into place when the rear doors were opened, protecting the legs of the men following the vehicle.

When the Saracen was withdrawn from Northern Ireland in 1984 the Pig had to take over its role and this led to a number of specialist conversions with exotic sounding names. The "Kremlin Pig" was covered with wire mesh as a protection against the Soviet RPG-7 rocket launcher. The "Flying Pig" has large side-mounted riot screens fitted to the vehicle. These fold back along the length of the crew compartment when not in use, but when in the open position have the appearance of wings and give troops protection from stones or other objects thrown at them. The "Holy Pig" has a Plexiglas fixed observation turret in the roof, the front of which can be folded down. Other Pig variants had smoke and CS gas launchers placed in the roof which can be fired from inside the vehicle, and large bull-bar bumpers have been fitted to the front.

The Pig proved to be a very reliable and "squaddy-proof" AFV especially given the "interim" nature of the design, and it proved to be an extremely valuable vehicle. The Saxon has replaced the Humber Pig in many roles.

ABOVE: This is a "Flying Pig" in operation in Northern Ireland during the "Troubles" of the 1970s. The wire-mesh screens looked like a set of wings when deployed. Behind the wings of the vehicle are British troops. The soldier in the front is firing a baton-round gun, which could discharge either CS gas or rubber bullets.

Humber "Pig" APC

Country: UK
Entered service: 1955
Crew: 2 plus 8 infantry
Weight: 6,909kg/6.8 tons
Dimensions: Length – 4.93m/16ft 2in
  Height – 2.12m/7ft
  Width – 2.04m/6ft 8in
Armament: Main – None
  Secondary – Small arms
Armour: Maximum – 10mm/0.394in
Powerplant: Rolls-Royce B60 Mk 5A 6-cylinder 89kW/120hp petrol engine
Performance: Speed – 64kph/40mph
  Range – 402km/250 miles

LEFT: **This HUMVEE has been fitted with an extended exhaust system, which allows the vehicle to wade through 1m/39in of water. The bonnet of the vehicle tilts forward to give access to the engine.** ABOVE: **The driver's position is on the left with the vehicle commander on the right. The large console in the middle of the vehicle has the communications equipment mounted in it. When the vehicle is fitted with a roof-mounted machine-gun, the turret gunner stands between the rear seats.**

Humvee Multi-Role Vehicle

Development of the High Mobility Multipurpose Wheeled Vehicle (HMMWV or HUMVEE) started in the 1970s. In 1983, the US armed forces signed a 1.2 billion dollar production contract with the AM General Corporation under which AM General would produce 55,000 of these new vehicles for them between 1984 and 1989. Better known to the troops who use the vehicle as the "Hummer", it was given the official designation of M998. A further option was exercised by the US military for an additional 15,000 vehicles, while in 1989 another order was placed for 33,000 vehicles. More orders have since been placed for up-armoured variants, as a result of combat experience, which will bring the total production run to over 280,000.

The basic HMMWV has the engine in the front of the vehicle, the crew compartment in the middle and a load-carrying area in the rear. The vehicle is permanently in the 4x4 configuration and the bonnet tilts forward to allow easy access to the air-cooled 6.2-litre diesel engine. The crew compartment has a box frame steel roll-cage fitted to it, while the rest of the body is made from aluminium that is riveted and glued into position. This makes the replacement of damaged panels easier and

quicker than if it were an all-welded construction. The four-man crew sit either side of the power transfer, two in the front and two in the rear of the compartment. There is a hatch in the roof above the crew compartment when the vehicle is fitted with a machine-gun or other weapon system. The HMMWV can be fitted with a wide selection of armament ranging from a basic 7.62mm/0.3in machine-gun to a 30mm/1.18in cannon, Hellfire ATGMs or Starstreak AAGMs.

The Humvee was designed to be air-transportable, air-droppable (including by the very dramatic low-altitude parachute extraction system), and can be carried by large helicopters when sling-loaded. The USAF C-130 transport

BELOW LEFT: **The front of the HUMVEE, with the recessed lights and a cow-catcher on the front of the vehicle. Increased cooling is supplied to the engine from the grill in the bonnet. The vehicle now carries the official American designation of M998.**
BELOW RIGHT: **The M1151 Enhanced Armament Carrier is an improved version of the standard Humvee. It has a heavier chassis and improved engine to handle additional armour. It is built on an Expanded Capacity Vehicle chassis which allows for more passengers or up to 1043kg/2300lbs of additional supplies.**

aircraft could carry three while the C-5A Galaxy could accommodate an impressive 15 at a time. The HMMWV has been built in 18 different variations and development has continued with many improvements based on combat experience and evolving battlefield threats. The engine has also been improved to produce more power several times.

The Humvee A2 Series featured an improved steering wheel and column, new rear seats, increased cargo capacity and an increased (9,000lb) rated winch. A2s were fitted with a 119kW/160hp 6.5 litre V8 diesel engine and a four-speed automatic transmission. The standard A2s can carry a payload of 4400lb at a maximum speed of 112kph/70mph.

From 2006, what were termed "Reliability Extended HMMWVs" went into development with AM General. These are upgraded, uprated refurbished machines and included improved engine cooling, new shock absorbers, improved suspension, re-engineered geared hubs and new parking brakes.

ABOVE: **A US Army Humvee fires a BGM-71 TOW (Tube-launched, Optically tracked, Wire-guided) missile.** BELOW LEFT: **A fording Humvee launches from a US Navy landing craft utility (LCU), 2011.**

The expanded capacity vehicle (ECV) HMMWV variant was developed to carry heavier payloads without any loss in performance. These versions, powered by a turbocharged 6.5 litre V8 diesel engine typically weigh 2,500kg/ 2.5 tons and have a payload capacity of 5100lb. A number of derived international models have been produced through AM General collaboration with, for example, Swiss MOWAG Corporation (the Eagle) and the Turkish company Otokar (the Cobra).

The HMMWV has been the most widely-used military light utility vehicle in the world and has been in service with over 50 nations. While the US Army is introducing the replacement Joint Light Tactical Vehicle in great numbers, Humvees are expected to remain in US Army service in quantity well into the 2040s.

HMMWV M1114

Country: USA
Entered service: 1985
Crew: 1 plus 3 infantry
Weight: 5,489kg/5.4 tons
Dimensions: Length – 4.99m/16ft 4in
    Height – 1.9m/6ft 3in   Width – 2.3m/7ft 7in
Armament: Main – 1 x 7.62mm/0.3in
    GP machine-gun (basic variant)
    Secondary – Small arms
Armour: Protection against 7.62mm/0.3in
    armour-piercing rounds and artillery shell
    splinters
Powerplant: General Motors 6.5-litre 8-cylinder
    142kW/190hp diesel engine
Performance: Speed – 125kph/78mph
    Range – 443km/275 miles

Land Rover Defender Multi-Role Vehicles

The Land Rover has been in service with the British Army since 1949 and has gone through many changes and improvements in that time. Development of a civilian Land Rover Defender derivative started in 1983 when the then-current range of Land Rover vehicles was beginning to show its age and was in need of updating with more modern design and technology. The Defender inspired series were in service from 1985 and produced in three chassis variations: 2.29m/90in, 2.79m/110in and 3.3m/130in. This is the distance between the wheel centres of the vehicle, known as the wheelbase and the distance in inches gives the version its model number – 90, 110 and 130. The Land Rover 90 and 110 were the core vehicles at that time while the 130 was a special conversion vehicle, for example in the ambulance role. At first an order was placed for 950 of all types, followed by an order for 500 of the 90 version and 1,200 of the 110 version.

The Defender series used the chassis and coil-spring

ABOVE: **Given a new lease of life, saving lives, this vehicle combination is a British Army Mastiff fitted with Choker Mine Rollers following behind a Panama remote control Land Rover which carries a ground penetrating radar used for mine and IED route clearance operations.**

suspension of the proven Range Rover so was a stronger and more comfortable vehicle than the previous series of vehicles. In appearance, it was similar to other earlier Land Rover models except that there are bulges over the wheel arches and there is a revised radiator grill. The windscreen is a one-piece unit and the vehicle was fitted with permanent four-wheel drive. The military Defender was normally fitted with a diesel engine but an 8-cylinder petrol engine was also available. The roof was constructed from roll-bars and the gun-mounting.

The weapons fit of the vehicle could be very varied, but the basic configuration is three 7.62mm/0.3in GPMGs, one fitted in the front for use by the vehicle commander and two on a twin mount in the roof of the rear area. Other weapons available are a 30mm/1.18in cannon, TOW missiles, LAW 80 ATM or Browning 12.7mm/0.5in heavy machine-guns.

A Special Operations Vehicle (SOV) version was developed for the British SAS forces and the US Rangers. These vehicles were fitted with the 300Tdi direct injection intercooled diesel engine. The SOV was fully air-portable by heavy-lift aircraft

LEFT: **The famous SAS "Pink Panther"; this is a long wheelbase Land Rover. The vehicle has been fitted with several machine-guns and has smoke dischargers fixed to the top of the bodywork on the rear of the vehicle.**

LEFT: **A trio of long wheelbase reconnaissance Land Rover Defenders. The vehicles have been fitted with several heavy machine-guns, and smoke dischargers have been fixed to the top of the front bumper of the vehicle. The vehicles are all covered in extra equipment.** ABOVE: **The inside of "Dinky", the short wheelbase Land Rover Defender derived vehicle developed for the British Army. The vehicle is fitted with a roll-bar to protect the crew if the vehicle turns over. In the rear of the vehicle is a pintle mount for a machine-gun or MILAN AT missile system.**

such as the C-130 or could be under-slung from helicopters like the Puma and Chinook.

By the end of 1998, almost eight thousand examples of the Defender XD Wolf in both Truck Utility Light (TUL) short wheelbase and Truck Utility Medium (TUM) long wheelbase version had entered British Army service. Powered by a 300TDi engine, it was a new design compared to the 90/110s and was far stronger (all new axles) and more reliable than the original Defender-derived models. A roll-cage was supplied as standard and some models destined for use in especially harsh or high-risk environments were fitted with an extra front roll cage. Around thirty different versions of the Land Rover Wolf, each specially adapted, were developed for British Army use.

Some obsolete surplus Land Rovers were converted to become Panama Remotely Operated Vehicles (ROV) as part of a mine-clearing system used by the British Armed Forces. The system was developed very quickly as a cost effective

solution to mine detection in Afghanistan where an average of one person a week was killed and up to six more seriously injured. The Panama is fitted with a large piece of mine-detection equipment mounted on the vehicle's front. The vehicle is towed behind another vehicle – usually a Buffalo, then automatically unhitched and driven by remote control to search for explosive devices.

In broader use however, while suitable replacements are sought and brought into service, several thousand military Land Rovers remain in British Army service, and are expected to continue to, for the foreseeable future. Several hundred remain in use with export customers around the world.

BOTTOM LEFT: **This variant of the Wolf TUM, the Weapons Mount Installation Kit (WMIK, referred to as 'Wimik') is used as a reconnaissance and close fire support vehicle. WMIKs are stripped down, have a strengthened chassis and are fitted with roll cages and weapon mounts.**

Land Rover Defender 110 SOV	
Country: UK	
Entered service: 1990	
Crew: 1 plus up to 5 infantry	
Weight: 3,050kg/3 tons	
Dimensions: Length – 4.67m/15ft 4in	
Height – 2.04m/6ft 8in	
Width – 1.79m/5ft 10in	
Armament: Main – 3 x 7.62mm/0.3in GPMGs	
Secondary – Small arms	
Armour: None	
Powerplant: Rover 300Tdi 8-cylinder 100kW/134hp diesel engine	
Performance: Speed – 90kph/56mph	
Range – 450km/280 miles	

LAV-25 Light Armoured Vehicles

In September 1981 General Motors Defense, who also own MOWAG of Switzerland, was awarded a 3.1 million-dollar contract to build four 8x8 Piranha vehicles for a selection competition to provide a new Light Armoured Vehicle (LAV) for the US Marine Corps and the US Army. The first two vehicles were delivered in October 1981. One was fitted with an Arrowpointe two-man turret armed with a 25mm/0.98in chain gun, while the other vehicle had the same turret armed with a 90mm/3.54in Cockerill Mk III gun.

Both turrets had an M240 coaxial machine-gun and eight smoke dischargers fitted as standard. In September 1982, GM won the LAV competition, annual orders were placed for the vehicle and 758 had been built for the USMC by 1985. The first production LAV-25 vehicles, similar to the 8x8 Piranha, were delivered in 1983 and the last one in 1987.

The all-welded steel hull of the LAV-25 protects the crew from small-arms fire and shell splinters. The driver sits in the front of the vehicle on the left-hand side, next to the engine which is on the right with the air-inlet and outlet louvres on the hull top. The exhaust outlet is mounted on the right-hand side of the vehicle. In the middle of the vehicle is the two-man turret and the infantry compartment is in the rear of the vehicle. Access to the rear compartment is by two doors that open outwards, each of which has a vision port fitted. The troop compartment is connected to a centralized NBC system, but the six troops that sit in this area, three down each side facing inwards, are very cramped. Above the compartment are two hatches that can give access to the outside and there is also an escape hatch in the body of the vehicle. The Delco two-man turret has the

ABOVE: **A LAV-25 armoured ambulance. This is a development of the logistics vehicle, which can be seen behind the ambulance. The ambulance is fitted with two clusters of four smoke dischargers on the rear roof of the vehicle.**

commander on the right and the gunner on the left and is fitted with an M242 25mm/0.98in McDonnell Douglas Helicopter Company chain gun as the main armament. The vehicle commander can also have a 7.62mm/0.3in M240 machine-gun fitted on a pintle mount in front of the turret hatch, and on each side of the turret front are four smoke dischargers. The turret is fitted with laser range-finding and a full range of night-fighting optics. The driver also has night-driving optics fitted. When the vehicle is travelling cross-country full eight-wheel drive can be engaged, but in less demanding situations the vehicle is driven in the more economic mode which supplies power only to the rear four wheels. The steering controls the front four wheels, and the vehicle is fully amphibious. The LAV-25 is fitted with two propellers that propel the vehicle when in the water and steering is achieved using four rudders. A trim vane is fitted to the front of the vehicle and it takes just three minutes to make the LAV ready for the water.

The LAV has been built in a number of variants. The LAV Logistics Vehicle has a crew of two, a higher roof and a crane is fitted to the vehicle. The LAV Mortar Carrier has a crew of five, with the mortar fitted in the middle of the vehicle on a turntable where the turret would normally be. A large double folding hatch covers the space left by the turret opening. The LAV-ARV has a crew of five and has a boom with a 265-degree traverse. An "A"-frame support is fitted to be used when lifting heavy loads. The LAV Anti-Tank Vehicle mounts a twin TOW launcher that can traverse through 360 degrees. Fourteen reload missiles are carried in the vehicle.

The last version to enter service was the LAV Air Defence System, fitted with the General Electric Blazer system. This has two four-round Stinger missile pods on the side of a turret that is also fitted with the GAU-12/U 25mm/0.98in Gatling gun. These vehicles have proved to be very reliable in service, but suffer from lack of internal personal equipment storage space for the crew.

In 2019, General Dynamics was awarded a $37.2 million contract to upgrade the USMC fleet to LAV-25A3 standard with powerpack improvements, diagnostics, better fuel economy, new drivetrain, and a digitized drivers' instrument panel.

ABOVE: **This LAV-25 is fitted with an Emerson twin TOW AT missile launcher. Two missiles are carried in the launcher, with a further 14 reloads carried inside the vehicle. This vehicle has a crew of three. The twin rear doors can be clearly seen in this picture.**

ABOVE: **A column of LAV-25 vehicles of the US Marine Corps in the Middle East. The large exhaust system on the side of the vehicle can be clearly seen. The front four wheels are used to steer the vehicle. These vehicles are not in a combat zone as they have no personal equipment stored on the outside.**

ABOVE: **This shows how cramped the command vehicle is when all the communication equipment is fitted. The vehicle has a crew of two but can carry five HQ staff in the rear.**

LEFT: **This mobile AA system was developed for the US Air Force. The one-man turret was armed with a 30mm/1.18in Gatling gun and four Stinger missiles. The project was dropped when the US Army took over airfield defence.**

LAV-25 Light Armoured Vehicle

Country: Canada
Entered service: 1982
Crew: 3 plus 6 infantry
Weight: 12,792kg/12.6 tons
Dimensions: Length – 6.39m/21ft
  Height – 2.69m/8ft 8in
  Width – 2.5m/8ft 2in
Armament: Main – M242 25mm/0.98in chain gun, and coaxial M240 7.62mm/0.3in machine-gun   Secondary – Pintle mounted M240 7.62mm/0.3in machine-gun
Armour: Maximum – 10mm/0.394in (estimated)
Powerplant: Detroit 6V-53T 6-cylinder 205kW/275hp diesel engine
Performance: Speed – Road 100kph/62mph; Water 10kph/6mph
  Range – 668km/415 miles

LMV/VTLM Panther Multi-role Vehicle

The Iveco-designed and built LMV (Light Multirole Vehicle) is a lightly armoured four-wheel drive tactical military vehicle that was designed in the 1990s and produced from the early 2000s. It first entered service with the Italian Army as the Veicolo-Tattico-Leggero-Multiruolo (VTLM) Lince (Light tactical multirole vehicle Lynx). Italian Linces were used in action in both Afghanistan and Lebanon. The LMV uses modular armour packs to adjust its level of protection depending on mission requirements and the level of threat it faces. The vehicle went on to be bought by Albania, Austria, Belgium, Brazil, the UK, Norway, Russia and Spain.

The vehicle won the UK Ministry of Defence Future Command and Liaison Vehicle (FCLV) competition to identify a vehicle to replace assets including the Combat Vehicle Reconnaissance – tracked (CVRT) family of vehicles, the Ferret, the FV432, the Saxon and Land Rover TUM in British Army service where it was known as the Panther CLV. The outcome was controversial in that the larger, cheaper and proven Vickers RG32M was a clear favourite for many senior Army personnel. The UK Panther version featured UK-specific design modifications and it went into production at the BAE Systems Land Systems' factory in Newcastle upon Tyne, UK, and more than 300 Panthers were built between 2006 and 2009 at a cost of around £160m.

The first Panthers were delivered to the British Army's 1st Mechanised Brigade and some underwent hot weather trials in Afghanistan. It was found to be too small once essential equipment was installed and had an alarmingly poor

ABOVE: **The Russian-built Rys version of the Iveco LMV Lynx.** BELOW: **British Panther CLV. The British Army found that the Panther was unacceptably unsuited for most of the operations for which it had been procured and the whole fleet was sold off in 2018.**

serviceability record. Most damning of all however was the fact that the Panther could not protect its occupants in the very dangerous environments of Iraq and Afghanistan. It was realised, perhaps better late than never, that the Panther simply did not meet the evolving needs of the British Army, particularly

RIGHT: **Italian Army Lince during NATO exercises in Germany, 2016.** MIDDLE RIGHT: **Italian Army VTLM Lince during an exercise in Sardinia** BELOW: **Norwegian soldiers running operations in Faryab province, Afghanistan, 2010.**

regarding its involvement in counter-insurgency operations in Afghanistan and Iraq where landmines, improvized explosive devices and rocket propelled grenades became the dominant threats to British troops.

Some examples were upgraded at great cost to the UK taxpayer for service in Afghanistan but they saw little use. The Panther had not been acquired to answer an Urgent Operational Requirement where needs are clearly understood and defined. Rather it was acquired to fill a generic type-of-vehicle gap in the Army inventory. As a result, and in a rare move, in April 2018 the entire fleet of British Panthers was put up for disposal.

The LMV has been the subject of continuous development and innovation since it first appeared in 2006. The latest significant development is the LMV2, which offers better performance as a result of the FPT F1C engine coupled to a ZF automatic 8-speed transmission, increased payload, improved reliability and enhanced crew safety and comfort. New suspension and new tyres enhances the vehicle's all-terrain capability. The crew cell is decoupled from all other components, minimizing the transmission of blast energy from the chassis by employing a range of technical solutions including an underhull blast shield, multi-layered floor structure, suspended and shock-dampened seats, supporting structures and the use of composite materials.

The new vehicle top is made of a ballistic steel monocoque framework with lightweight aluminium/steel roll-bar, allowing the vehicle to be equipped with either a manual turret or Remote Weapon Station (RWS), both of which can be quickly and easily fitted and removed in the field, ensuring greater deployment flexibility. The LMV2 is designed to accommodate major electronic fits such as Battlefield Management System and Electronic Counter Measures. Management of essential maintenance has been made easier by improving the type and location of certain subsystems and by tailoring the vehicle service regime. A digitized dashboard option provides on-demand maintenance-based data enabling crews to accurately review and schedule maintenance tasks rather than predicting and scheduling preventive maintenance.

LMV

Country: Italy
Entered service: 2001
Crew: 1, 4 infantry
Weight: 65,000kg/71.65 tons
Dimensions: Length – 5.5m/18ft
  Height – 1.95m/6ft 4in
  Width – 2.05m/6ft 7in
Armament: Remote controlled weapon station
Armour: Modular, dependent on mission requirements
Powerplant: 137.7kW/182hp Iveco F1D Common Rail EURO 3 engine
Performance: Speed – 130kph/81mph
  Range – 5200km/310 miles

LVTP-7 Armoured Amphibious Assault Vehicle

ABOVE: **An LVTP-7 on a training exercise. The driver can be seen with his head just out of his cupola. Behind him is an instructor squatting next to the vehicle commander's cupola. The vehicle commander and gunner are beside the gun turret.**

The standard LVT of the US Marine Corps post World War II was the LVTP-5A1. This was an unsatisfactory vehicle as it had a very limited land and water range, was unreliable, and difficult to maintain. In 1964, the Marine Corps issued a requirement for a new LVTP and a development contract was awarded to the FMC Corporation. Development started in 1966 and the final 15 vehicles commissioned were delivered in 1967. Trials were completed in 1969 and in June 1970 a contract was signed with FMC to supply 942 LVTP-7 (Landing Vehicle Tracked Personnel Model 7). The first vehicles were delivered to the Marine Corps in August 1971 with the first unit being equipped in March 1972 and the final deliveries to the Marines being made in 1974.

The all-welded aluminium hull gives the crew protection from small-arms fire and shell splinters. The engine is in the front of the vehicle and is placed on the centreline. The driver's position is alongside the engine on the right-hand side and is fitted with all-round vision blocks. Behind the driver on the left-hand side is the vehicle commander's position which is also fitted with all-round vision blocks while a periscope in the front of the commander's cupola allows him to see over the driver's position. The turret is on the right-hand side of the vehicle beside the engine. The gunner has all-round vision from nine vision blocks fitted into the cupola and the turret is armed with a 12.7mm/0.5in M85 machine-gun with two rates of fire: either 1,050 or 480 rounds per minute. The vehicle carries 1,000 rounds of ammunition for this weapon. The turret traverse mechanism is electro-hydraulic and has a full 360-degree traverse in under five seconds.

The LVTP has no NBC system, but is fitted with infrared night-driving lights. The suspension consists of six dual rubber-shod road wheels on each side and the track is single pin type, fitted with replaceable rubber pads. The main troop compartment is situated behind the turret and extends to the rear of the vehicle providing accommodation for 25 men. There

LEFT: **This LVTP-7 is moving at speed in deep snow. The boat-shaped hull can be clearly seen along with the long track length, which gives the vehicle a low ground pressure.**

are three bench seats in the rear: one down each side and one in the middle, each seating eight men, while the other seating position is available behind the vehicle commander's position. The centre bench seat can be removed and stored on the left-hand side of the compartment and the other two bench seats can be folded up so the vehicle can be used for moving supplies or wounded.

The LVTP is fully amphibious and requires no preparation time when entering the water. It is propelled by two water jets mounted on the rear of the vehicle in the sponsons, each jet having a hinged water deflector fitted at the rear which acts as a protective cover when not in use. The tracks of the vehicle can also be used to provide additional propulsion when the vehicle is in the water. The Marines enter and leave the vehicle by a power-operated ramp. In the left-hand side of the ramp there is a small access door, and above the troop compartment two very large spring-balanced hatches are installed. These are used for loading the vehicle when it is waterborne while taking on supplies alongside a ship.

In March 1977, FMC was awarded a contract for the conversion of 14 LVTPs to a new configuration known as the LVTP-7A1. This upgrade included an improved engine, better night-driving equipment and fighting optics, improved radios, an improved fire-suppression system, better troop compartment ventilation, improved weapon stations and an ability to generate smoke. Subsequently, the Marine Corps decided to upgrade all of their LVTP-7 vehicles to the new

standard in 1982, and this was completed by 1986. These vehicles have also been fitted with a new turret that has an additional 40mm/1.58in grenade launcher installed along with the 12.7mm/0.3in machine-gun. RAFAEL appliqué armour has also been fitted to a large number of the new LVTP-7A1 vehicles since 1987. Having served for over half a century, these vehicles will be replaced in USMC service by the BAE Systems/Iveco SuperAV.

ABOVE: **A column of LVTP-7 vehicles moving through the surf on the soft sand of a beach. The three-man crew are in their crew positions in the vehicle. The lights on the front of the vehicle are recessed into the hull to help protect them.** LEFT: **The three crew cupolas can be clearly seen. The driver's position is in the front on the left with the commander's behind. On the right of the vehicle is the gunner's turret.**

RIGHT: **In service for over 50 years, in 2018, the US Marine Corps announced that the BAE Systems/Iveco wheeled SuperAV would supplement and ultimately replace the LVTP in USMC service.**

LVTP-7A1 Armoured Amphibious Assault Vehicle

Country: USA
Entered service: 1977
Crew: 3 plus 25 infantry
Weight: 23,936kg/23.6 tons
Dimensions: Length – 7.94m/26ft 1in
Height – 3.26m/10ft 8in
Width – 3.27m/10ft 9in
Armament: Main – 12.7mm/0.5in M2 HB machine-gun, and 40mm/1.58in grenade launcher
Secondary – Small arms
Armour: Maximum – 45mm/1.77in
Powerplant: Cummins VT400 8-cylinder 298kW/400hp turbocharged diesel engine
Performance: Speed – Road 72kph/45mph;
Water 13kph/8mph
Range – 482km/300 miles

M42 Duster Self-Propelled Anti-Aircraft Gun

In August 1951, the US Army authorized the development of a replacement vehicle for the M19A1 SPAAG and initially an interim design called the T-141 was developed. The final design was to be the T-141A1, and a fire control vehicle, the T-53, was also going to be developed but both were cancelled in 1952. However, the T-141 put into production and standardized as the M42. The first vehicle was produced in April 1952, with the last vehicle being handed over to the Army in December 1953. Total production was 3,700 vehicles.

The M42 used many of the same automotive components as the M41 light tank. The driver and radio operator/commander sat side by side in the front of the vehicle with the driver on the left. Behind them was the gun turret which was armed with twin 40mm/1.58in M2A1 cannon and had a crew of four, two gunners and two loaders. The turret had a power traverse and could complete a full 360-degree traverse in nine seconds. The guns could be fired in single shot or fully automatic modes and could discharge 120 rounds per minute when in the latter. When engaging ground targets the vehicle had a maximum range of 3,000m/9,842ft and a maximum ceiling of 3,962m/13,000ft. The Duster could carry 480 rounds of 40mm/1.58in ammunition in bins around the inside of the turret, which had a 7.62mm/0.3in machine-gun mount on the right-hand side. The engine and transmission were

in the rear of the vehicle and there were only had three gears – two forward and one reverse. The suspension was a torsion-bar type supporting five road wheels per side. The M42 had no NBC system and was not capable of any deep fording, but was fitted with infrared night-driving lights.

The Duster had a new engine fitted in 1956 which gave the vehicle an increased range and was redesignated the M42A1. The turrets of both vehicles could be manually operated and could track aircraft at up to 966kph/600mph, but they could only be used effectively during daylight.

TOP: **The chassis of the Walker Bulldog M41 light tank was used for the development of this vehicle. The gun turret was very open and so gave the gun crew no protection.** ABOVE: **A column of American armoured vehicles being led by two M42 Dusters in the early 1950s. The driver and co-driver are in their positions in the front of the M42, while the rest of the gun crew are riding on the open gun turret.**

LEFT: **Two American M42 Dusters with a crewman standing between them. The small size of the vehicle can be seen by the size of the crewman. Some of the vehicles were improved upon by fitting anti-grenade screens to the top of the turret.**

M42 Duster SPAAG

Country: USA
Entered service: 1952
Crew: 6
Weight: 22,452kg/22.1 tons
Dimensions: Length – 6.36m/19ft 5in
 Height – 2.85m/9ft 4in
 Width – 3.22m/10ft 7in
Armament: Main – 2 x 40mm/1.58in M2A1
 cannon
 Secondary – 7.62mm/0.3in machine-gun
Armour: Maximum – 25mm/0.98in
Powerplant: Continental or Lycoming 6-cylinder
 373kW/500hp petrol engine
Performance: Speed – 72kph/45mph
 Range – 160km/100 miles

LEFT: The lowered idler wheel, which is now on the same level as the road wheels, is clear from this profile. The short barrel length is also clearly shown; it does not overhang the front of the vehicle.

ABOVE: This M44 has been fitted with a canvas roof which gives the crew some protection from the weather. The exhaust system is located on the right-hand side of the vehicle. The engine is mounted in the front of the vehicle, hence all the engine intake grills on the glacis.

M44 155mm Self-Propelled Gun

Development of this vehicle started in 1947 and two prototypes, given the designation T99, were built. The vehicle was to utilize as many automotive parts from the M41 light tank as possible to make maintenance and sourcing spare parts easier to manage. The vehicle was redesignated the T99E1 and a contract was issued in 1952 when production started. A number of changes were required due to problems with the pilot models, but by the time these had been finalized 250 of the production vehicles had been built. The new improved vehicle, now called the T194, was standardized in September 1953 as the M44, and all the service vehicles already produced were upgraded to the new T194 standard.

The hull of the M44 was an all-welded steel construction, with the engine and transmission in the front of the vehicle. The transmission was a General Motors Model CD-500-3 cross-drive unit which gave the vehicle two forward gears and one reverse. The suspension was a torsion-bar system and the rear idler was lowered to form a sixth road wheel. The crew compartment was mounted high up on the vehicle and included the vehicle driver who was positioned at the front on the right-hand side. The crew compartment was open-topped but could have a canvas cover fitted to protect the crew from the weather. The gun was an M45 howitzer which was installed on an M80 mount, while a close-defence 12.7mm/0.3in machine-gun

was fitted to the left-hand side of the vehicle behind the driver. At the rear of the vehicle a recoil spade was fitted and when this was lowered into position a platform could be folded down from the rear of the vehicle. This allowed the twin rear doors, which serve as ammunition storage, to open. The exhaust system was fitted to the top of the front track guards and was the source of a major problem as engine fumes travelled back into the crew compartment, gassing the crew.

The M44 later received an improved engine giving greater range and fuel economy and this new vehicle was standardized in 1956 as the M44A1. The British Army also used the M44.

LEFT: The driver's position was located in the turret of the vehicle on the left-hand side. In front of his position was a small windscreen, while behind the driver was the close-support machine-gun. A model with overhead armour was built and trialled, but was not adopted for service by any country.

M44 155mm SPG

Country: USA
Entered service: 1953
Crew: 5
Weight: 28,346kg/27.9 tons
Dimensions: Length – 6.16m/20ft 3in
    Height – 3.11m/10ft 3in
    Width – 3.24m/10ft 8in
Armament: Main – 155mm/6.1in M45 howitzer
    Secondary – 12.7mm/0.5in machine-gun
Armour: Maximum – 12.7mm/0.5in
Powerplant: Continental AOS-895-3 6-cylinder
    373kW/500hp petrol engine
Performance: Speed – 56kph/35mph
    Range – 122km/76 miles

LEFT: **The crew compartment of the M52 is a covered armoured turret and gives the gun crew full protection from the weather and small-arms fire. The driver of the vehicle sits at the front of the turret. In this picture, he has his seat in the raised position, with the vehicle commander at the rear on the opposite side of the turret.** ABOVE: **The engine is positioned in the front of the vehicle with the exhaust systems on the front track guards. The front of the glacis is covered in air intake grills.**

M52 105mm Self-Propelled Gun

In February 1948, development was started on a replacement 105mm SPG for the M7 which was showing its age. Two prototypes, known as the T98E1, were built at the Detroit Tank Arsenal in 1950. They were to be constructed using as many parts from the M41 light tank as possible and the engine, transmission, tracks and suspension were all used. The T98E1 was standardized in 1953 as the M52 and entered service in 1954 with a total production run of 684 vehicles. In 1956 a new vehicle with an improved engine and fuel injection system was standardized as the M52A1.

The hull of the M52 was an all-welded steel construction, with the engine and transmission mounted at the front of the vehicle. The transmission was a General Motors Model CD-500-3 cross-drive unit which gave the vehicle two forward gears and one reverse. The suspension was a torsion-bar system and the rear idler was lowered to form a sixth road wheel. The large turret was mounted on the top of the hull towards the rear of the vehicle. All the crew were seated in the turret with the driver on the front left-hand side with a cupola above and a door in the side of the turret for access to the driving position. The gun layer was on the right-hand side of the turret at the front with the commander behind. The commander's cupola could be fitted with

a 12.7mm/0.3in machine-gun for close defence. On the rear, left-hand side of the turret a revolving drum was fitted which held 21 rounds of ready-to-use ammunition and a total of 102 rounds were carried in the vehicle. The turret had a 60-degree traverse to the left and right of the vehicle's centreline. No recoil spade was fitted to the rear of the vehicle, as it was not required.

The vehicle had no NBC system installed but was fitted with an over-pressurization system and infrared night-driving lights. It was the first NATO SPG to give the crew full protection on the modern nuclear battlefield.

RIGHT: **The compact size of the chassis can be seen, but the large turret takes up most of the space on the top of the vehicle. Driving the vehicle was not easy, but the crews did get used to it. Ammunition is stowed both in the turret and in the body of the vehicle.**

M52 105mm SPG

Country: USA
Entered service: 1954
Crew: 5
Weight: 24,079kg/23.7 tons
Dimensions: Length – 5.8m/19ft
Height – 3.06m/10ft 1in
Width – 3.15m/10ft 4in
Armament: Main – 105mm/4.13in M49 howitzer
Secondary – 12.7mm/0.5in machine-gun
Armour: Maximum – 12.7mm/0.5in
Powerplant: Continental 6-cylinder 373kW/500hp petrol engine
Performance: Speed – 56kph/35mph
Range – 160km/100 miles

M107 175mm Self-Propelled Gun

All SPGs in service in the early 1950s were too large and heavy to be transported by air, but in 1956 the Pacific Car and Foundry Company was awarded a contract to build six prototype air-transportable SPG vehicles, two armed with the new 175mm/6.89in gun, three with the 203mm/8in howitzer and one with the 155mm/6.1in gun. Trials began in late 1958 but the engine was changed in 1959 when the American armed forces made a policy decision that all future vehicles would be fitted with diesel engines rather than petrol. Trials were completed in early 1961. The T235E1 (175mm) was standardized as the M107 and the T236E1 (203mm) as the M110, while the other vehicle was dropped. Production started in 1962 and was completed in 1980 by which time 524 vehicles had been built. After a short period of time in service, a large number of faults were discovered and these were rectified.

The M107 hull is an all-welded construction made from cast armour and high-tensile alloy steel. The driver is positioned in the front of the vehicle on the left-hand side with the engine on the right, while the main gun mount is at the rear of the vehicle. The driver is the only member of the crew to sit inside the vehicle and therefore be protected by armour. The torsion-bar suspension has five twin rubber tyre wheels per side with the drive sprocket at the front and the fifth road wheel acting as an idler. There is a shock absorber fitted to each road wheel and this helps transfer the recoil shock directly into the ground. In

ABOVE: The M107 returned to the idea that artillery was not in the front line, so crew protection was not needed. The large full-width recoil spade can be seen in the raised position on the rear of this vehicle.

LEFT: The extremely long gun barrel stands out well in this picture. The driver and two of the crew can be seen in their travelling positions on the gun. The other two members of the gun crew were on the other side of the gun mount.

addition there is a hydraulically operated recoil spade at the rear of the vehicle.

The M107 has a crew of 13; 4 of them – including the vehicle commander – travel on the vehicle with the driver inside, the other 8 are transported in an M548 ammunition vehicle. The M107 has internal storage space for only two ready-to-use 175mm/6.89in rounds

and the barrel of the 175mm/6.89in gun can be interchanged with the M110 203mm/8in barrel. This operation takes two hours and can be undertaken in the field.

M107 175mm SPG

Country: USA
Entered service: 1963
Crew: 4 plus 9 gunners
Weight: 28,143kg/27.7 tons
Dimensions: Length – 11.26m/36ft 11in
 Height – 3.67m/12ft
 Width – 3.15m/10ft 4in
Armament: Main – 175mm/6.89in M113 gun
 Secondary – Small arms
Armour: Classified
Powerplant: Detroit Diesel Motors 8V-71T 8-cylinder 302kW/405hp diesel engine
Performance: Speed – 55kph/34mph
 Range – 725km/450 miles

LEFT: Two M107 guns on exercise. The gun in the rear has just fired a round, while the vehicle in the foreground is on the move with the five-man crew at their travelling stations. The barrel of the gun has been covered in camouflage netting.

M108 105mm Self-Propelled Gun

Take a 22,353kg/22-ton aluminium armoured vehicle and mount a relatively small 105mm/4.13in howitzer on it, and the result would appear to be a massively under-gunned self-propelled howitzer. A clean and simple design, the M108 represented a more sophisticated approach than the M52 but, not surprisingly, was only built in small numbers.

Development started in 1953 when it was decided to develop a 110mm/4.33in-armed SPG which was designated the T195. The first mock-up vehicle was built in 1954. Permission was subsequently given for prototype vehicles to be built and orders were placed for engines and transmissions. However, later that year it was decided to freeze the project, as there were doubts over the 110mm/4.33in gun. The engines and other parts were passed over to the T196/M109 project. It was

ABOVE: The large size of the vehicle can be seen against the small size of the gun barrel. This Taiwanese M108 is preserved at a ROCA base.

BELOW LEFT: This was the first turreted SPG to have the driver placed in the hull of the vehicle. The box on the rear of the turret is the air filtration system for the NBC system. These vehicles were produced for less than a year. BELOW: The M108 chassis was used for the American trials of the Roland Low-Altitude SAM system. It was converted in 1977 and the first firing trials were carried out in November 1977. The vehicle has a crew of four. From shut-down to fully operational takes under four minutes.

finally decided to drop the 110mm/4.33in gun in favour of the 105mm/4.13in, as there was a plentiful supply of ammunition for this weapon. The first prototype was finally completed in 1958 but the suspension failed in its first firing trials. When the

American military ordered in 1959 that all vehicles were to have diesel engines fitted as standard from now on, the T195 had its petrol engine replaced by a diesel unit and was given the new designation T195E1. Trials started again, with suspension failures being repeated, but this time they were corrected, and in 1961 the T195E1 was finally standardized as the M108. Production started in October 1962 after a number of changes to the design including the addition of an idler wheel at the rear of the vehicle, the removal of the muzzle brake and changes to the turret shape. The very short production run finished in September 1963 with only a few vehicles completed, production being halted because the US military decided to concentrate on the T196/M109 155mm/6.1in SPG, a unit that is still in service today.

The hull and turret of the M108 is an all-welded aluminium construction. The transmission is located in the front of the vehicle with the driver behind this on the left-hand side and the engine on the right. The torsion-bar suspension system of the M108 is the same as that of the M113 with seven dual rubber-shod road wheels per side. The drive sprocket is at the front of the vehicle and an idler is at the rear. The top of the tracks can be covered with a rubber skirt but the crews rarely fit this.

At the rear of the vehicle is the manually operated turret which can rotate through 360 degrees and houses the rest of the crew and the gun. The gun-layer is on the left-hand side of this with the commander on the right, while the two ammunition handlers are positioned in the rear. In the roof of the turret above the commander is a cupola, and this can be traversed through 360 degrees and can be armed with a 12.7mm/0.5in local defence machine-gun. The gun-layer also has a hatch in the roof of the turret, and two side hatches which open towards the rear of the vehicle are also fitted. In the rear of the turret are two more hatches in the rotating top section, while in the lower fixed rear of the hull a large door is installed which is used for supplying ammunition to the gun. The M108 carries 87 rounds of ammunition. The vehicle is capable of firing three rounds per minute but this is only for a short period of time, the normal fire rate being one round per minute

The M108 can be fitted with an NBC system but this is not fitted as standard, though infrared night-driving lights are. The vehicle can wade to a depth of 1.8m/5ft 11in but can also be fitted with nine flotation bags, one bag on the front and four down each side, which are inflated from the vehicle. However, these are not carried on the vehicle as standard. Propulsion in the water is supplied by the vehicle's tracks. Although an unmitigated failure in its original role and long out of service with the US Army, examples are believed to still be in service in Chile and Uruguay.

LEFT: Only three other countries bought the M108 from new: Belgium, Brazil and Spain. Belgium turned out to be the largest overseas customer. ABOVE: The very short length of the barrel can be clearly seen. The drive sprocket is at the front of the vehicle, which makes for a very compact drive train. The engine and drive train proved to be very reliable and were used in several vehicles.

LEFT: The headlights were initially mounted on the glacis plate, but on later production vehicles they were moved to the front of the track guards, as seen on this example in a US museum.

M108 105mm SPG	
Country: USA	
Entered service: 1962	
Crew: 5	
Weight: 22,454kg/22.1 tons	
Dimensions: Length – 6.11m/20ft 9in	
Height – 3.15m/10ft 4in	
Width – 3.3m/10ft 10in	
Armament: Main – 105mm/4.13in M103 howitzer	
Secondary – 12.7mm/0.5in M2 machine-gun	
Armour: Classified	
Powerplant: Detroit Diesel Motors 8V-71T	
8-cylinder 302kW/405hp diesel engine	
Performance: Speed – 55kph/34mph	
Range – 350km/220 miles	

LEFT: **The M109 had basically the same chassis and running gear as the M108. A few problems were experienced with the running gear but these have been fixed. It remains in service with a large number of countries to the present day.**
BELOW: **This vehicle is an improved M109A1. The new vehicle has an extended barrel, which now has a long overhang over the front of the vehicle. The travel lock for the gun barrel has been moved to the front edge of the glacis.**

M109 155mm Self-Propelled Gun

The first prototype M109, then designated the T196, was finally completed in 1959 but during its first firing trials the suspension failed. When in the same year the American military ordered that all future new vehicles were to have diesel engines fitted as standard, the petrol engine was replaced by a diesel and the vehicle was given the new designation T196E1. Trials started again and again there were suspension failures, as with the M108 which had the same chassis. These problems were corrected, and the first vehicles were completed in October 1962 as Limited Production Vehicles. Finally, in 1963 the T196E1 was standardized as the M109. A number of changes were made to the design including the addition of an idler wheel at the rear of the vehicle and changes to the turret shape before the M109 entered service with the American Army in June 1963. The vehicle has gone through many changes and upgrades during its service life to keep it up-to-date and as a result remains in widespread use around the world.

The hull and turret of the M109 is an all-welded aluminium construction. The transmission is in the front of the vehicle with the driver located behind this on the left-hand side. The engine is next to the driver on the right, and the turret, which houses the rest of the crew and gun, is behind. The gun-layer is positioned on the left-hand side of the turret with the commander on the right. A cupola for the commander, which can be traversed through 360 degrees and can be armed with a 12.7mm/0.5in local defence machine-gun, is installed in the roof of the turret. The gun-layer also has a hatch in the roof of the turret, and two side hatches, which open towards the

rear of the vehicle, are also fitted. In the rear of the turret are two more hatches in the rotating top section, and there is a large door in the rear of the hull which is used for supplying ammunition to the gun. Mounted on the rear of the vehicle is a large recoil spade that is manually operated from within the turret. The main armament is the M126 155mm/6.1in gun on the M127 mount. The barrel is fitted with a double-baffle muzzle brake and a fume extractor two-thirds of the way up.

The turret can traverse through 360 degrees and is power operated, but can be operated manually. The normal rate of fire is one round per minute but for short periods, three rounds per minute can be fired. The latest version of the vehicle, the M109A6 Paladin, is armed with the M284 L/39 155mm/6.1in howitzer and a new fire-control system.

LEFT: **A Swiss Army M109A2. On the roof of this vehicle is a new armoured hood for the optical fire-control system. This vehicle is known as the Pzhb 74 In the Swiss Army.** ABOVE: **A British M109A2 vehicle taking part in a live-firing exercise. The optical hood is on the front left of the turret. The turret of the M109A2 is fitted with a bustle that can hold an additional 22 rounds of ammunition. The gun has been heavily covered in camouflage netting and spare ammunition is laid out on a sheet behind the gun.**

The first improvements were made to the vehicle in 1972 and it was redesignated the M109A1. These were mainly to the gun that had a much longer and more slender barrel increasing the range to 18,288m/60,000ft. Further developments came in 1978 when the M109A2 went into production, with improvements to the ammunition storage, the rammer, and hull doors. A bustle was also fixed to the rear of the turret to take a further 22 rounds of ammunition. The M109A3 upgrade was M109A1s brought up to M109A2 standard. The vehicle became the M109A4 in 1990 with the fitting of an NBC kit as standard. The M109A5 designation was the upgrading of all the older marks to A4 standard, and the gun barrel was also changed to one that could fire rocket-assisted ammunition.

The A6 Paladin was developed for the US Army. Development of this started in 1990 and production began in 1992 with the new vehicle entering service in 1993. The Paladin has the same chassis and hull as the basic M109 but everything else was changed. The turret is bigger, the rear doors in the upper part of the turret have been removed, as the bustle is now full width, and there is also a new muzzle brake. A new gun-control system has been fitted which is

linked to a GPS (Global Positioning System), allowing the automatic gun controls to point the gun at the target with no human intervention.

During the 2022 Russian invasion of Ukraine, Ukraine used M109 howitzers, donated by Western countries.

ABOVE: **A line-up of American M109A6 vehicles. The M109A6 is better known as the "Paladin", and is the first vehicle in the series to be given a name. The large muzzle brake has a double baffle, and behind this on the barrel of the gun is the fume extractor.**

LEFT: **This vehicle is fording a stream at some speed. The M109 can ford water obstacles to a depth of 1m/39in. The vehicle commander can be seen standing in his cupola giving directions to the driver, who has very poor vision from his position.**

M109A6 155mm Paladin SPG

Country: USA
Entered service: 1993
Crew: 6
Weight: 28,753kg/28.3 tons
Dimensions: Length – 9.12m/29ft 11in
　Height – 3.24m/10ft 7in
　Width – 3.15m/10ft 4in
Armament: Main – 155mm/6.1in M284 L/39 howitzer
　Secondary – 12.7mm/0.5in M2 machine-gun
Armour: classified
Powerplant: Detroit Diesel Motors 8V-71T 8-cylinder 302kW/405hp diesel engine
Performance: Speed – 56kph/35mph
　Range – 405km/252 miles

LEFT: **The gun crew of the M110 are very exposed when operating the gun, as can be seen with this vehicle. The recoil spade on this SPG is in the down position.** BELOW: **A line-up of three batteries of M110 vehicles. The gun has no muzzle brake or fume extractor. The vehicle can carry 5 of the 13-man crew; the rest travel in an M548 ammunition vehicle.**

M110 203mm Self-Propelled Howitzer

In 1956 the Pacific Car and Foundry Company (PCF) was given a contract to build six prototype SPG vehicles for the US Army, two armed with the new 175mm/6.89in gun (T235), three with the 203mm/8in howitzer (T236) and one with the 155mm/6.1in gun (T245). The main design priority for these vehicles was that they all had to be air-portable to fill a requirement not met by the then available American SPGs, which were either too large or too heavy. The three prototype designs all used the same M17 lightweight gun mount and were all to have the ability for their gun barrels to be interchangeable. The T245 development was halted at the prototype stage as it was felt to be unnecessary. The T235 went on to become the M107, while the T236 became the M110. The M108, M109 and M110 all utilized the same transmission and engine.

Testing of the M110 prototype began in late 1958 but in 1959 the American military made a policy decision that all future vehicles would be fitted with diesel engines rather than petrol. The T236 with a diesel engine fitted was renamed the T236E1. Trials were completed in 1961 and the T236E1 was standardized as the M110. In June 1961, PCF was awarded a production contract for the new vehicle and the first production models were finished in 1962, entering service with the US Army in 1963. The original contract was for 750 vehicles, all built by PCF, which were completed by late 1969. Once the vehicle had entered service, it was found that improvements to the engine-cooling, electrical and hydraulic systems, the loader/rammer and the recoil spade were necessary. In March 1976, an improved vehicle incorporating these modifications was standardized as the M110A1. These vehicles included

RIGHT: **The eight circular holes in the right-hand side of the vehicle are the exhaust outlets. This caused a lot of discomfort for the crew of the vehicle when it was stationary. The short, stubby gun barrel can be clearly seen on this SPG.**

both M110s and some M107s, as a number of M107 vehicles were no longer required. A new longer gun barrel, the M201, was fitted to the vehicle so it could fire tactical nuclear shells as the M107 had done and which the M110A1 would eventually replace. In 1980, the last version of the M110 entered service, as the M110A2. This had an improved barrel and was fitted with a muzzle brake. Improvements were also made to the electrical and recoil systems. With this last upgrade the gun crew at long last had some protection from small-arms fire, shell splinters and the weather, as a Kevlar
and aluminium shelter was built over the open gun area.

The M110 hull is an all-welded construction made from cast armour and high tensile alloy steel. The driver is located in the front of the vehicle on the left-hand side with the engine on the right, while the main gun mount is at the rear. The driver is the only member of the crew to sit inside the vehicle and therefore be protected by armour. The torsion-bar suspension has five twin rubber-tyred wheels per side with the drive sprocket at the front and the fifth road wheel acting as an idler. There is a shock absorber fitted to each road wheel and this helps transfer the recoil shock directly into the ground. There is also a hydraulically operated recoil spade at the rear. On the right-hand side of the vehicle are a series of holes in the sponson that act as exhaust outlets.

The vehicle commander and three members of the gun crew sit in the open, two either side, exposed to small-arms fire, shell splinters and above all the weather. The other eight crewmen are transported in an M548 ammunition vehicle along with all the personal kit of the gun crew. The main armament is fitted with a hydro-pneumatic recoil system and an automatic loader and rammer is located at the rear of the vehicle on the left-hand side. The M110 only has storage for two ready-to-use rounds, the remaining being carried in the ammunition vehicle. The normal rate of fire is one round every two minutes, but for short periods, two rounds per minute can be fired. Several hundred examples remain in front-line service with export customers worldwide.

TOP: An American M110 with the recoil spade in the raised position. One improvement the Americans made to this vehicle was the construction of a canvas tent around the exposed gun position on the rear of the vehicle.
ABOVE: The M110 has five road wheels on each side and the drive sprocket is at the front. No return roller is fitted to the chassis. BELOW LEFT: These vehicles are the improved M110A1. They have much longer barrels but still no muzzle brake or fume extractor fitted; the M110A2 would have a large double-baffle muzzle brake.

These M110A1 SPGs are at maximum elevation and the hoop frame of the canvas screen can be seen.

M110A2 203mm SPG

Country: USA
Entered service: 1980
Crew: 5 plus 8 gunners
Weight: 28,346kg/27.9 tons
Dimensions: Length – 7.5m/24ft 7in
Height – 3.15m/10ft 4in
Width – 3.15m/10ft 4in
Armament: Main – 203mm/8in M12A2 howitzer
Secondary – Small arms
Armour: Classified
Powerplant: Detroit Diesel Motors 8V-71T
8-cylinder 373kW/500hp diesel engine
Performance: Speed – 55kph/34mph
Range – 523km/325 miles

M113 Armoured Personnel Carrier

In January 1956 the Food Manufacturing Corporation (FMC) were awarded a contract to start development on the T113 and the T117 APCs. These new vehicles had to be fully air-portable, amphibious, lightweight and have a good cross-country performance. They had to be adaptable and be able to take modification kits with a long projected service life. Testing started and the steel-bodied T117 was quickly dropped in favour of the aluminium-constructed T113. The T113E1 was developed with a petrol engine and four prototypes were built, but the diesel-engined T113E2 was also developed following the US Army's 1959 requirement for diesel engines in all its new vehicles. Despite this, the T113E1 was standardized in 1960 as the M113 and FMC began production with an order for 900 vehicles, all with petrol engines. In 1963 the diesel-engined T113E2 was standardized as the M113A1 and entered production in 1964, replacing the basic M113.

The next version of the M113, the M113A2, entered production in 1978. This involved a number of improvements to the engine-cooling system, radiator, and suspension. All M113s and M113A1s were also to be brought up to the same standard, involving some 20,000 vehicles, and a further 2,660 new M113A2s were to be built. The whole programme had to be finished by 1989. In 1980 development started on a further improvement programme including a new engine, giving better performance, and improved cooling and suspension systems. Production of the new M113A3 began in 1987 and is still continuing today. It includes improvements such as external fuel tanks and the provision for the installation of external

ABOVE: **This Israeli M113 has been fitted with additional add-on armour. The crew of the vehicle are at action stations. The trim vane has been removed to allow the armour to be fitted.**

optional appliqué armour. Experience gained in the Gulf War of 1991 has influenced a number of these developments.

The hull of the M113 is an all-welded aluminium construction. The transmission, providing six forward and two reverse gears, is in the front of the vehicle. The driver sits behind this on the left-hand side, with the engine immediately on the right. The air inlet and outlet louvers for the engine are located on the roof of the hull. The commander's position is in the centre of the vehicle, and is provided with a cupola that can be traversed through 360 degrees and is fitted with a single

LEFT: **This is an M113 armed with a TOW AT missile. The TOW is mounted on a pedestal mount, which when not in use is retracted inside the hull and covered by the large hatches on the roof of the vehicle.** BELOW: **An Israeli M113 in a combat area in the Middle East. The vehicle is armed with a TOW missile and two 12.5mm/50cal machine-guns. The front machine-gun is mounted over the commander's hatch. The M113 is covered in extra storage racks that have been added by the crew.**

M2 12.7mm/0.5in machine-gun. In the rear of the vehicle is the troop compartment with accommodation for 11 men. These sit five down each side facing each other, with one single seat behind the vehicle commander. A large single hatch which opens to the rear of the vehicle covers the troop compartment. In the rear is the main entry and exit hatch that is a hydraulic ramp, with an integral door fitted to the left-hand side for use in the event of the ramp mechanism failing. The vehicle is fully amphibious and is ready to enter the water once the trim vane at the front of the vehicle has been raised. Propulsion in the water is provided by using its tracks.

In 2005 the M113A3 fleet had some 16 different models in service with the US Army and many others around the world. The vehicle has been modified into 40 specific variations with a further 40 unofficial variations and is the most widely produced, in-service vehicle in the Western World. The basic armament is a single 12.7mm/0.5in machine-gun, but after this, whatever is required seems to have been fitted to the vehicle. Cannon such as 20mm/0.79in and 30mm/1.18in and even up to a 90mm/3.54in-armed turret have been fitted, as well as various missile systems. The vehicle does possess one rather alarming fault which has not been eliminated despite numerous

improvements. If it loses a track or breaks a track shoe then extreme care must be taken when slowing the vehicle. Use of the foot brake or any other means of braking can cause the vehicle to pull to the side of the unbroken track and roll over.

The M113 family was in production until 2007 by which time over 80,000 had been built in a variety of forms. This vehicle is still a good basic reliable battlefield taxi and is well liked by its crews. As a result, thousands remain in service around the world and are expected to remain so for some time.

LEFT: **This basic M113 is travelling across rough ground at speed. A number of countries have improved the armament of their basic M113 vehicles by adding various turrets. The largest of these is the 90mm/3.54in Cockerill Mk III turret.**

M113A3 APC

Country: USA
Entered service: 1987
Crew: 2 plus 11 infantry
Weight: 12,339kg/12.1 tons
Dimensions: Length – 4.86m/15ft 11in
Height – 2.52m/8ft 3in
Width – 2.69m/8ft 10in
Armament: Main – 12.7mm/0.5in M2 HB
machine-gun
Secondary – Small arms
Armour: Maximum – 38mm/1.5in
Powerplant: Detroit Diesel model 6V53T
6-cylinder 205kW/275hp
Performance: Speed – Road 65kph/41mph;
Water 5.8kph/3.6mph
Range – 497km/309 miles

LEFT: **This M577 has had a wire-mesh storage basket fitted to the front of the vehicle next to the driver. Even with the increased height of the vehicle, the M577 retains its amphibious capability, hence this vehicle has its trim vane fitted to the front.** ABOVE: **An American M577 command vehicle, with an M60 MBT behind it. The driver has his hatch open and the vehicle commander is standing in his hatch in the roof of the vehicle.**

M577 Command Vehicle

Once the basic M113 had entered production, FMC started development of the command post variant. Production commenced in 1962 and the first M577, the first true command post vehicle developed for the US Army, entered service in 1963. The M577 has gone through the same upgrades as the M113 APC with numerous improvements to the cooling and suspension systems, the driving controls and the engine. The M577A3 has also had the auxiliary petrol APU replaced with a 5kW/6.7hp diesel-powered unit. The first upgrade in 1964 produced the M577A1. From the mid-2000s, the main version of the vehicle in service was the M577A3 which had

been considerably updated since then by its many operators around the world. The US Army continued to operate large numbers of the A3 into the 2020s.

The hull of the M557 is an all-welded aluminium construction. The transmission is located in the front and provides the vehicle with six forward and two reverse gears. The driver sits behind the transmission at the front of the vehicle on the left-hand side, with the engine located on the right. Air inlet and outlet louvres for the engine are located on the roof of the hull. Behind the driver is the crew area, with a roof that is raised more than 91cm/3ft higher than the original hull top. This allows the command crew to work in the rear of the vehicle and

provides the extra space required for the additional communication equipment. On the front of the raised crew area is the APU, and there is a cupola that can be fitted with an M2 12.7mm/0.5in machine-gun in the roof of the crew area for use by the vehicle commander.

In addition to its use as a command post, the M577A3 is used for several other tasks such as a fire-direction centre, field treatment centre and a communications vehicle.

The modernised A4 version of the M577 Command Post Vehicle production version had upgraded digital systems and communications suites, retro-fitted applique armour and increased internal space through use of armoured external fuel tanks.

LEFT: **The increased height and bulk of the M577 can be clearly seen, compared to the original M113 APC. The top of this vehicle is covered in personal equipment. A number of these vehicles have been converted into mobile medical units.**

M577A3 Command Vehicle

Country: USA
Entered service: 1987
Crew: 4
Weight: 14,424kg/14.2 tons
Dimensions: Length – 4.86m/15ft 11in
　　Height – 3.89m/12ft 9in
　　Width – 2.69m/8ft 10in
Armament: Main – 7.62mm/0.3in M60
　　machine-gun
　　Secondary – Small arms
Armour: Maximum – 38mm/1.5in
Powerplant: Detroit Diesel model 6V53T
　　6-cylinder 205kW/275hp diesel engine
Performance: Speed – Road 65kph/41mph;
　　Water 5.8kph/3.6mph
　　Range – 497km/309 miles

LEFT: An M901 with the TOW launcher in the reload position. A member of the crew is feeding a missile into the rear of the launcher. Two missiles are carried in the launcher while ten others are carried in the body of the vehicle. BELOW: An M901 with its TOW launcher in the raised position. The turret can traverse through 360 degrees, and can elevate to 34 degrees. When on the move, the turret can be retracted so that it sits on the roof of the vehicle.

M901 Improved TOW Vehicle

By 1979, the US Army had some 1,400 TOW-armed vehicles in service. These first TOW (Tube-launched, Optically-tracked, Wire-guided) vehicles were basic M113 APCs fitted with a pedestal-mounted weapon system that retracted into the troop compartment. However, development work was started in 1976 on a new and better Improved TOW Vehicle (ITV) system that could be fitted to the M113A2 vehicle; this would become the M901A1. The M901 would be developed in the same way as the M113 and went through the same upgrades of suspension, cooling, driving controls and engine. The M901A3 version was the final production variant and this has the better driver controls of the M113A3 plus the RISE (Reliability Improvements for Selected Equipment) powerback

upgrade with a turbocharged engine and new transmission. Production of the M901 started in 1979. The US Army had a requirement for 2,526 of these vehicles, and 1,100 of these vehicles were deployed in Europe by 1981. Although the US Army phased out the vehicle, it continues in the service of export customers.

The hull of the M901 is an all-welded aluminium construction. The transmission, giving six forward and two reverse gears, is located in the front of the vehicle. The driver sits behind the transmission at the front of the vehicle on the left-hand side, with the engine on the right. Behind the driver and engine position is an M27 cupola. This is fitted with an image-transfer system, armoured launcher, missile guidance equipment and an auxiliary back-up battery pack. Two

TOW missile tubes are fitted to the armoured launcher, the acquisition sight is mounted on the top and between the TOW tubes is the TOW sight. A further 10 TOW missiles are carried inside the vehicle. Behind the M27 cupola is a large hatch that provides access to the TOW launcher so that spent missile tubes can be removed and jettisoned over the side of the vehicle allowing reloading to take place. Once the vehicle comes to a halt the TOW launcher is raised to the firing height and the first target engaged. This takes 20 seconds and reloading can be completed in 40 seconds. When in the travelling mode the launcher is retracted and sits on the hull roof, making the vehicle more difficult to identify.

M901A3 ITV

Country: USA
Entered service: 1989
Crew: 3
Weight: 12,339kg/12.1 tons
Dimensions: Length – 4.86m/15ft 11in
 Height – 3.36m/11ft
 Width – 2.69m/8ft 10in
Armament: Main – TOW launcher
 Secondary – 7.62mm/0.3in M60 machine-gun
Armour: Maximum – 38mm/1.5in
Powerplant: Detroit Diesel model 6V53T
 6-cylinder 205kW/275hp diesel engine
Performance: Speed – Road 65kph/41mph;
 Water 5.8kph/3.6mph
 Range – 497km/309 miles

RIGHT: A US Marine Corps vehicle heading into the water. The launcher turret is built by Emerson. This is made up of the M27 cupola, image-transfer equipment, armoured launcher, missile guidance set and a battery back-up pack.

LEFT: This German Marder 1 is armed with a 20mm/0.79in MK20 cannon, while above the rear exit of the vehicle is the remote-control 7.62mm/0.3in machine-gun. The Marder has a well-sloped glacis with the driver's position on the left-hand side of the vehicle. BELOW: This Marder 1 is taking part in an exercise in Germany. Some of the infantry section are standing up in the rear infantry compartment and are using their small arms from the safety of the vehicle.

Marder 1 Infantry Combat Vehicle

In the late 1950s, development started on a chassis that could be used for a family of military vehicles for the Federal German Army. The first vehicles in the series required by the German Army were the tank destroyers – the Jagdpanzer Kanone and Jagdpanzer Rakete. The Kanone entered production in 1965 while the Rakete entered production in 1967, and both were still in service in 2005. The next vehicle to be developed was the Infantry Combat Vehicle (ICV). The contracts were issued in 1960 to three companies to be involved in prototype production; Rheinstahl-Hanomag, Henschel and MOWAG. Between 1961 and 1963, a second series of prototype vehicles were built and the final series of prototype vehicles were produced in 1967–68. In April 1969, the three companies were invited to tender for the production of the ICV. In May 1969, the new vehicle was given the name Marder, and Rheinstahl-Hanomag won the contract. The first production vehicles were completed in December 1970, but did

not officially enter service with the Federal German Army until May 1971. In total, 3,100 Marder 1 ICVs were produced.

The hull of the Marder is an all-welded aluminium construction, and provides protection from small-arms fire and shell splinters. The front of the Marder is proof against direct fire from 20mm/0.79in ammunition. The driver sits at the front of the vehicle on the left-hand side and has a single-piece hatch in front of which are three vision blocks. Next to the driver on the right-hand side is the engine; the radiators for this are mounted on the rear of the vehicle on either side of the ramp. Behind the driver is the squad commander who has a hatch in the roof of the vehicle.

The two-man turret is mounted on the centreline just behind the squad commander and engine. The vehicle commander sits in the turret on the right-hand side with the gunner on the left. Both have their own hatches in the turret and the

LEFT: This overhead view of the Marder shows the vehicle driver in his position with his hatch open to the right. Most of the hatches above the rear infantry compartment are in the open position with men manning their positions.

LEFT: **This Marder is taking part in a NATO exercise in Germany. The crew of the Marder are servicing their vehicle's armament, while the vehicle itself is covered in camouflage netting.** ABOVE: **Six smoke dischargers are fitted to the main support arm of the 20mm/0.79in cannon. In the side of the infantry compartment are two MOWAG ball mountings for the infantry to fire their weapons from inside the vehicle.**

commander has all-round vision from eight different vision blocks. The 20mm/0.79in Rheinmetall MK20 Rh202 cannon is mounted externally on the vehicle and can traverse through 360 degrees. The cannon is fed from two different ammunition belts which can be loaded with different types of ammunition and has a rate of fire of 800–1,000 rounds per minute. The vehicle carries 1,250 rounds of ammunition for this main gun. Mounted coaxially on the-left hand side of the turret is a 7.62mm/0.3in machine-gun.

In the rear of the vehicle is the troop compartment with accommodation for six men sitting in the middle of the compartment, three on each side, facing outwards. There are also two firing ports on each side and four hatches in the roof. The main exit and entrance to the troop compartment is via a power-operated ramp that folds down from the top of the vehicle. A remote-controlled 7.62mm/0.3in machine-gun with a traverse of 180 degrees was originally fitted above the troop compartment at the rear of the vehicle, but this has now been removed on many vehicles. All Marder vehicles in German Army service have now been fitted with the MILAN anti-tank guided missile and a full NBC system.

In 1982 the Marder went through an upgrade programme which improved the main armament, night-vision lights, thermal pointer, and NBC system and gave better personal equipment stowage in the troop compartment. This vehicle became the Marder A1. The Marder A1A was also produced having all the same improvements as the A1 except the improved night-vision equipment. The Germans brought 670 Marder vehicles up to A1 standard and 1,400 vehicles to the A1A standard. The Marder 1A3 had improved armour and new improved roof hatches.

The Marder 1A5 1 A5 was an upgrade of some A3 vehicles and featured additional anti-mine armour and a completely remodelled interior to reduce blast and shock injuries to the crew. The Marder ICV was only in service with the German Army but the chassis has been used to mount the Roland Surface-to-Air Missile system which came into service in 2005 with several countries in the NATO Alliance. Although Germany is phasing out the Marder, it remains in front-line service with export customers including Chile, Greece and Indonesia.

LEFT: **The infantry section of this Marder are boarding their vehicle. The rear ramp is not fully lowered. A MILAN AT missile launcher has been fitted to the side of the main turret, which can traverse through 360 degrees and has a maximum elevation of 65 degrees.**

Marder 1 ICV

Country: West Germany
Entered service: 1971
Crew: 3 plus 6 infantry
Weight: 29,210kg/28.75 tons
Dimensions: Length – 6.79m/22ft 3in
    Height – 2.98m/9ft 9in
    Width – 3.24m/10ft 7in
Armament: Main – 20mm/0.79in MK20 Rh202
    cannon, and coaxial 7.62mm/0.3in machine-gun
    Secondary – Small arms
Armour: Classified
Powerplant: MTU MB 833 Ea-500 6-cylinder
    447kW/600hp diesel engine
Performance: Speed – 75kph/46mph
    Range – 520km/325 miles

LEFT: **This Marksman turret is fitted on a Chieftain chassis. The large adapter ring on which the turret sits has been designed to fit a number of tanks from other countries.**
BELOW: **The large ventilator grill is visible in the rear of the turret. The height and bulk of the turret can also be clearly seen.**

Marksman Self-Propelled Anti-Aircraft Gun

The Marksman twin 35mm/1.38in turret was developed by Marconi Command and Control Systems as a private venture and was very similar in concept to the German 35mm/1.38in Gepard. The Marksman system had to be able to function at any time of the day or night and in all weather conditions. Development started in 1983 and the first prototype was finished in time to go on display at the British Army Equipment Exhibition in 1984, where it was shown mounted on a Vickers Mk 3 MBT (Main Battle Tank) chassis. The second prototype was completed in 1986 and was an all-welded steel construction; the turret was built by Vickers and the guns by Oerlikon.

The turret has been designed to be fitted to some 11 different MBT chassis, both NATO and ex-Warsaw Pact, and is easily fitted to this wide range of vehicles by using an adaptor ring where necessary. The only other part required is an electrical and communication interface so the turret crew can talk to the driver of the vehicle. The turret provides the crew with protection from bullets and shell splinters; the commander sits on the left-hand side with the gunner on the right. Both have all-round vision periscopes as well as a roof-mounted gyro-stabilized sight for optically acquired air or ground targets, while the gunner also has a laser range finder. In the rear of the turret is a diesel APU that is the main power supply to the turret.

The main armament is the Oerlikon 35mm/1.38in KDA cannon and one is mounted on each side of the turret. Each gun is supplied with 250 rounds,

20 of them anti-tank. The ammunition is containerized and so reloading of the turret can be completed in 10 minutes. The guns are fully gyro-stabilized, to engage targets on the move and the vehicle radar has a 12km/7.5 miles range. The only country to buy the Marksman was Finland which used it on the T-55 MBT chassis. The Leopard 2 Marksman, now in service with Finland, combines the turret of the T-55 Marksman with the chassis of the Leopard 2A4.

LEFT: **The search radar is fitted to the rear of the turret, and stands 1m/39in above the top of this. Behind each gun barrel on both sides of the turret are a cluster of smoke dischargers.**

Marksman 35mm SPAAG on Chieftain Chassis

Country: UK
Entered service: 1987
Crew: 3
Weight: 54,864kg/54 tons
Dimensions: Length – 8.13m/26ft 8in
　　　Height – 3.07m/10ft 1in
　　　Width – 3.5m/11ft 6in
Armament: Main – 2 x 35mm/1.38in KDA cannon
　　　Secondary – 7.62mm/0.3in machine-gun
Armour: Classified
Powerplant: Leyland 12-cylinder 559kW/750hp multi-fuel engine
Performance: Speed – 48kph/30mph
　　　Range – 500km/310 miles

LEFT: **An MT-LB fitted with a SNAR 10 counter-battery radar. The SNAR 10 has the NATO codename of "Big Fred". The radar is fitted in a turret sited at the rear of the vehicle. The radar dish is in the raised position but when travelling the dish is folded down on top of the radar turret. The driver's and the vehicle commander/gunner's front visors are in the open position.** ABOVE: **A crew member is entering the front compartment of the vehicle. This compartment holds two: the driver and vehicle commander, while in the rear of the vehicle there is space for 11 men.**

MT-LB Infantry Carrier

In the late 1960s the Soviet Army required a replacement for the ageing AT-P armoured tracked artillery tractor, so a new vehicle based on the MT-L unarmoured tracked amphibious carrier was developed and called the MT-LB. Production started at the Kharkov Tractor Plant in the late 1969 and it was seen in public for the first time in 1970. The new vehicle can fill many roles including APC, prime mover for 100mm/3.94in AT guns and 122mm/4.8in howitzers, command and radio communication vehicles, and cargo carrier. It is also very good at crossing difficult terrain such as snow or swamp, gets updated, and is still in service in large numbers with a number of different countries.

The MT-LB is an all-welded steel construction, and gives the crew protection from small-arms fire and shell splinters. The crew compartment is in the front and occupies the full width of the vehicle with the driver on the left-hand side and the commander on the right. A manually operated turret, armed with a 7.62mm/0.3in PKT machine-gun is mounted in the roof above the commander's position. Next to the turret in the roof of the crew compartment is the commander's hatch and there is also a hatch above the driver's position. Both the driver and the commander have a windscreen to their front, and these are covered by an armoured flap when in action. The engine is mounted behind the driver, but does not run the full width of the vehicle. The air intake and outlet louvers

for this are on the roof. Between the crew compartment and the troop compartment is an aisle which allows access to both compartments. The troops sit down each side of the vehicle facing inwards. There are two hatches in the roof and the main entrance and exit is via two doors in the rear of the vehicle which open outwards.

The MT-LB is fully amphibious and is propelled in the water by its tracks. A trim vane, mounted on the front of the vehicle, is raised before entering the water. This operation only takes a few minutes. The vehicle is fitted with a full NBC system and night-driving equipment.

LEFT: **This MT-LB is seen towing a T-12A 100mm/3.94in AT gun during a November Parade. The vehicle could carry the six-man gun crew and ammunition. The twin large hatches in the rear of the roof of the vehicle are visible.**

MT-LB Infantry Carrier

Country: USSR
Entered service: 1970
Crew: 2 plus 11 infantry
Weight: 11,887kg/11.7 tons
Dimensions: Length – 6.45m/21ft 2in
  Height – 1.86m/6ft 1in
  Width – 2.86m/9ft 5in
Armament: Main – 7.62mm/0.3in PKT machine-gun
  Secondary – Small arms
Armour: Maximum – 10mm/0.394in
Powerplant: YaMZ 238V 8-cylinder 179kW/240hp diesel engine
Performance: Speed – 62kph/38mph
  Range – 500km/320 miles

MXT-MV Husky

At the time of writing, the British Army has been the major customer for the International MXT-MV (Military Extreme Truck – Military Version). This infantry mobility vehicle is produced by US company Navistar Defense. The MXT-MV, optimized for military use, was introduced in 2005 and is very different to the civilian version of the vehicle even though they were developed at the same time.

In 2006, the MXT-MVA (A for armoured) version was demonstrated for the United States Army as part of the competition for their MRAP All Terrain Vehicle (M-ATV) programme, but without success. The MXT-MVA was developed in partnership with Israeli vehicle manufacturer Plasan and is available with different, removable armour fits offering increasing levels of protection against bullets, improvized explosive devices etc, depending on mission requirements.

While the US Army may not have procured the MXT-MVA, the British Army were however embroiled in fighting counter-insurgency actions in both Iraq and Afghanistan. Britain had an urgent operational requirement to find a more effective replacement for its Snatch Land Rovers in Afghanistan. These ageing vehicles, in no way suited to this dangerous environment, had proved to be dangerously inadequate when it came to protecting crew and passengers from exploding improvized explosive devices.

After stringent but swift evaluation, in 2009 a specially modified version of the MXT-MVA was ordered for service with the British Army to satisfy this urgent operational need, the Tactical Support Vehicle (TSV) programme. In British service the variant was

LEFT: Soldiers from 1st Battalion, The Scots Guards, are pictured patrolling Lashkar Gar in Helmand Province, Afghanistan, in a Husky, 2010. Early in its deployment, the Husky proved itself protecting its passengers from small arms fire, RPGs and IEDs.

known as the Husky, in keeping with giving dog breed names to all-wheeled armoured vehicles in Army service. Its addition to the inventory gave British Army commanders a highly mobile and flexible load-carrying armoured vehicle, equally suited to transporting troops, food, water and ammunition, acting as a command vehicle or as a protected ambulance.

262 examples of the Husky TSV were procured initially, followed by another 89 and these vehicles were used extensively for operations in both Iraq and Afghanistan.

The Husky TSV is an all-terrain 4x4 armoured vehicle deployed to support infantry – it can transport, subject to its configuration, four to eight people. Typical Husky armament would be a 12.7mm/0.5in machine-gun as well as a remote-controlled weapon system. The Husky powerplant was usually the 242kW/325 hp Navistar VT 365 V8 diesel engine but some vehicles were known to have 253kW/340hp MaxxForce D6.0L V8 engine also manufactured by Navistar VT.

International offers three versions of the MXT-MV, based on

ABOVE: **At Sunset in Afghanistan, 2014, a convoy is led by a British Army Husky, followed by a Foxhound Protected Patrol Vehicle, with another Husky at the rear.**

different cab configurations to suit different operational needs. These are Standard, Extended Cab, and Crew Cab.

As Britain's commitments in Iraq and Afghanistan reduced, so did the need for the fleet of Huskys that had served with distinction in both areas of conflict and Britain retired its fleet in 2022. Seventy ex-British Army machines had already been given as military aid to Ghana in 2022 and then, following the Russian invasion of Ukraine in that same year, an undisclosed number of the British Husky fleet was sent to Ukraine, also as military aid.

The MXT-MV is air-transportable in aircraft from the size of a Lockheed C-130 Hercules and above.

BELOW: **A Husky being loaded onto an Oshkosh, Medium Tactical Vehicle Replacement truck in "field conditions". Note how much room the vehicle has as open storage on its rear "flatbed".**

MXT-MV Husky

Country: USA
Entered service: 2006
Crew: 2 plus 10 infantry
Weight: 14,288kg/15.75 tons
Dimensions: Length – 6.4m/21ft
  Height – 2.5m/8ft 2in
  Width – 2.92m/9ft 5in
Armament: Manual turret armed with machine-gun, or Protector remote weapon station
Armour: Removable armour kits – A-Kit and B-Kit for increasing levels of protection
Powerplant: 242kW/325hp Navistar VT 365 V8 diesel engine
Performance: Speed – 112kph/70mph
  Range – 700km/435 miles

LEFT: **An MLRS firing a salvo of missiles. The missiles are fired one at a time so the vehicle does not become unstable.** ABOVE: **A loaded MLRS at maximum elevation. The armoured louvres in front of the windscreen are in the closed position. The MLRS uses the same chassis as the M2 Bradley, and the Cummins diesel engine is mounted in a small compartment behind the crew cab.**

Multiple Launch Rocket System

In 1972, the Americans started development on a new rocket system that would use a low-cost rocket and had to be as easy to use as a conventional artillery round. The two main companies involved in the project were Boeing and Vought; each company had to develop a Self-Propelled Launcher Loader (SPLL) and 150 rockets. In 1978 France, West Germany, Italy and the United Kingdom asked to join the project and some changes were made to the rockets. A larger rocket motor was to be fitted and the diameter of the rocket increased to 227mm/8.9in. In May 1980, Vought won the competition and were awarded the contract to manufacture the SPLL and rockets. The US Army ordered 491 SPLL and 480 reload vehicles together with 400 rockets, all to be delivered

by 1990. These new vehicles would play a major part in the 1991 Gulf War (nicknamed "Steel Rain" by the Iraqi Army), and are expected to remain in service with operators for the foreseeable future.

The vehicle uses many of the M2/M3 Bradley automotive components and running gear and is an all-welded aluminium construction. In the front of the vehicle is the three-man armoured cab, which houses the driver on the left, vehicle commander on the right and the gunner in the middle. Entry and exit to the cab is via two side doors, one on each side, and each man has a windscreen which is protected by armoured louvres. Only the vehicle commander has a roof hatch. Behind the armoured cab is the engine housing

which is in an armoured box, on the top of which is the main air intake for the engine. Behind this is the main rocket pod, which is mounted on a turntable that allows a traverse of 180 degrees. The rocket pod houses 12 solid fuel rockets which are ripple-fired and can be reloaded in less than 10 minutes.

Various warheads can be fitted to the rockets: high-explosive sub-munitions, anti-tank mines and chemical warheads. The basic M77 rocket has a shelf life of 10 years and contains 644 pre-programmed shaped bomblets.

MLRS	
Country: USA	
Entered service: 1982	
Crew: 3	
Weight: 25,191kg/24.8 tons	
Dimensions: Length – 6.8m/22ft 4in	
Height – 2.6m/8ft 6in	
Width – 2.92m/9ft 7in	
Armament: Main – 12 x 227mm/8.9in	
M77 rockets	
Secondary – Small arms	
Armour: Classified	
Powerplant: Cummins VTA-903T turbocharged	
8-cylinder 373kW/500hp diesel engine	
Performance: Speed – 64kph/40mph	
Range – 483km/302 miles	

LEFT: **An MLRS in travelling mode. These vehicles replaced long-range towed artillery in most NATO armies and with updates are expected to remain in service for some time to come.**

OT-64 Armoured Personnel Carrier

The OT-64 (Obrneny Transporter) 8x8 was jointly developed by Czechoslovakia and Poland, the project starting in 1959. It uses many of the automotive parts of the Tatra 813 heavy truck series and entered service in 1964. The Czechoslovak company Tatra produced the chassis and automotive parts while the Polish firm FSC of Lubin produced the armoured body. The Polish designation for the vehicle was Sredni Kolowy Opancerzny Transporter; OT-64 being the Czech designation. It is still in service with many nations at the time of writing.

The hull of the OT-64 is an all-welded steel construction. The crew compartment is in the front of the vehicle, with the driver on the left-hand side and the vehicle commander on the right. Each has a large single door in the side of

the vehicle for access to the crew cab and also a hatch in the roof of the compartment. The driver has three vision blocks which provide views to the front and sides. The engine compartment is behind the crew cab and is mounted over the second axle with the air inlet and outlets on the roof and the exhaust pipes on either side of the vehicle. Behind the engine is an octagonal plinth on top of which sits the turret. The turret is operated by one man and has no hatch

ABOVE: **Three OT-64 APC vehicles taking part in a November Parade. The vehicle commanders are standing in their turrets. Half of the possible eight-man infantry sections are standing in the rear of the vehicles, and the doors of the rear roof hatches have been removed.** LEFT: **An OT-64 being guided around a tight corner. The front four wheels of the vehicle are used for steering, but the turning circle is very large. The exhaust system is fitted to each side of the hull of the vehicle. This APC does not have a turret fitted.**

in the top of it. To the rear of this is the troop compartment which runs to the rear of the vehicle and has room for eight men inside. At the rear are the main entry and exit doors, both of which are fitted with firing ports. There are four roof hatches above the troop compartment, all of which are also fitted with firing ports, which can be locked in the vertical position and used as shields when using the firing ports. There are also a further two ports in each side of the troop compartment.

The OT-64 is fitted with a basic NBC over-pressure system. Steering is on the front four wheels and the vehicle is fully amphibious, being propelled in the water by two propellers at the rear.

ABOVE: **The trim vane on this vehicle is folded back against the glacis. The driver's side door is in the open position, folded back against the hull of the vehicle. Above the driver's position is the driver's cupola.**

OT-64 Armoured Personnel Carrier

Country: Czechoslovakia
Entered service: 1964
Crew: 2 plus 8 infantry
Weight: 14,326kg/14.1 tons
Dimensions: Length – 7.44m/24ft 5in
 Height – 2m/6ft 6in
 Width – 2.5m/8ft 3in
Armament: Main – 14.5mm/0.57in KPVT machine-gun, and coaxial 7.62mm/0.3in PKT machine-gun
 Secondary – Small arms
Armour: Maximum – 14mm/0.55in
Powerplant: Tatra 928-14 8-cylinder 134kW/180hp diesel engine
Performance: Speed – 60kph/37mph
 Range – 500km/310 miles

OT-810 Armoured Personnel Carrier

ABOVE: **The OT-810 was a copy of the World War II German Sd Kfz 251 half-track. The crew compartment has three pistol ports down each side of the hull. The frame above the vehicle commander's position was for a 12.7mm/0.5in heavy machine-gun.**

During World War II, the Germans manufactured the Sd Kfz 251 half-track at the Skoda plant in Pilsen, Czechoslovakia. After the war had finished, the Czechoslovakian Army were desperate for vehicles and as the Skoda factory was tooled up for Sd Kfz production, they started to make the vehicle again. The first vehicles, unchanged from the basic German design, were delivered in 1948. The first major redesign occurred in the early 1950s when an armoured roof was placed over the troop compartment and the German engine was replaced with a Czech Tatra engine. When the OT-810 was replaced in 1964 on the introduction of the OT-64, a large number of the earlier carriers were converted to anti-tank vehicles. The rear of the vehicle was modified and the gun placed on to it. These variants would remain in service until the late 1980s.

The hull of the vehicle was an all-welded steel construction, with the engine in the front. Behind this was the joint crew and troop compartment. The driver sat in the front of the compartment on the left-hand side, with the vehicle commander, who also acted as the radio operator and gunner, on the right. The driver and commander had small vision ports to their front and side, and the commander also had a hatch in the roof of the vehicle. The troop compartment held 10 men, five on each side facing each other. In the rear of the vehicle were two large doors that were the sole means of access for the troops and the crew. The OT-810 had neither night-driving equipment nor an NBC system.

The only variant of the OT-810 ever produced was the anti-tank conversion, which had a crew of just four men. This was armed with the M59A recoilless gun, which was carried in the troop compartment and could be fired from inside the vehicle. Alternatively, it could be dismounted and fired from the ground. Forty rounds of ammunition for this weapon were carried in the vehicle. The twin doors at the rear were removed and replaced with a single hatch.

ABOVE: **A number of these vehicles have been converted back into Sd Kfz 251s by collectors. This example has had a 7.5cm/3in PaK 40 added.**

OT-810 APC

Country: Czechoslovakia
Entered service: 1948
Crew: 2 plus 10 infantry
Weight: 8,534kg/8.4 tons
Dimensions: Length – 5.92m/19ft 1in
 Height – 1.75m/5ft 8in
 Width – 2.1m/6ft 9in
Armament: Main – 7.62mm/0.3in M59
 machine-gun
 Secondary – Small arms
Armour: Maximum – 12mm/0.47in
Powerplant: Tatra 6-cylinder 89kW/120hp
 diesel engine
Performance: Speed – 52kph/32mph
 Range – 320km/198 miles

Panhard AML 90H Armoured Car

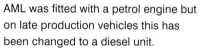

In the late 1950s, the French Army issued a requirement for an armoured car similar to the British Ferret, which they had used in North Africa. Panhard produced the first prototype in 1959 as the Model 245. It passed the trials and was accepted into French Army service as the AML (*AutoMitrailleuse Légère*), the first production vehicle being delivered in 1961. The AML has been built in large numbers, and some 4,800 cars had been produced by 2002. It has served with over 50 countries and government agencies and it remains in service with more than 30 nations.

The hull of the AML is an all-welded steel construction. The driver is in the centre front of the vehicle, and has a single hatch that opens to the right. Behind and above the driver is

the turret, which is manufactured by Hispano-Suiza and is armed with the 90mm/3.54in D 921 F1 gun. It also has a 7.62mm/0.3in coaxial machine-gun. The turret houses the vehicle commander on the left-hand side and the gunner on the right; both have hatches in the roof of the turret. There are two large hatches in the sides of the vehicle below the turret, which are the main methods of access to the vehicle. The left-hand hatch has the spare wheel mounted on it and opens to the rear while the right-hand door opens towards the front of the vehicle.

A 7.62mm/0.3in or 12.7mm/0.5in machine-gun can be mounted on the roof of the vehicle as an anti-aircraft weapon. The engine is in the rear and has two access hatches. Originally the

AML was fitted with a petrol engine but on late production vehicles this has been changed to a diesel unit.

The AML has been produced in many different variants. The body has remained the same but the turret has been changed and fitted with a variety of weapons. These include mountings for 60mm/2.36in mortars and a twin 20mm/0.79in anti-aircraft gun turret. The latest version has an open-topped turret and is known as the AML Scout Car.

LEFT: This AML 60 variant equipped a French mobile reserve to provide interior seccurity during wartime. Stripped of main armament, the crew would have relied on secondary automatic weapons. Note the two unditching channels fitted to the front of the vehicle.

Panhard AML 90H Armoured Car

Country: France
Entered service: 1961
Crew: 3
Weight: 5,486kg/5.4 tons
Dimensions: Length – 3.79m/12ft 5in
  Height – 2.07m/6ft 10in
  Width – 1.98m/6ft 6in
Armament: Main – 90mm/3.54in D 921 F1 gun, and coaxial 7.62mm/0.3in machine-gun
  Secondary – 7.62mm/0.3in machine-gun
Armour: Maximum – 12mm/0.47in
Powerplant: Panhard Model 4 HD 4-cylinder 67kW/90hp petrol engine
Performance: Speed – 100kph/62mph
  Range – 600km/370 miles

Panhard ERC-90-F4 Sagaie

Panhard started development of the ERC (*Engin de Reconnaissance Cannon*) in 1975 as a private venture aimed at the export market. The first production vehicles were completed in 1979. The French Army carried out an evaluation between 1978 and 1980 and in December 1980, it was accepted for service. However, further trials were carried out until 1983, the first ERC cars entering French Army service in 1984. An order for 176 ERC-90-F4 Sagaie was placed with the final delivery being made in 1989.

The hull of the ERC is an all-welded steel construction which gives the crew protection from small arms and shell splinters. The hull bottom is made of two plates that are welded together, stiffening the floor and helping protect the vehicle from mines. The driver's position is in the front of the vehicle but is offset to the left-hand side. It can be fitted with night-driving equipment. The two-man turret, armed with a 90mm/3.54in Model 62 F1 gun, is behind and above the driver. The commander is on the left-hand side with the gunner on the right. The commander's cupola has periscopes all round providing a 360-degree field of vision and can also be fitted with a 7.62mm/0.3in or 12.7mm/0.5in machine-gun. The engine is in the rear of the vehicle and is a militarized Peugeot V-6 petrol engine, with six forward and one reverse gear. All six wheels are permanently driven, even the middle pair when raised. The central pair is raised off the ground when the car is driven on hard roads but lowered when traversing rough terrain cross-country.

The ERC range of vehicles use many of the same automotive parts as the VCR

ABOVE LEFT: **This is the original version armed with the TTB 190 turret, but it is being replaced in service with the French Army by cars fitted with the Lynx turret.** ABOVE: **An ERC-90 fitted with the Lynx turret, which is the same as the one fitted to the AML. Steering is only available via the front wheels of the car. The centre wheels can be raised when travelling on roads.**

series of vehicles. The ERC-90-F4 has a full NBC system and is fully amphibious; normally it is propelled in the water by its wheels but it can be fitted with two water jets mounted at the rear of the vehicle. The vehicle can also be fitted with one of up to ten different turrets.

Although France is phasing out its Sagaie fleet, other nations plan to keep ERC-90 variants in service for some years to come.

LEFT: **Two Lynx-armed vehicles training in the water. The trim vane folds into three and then folds back on to the glacis plate between the front wheels. When raised and unfolded, the trim vane is full vehicle width. It has clear panels in it so the driver has some forward vision when in the water.**

Panhard ERC-90-F4 Armoured Car

Country: France
Entered service: 1984
Crew: 3
Weight: 8,331kg/8.2 tons
Dimensions: Length – 5.27m/17ft 3in
  Height – 2.32m/7ft 7in
  Width – 2.5m/8ft 3in
Armament: Main – 90mm/3.54in Model 62 F1 gun, and coaxial 7.62mm/0.3in machine-gun
  Secondary – 7.62mm/0.3in machine-gun
Armour: Classified
Powerplant: Peugeot 6-cylinder 108kW/145hp petrol engine
Performance: Speed – 95kph/60mph
  Range – 700km/435 miles

LEFT: **Showing a very distinctive front profile, this rare South African example is one of only three M3 VTT Bosboks produced in South Africa under licence.** ABOVE: **The large square rear of the M3, with two large doors for the infantry section to use. The vehicle is wider in the middle than at the end and also tapers down slightly towards the middle.**

Panhard M3 Armoured Personnel Carrier

Panhard started development of the M3 as a private venture for the export market. The first prototype was completed in 1969 and put through a series of trials. The design was subsequently changed, and in 1971 the first vehicle came off the production line. Some 1,500 M3 vehicles have been produced and exported to 26 countries and is still in service with 20 nations at the time of writing. The M3 uses 95 per cent of the same automotive parts as the AML armoured car.

The hull of the M3 is an all-welded steel construction and gives the crew protection from small arms and shell splinters. The driver's position is on the centreline in the front of the vehicle and may be fitted with night-driving equipment. The engine compartment is behind this, with the air intake above and behind the driver. The air outlets are on either side of the roof along with one exhaust system tube per side. Behind the engine is the troop compartment with accommodation for ten men. There

are four doors in this compartment: two, both fitted with firing ports, mounted in the rear of the vehicle, and a large single door on each side of the M3. There are three firing ports down each side of the infantry compartment. Behind the engine in the roof of the vehicle is a forward hatch that can mount a wide range of turrets, cupolas and machine-gun mounts, which can in turn be armed with a variety of machine-guns and cannon. Anti-tank missiles such as MILAN can also be fitted to the M3. There is a second hatch in the rear of the roof of the troop compartment and this is normally fitted with a pintle mount for a 7.62mm/0.3in machine-gun. The M3 is fully amphibious and uses its wheels to propel itself through the water.

There are five variations on the basic vehicle; these are M3/VAT repair vehicle, M3/VPC command vehicle, M3/VLA engineering vehicle, M3/VTS ambulance and the M3 radar vehicle. In 1986 the Panhard Buffalo replaced the M3, on which it is based, in production.

ABOVE: **An M3 armed with an automatic 7.62mm/ 0.3in machine-gun. The vehicle has a cluster of two smoke dischargers on each side of the vehicle. The driver's hatch is open and swung out to the right of the vehicle.**

Panhard M3 Armoured Personnel Carrier

Country: France
Entered service: 1971
Crew: 2 plus 10 infantry
Weight: 6,096kg/6 tons
Dimensions: Length – 4.45m/14ft 6in
    Height – 2.48m/8ft 2in
    Width – 2.4m/7ft 9in
Armament: Main – 7.62mm/0.3in machine-gun
    Secondary – 7.62mm/0.3in machine-gun
Armour: Maximum – 12mm/0.47in
Powerplant: Panhard 4HD 4-cylinder 67kW/90hp
    petrol engine
Performance: Speed – 100kph/62mph
    Range – 600km/372 miles

Piranha Armoured Personnel Carrier

The MOWAG Piranha is a complete range of armoured vehicles and is available as 4x4, 6x6 and 8x8 chassis. This collection of vehicles started life as a private venture and was designed for the domestic and export market. Development started in 1972 and production started in 1976. The first customer was the Canadian Armed Forces and in February 1977 they placed an order for 350 6x6 vehicles which was very quickly increased to 491 6x6s.

The Piranha has an all-welded steel construction that protects the crew from small-arms fire and shell splinters. The driver sits at the front of the vehicle on the left-hand side and has a single-piece hatch with three periscopes in the front of it. The driver's position can also be fitted with night-driving equipment. The engine is next to the driver on the right-hand side of the vehicle with the air intake and outlet louvers on the top of the hull. The exhaust exit is on the right-hand side of the hull. The main armament is normally turret-mounted and this is positioned behind the driver on the centreline of the vehicle.

In the rear of the vehicle is the troop compartment that usually holds 11 men, although this number can be lower depending on the type of turret fitted to the vehicle. The main exit and entry to the compartment is via two large doors that open outwards. There are two hatches in the roof of the troop compartment and, depending on the customer's requirements, firing ports can be fitted into the sides of the vehicle and in the rear doors. Steering is on the front axle for the 4x4 and 6x6 vehicles, and on the front two axles on the 8x8. The fixed rear axles have torsion-bar suspension while the axles that can steer are fitted with coil springs. All the Piranha family are fully amphibious and are propelled in the water by two propellers. Once the trim vane, which is stowed under the nose of the APC, is raised, the vehicle is ready for the water in only a few minutes. The Piranha comes with an NBC kit fitted as standard and a full air-conditioning system.

ABOVE: **This Piranha prototype is fitted with a 90mm/3.54in Cockerill Mk III gun. On the front of the turret on each side is a cluster of three smoke dischargers. The vehicle commander's and gunner's hatches are open.**
LEFT: **This Piranha is fitted with a Blazer 25 air-defence gun turret. This is fitted with 25mm/0.98in GAU-12/U cannon, and four Stinger SAMs are fitted above the gun barrel. The gun is firing and the large number of empty shells can be seen being ejected from the weapon.**

All members of the Piranha family share many of the same components such as the front and rear hull sections, doors, hatches, wheel drives, wheels, differentials, suspension, steering and propellers, which makes maintenance of the vehicles easier and cheaper. The Piranha family has been designed to fill a wide variety of roles for both the military and internal security forces, for example ambulance, anti-tank, armoured personnel carrier, command, mortar carrier, recovery and reconnaissance. The most popular version of the Piranha family is the 6x6 which can be fitted with a wide array of armaments. This includes a remote-controlled 7.62mm/0.3in machine-gun, a 12.7mm/0.5in machine-gun turret, 20mm/0.79in GAD-AOA Oerlikon turret, 25mm/0.98in GBD series turret, a 30mm/1.18in turret and a two-man turret armed with a 90mm/3.54in Cockerill or Mecar gun. The Canadians and Australians have fitted the British Scorpion 76mm/2.99in L23A1 gun turret to a number of their vehicles.

The Swiss Army had a requirement for 400 6x6 Piranha anti-tank vehicles to replace the ageing 106mm/4.17in M40 recoilless rifle in Swiss Army service. Each Swiss infantry regiment has nine of these anti-tank vehicles in a tank-destroyer company. They are armed with the Norwegian Thune-Eureka twin TOW turret, which has a hatch in the rear for the gunner. In the forward part of the turret are the sight and guidance systems and these are the same as for the basic infantry version of the TOW. Within two seconds of the first

ABOVE: **This Piranha is fitted with a remote-controlled Oerlikon 25mm/0.98in GBD-COA turret. The gunner sits inside the vehicle and can select two different types of ammunition. The driver's hatch is at the front of the vehicle with the commander's hatch behind, while the engine intake grills are to the left.**

missile impacting, the turret can lock on to another target ready to fire again. Reloading is carried out from the rear of the turret and can be completed in 40 seconds for the two missiles.

The Piranha has been built under licence in a large number of countries and has proved to be very successful, reliable and well-liked by its crews. It has been produced in a variety of forms and has been frequently updated. Versions remain in service around the world.

RIGHT: **This is a Blazer 30 air-defence system fitted to a Piranha. The turret is armed with a 30mm/1.18in cannon, while above the cannon are four Javelin SAMs. The radar is mounted to the rear of the turret on a pintle mount.**

ABOVE RIGHT: **The Piranha armed with a Belgian CM90 turret. This turret is also armed with the Cockerill 90mm/3.45in gun and has a row of seven smoke dischargers on each side of the turret.** LEFT: **This MOWAG Piranha is armed with the Italian OTO Melara Quad 25mm/0.98in AA system. The gunner sits in the middle of the turret, with his hatch opening to the rear. The turret can complete a full traverse in just three seconds.**

Piranha 6x6 APC

Country: Switzerland
Entered service: 1977
Crew: 3 plus 11 infantry
Weight: 10,465kg/10.3 tons
Dimensions: Length – 5.97m/19ft 6in
　　　　　Height – 1.85m/6ft 1in
　　　　　Width – 2.5m/8ft 2in
Armament: Main – Variable
　　　　　Secondary – Small arms
Armour: Maximum – 10mm/0.394in
Powerplant: GM Detroit Diesel 6V-53T 6-cylinder
　　　　　261kW/350hp diesel engine
Performance: Speed – 100kph/62mph
　　　　　Range – 600km/370 miles

LEFT: **The trim vane of the vehicle is folded back against the glacis plate. In the front of the hull are the headlights, and the commander's cupola is fitted with a 7.62mm/0.3in machine-gun. On each side of the turret is a row of four smoke dischargers.**

ABOVE: **This Luchs is negotiating a German driver-training course. The suspension is operating in several directions on all the wheels of the vehicle. The searchlight on the left-hand side of the turret is covered. The Luchs has developed a very good reputation for its cross-country ability.**

Radspahpanzer Luchs Reconnaissance Vehicle

In 1964, the Federal German Army issued a requirement for a new family of vehicles, including an 8x8 armoured amphibious reconnaissance vehicle, to enter service in the 1970s. The prototypes were delivered for testing in 1968 and in 1971, the Daimler-Benz candidate was chosen, with a contract for 408 vehicles being placed in 1973. The first production vehicles were completed in May 1975 and the first vehicle was handed over to the army in 1975. In German Army service it was known as the Luchs. Production continued until 1978.

The hull of the Luchs is an all-welded steel construction which gives the crew protection from small-arms fire and shell splinters, while the front of the vehicle is proof against 2cm/0.79in cannon fire. The driver is located in the front of the

Luchs on the left-hand side and this position can be fitted with night-driving equipment. The two-man Rheinmetall TS-7 turret is situated to the rear of the driver, with the commander stationed on the right-hand side and the gunner on the left. This turret is fitted with spaced armour to improve protection. A searchlight is fitted to the left-hand side of the turret and is connected to the elevation controls of the gun. This can also be used in the infrared mode. Both the commander and the gunner are equipped with sights for the main gun.

The fourth man in the crew is the radio operator/rear driver, and they are seated behind the turret facing the rear of the vehicle on the left-hand side with the engine compartment on the right. There is a large hatch that gives access to all crew positions in the left-hand side of the

hull between the front four and rear four wheels. The Luchs is fully amphibious and is propelled through the water by two propellers mounted at the rear of the vehicle. Steering is on the front and rear axles which makes this vehicle very manoeuvrable.

The Luchs developed a very good reputation for its cross-country ability, reliability and quietness. After 34 years of Bundeswehr service the Luchs was phased out in 2009 to be replaced by the Fennek.

Radspahpanzer Luchs Reconnaissance Vehicle

Country: West Germany
Entered service: 1975
Crew: 4
Weight: 19,507kg/19.2 tons
Dimensions: Length – 7.74m/25ft 5in
  Height – 2.9m/9ft 6in
  Width – 2.98m/9ft 9in
Armament: Main – 2cm/0.79in MK20 Rh202 cannon
  Secondary – 1 x 7.62mm/0.3in MG3 machine-gun
Armour: Classified
Powerplant: Daimler-Benz OM 403A 10-cylinder 291kW/390hp diesel engine
Performance: Speed – 90kph/56mph
  Range – 730km/455 miles

LEFT: **A Luchs leaving the water with its trim vane in the raised position. To give the driver some forward vision when in the water, the trim vane has several clear panels fitted in it.**

Rapier Tracked SAM Vehicle

LEFT: **A Rapier Tracked SAM Vehicle that has just launched a missile. The tracking radar on the rear of the turret can be seen in the raised position. The vehicle is divided into two clear parts: the crew and engine compartment to the front and the missile launcher/radar to the rear.**

Rapier Tracked SAM Vehicle

Country: UK
Entered service: 1984
Crew: 3
Weight: 14,010kg/13.8 tons
Dimensions: Length – 6.4m/21ft
    Height – 2.5m/8ft 2in
    Width – 2.78m/9ft 1in
Armament: Main – 8 x Rapier SAM
    Secondary – Small arms
Armour: Classified
Powerplant: GMC 6-cylinder 186kW/250hp
    diesel engine
Performance: Speed – 80kph/50mph
    Range – 300km/190 miles

Development of this vehicle commenced in 1974, initially using the chassis of the M548, but this was quickly changed for the RCM 748, part of the M113 APC family of vehicles. Originally developed for the Imperial Iranian Armed Forces, British Aerospace was left with a number of these vehicles and no customer following the overthrow of the Shah in 1979. Subsequently, the British Army agreed to conduct vehicle trials and in 1981 placed an order for 50 units. It entered service in 1984 with two Royal Artillery Regiments, each deploying 24 Rapier vehicles.

The hull is an all-welded aluminium construction, and is proof against small-arms fire and shell splinters. The driver, commander and gunner all share the very small and cramped cab in the front of the vehicle. The driver is on the left-hand side, while the engine is installed behind the crew compartment. The eight-round Rapier system is mounted on the rear of the vehicle. The time taken from the vehicle stopping to the first target being engaged is 15 seconds.

Rooikat 105mm Armoured Car

Development on this vehicle started in 1978. The first production vehicles were completed in 1989 and entered service in 1990, armed with a 76mm/2.99in fully stabilized gun.

Rooikat 105mm Armoured Car

Country: South Africa
Entered service: 1994
Crew: 4
Weight: 28,042kg/27.6 tons
Dimensions: Length – 7.09m/23ft 3in
    Height – 2.8m/9ft 2in
    Width – 2.9m/9ft 6in
Armament: Main – 105mm/4.13in GT7 gun,
    and coaxial 7.62mm/0.3in machine-gun
    Secondary –1 x 7.62mm/0.3in machine-gun
Armour: Classified
Powerplant: 10-cylinder 420kW/563hp
    diesel engine
Performance: Speed – 120kph/75mph
    Range – 1,000km/620 miles

In 1994, further development resulted in a 105mm/4.13in version of the vehicle entering service with the South African National Defence Force. Total production so far has been 240 vehicles.

The hull is an all-welded steel construction, and is proof against small-arms fire, shell splinters and anti-tank mines. The front of the vehicle is proof against 24mm/0.94in cannon fire. The driver's position is located in the front on the centreline, while the other three members of the crew are situated in the turret. The commander and gunner are on the right-hand side of the turret with the loader on the left. The engine is in the rear of the vehicle, which can be driven in either 8x4 mode or 8x8 mode and accelerate

ABOVE: **The driver's position is under the main gun, which has to be cantered off to one side to allow the driver to access the vehicle. There is a mount for a machine-gun at the rear of the commander's cupola.**

from 0–30kph/0–18.6mph in under eight seconds.

The Rooikat is designed for the reconnaissance role but can also carry out "seek and destroy" missions.

SA-8b SAM Vehicle

The SA-8 has the NATO designation "Gecko" and is an all-weather low-altitude Surface-to-Air Missile (SAM) system. The Gecko entered service in 1974 with the Soviet Armed Forces and was seen for the first time at the November Parade in Moscow in 1975. It was designed to fill the gap between the SA-7/SA-9 and the SA-6 and was developed in conjunction with the Soviet Navy SA-N-4 system. The Gecko is known in the Russian Army as the ZRK-SD Romb (*Zentniy Raketniy Komplex*) which indicates that the system is a complete SAM system.

Each anti-aircraft division has 20 of these vehicles. This was the first anti-aircraft system to combine the surveillance, target-acquisition and missile launcher all-in-one vehicle.

The chassis of the Gecko, an all-welded steel construction, is based on the ZIL-167 6x6 truck and is not proof against small arms or shell splinters. The crew compartment is at the front of the vehicle where all three crew members sit in a row with the driver in the centre. In the roof above the driver is a small hatch which is the only access to and from the vehicle. The main missile control consoles, operated by all three crew members, are behind the crew. The vehicle is very spacious and the crew can even sleep in it. The engine is in the rear of the vehicle with the air intakes and outlets built into the top of the hull, while the exhaust is at the rear of the engine compartment.

The central radar dish is the main tracking system with the two smaller dishes acting as target-acquisition radar. On the top of the radar mount is a television camera which is used to acquire targets without having to switch on the radar. The SA-8b variant can

ABOVE LEFT: **The boat-shaped hull of the vehicle can be clearly seen, with the trim vane folded back in front of the windscreen. The missile turret sits high on the top of the vehicle.** ABOVE: **The main entry and exit hatch for the crew of the Gecko is in the roof of the vehicle immediately in front of the main radar dish and is seen here in the open position.**

carry six missiles (the SA-8a carries only four) and no reloads. The Gecko is fully amphibious, propelled in the water by two water jets built into the rear of the vehicle, and is also air-transportable. The vehicle has been used in combat and is very popular with several armies in the Middle East.

LEFT: **The main search radar of the Gecko is in the travel mode; it is folded down against the missile launching boxes. The water jet entry hatch is sited above the rear wheel with the exit in the rear of the vehicle.**

SA-8b SAM Vehicle

Country: USSR
Entered service: 1974
Crew: 3
Weight: 17,499kg/17.2 tons
Dimensions: Length – 9.14m/30ft
Height – 4.2m/13ft 10in
Width – 2.8m/9ft 2in
Armament: Main – 6 x SA-8b missiles
Secondary – Small arms
Armour: Classified
Powerplant: 5D20 B-300 223kW/299hp
diesel engine
Performance: Speed – 80kph/50mph
Range – 250km/155 miles

Saladin Mk 2 Armoured Car

In 1947, a contract was issued to Alvis Ltd to develop a new 6x6 armoured car for the British Army. A mock-up was completed in 1948 and was given the designation of FV 601. This first vehicle was to be armed with a 2pdr gun (FV 601A) but this was quickly dropped in favour of a 76mm/2.99in gun (FV 601B). The first prototype vehicles were delivered in 1952–53 and were followed by six pre-production vehicles. Further modifications were made to these vehicles as a result of trials, in particular the turret was redesigned. In 1958 the FV 601C or Saladin Mk 2 entered production with the first vehicles being completed in 1959 and entering service the same year. Production continued until 1972, by which time 1,177 Saladins had been built.

The hull and turret of the vehicle were all-welded steel constructions and were proof against small-arms fire and shell splinters. The driver was located in the front of the vehicle on the centreline with a hatch in front that folded down on to the glacis plate. There was powered steering to the four front wheels. The steering wheel was rather oddly fitted sloping into the driver's chest, which took some getting used to. Behind and above the driver was the turret which housed the other two members of the crew. The commander was on the right-hand side of the turret with the gunner on the left. Both had hatches in the roof of the turret and the commander had a pintle mount for a 7.62mm/0.3in machine-gun. There was an escape hatch for the crew below the turret in each side of the hull, while the engine and three fuel tanks were in the rear of the vehicle. The Saladin was not fitted with any form of NBC system, and did not carry night-driving or night-fighting equipment.

The Scorpion finally replaced the Saladin in British Army service. Saladins have seen service in many parts of the world including the defence of Kuwait City during the 1991 Gulf War when they destroyed severa T-55 MBTs. Despite their age, Saladins, many of them updated, remain in service with a number of nations.

RIGHT: **A detail of the front of a Saladin. On each side of the front of the turret are two clusters of six smoke dischargers. The driver's hatch has been pushed open; this makes a very useful shelf for a mug of tea.**

Saladin Mk 2 Armoured Car	
Country: UK	
Entered service: 1959	
Crew: 3	
Weight: 11,582kg/11.4 tons	
Dimensions: Length – 4.92m/16ft 2in	
Height – 2.92m/8ft 7in	
Width – 2.53m/8ft 4in	
Armament: Main – 76mm/2.99in L5A1 gun, and coaxial 7.62mm/0.3in machine-gun	
Secondary – 7.62mm/0.3in machine-gun	
Armour: Maximum – 16mm/0.63in	
Powerplant: Rolls-Royce B80 Mk 6A 8-cylinder 127kW/170hp petrol engine	
Performance: Speed – 72kph/45mph	
Range – 400km/250 miles	

LEFT: **A Saracen command vehicle. The tube frame on the rear of the vehicle is for a tent extension to be fitted to increase the working space. This vehicle has been fitted with a turret with a cluster of four smoke dischargers on each side on the top of the vehicle,** BELOW: **This vehicle has a light machine-gun fitted to the ring mount that is set in the rear of the roof. Most of the vision ports are in the open position; these are not fitted with any form of glass. A fire extinguisher is fitted to the rear mudguard of the Saracen, while camouflage netting has been stored above the centre road wheel.**

Saracen Armoured Personnel Carrier

After World War II, the British Army issued a requirement for a family of vehicles that were all 6x6 configurations. These were given the family designation FV 600. The family was made up of the FV 601 Saladin Armoured Car, the FV 602 Command Vehicle (which was cancelled but was later reincarnated as the FV 604) and the FV 603 Saracen Armoured Personnel Carrier. Development of the Saracen started in 1948 with the first prototype completed in 1952. The first production vehicle was completed in December 1952 and the type entered service in early 1953. The Saracen was rushed into production and given priority over the other vehicles in the family as a result of the emergency in Malaya. The Saracen would remain the main APC of the British Army throughout the 1950s and 1960s until replaced by the FV 432. Production continued until 1972, by which time 1,838 vehicles had been produced. Some of these vehicles are still in service with a few armed forces around the world. All vehicles in the family would share many of the same automotive parts and the unusual steering-wheel angle (see the Saladin). The last vehicle in the family was the Stalwart Amphibious Load Carrier (FV 620).

The hull of the Saracen is an all-welded steel construction, and is proof against small-arms fire and shell splinters. The radiator is in the front of the vehicle with the engine behind. The crew and troop compartments are all one in this vehicle, with the driver's position situated on the centreline in the front of the compartment directly behind the engine. There is no windscreen; the driver looks through a hatch that folds down and lays on the top of the engine in non-combat situations. The troop commander sits behind the driver facing forwards on the left-hand side of the vehicle, and also doubles as vehicle commander. The radio operator sits behind the driver on the right-hand side of the vehicle and also faces forwards. Between the commander and the radio operator is the machine-gun turret position. This is the same type of turret as that fitted to the Ferret Mk 2 armoured car and is un-powered.

LEFT: **This aerial view shows the front turret and the rear ring mount on the roof of the Saracen APC. The turret is fitted with a searchlight on the left-hand side, while two fixed steps at the rear make boarding quicker for the infantry.**

LEFT: **This Saracen has all the vision ports in the open position and the driver's hatch is in the half-open position. The Saracen has a cluster of three smoke dischargers on each front mudguard. The headlights proved to be very vulnerable to damage.**
ABOVE: **A Saracen on exercise in Britain. The driver has his hatch in the open position, while the vehicle commander is talking into the radio. The Saracen can continue to operate with a damaged wheel on each side of the vehicle.**

In the rear of the compartment is accommodation for eight troops, who sit four down each side facing inwards. There are two large doors in the rear of the vehicle, each of which has a firing port. These are the main entrance and exit from the vehicle for the crew and the troops. Below the doors are two steps and between them is a large towing hitch. In the rear of the roof behind the turret is a large sliding hatch which gives access to a ring-mounted anti-aircraft machine-gun which was initially an LMG, better known as the World War II Bren gun. Subsequently, this was replaced by a 7.62mm/0.3in machine-gun. There are also three firing ports in each side of the vehicle. The Saracen has no NBC system, night-driving or night-fighting equipment and is not amphibious, but can ford shallow water. Along with the other vehicles in the family, the Saracen can continue to operate on the battlefield even if it loses two wheels as a result of mine explosions, provided the wheels are lost one from each side.

The FV 603C was a tropical version of the Saracen. These were built mainly for Kuwait and had reverse-flow cooling. The air was sucked in at the rear of the engine, passed over the engine and out through the radiator. Libya also placed an order for these vehicles but they were never delivered due to the political situation, the Libyan vehicles being taken over by the British Army and sent to Northern Ireland. The FV 604 Command Vehicle was modified for the command role and had a crew of six, with map-boards and extra radios inside. The FV 610 was another command vehicle but was taller and wider than the FV 604 and saw service with the British Army in Northern Ireland. The FV 610 could also be fitted with FACE (Field Artillery Computer Equipment) and was trialled with the Robert Radar System but this progressed no further than a trials vehicle. The FV 611 was the ambulance version of the Saracen and could accommodate ten walking-wounded or three stretcher cases and medical personnel. Some of these vehicles remain in service around the world to this day.

BELOW: **This Saracen command vehicle has been fitted with an additional layer of armour. The cut-out around the driver's visors can be seen. The ring mount from the rear of the roof has been moved forward for the vehicle commander, as the turret has been removed.**

Saracen Armoured Personnel Carrier

Country: UK
Entered service: 1953
Crew: 2 plus 10 infantry
Weight: 10,160kg/10 tons
Dimensions: Length – 5.23m/17ft 2in
    Height – 2.46m/8ft 1in
    Width – 2.53m/8ft 4in
Armament: Main – 7.62mm/0.3in machine-gun
    Secondary –7.62mm/0.3in machine-gun
Armour: Maximum – 16mm/0.63in
Powerplant: Rolls-Royce B80 Mk 6A 8-cylinder
    127kW/170hp petrol engine
Performance: Speed – 72kph/45mph
    Range – 400km/250 miles

LEFT: **The vehicle commander is in his turret. Note the prominent engine grills and the large single door in front of the storage boxes on the side of the vehicle. The driver's vision blocks are bullet-proof and provide a good view from his position high up in the front of the vehicle.**

Saxon Armoured Personnel Carrier

In 1970, GKN Sankey started a private venture development of a wheeled personnel carrier for use in the internal security role. The development vehicle was known as the AT 104. It had the engine mounted at the front of the vehicle similar to the Saracen and although the armour around the engine was poor, the floor of the vehicle was redesigned to give better anti-mine protection. The first prototype vehicle of an improved design was produced in 1974, entering production in 1976 for the export market only with the designation AT 105. The name "Saxon" was not given to the vehicle officially until 1982. After further development, production would start for the British Army in 1983 and the Saxon entered service in 1984. Over 800 of these vehicles have been produced, with some 600 serving with the British Army.

The hull of the Saxon is an all-welded steel construction that gives the crew protection from small-arms fire and shell splinters. The floor of the vehicle is V-shaped, giving the crew and troops inside some protection from mines. The axles, however, are not protected. The chassis and automotive parts are taken from the Bedford MK design and these standard parts make logistics easier. However, to remove the engine the roof of the vehicle needs to be taken off which is time-consuming, requires heavy equipment, and makes maintenance in the field difficult.

The Saxon can be built in left- and right-hand drive versions. The driver's compartment is in the front of the vehicle on either the left- or right-hand side as required and can be accessed from the main troop compartment or from a large single hatch

RIGHT: **A convoy of three Saxon APCs on exercise with the vehicle commanders positioned in their turrets. Wire-mesh storage baskets are installed on the roof of each vehicle and a spare wheel is carried under the side door on the right-hand side.**

in the roof of the driving compartment. The driver has three large bullet-proof vision blocks, one to the front and one in each side. The engine compartment is next to the driver, on either the right or the left of the vehicle depending on the configuration. The radiator grill is mounted in the front of the vehicle with the air outlet on the side of the vehicle, and again this is installed on one side or the other depending on the driving position.

Behind and above the driver's position is the vehicle commander's fixed cupola which is a four-sided box with all-round vision blocks and a large single hatch in the roof. There are machine-gun pintle mounts on each side of the cupola for a single 7.62mm/0.3in GPMG. As this cupola is only bolted to the roof of the vehicle, it can be replaced very quickly with a manually traversed machine-gun turret which can be armed with a single or twin 7.62mm/0.3in machine-gun. Alongside the commander's position in the hull of the vehicle is a single large door which in British service is normally fitted on the right-hand side of the vehicle, but again this door can be moved to the other side of the vehicle or two side doors can be fitted as required. The main troop compartment holds eight men, four down each side of the vehicle facing inwards. In the rear of the Saxon are two large doors that are the main exit and entrance for the infantry section using the vehicle. Each door is fitted with both a vision block and a firing port and there is another firing port in the front of the vehicle next to the driver. The British Army has fitted large storage boxes to the sides of the vehicle and a mesh rack to the roof behind the commander's cupola to improve personal equipment storage.

A Saxon recovery vehicle variant was designed to recover vehicles of its own type and soft-skin trucks. With a crew of four it had a 5,080kg/5-ton hydraulic winch mounted on the left-hand side of the vehicle. A tent could be fitted to the vehicle to act as a covered workshop.

A command vehicle was also developed for the British Army and the Royal Air Force for use with the Rapier missile batteries. The Saxon APC was in service with the British Army from 1983 to 2008, and Saxons were supplied to Ukraine in 2015.

ABOVE: **This is a British Army Saxon recovery vehicle, which is fitted with a 5,080kg/5-ton hydraulic winch. The large side-mounted hull door was removed from these vehicles to allow for increased equipment storage.**

ABOVE: **The headlights of the Saxon are built into the front of the vehicle to give them better protection. The high ground-clearance of the body of the vehicle, which gives the infantry inside the Saxon some protection from land mines, can be clearly seen.** BELOW: **The turret of this Saxon has been fitted with a 7.62mm/0.3in GPMG. A hessian screen, which is rolled down when the vehicle is parked to help camouflage it, has been attached to the lower hull of the Saxon. The driver's hatch is open and folded forward. The spare wheel can be clearly seen attached to the underside of the vehicle.**

Saxon Armoured Personnel Carrier

Country: UK
Entered service: 1984
Crew: 2 plus 8 infantry
Weight: 11,684kg/11.5 tons
Dimensions: Length – 5.17m/17ft
Height – 2.63m/8ft 7in
Width – 2.49m/8ft 2in
Armament: Main – 7.62mm/0.3in GPMG
Secondary – Small arms
Armour: Classified
Powerplant: Cummins 6BT 6-cylinder 122kW/160hp diesel engine
Performance: Speed – 96kph/60mph
Range – 510km/317 miles

Scud Missile System TEL

The Scud missile system was developed in response to the Soviet Army's requirement in the early 1950s for a tactical missile system that could deliver both conventional and nuclear warheads. This was to replace the Soviet-developed R-1 and R-2 missiles, which were based on the German V2 ballistic missile. These battery systems required 152 trucks, 70 trailers and over 500 men and could only fire 9 missiles per day. The new missile was called the R-11 (NATO codename Scud A). Its first test flight was in April 1953 and production began in 1955. The first TEL (Tractor, Erector and Launcher) was developed using the ISU-152 (Obiekt 218) tank chassis. These TEL vehicles, known as 8U218, entered service with the Soviet forces in 1955. They were deployed at the density of one regiment per army; each regiment being composed of three batteries, each of which had three TEL vehicles. These 9 TEL vehicles were supported by 200 trucks and 1,200 personnel and had an allocation of 27 missiles per day. It is believed that 100 TEL vehicles were built for the Soviet Army. In 1960 Khrushchev ordered that Soviet heavy tank production should be stopped and the decision was taken to develop a new TEL.

This new vehicle was based on the MAZ-543LTM 8x8 heavy truck, a standard Soviet heavy truck design. The wheeled chassis has many advantages over the tracked chassis. It provides a smoother ride which causes less vibration damage to the missile and the control and test equipment on the vehicle, and is a more reliable and cost-effective vehicle, with only a slight decrease in cross-country performance compared to the tracked chassis. The vehicle has a full set of power-assisted controls for the steering and gearbox which makes it easy to drive. All the wheels are connected to a central tyre pressure system that is regulated from the driver's position.

The vehicle was given the official designation of 9P117 TEL and the official name of "Uragan" (Hurricane) but was

TOP: **A Soviet Scud missile TEL about to take part in a November Parade. The compartment between the second and third wheels is the main fire control centre. The compartment on the other side of the vehicle holds the auxiliary power unit.** ABOVE: **A Soviet Scud B is halfway up to the vertical firing position, while the Scud behind is in the firing position. The six-man launch crew is attaching the control cables to the missile as it is being raised.**

popularly known as the "Kashalot" (Sperm Whale) by the Soviet Army because of its size. The driver is situated in the front of the left-hand crew compartment and has a very simple set of controls. Behind the driver is a member of the launch crew with a set of compressed air bottles between them which supply the power for the cold weather starter. The other crew compartment on the right side of the vehicle has the vehicle commander, the main communications equipment and the fourth crew member in it. Between the two crew compartments is the radiator and main engine, which is not shielded and can betray the vehicle's position with its heat signature. The exhaust from this comes out between the first and second wheels. Behind the crew cabins is an APU that is used when the main engine is shut down.

The missile and its erector are carried in a cavity down the centre of the vehicle when in the travelling mode. In the centre of the vehicle are two control cabins. The left-hand cabin houses the main selector switches and an auxiliary power unit. The right-hand cabin has accommodation for the targeting controls and missile testing equipment, along with seats for two crew members. The vehicle carries its own launching base-plate which is hydraulically operated and is folded up against the rear of the vehicle when in the travelling mode. Between this base-plate and the vehicle are two large stabilizing jacks that help support the weight of the missile when it is in the erect position. On the left-hand side at the rear of the vehicle is the main safety catch for the missile; this is a simple mechanical slide that is moved under the fuel pump switches.

The Scud B was used during the 1973 war between Egypt and Israel. The next major use of Scud was between 1986 and 1988 during the "War of the Cities" between Iran and Iraq. Long-range versions of the Scud were fired against Israel and Saudi Arabia during the 1991 Gulf War, but the largest number of missiles was fired by the Soviets during the Afghan War (1979–89) when 1,000 were fired against mountain villages. Updated versions remain in front-line use and earlier versions are still deployed by a number of Scud export customers.

TOP: **The two separate crew compartments with the radiator and missile warhead between them can be clearly seen. The driver's cab is on the left-hand side of the vehicle, while in the rear of the cab are a crew member and the compressed-air starting system for the vehicle.** ABOVE: **On the rear of the vehicle are two hydraulic jacks that are lowered into position before the missile is raised. The firing platform swings down with the missile resting on it. There are access ladders on the arms of the cradle.** MIDDLE LEFT: **A Scud TEL taking part in a parade. The front four wheels are used for steering the vehicle, with the exhaust system exiting between the first and second wheels. The large clamp just behind the warhead attaches the missile to the TEL.**

LEFT: **The red dot on the vehicle is a heavy canvas security blind covering the little window in the control cabin. The small ladder above the third wheel swings down to give access to the top of the TEL.**

MAZ 9P117 TEL

Country: USSR
Entered service: 1965
Crew: 4
Weight: 37,400kg/36.4 tons
Dimensions: Length – 13.36m/43ft 9in
　　　　Height – 3.33m/10ft 10in
　　　　Width – 3.02m/9ft 10in
Armament: Main – R300 missile
　　　　Secondary – None
Armour: None
Powerplant: D12A-525A 12-cylinder
　　　　391kW/525hp diesel engine
Performance: Speed – 45kph/28mph
　　　　Range – 450km/280 miles

Spartan Armoured Personnel Carrier

Designed by Alvis, the Spartan was an early 1970s development of the Scorpion CVR(T) and entered service with the British Army in 1978. It was designed to perform in a number of roles that the Saracen 6x6 APC had previously filled, but was not designed as a direct replacement for the FV 432 APC. Rather than being a vehicle to move general troops from A to B, this very adaptable vehicle was deployed as a carrier for specialist teams including the Royal Artillery Blowpipe/Javelin surface-to-air missile teams, as a missile reload resupply vehicle for the FV102 Striker, carrying extra Swingfire missiles, and as a carrier for Royal Engineer assault teams. The

ABOVE: **A British Army Spartan APC hits the beach during an amphibious demonstration in Hampshire, UK, 2010.** BELOW LEFT: **This exported Spartan is preserved at the Royal Military History Museum, Brussels, Belgium. Note the engine's air intakes and outlets on the glacis plate and the exhaust is on the roof on the left-hand side of this photo.**

Spartan was also operated by the Royal Air Force Regiment for airfield defence and related activities.

By 2001, 960 Spartan vehicles had been built. The late production vehicles have an improved suspension and a new, more fuel-efficient Cummins diesel engine fitted, and a large number of the early production vehicles also had these improvements fitted. While officially the Spartan is designated as an APC, it can only carry four men in the rear of the vehicle.

Its hull is an all-welded aluminium construction which is proofed against small-arms fire and shell splinters. It can withstand, over its frontal area, up to 14.5mm/0.57in projectiles and 7.62mm/0.3in armour-piercing rounds over the rest of the vehicle.

The driver is located in the front of the vehicle on the left-hand side and has a wide-angle periscope which can be replaced by passive night-driving equipment. Next to the driver on the right-hand side is the Jaguar 4.2-litre petrol engine giving an impressive top speed of 96kph/60mph and an unrefuelled range of 510k/320m. The engine's air intakes and outlets can be seen on the glacis plate while the exhaust is on the roof on the right-hand side.

ABOVE LEFT: **A Spartan fitted with the Euromissile MILAN MCT turret. The launcher rails are empty on this vehicle. The long sloping glacis plate can clearly be seen.** ABOVE: **This Spartan has both the driver's and commander's hatches open. The driver's hatch opens towards the front of the vehicle. The Spartan has two clusters of three smoke dischargers fitted to the glacis plate.** LEFT: **The Spartan is very similar in appearance to the FV102 Striker and can be distinguished by the lack of the Striker's missile launcher.**

The vehicle commander/gunner is behind the driver and is provided with a cupola mounted in the vehicle roof with eight periscopes, which provide all-round vision. Mounted on the right of the cupola is a 7.62mm/0.3in machine-gun which can be aimed and fired from inside the vehicle. Four smoke dischargers could be mounted on each side.

Next to the commander on the right of the vehicle is the troop commander/radio operator, who also has a hatch in the roof. In the rear of the vehicle is the troop compartment which holds four men, one seated behind the troop commander and three others on a bench seat on the left-hand side. Entry and exit from the vehicle is via a large single door in the rear.

The FV120 Spartan MCT (Spartan with MILAN Compact Turret) was developed as an anti-tank version. With a two-man turret, the MCT could carry 13 MILAN Anti-Tank Light Infantry Missiles, with two in ready-to-fire launch positions.

In 2006, 478 FV103 vehicles were known to be in service with UK armed forces and these were gradually replaced from 2009 on. Export customers included Belgium (from 1975), Oman and the Philippines. Following the 2022 Russian invasion of Ukraine, the UK agreed to supply Spartans to Ukraine. These machines were complemented in the front line by another 50 surplus ex-British Army Spartans acquired by a charity through an online crowdfunding campaign.

ABOVE: **A group of soldiers loading their sleeping bags into the back of the Spartan. The commander's cupola has its hatch in the open position.**

Spartan APC

Country: UK
Entered service: 1978
Crew: 2 plus 4 infantry
Weight: 8,128kg/8 tons
Dimensions: Length – 5.13m/16ft 11in
    Height – 2.26m/7ft 5in
    Width – 2.24m/7ft 4in
Armament: Main – 7.62mm/0.3in machine-gun
    Secondary – Small arms
Armour: Classified
Powerplant: Jaguar J60 No.1 Mk 100B 6-cylinder
    142kW/190hp petrol engine
Performance: Speed – 80kph/50mph
    Range – 483km/301 miles

Stormer Armoured Personnel Carrier

Development of the FV 4333 started at the UK Military Vehicle and Engineering Establishment in the 1970s and the first prototype was displayed in 1978. Alvis took over the development of the vehicle in June 1981, giving it the name "Stormer" and making it part of the CVR(T) family, as it uses many of the same automotive parts as the other members of this group. The Stormer is actually a stretched version of the Spartan with increased chassis length and an extra road wheel on each side.

Production began in 1982, for export orders only at first, with the first vehicles entering service with the Malaysian armed forces in 1983. In 1986 the British Army selected the

ABOVE: **British Army Stormer vehicle firing a Starstreak High Velocity Missile (HVM) on exercise in Canada, 2014.**

Stormer for three roles: the Shielder anti-tank mine dispenser vehicle which first entered British Army service in 1999; a launch vehicle for the Starstreak and Martlet SAM high-velocity missile (Stormer HVM) which entered service in 1989 ; and a reconnaissance vehicle for the Starstreak. Now supplied by BAE Systems Land & Armaments, the Stormer is also marketed as being available in additional configurations with a two-man 25mm/0.98in cannon-armed turret, for air defence with guns or missiles, a command and control vehicle, as an engineer vehicle, as a recovery vehicle, an ambulance, an 81mm/3.2in or 120mm/4.72in mortar carrier, or as a bridge layer.

The Stormer HVM provides effective short range low-level air defence with excellent mobility. The vehicle is armed with eight ready-to-fire missiles and a further nine can be stowed inside. The system's rapid engagement capacity is optimized to counter the threat of attack helicopters. Each missile employs a system of three dart type projectiles which can make multiple hits on the same target – each of these darts has an explosive warhead. The system entered British Army service in 1997.

LEFT: **A Stormer air defence vehicle armed with the Starstreak SAM system. The missiles are stored in their launch boxes, each box holding four missiles. A full reload is carried inside the vehicle. The flotation screen can be seen in its stored position around the edge of the vehicle.**

LEFT: **An infantry section debussing from a Stormer IFV. The vehicle is armed with a Helio FVT 900 turret which is fitted with a 20mm/0.79in cannon. In the hull of the vehicle are firing ports for the infantry to use from inside the vehicle.** BELOW: **A Stormer fitted with a two-man turret, armed with a 30mm/1.18in cannon and coaxial 7.62mm/0.3in machine-gun. The vehicle can carry 165 rounds of ammunition for the main gun.**

The hull of the Stormer is an all-welded aluminium construction and is proofed against small-arms fire and shell splinters. The driver is located in the front of the vehicle on the left-hand side and has a single wide-angle periscope that can be replaced by passive night-driving equipment. The engine compartment is located next to the driver on the right.

Behind the driver is the vehicle commander/gunner's position, which has a cupola in the roof with eight periscopes providing all-round vision and also mounts a 7.62mm/0.3in machine-gun. The radio operator/troop commander's position is next to the vehicle commander, and behind this is the crew compartment, which accommodates eight infantry, four down each side on bench seats facing inwards. The main access

point, a single large door with a vision block, is at the rear of the vehicle.

The Stormer and other members of the CVR family have a full NBC system and are air-portable. They can ford water to a depth of 1.1m/3ft 7in in their normal combat mode but, with a little preparation and the raising of a flotation screen, they become fully amphibious, propelling themselves in the water with their tracks.

Export customers for the Stormer included Indonesia, Malaysia and Oman. The latter nation acquired vehicles fitted out to be command vehicles to support their Chieftain tanks force. Stormer HVMs were also supplied to Ukraine following the 2022 Russian invasion.

LEFT: **A Stormer HVM in Ukrainian service, 2022. Part of the CVR(T) family, Stormer uses many of the same automotive parts as the other members of this AFV group and is a stretched version of the Spartan.**

Stormer APC

Country: UK
Entered service: 1983
Crew: 3 plus 8 infantry
Weight: 12,700kg/12.5 tons
Dimensions: Length – 5.33m/17ft 6in
    Height – 2.27m/7ft 5in
    Width – 2.69m/8ft 10in
Armament: Main – 7.62mm/0.3in machine-gun
    Secondary – Small arms
Armour: Classified
Powerplant: Perkins T6/3544 6-cylinder
    186kW/250hp diesel engine
Performance: Speed – 80kph/50mph
    Range – 650km/400 miles

Striker Self-Propelled Anti-Tank Guided Weapon Vehicle

ABOVE: This example of a Striker is preserved in the UK in private ownership. Note the 35-degree angle of the raised missile "bin" and the top-mounted machine-gun.

The Striker (FV 102), built by Alvis, is part of the Scorpion CVR(T) family and was designed to carry the Swingfire anti-tank missile. The first production vehicles entered service at the height of the Cold War with Royal Artillery anti-tank guided missile batteries that formed part of the British Army of the Rhine (BAOR) in then West Germany during 1975. These vehicles would have been an element of the forces deployed to try to halt the advance of Warsaw Pact tanks, had the Cold War heated up.

The Striker uses many of the same automotive parts as the other members of the CVR family and has been designed to be an air-portable anti-tank missile system capable of destroying MBTs. Having a similar performance to the Scorpion, the Striker can move in and out of unprepared positions very quickly (up to 80kph/50mph) and is well suited to "shoot and scoot" missions.

The hull of the Striker is an all-welded aluminium construction, and is proofed against small-arms fire and shell splinters. The driver is located in the front of the vehicle on the left-hand side, with the engine next to him on the right of the vehicle. Initially power came from the Jaguar J60 4.2 litre 6-cylinder petrol engine, the same used by some Jaguar cars. As part of the CVR(T) life extension programme, the petrol engine was replaced by a Cummins 5.9 diesel engine, as was used in British Army Scimitars.

The commander/gunner is situated behind the driver, and has a cupola above his position that has all-round vision and is armed with a 7.62mm/0.3in machine-gun with 3,000 rounds. Next to the vehicle commander is the guided-weapons controller. As the Swingfire is a wire-guided system, the controller has a sight mounted above his position – the controller has to follow the flight of the missile, which can be guided on to the target by using a joystick.

Behind the vehicle commander's cupola is a "bin" holding five ready-to-fire Swingfire missiles which would be elevated to 35 degrees from the horizontal for firing. The targeting sight could even be demounted to be operated at a distance from the vehicle which could remain parked and totally hidden from the enemy by cover, facing a different direction. The

LEFT: On the front of the Striker are two clusters of three smoke dischargers. The headlights are attached to the front of the vehicle by simple brackets.

LEFT: **The Striker was designed to move in and out of unprepared positions very quickly for "shoot and scoot" missions. The upgrade to the Cummins 5.9 diesel engine enabled the vehicle to better cope with demanding terrain.** BELOW: **The driver of this Striker is in his position with his hatch lying on the glacis plate. The exhaust system runs back down the right-hand side of the vehicle. At the end of the protective cover, the exhaust turns through 90 degrees and goes straight up for about 31cm/12in.**

missile's operational range was between 150 – 4,000m/492ft – 4,374yd and would accelerate towards the target at a speed of 185m/606ft per second. The missile could turn in flight by up to 90 degrees following launch which meant that enemy tanks would not even know the Striker was there until a Swingfire was bearing down on them. Early Swingfires were steered to the target by a joystick using manual command to line of sight (MCLOS). The system was later refined to the semi-automatic command to line of sight (SACLOS) system where the target simply had to be sighted by the guided-weapons controller.

Five additional missiles, accessed through a large single door, are carried in the rear of the vehicle. Reloading is performed outside the vehicle. The missile system can operate either in daylight or in nighttime conditions. The Striker is

capable of fording 1.1m/3ft 7in of water without preparation, but the vehicle becomes fully amphibious by fitting a flotation screen, using its tracks to propel itself through the water.

British Army Strikers served in both the Gulf War of 1991, and Operation Enduring Freedom, the invasion of Iraq, in 2003, during which a British Army Striker destroyed an Iraqi T-55 tank with an anti-tank missile. During their service careers, both the Striker vehicle and the Swingfire missile system were upgraded but were ultimately phased out of British Army service in 2005.

BELOW: **A Striker on a live-firing exercise. This vehicle has just launched one of the five Swingfire AT missiles that are carried in the launcher at the rear of the vehicle. The back-blast generated by the Swingfire on launching is small and so does not give away the position of the vehicle.**

Striker SP ATGW Vehicle

Country: UK
Entered service: 1975
Crew: 3
Weight: 8,331kg/8.2 tons
Dimensions: Length – 4.83m/15ft 10in
Height – 2.28m/7ft 6in
Width – 2.28m/7ft 6in
Armament: Main – 10 x Swingfire Wire-Guided Missiles
Secondary – 7.62mm/0.3in machine-gun
Armour: 12.7mm/0.5in resistant
Powerplant: Jaguar J60 No.1 Mk 100B 6-cylinder 142kW/190hp
Performance: Speed – 80kph/50mph
Range – 483km/301 miles

LEFT: **Two of the driver's vision blocks have been covered to protect the vision port. The turret on the roof of the vehicle is a Creusot-Loire TLI 127, and is armed with a 12.7mm/0.5in heavy machine-gun and a coaxial 7.62/0.3in machine-gun.** ABOVE: **A Belgian BDX APC used by the air force for airfield defence. A 7.62mm/0.3in machine-gun is mounted on the top of the shield on the vehicle roof. Just in front of the turret on each side of the hull is a bank of three smoke dischargers.**

Timoney Armoured Personnel Carrier

Due to the troubles in Northern Ireland, the Government of the Irish Republic decided to expand the army in the early 1970s, aiming for between 100 and 200 APC vehicles. In 1972 the Irish Army issued a requirement for a 4x4 armoured personnel carrier that could be used anywhere in the world operating under United Nations control. The Timoney brothers came up with a design, producing the first prototype in 1973. There were a large number of technical faults with this prototype vehicle, which were rectified to produce the Mk II in April 1974, and this was then put on trial with the Irish Army. After further improvements to the basic design, the Mk III was produced in 1976. Further development produced the Mk IV, of which only five vehicles were built. The final vehicle produced by Timoney in the series was the Mk VI, but again only five units were ever manufactured.

The hull of the Mk V was an all-welded steel construction, which was proof against small-arms fire and shell splinters. The vehicle could also withstand the blast from a 9kg/20lb mine. The driver was positioned in the front of the vehicle on the centreline, and had a windscreen to the front and one to each side. There were three doors in the vehicle, one in each side and one in the rear. The engine compartment was to the rear of the driver with the air louvres in the roof. There was a manual machine-gun turret armed with a single 7.62mm/0.3in machine-gun in the centre of the roof. The troop compartment in the rear had seats for ten men. The vehicle was fully amphibious, propelling itself through the water using its wheels.

The Belgian company Beherman Demoen negotiated a licence to produce the APC in 1976. Their vehicle, put into production in 1982, was called the

BDX Armoured Personnel Carrier. In total 123 of these were produced, 43 for the Belgian Air Force and 80 for the Gendarmerie. The design was then bought by Vickers who developed the vehicle further and called it the "Valkyr", but no further vehicles were sold.

Timoney Mk V/BDX APC

Country: Eire (Republic of Ireland)
Entered service: 1982
Crew: 2 plus 10 infantry
Weight: 9,957kg/9.8 tons
Dimensions: Length – 4.95m/16ft 3in
  Height – 2.75m/9ft
  Width – 2.5m/8ft 3in
Armament: Main – 7.62mm/0.3in machine-gun
  Secondary – Small arms
Armour: Maximum – 12.7mm/0.5in
Powerplant: Chrysler 8-cylinder 134kW/180hp petrol engine
Performance: Speed – 100kph/62mph
  Range – 700km/430 miles

Timoney/ADI Bushmaster IMV

The Bushmaster Infantry Mobility Vehicle is an Australian-built four-wheel drive lightly armoured vehicle optimized for operations in northern Australia, but designed to protect its crew against land mines thanks to its innovative v-shaped hull to deflect the blast away from the vehicle. Its armour offers protection against small arms of up to 7.62mm/0.3in, large mortar fragments, and mines. Supplementary armour can be installed to protect against armour-piercing ammunition. With a road speed of up to 100kph/118mph and operational range of 800km/497m, it can carry up to nine troops and their equipment together with supplies for three days.

The vehicle's origins date to the early 1990s and an Australian government Defence Force Structure Review identified an Australian Army need for an Infantry Mobility Vehicle (IMV). This led to Project Bushranger and the 1994 release of a draft specification for the IMV. In 1996 Australian company Perry Engineering produced a prototype vehicle based on

the Irish-designed Timoney Technologies MP44 but featuring the Rockwell/Timoney independent suspension and significant elements from the US Army's Family of Medium Tactical Vehicles, including the engine and transmission. After modification and improvement in 1999 the design was chosen as the winning proposal for further development and production.

Heavy lifting for the Bushmaster design – which required cost effective merging of a number of different design elements which had originated from design teams in Australia, the US and Ireland – was undertaken by the then government-owned Australian Defence Industries (ADI), since acquired by Thales Australia.

As well as serving with the Australian Army and Royal Australian Air Force, the Bushmaster was also bought for service with the British Army, Royal Netherlands Army, Japan Ground Self Defense Force, Indonesian Army, Fiji Infantry Regiment, Jamaica Defence Force and New Zealand Army. The Bushmaster has seen considerable action in the

service of Britain (in Iraq), Netherlands (Afghanistan) and Australia (Afghanistan and Iraq).

Following the Russian invasion of Ukraine in 2022, Ukrainian President Zelenskyy specifically requested the supply of Bushmasters to bolster the Ukrainian war effort.

Bushmaster IMV

Country: Australia
Entered service: 1997
Crew: 1 driver, 9 infantry
Weight: 15,400kg/16.9 tons
Dimensions: Length – 7.18m/23ft 7in
  Height – 2.65m/8ft 10in Width – 2.48m/8ft 1in
Armament: Main – 12.7mm/0.5in heavy machine-gun or 40mm/1.6in grenade launcher
  Secondary – up to three 7.62mm/0.3in machine-guns
Armour: Protection against up to 7.62mm/0.3in ammunition, with additional applique armour, for AP ammunition up to 7.62mm/0.3in
Powerplant: Caterpillar 3126E 7.2L six-cylinder turbocharged diesel engine
Performance: Speed – 100kph/62mph
  Range – 800km/497 miles

LEFT: **A Warrior at speed during training in the Gulf. The driver and vehicle commander have their hatches open. Crews of AFVs had to be taught how to drive in the desert so as not to create a dust cloud. On the rear of the vehicle is a large storage bin for personal equipment.** ABOVE: **One of the Warrior development vehicles. The vehicle is fitted with several clusters of four infrared and smoke screening dischargers. On the turret are a further four smoke dischargers on each side. The driver's entry hatch is mounted on the sloped side of the vehicle hull.**

Warrior Mechanised Combat Vehicle

The British Army's FV 432 entered service in the 1960s and was due for replacement by 1985. Development of the MCV-80 as the replacement vehicle started with various studies being carried out between 1967 and 1977, when the detailed design work started. By 1980, three prototype vehicles were being tested and these were followed by a further seven vehicles which were completed in 1984. In the same year development of MCV-80 variants and derivative vehicles started. In 1985 GKN Defence Operations were awarded three contracts for 1,048 MCV-80 vehicles, and it was given the name "Warrior" by the British Army. Production started in January 1986, the first vehicle being produced in December 1986. The first batch of vehicles numbered 290, consisting of 170 section vehicles and 120 of the specialized vehicles. Once production started the British Army would take delivery of 140 vehicles per year, and 70 per cent of the 1,048 Warriors ordered would be section vehicles. Vickers Defence Systems manufacture the turret in a modular form ready to drop into a vehicle on the production line, while Rolls-Royce do the same with the engine pack which is made up of the engine, the transmission and the cooling system. The first three variants under development, the Infantry Command Vehicle, the Artillery Observation Vehicle and a Repair and Recovery Vehicle, were all completed in 1985. Unfortunately, the cost of the Warrior has meant that by 2004 it had still not fully replaced the FV 432.

The hull of the Warrior is of an all-welded aluminium construction, and is proof against small-arms fire and shell splinters. The driver is located in the front of the vehicle on the left-hand side, with a single large hatch over his position that is fitted with a wide-angle periscope which can be changed for a passive night-sight. The engine is next to the driver on the right-hand side and is a Rolls-Royce Condor. This is linked to a

ABOVE: **The RARDEN-armed turret is covered in camouflage netting. Modern camouflage netting helps hide the vehicle on the battlefield from infrared and other sensors that are now carried by modern reconnaissance aircraft. The headlight clusters are mounted on the leading edge of the glacis.**

Detroit Diesel automatic transmission with four forward and two reverse gears made under licence by Rolls-Royce. The Warrior is fitted with a full NBC system and night-fighting equipment.

The two-man turret is a steel construction mounted in the centre of the vehicle but slightly offset to the left of the centreline. The vehicle commander sits on the right-hand side of the turret, with the gunner on the left. The vehicle commander can also double as the infantry section leader and can debus with the troops. The turret is armed with a 30mm/1.18in L21A1 cannon and a coaxial 7.62mm/0.3in machine-gun. The cannon can fire single rounds, a burst of six rounds or a high rate of 80 rounds per minute, all spent

BELOW: **A pair of Warrior vehicles on a live-firing range. The low height of the turret can clearly be seen from the instructor standing on the rear of the vehicle. On each side of the rear door on the back of the Warrior are large equipment storage containers. A wire-mesh storage box has been fitted to one of the roof hatches in the rear of the Warrior.**

shell cases being expelled outside the turret. However, there have been a few problems with the main gun, in particular with accidental discharge.

The troop compartment is at the rear of the vehicle and holds seven men, four on the right and three on the left-hand side of the vehicle, each man having his own seat and seat belt. There is no provision for the infantry to fire their weapons from inside the Warrior. The main entrance and exit for the infantry section is a single power-operated door with a vision port in it in the rear of the vehicle, and above the troop compartment is a large double hatch which, when opened, lies flat on the top of the vehicle. There are storage baskets on the rear of the vehicle for personal kit as there is insufficient room for this inside.

There are three different Warrior command versions – Platoon, Company and Battalion, the main difference between these vehicles being the communications equipment fitted.

The Warrior Repair and Recovery Vehicle has a 6,502kg/6.4-ton crane and a 20,015kg/19.7-ton capstan winch, and also a hydraulically operated ground anchor which allows the vehicle to pull 38,000kg/37.4 tons. Other vehicles of the Warrior family serving with the British Army are the Artillery Observation Vehicle and the Battery Command Vehicle. A desert version of the Warrior was developed for the export market and this was bought by Kuwait as the Warrior proved to be a very reliable vehicle during the Gulf War of 1991.

In 2021 the UK Ministry of Defence announced that all of the British Army's Warriors would be replaced by the mid 2020s.

ABOVE: **This Warrior is on active service with British forces in Bosnia. It has been fitted with appliqué armour to the sides and front of the vehicle. The Warrior has proved to be a reliable and strong vehicle in combat.**

Warrior Mechanised Combat Vehicle

Country: UK
Entered service: 1985
Crew: 3 plus 7 infantry
Weight: 24,486kg/24.1 tons
Dimensions: Length – 6.34m/20ft 10in
Height – 2.79m/9ft 2in
Width – 3.03m/9ft 11in
Armament: Main – 30mm/1.18in RARDEN cannon, and coaxial 7.62mm/0.3in machine-gun
Secondary – Small arms
Armour: Classified
Powerplant: Perkins CV8 TCA 8-cylinder 141kW/190hp diesel engine
Performance: Speed – 75kph/47mph
Range – 660km/412 miles

LEFT: **The Varta has the capability to ford water bodies with a depth of 1m/3ft and can negotiate grades and side slopes of 60 per cent and 45 per cent, respectively.** BELOW: **Inside the Varta troop compartment. Note the advanced wall-mounted five-point seat belt anti-mine seats designed to absorb energy from under-vehicle blasts.**

Varta APC

The mine resistant ambush-protected (MRAP) Varta is a 4x4 all-terrain armoured personnel carrier designed and produced by defence vehicle company Ukrainian Armor and it entered service with the Ukrainian armed forces in December 2018. It is a versatile design that can also serve as a command post or ambulance. A Varta APC that appeared in the Ukraine's 30th Independence Day parade in August 2021 was fitted with an FGM-148 Javelin anti-tank missile.

The main vehicle compartment is made from specialized grade Swedish 560 steel which protects the crew from armour piercing incendiary ammunition up to 7.62mm/0.3in calibre from 10m/33ft distance. All of the vehicle's windows offer the same level of protection as the vehicle's armour and all panels have been designed for rapid removal and replacement. All windows and mirrors are heated.

The vehicle's v-shaped hull not only helps to minimize the effect of mine and IED blasts on the occupants but they also

have wall-mounted five-point seat belt anti-mine seats with an advanced energy damper attenuation system to absorb violent shocks generated by mines and IEDs. This, with general mine blast protection from the hull, offers crew members protection against nearby detonation of charges up to the equivalent blast of 6kg of TNT.

The cabin features an independent air conditioning and heating system to provide a comfortable environment in the cabin within the wide temperature range of –40 to +50 degrees Centigrade. The vehicle has an air filtering and ventilation device to ensure the air within the cabin remains clean whatever may be going on outside.

The vehicle is powered by a 283kW/380hp 6 cylinder in-line turbo diesel engine and 8 gear manual transmission which bestows a maximum road speed of 100kph/62mph. The engine can run on many types of fuel (including lower quality

LEFT: **The Varta's crew position seems more like delivery van than APC. Note the NBC warning console.**

fuel in combat situations) and is surrounded by ballistic plates for additional powerplant protection.

The Varta chassis has a central tyre inflation system which enables the crew to inflate or deflate tyres as required to get optimal performance from the vehicle for any conditions encountered. The system manages automatic maintenance of required air pressure in the tyres in the event they are damaged. The system will execute automatic wheel disconnection from the system in the case of significant damage when air leakage exceeds the rated compressor performance. This is a proven and reliable system that will get the Varta through even the most challenging and difficult terrain conditions. Rubber run-flat tyres permit continued operation even after a loss of some or all inflation pressure for up to 40km/25m on or off road.

With a crew of 2 and up to 8 dismounted troops, the vehicle has a gunner station with a gunner protection kit on the roof that can take various machine gun systems including 7.62mm/0.3in or 12.7mm/0.5in and also has 10 gun ports spaced around the vehicle, large enough to allow for rifle grenade installation. Each side of the hull has five windows and two doors. Entry and exit of the eight troops is via a large door at the rear of the vehicle.

ABOVE LEFT: **The Varta is fitted with a nine-ton winch to rescue other vehicles or to use for self-extraction in difficult positions.** ABOVE: **The Varta has two access doors on the side of the vehicle and a machine-gun position on the roof.**

The Varta can also come equipped with an enclosed turret (manual or powered options) mounting dual machine gun systems (14.5mm/0.57in and 7.62mm/0.3in). A smoke grenade launching system can also be fitted. Interior lighting is provided with several settings – full, partial camouflage and specific night lighting.

The vehicle is fitted with a winch with a nine-ton towing capacity using 25m/82ft of either synthetic rope or steel cable. This can be used to rescue other vehicles as well for self-extraction from difficult positions.

The Varta has a high speed fire extinguishing system for both the crew compartment and the engine compartment. The system has both UV and IR detectors that can detect and indicate fire in the vehicle within 3 milliseconds and then suppress it in 250 milliseconds.

BELOW: **This all-Ukrainian vehicle has been designed to operate in extremes of temperature and terrain.**

Varta APC

Country: Ukraine
Entered service: 2018
Crew: 2 plus 8 infantry
Weight: 17,500kg/19.29 tons
Dimensions: Length – 8m/26ft 3in
　　　　　Height – 3.6m/11ft 10in
　　　　　Width – 2.6m/8ft 6in
Armament: 7.62mm/0.3in or 12.7mm/0.5in macine-gun fixed on roof, or turret armed with machine-gun
Armour: Swedish 560 steel against up to 7.62mm/0.3in AP incendiary ammunition
Powerplant: 283kW/380hp 6-cyliner in-line turbo diesel engine
Performance: Speed – 100kph/62mph on road
　　　　　Range – 600km/373 miles

LEFT: **A 6x6 version of the VAB fitted with a Creusot-Loire TLi 52A one-man turret which is armed with a single 7.62mm/0.3in machine-gun.** ABOVE: **A basic 4x4 version of the VAB APC, as used by the French Army. All of the armoured shutters are in the open position on this vehicle. Behind the shutter the vision ports are protected by bullet-proof glass.**

VAB Armoured Personnel Carrier

In the late 1960s the French Army issued a requirement for a wheeled APC, as the tracked AMX-10 was proving to be too expensive and complex to fill all the roles required of it. This was further extended in 1970 when a requirement for a Forward Area Control Vehicle (*Véhicule de l'Avant Blinde*, VAB) was identified. The French Army tested 4x4 and 6x6 versions between 1972 and 1974, eventually selecting the Renault 4x4 vehicle to fulfil both roles. Production started in 1976 and the first vehicles entered service in 1977.

The basic vehicle used by the French is the VAB VTT (*Véhicule Transport de Troupe*). Its hull is an all-welded steel construction, proof against small-arms fire and shell splinters, with an NBC system. The driver sits at the front of the vehicle on the left-hand side, with the vehicle commander/gunner beside him on the right. In front of them is a bullet-proof windscreen. Both have access doors in the side of the cab opening towards the front of the vehicle and hatches above their positions. The commander also has a machine-gun mount, the Creusot-Loire type CB 52, armed with a 7.62mm/0.3in machine-gun. This can be replaced with a TLi 52A turret or CB 127 12.7mm/0.5in gun and shield.

The engine compartment is behind the driver with the air intake and outlet in the roof. On the right-hand side of the vehicle is a passageway between the crew compartment and the troop compartment in the rear. The ten men in here sit on bench seats, five down each side, while the main access to the vehicle is via two doors in the rear of the VAB. There are two firing ports in each side of the vehicle and one in each door. The VAB is fully amphibious and is propelled in the water by two water jets.

Renault developed a 6x6 vehicle for the export market and offered both for sale. By 1999 the French Army had taken delivery of over 4,000 vehicles and over 700 (6x6 and 4x4 vehicles) had been sold to the export market. The VAB is being gradually replaced by the VBMR Griffon and VBMR-L Serval.

LEFT: **Several 6x6 and 4x4 VAB APCs taking part in a French Army exercise. The VAB in the front of the picture has been fitted with a basic ring mount over the roof hatch for a 12.7mm/0.5in heavy machine-gun. The cylinder below the gunner is the exhaust system for the vehicle.**

VAB VTT

Country: France
Entered service: 1977
Crew: 2 plus 10 infantry
Weight: 13,614kg/13.4 tons
Dimensions: Length – 6.1m/20ft
　　　Height – 2.1m/6ft 11in
　　　Width – 2.5m/8ft 2in
Armament: Main – 7.62mm/0.3in machine-gun
　　　Secondary – Small arms
Armour: Classified
Powerplant: Renault MIDS 06.20.45 6-cylinder 175kW/235hp diesel engine
Performance: Speed – 92kph/57mph
　　　Range – 1,000km/621 miles

LEFT: **This Shilka has the driver's hatch in the open position. In front of the driver's position is the splash board which helps to prevent water entering there. The main armament is at maximum elevation, and the Gun Dish radar is in the raised position at the rear of the turret.** BELOW: **A Shilka in travelling mode. The radar has been lowered and the guns brought down to the horizontal. To the left is a T-72 MBT and to the right is a BTR-60 PB, in the snow.**

ZSU-23-4 Self-Propelled Anti-Aircraft Gun

In 1960 development started in the Soviet Union on a replacement for the ageing ZSU-57-2, which was too slow, inaccurate and did not have an all-weather capability. The replacement unit carries the Soviet designation *Zenitnaia Samokhodnaia Ustanovka* (ZSU), which mounts a 23-calibre armament (23mm/0.91in) of which there are four, hence ZSU-23-4. They also called it "Shilka" after the Russian river of that name. First seen during the 1965 November Parade, having entered service in 1964, its NATO reporting name is "Awl" but it is more popularly known as "Zoo-23". Production finished in 1983 with more than 7,000 vehicles being produced.

The hull and turret are an all-welded steel construction. The glacis plate is proof against small arms and shell splinters, but the turret is susceptible to shell splinter damage. The driver is located at the front of the vehicle on the left-hand side in a small cramped position, with the cold weather starter and battery compartment next to him on the right. His position can be fitted with infrared night-driving equipment. The other three members of the crew are positioned in the rear of the turret, the commander on the left-hand side with the other two beside him, and the guns are separated from the crew by a gas-tight armoured bulkhead. Access to the guns is via two large hatches in the front roof of the turret. The gun barrels are water-cooled, although this is not always satisfactory and when the gunner releases the trigger the guns can still fire several more rounds. The gunner can select either single, twin or all four gun barrels to engage a target. At the rear of the turret is the Gun Dish Radar System which can be folded down into the travel mode when on the move. The engine is in the rear of the Shilka which is fitted with a full NBC system.

The Shilka proved to be a very effective system and during the Middle East War of 1973 it accounted for 31 out of 103 Israeli aircraft shot down. It has been active in over 20 wars since, including both sides of the 2022 Russian invasion of Ukraine, and remains in front-line use with over 25 nations.

RIGHT: **The large ammunition magazine running down the side of the turret can be clearly seen. Above the driver's hatch is the very small vision port. The driver has a very poor field of vision when the hatch is closed.**

ZSU-23-4 Shilka SPAAG

Country: USSR
Entered service: 1964
Crew: 4
Weight: 14,021kg/13.8 tons
Dimensions: Length – 6.29m/20ft 8in
  Height – 2.25m/7ft 5in
  Width – 2.95m/9ft 8in
Armament: Main – 4 x AZP-23 23mm/0.91in cannon
  Secondary – None
Armour: Maximum – 15mm/0.59in
Powerplant: Model V6R 6-cylinder 179kW/240hp
Performance: Speed – 44kph/27mph
  Range – 260km/160 miles

Glossary

AA Anti-Aircraft.

AAGM Anti-Aircraft Guided Missile.

AFV Armoured Fighting Vehicle.

AP Armour-Piercing.

APC Armoured Personnel Carrier.

APU Auxiliary Power Unit.

ARV Armoured Recovery Vehicle.

ATGM Anti-Tank Guided Missile.

ATGW Anti-Tank Guided Weapon.

barbette An open-topped turret.

bustle Rear storage container on a vehicle (named after the "bustle", the bulge on the back of a lady's skirt in the early 20th century).

"buttoned up" All hatches are shut with the crew inside.

calibre Diameter of the bore of a gun barrel.

central tyre pressure system Tyre pressures are controlled from a central position, normally the driver's, to match driving conditions.

chain gun Machine-gun.

chassis Running gear of vehicles: axles, road wheels etc.

closed-down All hatches are shut.

coaxial The secondary armament mounted to fire alongside the main armament.

cupola Domed turret fitted with vision devices, frequently for use of vehicle commander.

CVR(T) Combat Reconnaissance Vehicle (Tracked).

Czech Republic Created in 1993, with Prague as its capital, from part of the former Czechoslovakia.

Czechoslovakia Country in central Europe, created in 1918 from part of the Austro-Hungarian empire, which divided in 1993 into two separate states, the Czech Republic and Slovakia.

double-baffle Muzzle brake with two holes.

ECM Electronic counter measures.

German Democratic Republic After World War II, Germany was divided into two parts. The eastern part, falling under the influence of the Soviet Union, was known as the German Democratic Republic (GDR) or East Germany. It reunited with the German Federal Republic in 1990.

German Federal Republic After World War II, Germany was divided into two parts. The western part, allied to the West, was known as the German Federal Republic (or West Germany). It reunited with the German Democratic Republic in 1990.

glacis Defensive sloping front plate on an armoured vehicle.

GP General Purpose.

GPMG General Purpose Machine-Gun, typically 7.62mm/0.3in calibre.

HE High-Explosive.

HEAT High-Explosive Anti-Tank.

HE-FRAG High-Explosive Fragmentation.

HMG Heavy Machine-Gun, typically 12.7mm/0.5in calibre.

hull The main body of the vehicle above the chassis.

IFV Infantry Fighting Vehicle.

LMG Light Machine-Gun, typically 7.62mm/0.3in calibre.

LVTP Landing Vehicle Tracked Personnel.

mantlet Protective covering for the hole in the turret where the main armament emerges.

MBT Main Battle Tank.

MILAN *Missile d'Infanterie Léger Anti-Char.*

muzzle brake Way of slowing down the recoil of the barrel by using the excess gases from the propellant charge.

NATO North Atlantic Treaty Organization. A military alliance of Western countries, set up in 1949 by the United States, Britain, Belgium, Canada, Denmark, France, Iceland, Italy, the Netherlands, Norway and Portugal against the perceived threat from the Soviet Union and its satellites. There are currently 30 members of NATO.

NBC Nuclear, biological, chemical. Typically used when describing systems which offer protection against these threats.

November Parade Annual military parade in the USSR to celebrate the successful Communist Revolution in 1917.

over-pressurization system/ over-pressure system Air pressure in a vehicle is raised by one or two atmospheres above outside atmospheric pressure as a crude form of NBC protection.

pdr Contraction of "pounder" – old British measurement for artillery pieces, which were measured by weight of their shell, e.g. "6pdr" – six-pounder.

pistol ports An opening in a vehicle allowing small arms to be used from inside.

portee Vehicle transporter for an artillery piece.

prime mover Dedicated tractor unit, for example one whose first job is to shift guns.

pulpit Slang term for a raised gunner's or driver's position.

RNAS Royal Naval Air Service: the naval arm of the British military air forces between 1911 and 1918.

run-flat tyres These can be driven on even after punctures for around 30km/ 18 miles.

Russia (rather than USSR) The old Russian empire before the foundation of the Soviet Union in 1917 and also the country known as Russia since the break-up of the Soviet Union in 1991. All vehicles from this region coming into service before 1917 or after 1991 are designated as being from Russia.

SAM Surface-to-Air Missile.

SAMM Surface-to-Air Mobile Missile.

Sd Kfz German abbreviation for *Sonderkraftfahrzeug*: Special Purpose Motor Vehicles.

section vehicle Either a platoon commander's vehicle or a vehicle which can carry an infantry section of 10 men.

"seek and destroy" missions Hunting missions.

"shoot and scoot" missions Ability to deliver approximately three rounds of fire on target and then speedily leave the area before the enemy can detect position and destroy.

Slovakia Created in 1993, with Bratislava as its capital, from part of the former Czechoslovakia.

Soviet Union Colloquial name for the USSR.

SPAAG Self-Propelled Anti-Aircraft Gun.

spaced armour Armour built in two layers with a space in between.

SP ATGW Self-Propelled Anti-Tank Guided Weapon.

SPG/H Self-Propelled Gun/ Howitzer.

standardized (of US vehicles) Term used when a vehicle is accepted into service with the US Army and given a military designation.

sustained rate of fire Rate of fire which a gun-crew can keep up over a period of time, not just for a short burst.

TOW missile Tube-launched, Optically-tracked, Wire-guided missile.

track grousers Attachments to tracks for extra grip over soft ground or ice.

uparmoured Increases in the original basic armour fitted to a vehicle.

USSR (rather than Russia) Union of Soviet Socialist Republics, founded in 1917 from the former Russian empire, and disbanded in 1991, when parts of this became known once again as Russia. All vehicles from this region coming into service between 1917 and 1991 are designated as being from the USSR.

vision slits/slots An opening in a vehicle fitted with a vision device.

Warsaw Pact A military alliance of the USSR and its satellite countries set up in 1955 to offer mutual assistance against any attacks. Members included the German Democratic Republic, Czechoslovakia and Poland.

water jet Hydro-drive underwater propellant system.

weapon station Weapons firing position.

White Russians Counter-revolutionaries in the civil war in the Soviet Union following the Revolution in 1917, opposing the Communist forces (the "Reds").

Key to flags

For the specification boxes, the national flag that was current at the time of the vehicle's use is shown.

 Australia

 Belgium

 Brazil

 Canada

 Czechoslovakia

 Eire (Republic of Ireland)

 France

 Germany: World War I

 Germany: World War II

 Germany: post-World War II

 India

 Italy (civil ensign)

 Italy

 Japan

 Netherlands

 South Africa: pre-democracy

 South Africa: post-democracy

 Switzerland

 UK

 Ukraine

 USA

 USSR

 USSR

Acknowledgements

The author would like to thank David Fletcher, historian at the Tank Museum, Bovington, and his staff, the DAS MT Section, Duxford, and the Cambridge Branch of MAFVA, for all their help and advice. A special thank you to Bridget Pollard for all her encouragement and help, especially "de-jargoning".

The publisher would like to thank the following individuals and picture libraries for the use of their pictures in the book. Every effort has been made to acknowledge the pictures properly. However, we apologize if there are any unintentional omissions, which will be corrected in future editions.

l=left, r=right, t=top, b=bottom, m=middle, um=upper middle, lm=lower middle

After the Battle: 77tl.

Imperial War Museum Photographic Archive: 8–9; 11br; 15tl; 15m; 15b; 17tl; 22tl; 22b; 23tl; 23tr; 23m; 23b; 24m; 25umr; 25lmr; 38m; 39ml; 46–7; 51tl; 52tr; 62tl; 62tr; 62b; 63tl; 64b; 65m; 65b; 66t; 66m; 66b; 67tl; 67tr; 67b; 69t; 70b; 71tl; 72; 76tl; 76b; 80tl; 80m; 80b; 81tl; 81tr; 81b; 82b; 86tl; 87t; 87m; 87b; 90m; 94b; 95tr; 98; 100b; 101tl; 101tr; 101b; 102tr; 103tl; 104b; 106b; 112t; 112b; 113tl; 113b; 115b; 116tl; 116br; 117b;

118t; 118m; 119t; 121t; 121m; 121b; 127t; 127bl; 127br; 128b; 133t; 137tr; 137m; 137b; 148t; 148br; 149tl; 149tr; 216tl; 216tr; 216b; 219b.

Jack Livesey Collection: 2; 6t; 7; 13; 21tr; 21br; 24t; 28; 30–3; 34b; 35tr; 35bl; 36–7; 38t; 39mr; 39b; 40mr; 41; 43tl; 43tr; 60b; 64t; 69m; 69b; 71tr; 71b; 77b; 79; 82tl; 82tr; 86tr; 86b; 88; 89t; 89um; 90t; 90b; 91–92; 93ml; 96b; 97; 99; 100t; 103b; 106tl; 104tr; 107; 112m; 113tr; 128tr; 130; 132; 133b; 136; 137tl; 141tl; 143tr; 146; 154–9; 161–62; 164–88 (unless indicated elsewhere); 199tl; 199b; 200–01; 202t; 202m; 203; 204tl; 204tr; 205–15 (unless indicated elsewhere); 218; 219t; 1219m; 220–55 (unless indicated elsewhere); 257t; 257mr; 257b; 258–62; 263tl; 263tr; 264–70 (unless indicated elsewhere); 72b; 276tr; 277m; 277b; 280–1; 283; 286; 287; 288.

Tank Museum Photographic Archive: 4; 5b; 6m; 10tl; 10m; 11tr; 11mr; 11ml; 12; 14; 15tr; 16; 17tr; 17m; 17br; 18–20; 21tl; 21ml; 21mr; 25t; 26–7; 34t; 35tl; 35br; 40ml; 40b; 42; 43mr; 43b; 48–50; 51tr; 51b; 52tl; 52b; 53–9; 60t; 61; 63tr; 63mr; 68; 70tl; 70tr; 73–5; 76tr; 77tr; 78; 83–5; 93t; 93b; 94tl; 94tr; 95tl; 95b; 96tl; 96tr; 102tl; 102b; 103tr; 104tl; 104tr; 105; 108–11; 114; 115tl; 115tr; 116tr; 116bl; 117t;

118b; 119b; 120; 122–6; 131; 134–5; 138–40; 141tr; 141b; 142; 143tl; 143b; 144–5; 147; 148bl; 149b; 150–1; 160; 163; 199tr; 202b; 204b; 217; 256; 257ml; 263b; 272tl; 272tr; 274; 282.

TRH Pictures: 89lm; 89b; 129b; 276tl; 276b; 277t.

Victory Memorial Museum: 5t; 25b; 128tl; 129t; 129m; 284.

Rheinmetall BAE Systems Land: 213b.

Defence Imagery: 1; 191t; 207; 213t; 248m; 248t; 249.

U.S. Department of Defence: 39t; 181t.

Ukrainian Armor: 278; 279.

Wikimedia Images: 44; 45; 152–3; 174; 175; 176; 177; 178; 179; 180; 181b; 182t; 183; 184t; 185tr; 185tl; 186; 187; 188t; 189; 190; 191m; 191b; 196; 197; 198m; 206; 212t; 220br; 221b; 222t; 223b; 224t; 226; 227; 234t; 235b; 248t; 252b ;253b; 255tl; 268; 269m; 270t; 271b; 272t; 273tl; 275.

Index

This edition is published by
Lorenz Books
an imprint of
Anness Publishing Ltd
www.lorenzbooks.com
info@anness.com

© Anness Publishing Ltd 2023

A CIP catalogue record for this book is available from the British Library.

Publisher: Joanna Lorenz
Editorial Director: Helen Sudell
Project Editor: Felicity Forster
Additional Text: Francis Crosby
Cover Design: Nigel Partridge
Designer: Design Principals
Production Controller: Ben Worley

NOTE
The nationality of each vehicle is identified in the relevant specification box by the national flag that was current at the time of the vehicle's use.

FRONT COVER: **Mastiff 3 Protected Patrol Vehicle.**
PAGE 1: **Buffalo MPCV.**
PAGE 2: **SA-8b "Gecko" SAM Vehicle.**
PAGE 3: **Boxer Multi-role AFV.**
ENDPAPERS: **Armoured Multi-purpose Vehicle (front); BMP-2 Saraths (back).**